HANDBOOK
Member Churches

HANDBOOK
Member Churches

World Council of Churches

Edited by Ans J. van der Bent

Cover design: Nel Witte-Brooymans

ISBN No. 2-8254-0725-9

© 1982 World Council of Churches, 150 route de Ferney
1211 Geneva 20, Switzerland

Printed in Switzerland

Contents

Foreword

Our common membership as churches in the World Council of Churches grants us access into a treasure-house of tradition and inspiration.

Those who are privileged to visit the churches in this fellowship are often overwhelmed by the spiritual richness and cultural diversity of the member bodies. But how do we share that experience of God's abundance with one another? That is a continuing problem of ecumenical education.

This handbook is a modest contribution towards that task of saying what we are as a World Council of Churches. Patiently and skillfully compiled by our librarian, the Rev. Ans van der Bent, the volume is the World Council's first ever attempt to gather in one readily accessible form an overview of all its member churches.

For preparation of the Sixth Assembly of the WCC, in Vancouver, Canada, this book will have special value. But even more important, it will provide a unique ongoing resource for unwrapping the riches of the fellowship we share.

Those riches cannot simply be measured by statistics of money and membership. They are, at the end of the day, records of how the gospel has been rooted and grounded in each place, and is being nurtured and enabled to come alive in witness and service to the world.

The purpose of this handbook, as of the WCC as a whole, is to ensure that these riches are seen and shared. The more that happens, the deeper and stronger becomes our ecumenical fellowship.

PHILIP A. POTTER
WCC General Secretary

Introduction

Much of the information contained in this handbook is based on answers to a questionnaire. The answers in many cases provided up-to-date statistical information, brief historical surveys and notes on the present concerns, programmes and activities of the churches. We have made use of information available at the offices of the WCC in Geneva when the answers were too short or too incomplete — or when no answer was received. We have also made substantial use of some existing handbooks of churches, eg. *Yearbook of the Orthodox Church* (1978), *Handbook of Lutheran Churches in the World* (1977), *Handbook of the World Alliance of Reformed Churches' Member Churches* (1974), *World Methodist Council Handbook of Information* (1976-1981).

We are conscious of the limitations of this Handbook. It is no more than a first attempt to make available some basic information on the churches which together form the WCC family. Further information on their past history and present situation can of course be obtained from the churches' head offices.

We begin with a chapter on the national and regional councils and conferences of churches to which WCC member churches belong. We have tried to include in it the basic historical facts, and a description of their work at present. Some among the national councils are associate councils and conferences of the WCC; some are affiliated with the Conference on World Mission and Evangelism; still others are councils and federations of churches in working relationship, though not in association, with the WCC.

In the chapter that follows we give a brief account of the world confessional families, recently renamed the "Christian world communions". These communions are active, and play an important role in the ecumenical movement. In this chapter we also take note of the growth of united and uniting churches during the last forty years.

Each member church is listed according to continent, sub-continent and then according to the country in the continent or region. An alphabetical index by country is provided for easy reference.

Perhaps at this point we should make a specific reference to the China Christian Council. With the normalization of religious policies after the period of the cultural revolution (1966-76) hundreds of churches in cities and towns, and numerous house groups in rural areas, have been making public witness to their faith. In the China Christian Council, they have come together (1980) as a national organization. It is responsible for theological training, Bible and hymnal publication, and many forms of pastoral support ministries. Its overall objective is to help the cause of the self-governing, self supporting and self-propagating church in China. Though the China Christian Council is not at present a member council of the WCC, the church in China must be recognized in the ecumenical movement because of historical ties — some churches in China being founding members of WCC — and its present independence, its unity, its open desire for friendship, and its place among the Chinese people.

The statistical details and names of office-bearers given under each church are based on the information received, and are correct only at the time of compiling. Statistics become out of date, and officers change. It should also be kept in mind that statistics of membership provided by the churches can be misleading. The questionnaire asked for the total membership of the church. Responding to it, some churches list the number of communicant members; others include all baptized members. Some churches, in particular in Asia, list all baptized members and sometimes even potential believers.

Churches which are associate members of the WCC are indicated by an asterisk.

When no address is given after the name of a patriarch, an archbishop, a bishop, a president, or a general secretary of a church, it may be assumed that the address is the same as that of the church's headquarters.

Following the date of joining the WCC, membership in or affiliations with national, regional or world organizations of an ecumenical or confessional nature are indicated.

An alphabetical list of abbreviations is provided at the end of the handbook. Also provided are alphabetical lists of the English names and of the actual names of the member churches.

In the maps provided for each section, the countries with member churches are shown in grey. There are a great many churches in (1) the Federal Republic and the German Democratic Republic, and (2) Indonesia. Maps of these countries indicate the approximate location of these churches.

The handbook is primarily meant for reference, but we would also recommend its use along with *For All God's People: The Ecumenical Prayer Cycle* published by the WCC in 1978. The prayer cycle includes not just WCC member churches but all churches confessing Jesus Christ as God and Saviour. It has been prepared to guide and deepen our intercession for the churches throughout the year in both public and private prayers.

We are aware that the entries are often uneven and sometimes incomplete. There may well be inaccuracies, names of people and places wrongly spelt, perhaps errors of an even more serious nature.

A handbook of this type needs to be revised and updated from time to time, and we would urge our readers to point out mistakes and inaccuracies so that the process of revision may begin early.

National and regional councils and conferences of churches

The English word "council" has two quite distinct meanings. According to the *Webster's International Dictionary* it refers firstly to an assembly of church representatives convened to consider matters of doctrine, discipline, law and morals, or the relation of the church to world problems (seven widely recognized ecumenical councils). Secondly, it refers to a federation of or a central body uniting a group of organizations for consultation and common action. Some languages have one term *(concile, Konzil, concilium)* that stands for the ecumenical "councils" of the ancient church, the governing bodies of some contemporary churches, and the "conciliar fellowship" envisioned by many Christians as the goal of the ecumenical movement. Another term *(conseil, Rat, consilium)* is used for the associations of churches and other bodies which are engaged in dialogue, attempt to overcome the misunderstandings and the divisions among them, and foster cooperation in programmes and common ventures. Such associations are the subject of this chapter.

Councils, understood as *conseils*, are still so diverse that it is quite difficult to apply a single label. Some are "federations of churches". Some include other church agencies. A number came into being in the early years of this century, were (and in some cases still are) free associations of more or less similar Protestant churches created to carry out common tasks. Many of the founders of these federations believed that the federal or cooperative structure was a sufficient expression of Christian unity. Missionary councils grew in the first half of the 20th century from the desire of Protestant missionary societies to substitute cooperation for competition in regions colonized by Europe and North America.

In countries of Africa and Asia, National Christian Councils began to develop at about the same time. In most of these councils, the constituent membership was composed mainly of mission bodies and other national organs of Christian cooperation. At a later stage many of them developed into national (or regional) councils of churches, and did not include organizations other than churches. Their purpose now was not primarily missionary cooperation but the creation of a fellowship of churches in one place in order to become servants of the ecumenical movement in its search for the visible unity of Christ's church.

National councils of churches

In 1910 there were only two national Christian councils. By 1948 there were thirty councils, which were members of the International Missionary Council. By 1980, 48 councils were affiliated with the Commission on World Mission and Evangelism. Several of the same councils are also associated with the WCC. The process by which missionary councils developed into Christian councils, and then, even if not always in name, into councils of churches, was already advanced by 1948. In the following years it was carried further, and that in a variety of ways.

In Asia and Africa there was the growing feeling that it was inappropriate for missionary agencies as such to have membership in a national Christian council. While their financial contributions were useful, and even necessary, their membership both obscured the nature of the councils and diminished their effectiveness in their relationships with national governments and communities. The National Christian Council of India is a typical example. First there was the Missionary Council (1912); then the National Christian Council of India, Burma and Ceylon (1921); then the National Christian Council of India and Pakistan (1947). According to its revised constitution of 1956 "only organized church bodies are entitled to direct representation in the Council". Missions which were still not integrated in a church in India could become associate members. Thereafter, and not only in India, the Christian councils have tended to become councils of churches. Four years ago the National Christian Council of India changed its name to the National Council of Churches of India. The Northern Rhodesia General Missionary Conference, founded in 1914, was in a similar way succeeded in 1945 by the Christian Council of Zambia.

There were similar trends in the development of regional councils. In 1948 we had the Near East Christian Council for Missionary Cooperation. It later became the Near East Christian Council, then the Near East Council of Churches, and more recently the Middle East Council of Churches. Contemporary ecumenical developments, the political struggles and tensions of the area, the vast and continuing problem of the Arab refugees, have all combined to bring the churches of the region into new and closer ecumenical relationships. The All Africa Church Conference, founded in 1958, became in 1963 the All Africa Conference of Churches. The "Prapat Plan" of March 1957 prepared for the East Asia Conference of Churches, led in 1959 to the formation of the East Asia Christian Conference, now known as the Christian Conference of Asia.

Developments have also taken place in other missionary councils. Member bodies of the International Missionary Council in 1948 included the National Missionary Councils of Australia and New Zealand, and the Foreign Missions Conference of North America. The first has become the Division of Mission of the Australian Council of Churches. The second member body is now the National Council of Churches in New Zealand.

Developments in North America have been far-reaching. The Foreign Missions Conference of North America, which had begun its notable history as far back as 1893, became in 1950 the Division of Foreign Missions of the National Council of the Churches of Christ in the United States of America (NCCCUSA). That organization itself grew out of the Federal Council of the Churches of Christ in America, which had been founded in 1908.

When the Federal Council was formed, its 28 member churches included Baptists, Methodists and Presbyterians, but the number was a small fraction of the total Protestant population. Its basis of union was modelled on the principle of American democracy. According to its constitution, the Council was to express the fellowship and catholic unity of the denominations, with a view to bringing them into common commitment to united service for Christ and the world.

The preamble of the constitution which the National Council of Churches adopted stated: "In the providence of God, the time has come when it seems fitting more fully to manifest oneness in Jesus Christ as Divine Lord and Saviour, by the creation of an inclusive cooperative agency of the Christian churches in the United States of America." This prelude has since become the guiding norm for Orthodox churches and many national denominational communities in the USA. The Council has many departments and sponsors many publications. In its yearly calendar are several ecumenical observances. The general assembly meets every three years. A general board governs the Council between triennial meetings.

The British Council of Churches came into being in 1942, amalgamating the Council on the Christian Faith and the Common Life (1937), the Commission of the Churches for International Friendship and Social Responsibility (1937), and the British Section of the World Conference on Faith and Order. Two years later, in 1944, the Canadian Council of Churches was inaugurated, incorporating various predecessor organizations. The Councils in Great Britain and Canada both have the same credal "basis" as the WCC.

The Second WCC Assembly at Evanston made provision for a more formal working relationship of National Christian Councils with the World Council by creating a category of "associated councils". The difference between "associated councils" and "affiliated councils" is that associated councils are formally related to the WCC as a whole. They are represented by fraternal delegates at WCC Central Committee meetings and Assemblies. "Affiliated councils" are legally members of the Conference on World Mission and Evangelism and support the work of the WCC Commission on World Mission and Evangelism. Some of these councils do not wish to become directly associated with the WCC because of certain conservative-evangelical reasons. A third category of 33 Christians councils are in a working relationship, though not in association, with the WCC. These councils frequently function as a channel of communication and cooperation with the WCC Commission on Inter-Church Aid, Refugee and World Service and the Commission on World Mission and Evangelism.

Today there are 30 associated councils — in Australia, Austria, Botswana, Burma, Canada, Czechoslovakia, Denmark, Finland, Germany (GDR), Germany (FRG), Ghana, Hong Kong, Hungary, India, Indonesia, Japan, Malaysia, Netherlands, New Zealand, Philippines, Poland, Singapore, South Africa, Sri Lanka, Sweden, United Kingdom, USA, Wales, Yugoslavia and Zimbabwe.

These national councils of churches have made a significant contribution to the ecumenical movement. They have served as important channels for the interpretation, support, and implementation of the work of the World Council of Churches. Some councils have reproduced in their own structures some parts of the organizational pattern of the WCC. This development not only indicates the growing commitment of national councils to the life and work of the ecumenical movement; it has meant a progressive involvement on their part both in the work of the WCC itself and in ecumenical activities in their own areas.

There are still gaps in the territories represented by the associated and af-
filiated councils, notably in Africa and in Latin America. Councils in "working
relationship" with the World Council are to be found in Angola, Antigua,
Belize, Burundi, Cameroon, Curaçao, Egypt, Fiji, Finland, France, Gambia,
Guyana, Iran, Ireland, Isle of Man, Israel, Italy, Kenya, Lesotho, Morocco,
Mozambique, Nigeria, Papua New Guinea, Portugal, Rwanda, St Vincent,
Scotland, Sudan, Swaziland, Tanzania, Uganda, Vanuatu (New Hebrides) and
Zaïre. It is obvious that the contribution which all these various councils can
make to the ecumenical movement is of vital importance; only through their
work can the ecumenical movement become rooted in the local situation.

The ecclesiological significance of Christian councils

The issue of councils of churches has received increased attention during the
last two decades. The Montreal meeting of the Faith and Order Commission
(1963) made "the ecclesiological significance of councils of churches" an important item on its agenda. A World Consultation on Christian Councils was held
from 28 June to 7 July 1971 in Geneva. The report commends that councils must
think of themselves as "temporary" servants of the movement towards visible
unity. The participants affirmed that unity, renewal and mission are inseparable
parts of a council's agenda. Churches in a council should not hesitate to examine
questions of faith and order alongside their efforts to render cooperative service.
The report asserts that "even now, when churches share in some common life,
and witness and act together, a new ecclesiastical reality appears". This ecclesiastical reality, however, inheres not in the councils themselves but in the
bonds of fellowship that bind member churches.

The report identifies the "self-contradictory attitudes" of member churches
towards councils as the crucial common problem facing councils of churches.
Frequently the churches impose a strictly limited mandate, and offer minimum
financial support, and still expect a large quantum of service.

The report calls on councils (and thus on their member churches) to give
greater attention to "spiritual ecumenism", especially through the search for appropriate ways of sharing eucharistic communion; to promote development,
social justice and racial understanding; to enlarge their fellowship (especially by
encouraging Roman Catholic participation) and to reach out in dialogue and
cooperation with other faiths and radical movements; to move towards financial
self-support; to improve communications, including those with the WCC; and to
pioneer in controversial areas as both servant and leader of the churches.

The Roman Catholic Church

Since 1972 the Joint Working Group between the Roman Catholic Church and
the World Council of Churches has on several occasions given attention to the
issue of councils. One of the results of this collaboration was the April 1972 issue
of *One in Christ*, in which a series of papers and documents dealing with councils
of churches was published.

In 1975 the Secretariat for Promoting Christian Unity published a pamphlet
entitled "Ecumenical Collaboration at the Regional, National and Local
Levels". Councils, this important document stresses, are not churches, nor the
beginnings of a new church. Their significance derives from the churches that

take part in them, but they are, nonetheless, "very important instruments of ecumenical collaboration, both for expressing the unity already existing among the churches and also advancing towards a greater unity and a more effective Christian witness". The pamphlet makes clear the Roman Catholic position that councils do not have responsibility for church union negotiations, but it does note that they are in a position to give important material help to union conversations and can, upon request, give consultative and organizational assistance.

By the time the World Consultation on Christian Councils took place in 1971, ten national councils had within them full Roman Catholic membership. Today there are 24 such councils. Two regional councils also have Roman Catholic membership. Despite these significant advances, several subsequent conferences have noted that the theological work is far from complete. The Nairobi Assembly of the WCC (1975) called for a new examination of "the role of ecumenical structures of collaboration such as regional, national and local councils". The conspectus of studies mandated by the 1978 Faith and Order Commission meeting recommended that "a study be initiated on the ways in which councils at the world, regional, national and local levels can contribute to the advance of the unity of the Church". In 1979 the Joint Working Group noted that "a common assessment of the role of regional and national councils, especially in terms of collaboration with the Roman Catholic church, would be a particularly useful contribution to the clarification of 'the way to unity'".

The Secretariat for Promoting Christian Unity is in touch with councils, especially those that have Roman Catholic membership, by means of correspondence and staff visits. A consultation was held in February 1982 between the Secretariat for Promoting Christian Unity (through the Joint Working Group) and the WCC. The findings of this consultation will be reported to the Vancouver Assembly through the JWG.

What has been said about national associations of churches applies to a considerable extent to the regional associations of churches. They are presented here in alphabetical order, according to the name of the continent or region (Africa, Asia, Caribbean, Europe, Middle East, North America, Oceania, South America).

All Africa Conference of Churches*

It was to the beating of African drums that the All Africa Conference of Churches came into existence in 1963 at Kampala, Uganda. As with the East Asia Christian Conference there had been an earlier period of preparation, and the decision to create the regional organization had been taken at a widely representative meeting at Ibadan, Nigeria, in 1958. In the brief period between 1958 and 1963 about twenty African nations had achieved political independence and this phenomenon, with all the turbulence and high expectation which accompanied it, inevitably coloured the thought and the definition of dominant concerns of the new all-Africa organization.

---

* The description of the history of regional councils until 1969 is partly based on a contribution by Hans-Ruedi Weber, *Out of All Continents and Nations*.

The historical and cultural background of the church in Africa gives a particular direction to ecumenical thinking and possibilities in this continent. The emphasis is on practice rather than theory, on experience rather than intellectual debate. The political situation, with a great emphasis on independence and liberation, and on the rejection of all traces of colonialism, brings special problems and possibilities for the movement for Christian unity. The independent churches offer a special vision of Christianity, posing many questions to traditional mainstream churches.

Further assemblies were held at Abidjan, Ivory Coast, 1969; Lusaka, Zambia, 1974; and Nairobi, Kenya, 1981. The AACC is made up of 114 member churches and associated councils in 33 countries. It represents over 50 million African Christians which is more than one-third of the total Christian population in Africa. The AACC headquarters are located in Nairobi.

The main concern of the AACC at present is to keep before the churches and national Christian councils the demands of the gospel pertaining to their life and mission, for witness in society, for service and unity, and to this end to promote consultation and action among the churches and councils.

Christian Conference of Asia (East Asia Christian Conference)

When Rajah Manikam (subsequently Lutheran Bishop of Tranquebar) began his work as secretary in East Asia for the World Council of Churches and the International Missionary Council, he was surprised to discover how little the Asian churches knew of one another. Many of them were well-informed about the churches in Europe and America, and some of them had strong links with Christian communities in the West. Yet these churches were often unaware of vital happenings within their neighbouring churches in Asia; sometimes they were even totally ignorant of one another's existence.

Three principle motives lay behind the creation of the East Asia Christian Conference. First, there was the desire of Asian Christian leaders to develop closer and more regular contacts with one another. Secondly, there was the concern for common enrichment and the strengthening of a common witness throughout the continent. Thirdly, there was the expressed desire that ways should be found for channelling more effectively the contribution of the Asian churches to the ecumenical understanding of faith, and of the life and witness of the church universal.

In 1973 the East Asia Christian Conference became the Christian Conference of Asia (CCA). There are 92 member churches and 15 national councils within the CCA fellowship today. Besides the two preparatory meetings in Bangkok, and the planning meeting at Prapat, Indonesia, 1957, assemblies were held in Kuala Lumpur, Malaysia, 1959; Bangkok, 1968; Singapore, 1973; Penang, Malaysia, 1977; and Bangalore, India, 1981. The CCA headquarters are in Singapore. The main concerns at present relate to evangelism, dialogue, communication, women, youth, education, laity, development, international affairs, urban and rural missions, medical service and theology.

Caribbean Conference of Churches

As regards ecumenical relations and actions, the Caribbean churches, including the Roman Catholic Church and a few evangelical churches, have come a long way in the past fifteen years. The Caribbean Conference of Churches (CCC), with its twin agencies CADEC (Christian Action for Development in the Caribbean) and ARC (Action for Renewal of the Churches), has carved out a place and a role for the regional ecumenical movement in the ongoing struggles of Caribbean peoples for unity, identity, change, justice, and development. It is deeply aware of the racial and religious pluralism of the region, as well as of the ideological pluralism.

The inaugural assembly of the CCC was held at Kingston, Jamaica, in 1973. The second assembly met at Georgetown, Guyana, in 1977; the third assembly at Curaçao in 1981. The main offices of the CCC are in Port of Spain, Trinidad.

The search for greater Christian unity is consciously charted via common participation in the human struggles of society, as evidenced in the preamble of the CCC constitution: "We are deeply concerned to promote the human liberation of our people, and are committed to the achievement of social justice and the dignity of man in our society." In the process of working towards these goals, the churches' understanding of the dimension of mission has expanded and their experience of "community" has become a greater reality.

Conference of European Churches

In 1939 Europe once again became the battlefield of the world. Contrary to experience in the 1914-18 war, however, in the Second World War the fellowship of Christians never ceased, and the WCC in process of formation played no small role in maintaining contacts. The story of the church struggles in Europe, of the various church renewal movements which sprang from them, and the remarkable saga of interchurch aid in post-war Europe, belong to the general ecumenical history. The largest operation of the WCC, the Division of Inter-Church Aid and Service to Refugees, worked almost exclusively for Europe until 1955.

The task of the Conference of European Churches (CEC) in trying to comprehend in one overall pattern the many differences, geographical, cultural, linguistic and ecclesiastical, is enormous. That task has become still more complicated because of the acute political differences between Western and Eastern Europe. A first unofficial conference of European churches was held at Liselung, Denmark, in 1957. Because the initiative came mainly from Reformed and United churches, many large Lutheran churches were cautious about committing themselves. Also the Anglican and Orthodox were not yet represented, except by a delegate of the Ecumenical Patriarchate. At a following meeting at Nyborg, Denmark, in 1959, a number of the larger Lutheran, Anglican and Orthodox churches were represented. For the participants of the small Protestant minority churches in the USSR, Poland, Czechoslovakia, Hungary, Yugoslavia, and Greece, as well as for those of the Latin countries of Europe, the first two gatherings were of great importance.

Organizationally things remained open, but the CEC had become a fact. The series of "Nyborgs" in the now famous hotel at Nyborgstrand continued: 1960, 1962, 1964, 1967, 1971. The last two assemblies were held at Engelberg, 1974, and in Crete, 1979. Already at the meeting in 1971, all countries in Europe were represented with the single exception of Albania. Today 114 churches are members of the Conference of European Churches. Its offices are located in the Ecumenical Centre in Geneva. The main concerns at present are ecclesiological questions bearing on church unity, peace questions in Europe, human rights in the area of Helsinki signatory states, interchurch aid in Europe and the churches and the Muslim communities in Europe.

Middle East Conference of Churches

Linking Asia and Africa lies the region of the Middle East. It is the cradle of Judaism, Christianity and Islam. Among the characteristics of this immensely diverse region, from Morocco to Iran and from Turkey to central Sudan, are the dominance of Islam, the Arab-Israeli tension, political instability, oil and poverty. Christians form a small minority; among them are various ancient Eastern churches, Roman Catholics, and numerous Protestant bodies. Political divisions and the unresolved refugee problem have created an atmosphere of mistrust in which cooperation and common worship, study and action is not easy.

We have already referred to the earlier history of the Middle East Council of Churches. It held two assemblies at Nicosia, Cyprus, in 1974 and Broumana, Lebanon, in 1977. The Council has at present 21 member churches. Its headquarters are in Beirut, Lebanon.

The main concerns of the MECC at present are: (a) continuity of Christian presence through the difficult, challenging, and radically changing situation in the Middle East; (b) church renewal — or deepening the spiritual quality of the Christian communities and helping them to transcend their socio-cultural identities; (c) Christian unity beyond ethnic, cultural, structural differences as the churches are called to witness together as one body of Jesus Christ; (d) witness through various ways including proclamation, life-style, diakonia, justice and service.

North America

North America remains the only continent which has no distinct regional body. This is mainly due to the fact that, especially in the USA, a strong national council has been built up which, together with the Canadian Council of Churches, almost covers the whole continent. Whenever necessary these two councils consult with each other and collaborate. The absence of a regional body has not excluded North American regional initiatives. The North American Ecumenical Youth Assembly at Ann Arbor in 1961, and the North American Faith and Order Conference at Oberlin in 1957, for instance, have shown what can be done regionally even without an established regional organization.

Pacific Conference of Churches

The vast area of the Pacific, more water than land, comes within the orbit of the Pacific Conference of Churches, another of the well-established regional expressions of the ecumenical movement. The discussion, initiated by the London Missionary Society (the pioneer mission in the area) with some of the churches and missions in the Pacific in 1959 resulted in a request that the International Missionary Council take responsibility for convening a regional gathering. After a period of intense preparation within the area itself, a conference was held at Samoa in 1961. All the main island groups, such as Fiji, Solomon Islands, Tahiti, Tonga, New Caledonia, the New Hebrides (Vanuatu), as well as Papua New Guinea, Australia and New Zealand, were represented. The need to overcome isolation and to consult on common problems was acutely realized.

It is not surprising, therefore, that at what was convened as an *ad hoc* consultation in Samoa the decision was taken to form a more permanent regional organization. This was formally constituted five years later in an inaugural assembly at Lifu, New Caledonia, in 1966. Other assemblies held were Davuilevu, Fiji, 1971; Port Moresby, Papua New Guinea, 1976; and Tonga, 1981.

The basic concerns of the Pacific Conference of Churches are related to the ministry, its nature, training and employment; the unity of the church, especially in a region where geographical isolation has combined with denominational insularity to harden separation; the nature of a Christian society and its implications for tribal communities; the special pressures and problems which have become universal in the aftermath of the Second World War and through the spread of a worldwide technological culture.

Currently twenty churches and the Episcopal Conference of the Pacific (including ten Catholic dioceses) are members of the PCC. Its offices are in Suva, Fiji.

Latin American Council of Churches

Historically Latin America has for centuries been the home of a dominant Roman Catholicism closely linked in many instances with traditional political and economic centres of power. It is also a continent where a strong minority of the leadership in the Roman Catholic Church is now involved in a far-reaching *aggiornamento*. Protestantism is largely the outcome of missions, chiefly from North America which, on conservative theological grounds, are hostile to, or lack sympathy with, the ecumenical movement. Many Christian groups are opposed to common worship, service and witness. Only four larger churches are members of the WCC: the Evangelical Pentecostal Church "Brazil for Christ", the Church of the Lutheran Confession in Brazil, the Methodist Church of Brazil, and the Pentecostal Church of Chile. There are 14 smaller churches which are also members of the WCC.

From the Panama Missionary Conference (1916) onwards, a number of councils and federations of churches were created under the influence of North American mission boards and churches. Several of these organizations were related to the International Missionary Council and to the USA Committee on Cooperation in Latin America (CCLA). In 1941 the Ecumenical Youth Movement in Latin America (ULAJE) was created. Church and Society in Latin America (ISAL) was born in 1961, which was related to the Church and Society concerns of the WCC, specifically to the programme of study on the church in rapid social change.

Movimiento pro Unidad Evangelica Latinoamericana (UNELAM), founded in a provisional form in 1965, was not a council of churches, but a loose alliance of Christian communities and organizations to promote cooperation and greater unity. It was preceded by two Latin American Evangelical Conferences at Buenos Aires in 1949 and at Lima in 1961. During the Fourth Latin American Protestant Conference (IV-CELA) at Oaxtepec, Mexico, in 1978, representatives of 110 churches and ten continental ecumenical organizations accepted the proposal of UNELAM to create a Latin American Council of Churches (CLAI) — which will be officially constituted at the end of 1982 in Lima, Peru. Meanwhile systematic efforts are being made to strengthen relationships with churches already in CLAI and to contact other churches in Latin America to bring them into its fellowship.

For further reading

"Christian Councils: Some Appraisals", in *One in Christ*, Vol. VIII, No. 2, 1972.

Directory of Christian Councils, Geneva, WCC, 1st ed. 1971, 2nd ed. 1975, 3rd ed. 1980.

Secretariat for Promoting Christian Unity, *Ecumenical Collaboration at the Regional, National and Local Levels*, London, Catholic Truth Society, 1975.

Short, Frank, "National Councils of Churches", in *A History of the Ecumenical Movement*, Vol. 2, 1948-1968, Philadelphia, Westminster Press, 1970, pp. 93-114.

Voices of Unity: Essays in Honour of W. A. Visser 't Hooft on the Occasion of his 80th Birthday, ed. Ans J. van der Bent, Geneva, WCC, 1981.

Weber, Hans-Ruedi, "Out of All Continents and Nations: a Review of Regional Developments in the Ecumenical Movement", in *A History of the Ecumenical Movement*, Vol. 2, 1948-1968, Philadelphia, Westminster Press, 1970, pp. 63-92.

Christian world communions

The term "Christian world communions" came into common use only in 1979. They used to be known as "world confessional church groups", "world confessional groups" and "world confessional bodies" until 1967 when, at a meeting of secretaries of such bodies, the term "world confessional families" was adopted. At that meeting these church families were described as consisting of "the various Christian traditions taken as a whole. Each world confessional family consists of churches belonging to the same tradition and held together by this common heritage; they are conscious of living in the same universal fellowship and give to this consciousness at least some structured visible expression."

The designation "world confessional families" is not entirely satisfactory. Several communions of churches (Orthodox, Anglican and others) do not understand themselves as a particular confession, that is, as churches marked by ties to particular creeds. They are also built on different ecclesiological assumptions. Yet all the participants at the 1967 meeting in Geneva accepted the collective term "world confessional families".

The forms of "structured visible expressions" of confessional organizations vary greatly. One Christian world communion has many employees and a large annual budget. Several have small staffs and moderate budgets. Some had origins which preceded the modern ecumenical movement by several decades. Others were formed or assumed their present level of activities since the World Council of Churches was officially launched in 1948.

Difficult as they are to define and varied as they are in their structure and purpose, the Christian world communions are very much alive, and must be studied in their relationship with the ecumenical movement. In their beginnings they were in fact the principal existing forms of the ecumenical movement, giving the members of their churches a new consciousness of universality through an understanding of the worldwide dimensions of their own fellowships. Many of their leaders participated in the formation of the World Council of Churches and today hold positions of leadership in it.

During the last three decades confessional groupings have increased in strength and in their scope of work. At the same time, their status, paradoxically, has become limited by the growth of the ecumenical movement. Shorn of any claim to absolutism, confessional organizations today seek and generally find constructive roles, or they examine reasons for separate existence even as they pursue their steadily expanding and deepening relations with other Christian world communions.

Even in their totality, the Christian world communions do not represent all branches of Christianity. Two groups of churches in particular exist outside a worldwide confessional framework: the independent or indigenous churches, especially in Africa, and the united churches which came into existence from the twenties onwards.

The issues of confessionalism had to be seriously considered from the time meetings began to be held for discussing the possible formation of a world council. The first meeting for the definitive projection of the Council was held in Utrecht, Holland, in 1938. Here Lutherans proposed that membership in the World Council should be composed of churches, and that seats in its Assembly and Central Committee should be allocated on a confessional basis. The argument for membership by churches prevailed, but the attempt to cluster churches in confessional blocks within the structure of the Council did not.

The first ecumenical document to mention the necessity for a certain coordination between the WCC and CWCs was the report of the Central Committee to the 1954 Evanston Assembly "concerning the structure and functioning of the Council in the period following the second Assembly". It said: "It may be noted with satisfaction that almost all world confessional associations have gone on record wishing to support the ecumenical movement, and it is suggested that the General Secretary shall arrange for informal consultations from time to time with three or four representatives from each association, to discuss the implementation of that desire and other common problems" (*The Evanston Report*, 1954, pp. 184-185).

A major factor in raising the confessional question in an inescapable form was the action of a new regional ecumenical organization — the East Asia Christian Conference (since 1973 the Christian Conference of Asia). Meeting in Bangalore, India, in 1961, the EACC commented that "the very vitality of these confessional loyalties often creates serious obstacles in the life of the younger churches". The Assembly which met in New Delhi in 1961 did not ignore this problem, but it did not pursue it too far. There are those who believe that a deeper understanding of the various confessions is necessary if the quest for unity in the truth is at length to be successful, the Assembly noted, and went on to suggest that it is the duty of the confessional organizations to advance that deeper understanding. On the other hand, the Assembly further observed, the churches have in their membership leaders who see the world confessional bodies as a threat to wider unity, particularly in Africa and Asia. The New Delhi Assembly had already endorsed the famous statement concerning "the centrality of unity of all Christians *in each place* which must of course always seek to be a 'unity of the truth'". It therefore concluded that, if the leaders of confessional bodies believe this, "they will not consider the union of one of their churches as a loss, but as a gain for the whole church".

The East Asia Christian Conference Assembly in Bangkok, 1964, recommended that representatives of confessional bodies and of the younger churches should be brought together in a major consultation. Asian Christians were asked to face three hard questions:

1. Do the world confessional organizations rest on a theological principle or do they simply gather together churches because of common history?

2. Even where world confessional organizations are seeking to preserve for the universal church some fundamental insight into an aspect of Christian truth, is this best done by an organization built around that truth?

3. Are the confessions and doctrines which are the historical basis of these world confessional organizations living realities among the people in these confessional families?

A response of the EACC was given by thirty-three representatives of nine world confessional bodies, gathered together in Geneva in October 1965. The conference dealt with the question of what is or should be the relation of the confessional movements to the "conciliar ecumenical movement and the future of the total mission of the church". It affirmed "that the present situation offers unprecedented challenges to the churches which call for a new and urgent response, both in the confessing of the faith and in the structures of church life". The report of this conference was published in *The Ecumenical Review* (Vol. XVIII, 1966, pp. 91ff.) under the title "Statement of a Joint Consultation Concerning Confessional Movements and Mission and Unity".

The Faith and Order Commission held a consultation on "Concepts of Unity and Models of Union" in Salamanca, Spain, in 1973. The term "conciliar fellowship" was considered there. This term has been frequently misunderstood. It does not envisage a conception of unity different from the full organic unity outlined in the New Delhi statement, but is rather a fuller elaboration of it. The term seeks therefore to integrate both aspects — regional diversity and organic unity. This interpretation was also accepted by the Fifth Assembly of the WCC at Nairobi in 1975.

The Salamanca consultation also urged the CWCs "to clarify their understanding of the quest for unity by cooperating with the World Council of Churches". It posed five questions about the role of the world confessional families, and the Nairobi Assembly later asked these same questions. The anxieties which the special role of the CWCs has caused in the ecumenical movement are clearly reflected in these questions. To overcome the tensions and conflicts which have often arisen in the past, the Nairobi Assembly made a number of suggestions:

1. Cooperation with the confessional families should be coordinated with the relevant regional ecumenical organizations.

2. There should be an effort to agree mutually on "the unity we seek" and "the witness we bear in the world".

3. The findings of the bilateral discussions should be "effectively" applied to the work of the WCC. A useful instrument for this purpose is a "forum" sponsored by the Faith and Order Commission.

4. Closer contacts should also be developed with the Commission on World Mission and Evangelism, with all the fields of interest of Unit II on Justice and Service, with the Programme on Theological Education, etc.

5. The Faith and Order Secretariat should assist the united churches in their conversation about the implications of church union for the future of the ecumenical movement.

The purpose of these proposals is that both the WCC and WCFs should find "a constructive and complementary way of contributing to the advance of the ecumenical movement" (*Breaking Barriers: Nairobi 1975*, pp. 196-198).

A document from the Executive Committee of the World Council, meeting in February 1977 in Geneva, entitled: "Towards a New Relationship with World Confessional Families" contains in the introduction the following key sentence: "Both sides should work towards a deeper mutual understanding and seek to overcome unnecessary competition. In their activities they should witness to the oneness and indivisibility of the ecumenical movement."

At the suggestion of the Conference of Secretaries of the World Confessional Families, its representatives met in Geneva with representatives of the WCC in October 1978, to consult together on mutual relationships. Three themes were discussed: the unity of the church; common witness and collaboration; and the appropriate form mutual relationships should take. This conference laid the basis for future discussions and paved the way for a consultation on relations between the World Council of Churches and the Lutheran World Federation, which was held at the Ecumenical Institute in Bossey in May 1981. It published an *aide-mémoire*. Apart from the recommendations made by the Central Committee, meeting in Kingston, Jamaica, in January 1979, with regard to deeper involvement of CWCs in the WCC's ongoing programmes the Central Committee agreed:

a) to request that ways be explored whereby the WCFs might assist the WCC in the task of communicating with WCC member churches which belong to the respective WCFs;

b) to encourage the General Secretary to explore maintaining and strengthening appropriate liaison with such WCFs as may be interested in building closer overall relationships, and to make maximum use of existing constitutional provisions for WCF involvement in developing WCC policies.

The Central Committee decided to review further developments at its meeting in 1981, with a view to considering what presentation should be prepared for submission to the Sixth Assembly. The question of the appropriate relationship between the three concepts of unity - "organic unity", "conciliar fellowship" and "reconciled diversity" remains undoubtedly crucial.

Confessions in Dialogue, in its third, revised and enlarged edition published by the WCC in 1975, contains accounts of various bilateral, international, regional and national dialogues between CWCs which have taken place from 1959 to 1974. The volume discusses the methods and procedures of the consultations, presents the prominent subjects of discussion — gospel, scripture and tradition, creeds and confessions, eucharist and intercommunion, ministry, unity and union, worship — and concentrates on the problems and possibilities of bilateral conversations, shifts in selfunderstanding, wider relationships, a permanent forum, and the challenge of the bilaterals to churches and Christian world communions.

After the publication of *Confessions in Dialogue* three forum meetings on bilateral conversations were held, with the participation of representatives of the world confessional bodies engaged in bilateral dialogues and members of the

Faith and Order secretariat. These were the first steps towards integrating the bilateral and multilateral levels of ecumenical dialogue. The first forum was held in Bossey in 1978 on the theme "Concepts of Unity"; the second met in Geneva 1979 on the theme "Joint Statements of Consensus"; the third took place in Glion in 1980 on the theme "Reception".

Since 1957 the Conference of Secretaries of World Confessional Families has met annually, normally in Geneva. (No meetings were held in 1960, 1961 and 1975.) It has discussed various concerns, like Corpus Confessionum, relationship with the Roman Catholic Church, the place and task of confessional families in the ecumenical movement, national loyalties: a help or hindrance to world fellowship, bilateral dialogues, the relationships between Bible Societies and the CWCs, religious liberty and human rights, the CWCs' commitment to the future of the ecumenical movement.

Besides the confessional groups described in the following pages, a representative each of the Salvation Army, the General Conference of Seventh-Day Adventists and the Reformed Ecumenical Synod participate in the discussions of the conference of secretaries of the Christian world communions. This participation indicates that the concerns of the debates go beyond the constituency of WCC member churches. Several conversations were held between the WCC and the General Conference of Seventh-Day Adventists and the Reformed Ecumenical Synod which have resulted in a number of publications (e.g. *Faith and Order Paper* No. 55, 1970).

Most of the minutes of the CWC conferences contain a rather extensive section of reports on the participating bodies, their plans, work and meetings. An appropriate dissemination of information, however, has not been achieved in a satisfactory way. As some of the minutes put it, there have always been "difficulties of intercommunication, both between the groups and the World Council".

Since 1968 the Secretariat for Promoting Christian Unity of the Roman Catholic Church has been regularly represented at the conference. It has therefore been unnecessary to keep the question of the relationship between the CWC conference and the Roman Catholic Church on subsequent agendas. The fact that an important network of interconfessional conversations has developed in recent years, in which the Roman Catholic Church is involved at the world level, reveals how seriously the Roman Catholic Church is taking the role of the various CWCs. In this field too the WCC and the CWCs complement each other on the ecumenical scene.

The following section presents short descriptions of the confessional groupings represented within the membership of the WCC. After the Eastern Orthodox Churches and the Oriental Orthodox Churches other Christian world communions follow in alphabetical order.

Eastern Orthodox Churches

At present Eastern Orthodoxy consists of the following autocephalous and/or autonomous churches: the four ancient Patriarchates of Constantinople, Alexandria, Antioch and Jerusalem; the four Patriarchates of more recent origin: Russia, Serbia, Romania, Bulgaria; the Catholicossate of Georgia; and the churches of Cyprus, Greece, Poland, Czechoslovakia, Albania and Finland. There is a strong Orthodox diaspora presence in the Americas, Australia and Western Europe. A section of the USA Orthodox has been granted autocephally, which nevertheless is not recognized by all Orthodox churches. The same applies for the Orthodox Church in Japan. The monastery of Sinai enjoys autonomy. All these churches are held together by a bond of unity in the faith and communion in the sacraments. The Patriarch of Constantinople is known as the Ecumenical Patriarch. He has a position of special honour, as "first among equals", with the right of convening, after consultation with primates of other Orthodox churches, pan-Orthodox conferences, but not the right of interfering in the internal affairs of the other local Orthodox churches.

Orthodoxy claims to be the unbroken continuation of the Christian Church established by Christ and his apostles. Its faith is based primarily upon the dogmatic definitions of the seven Ecumenical Councils. The Orthodox do not recognize as ecumenical any council held since the Second of Nicaea in 787. From the 9th century onwards there developed an increasing estrangement between the two great sees of Rome and Constantinople. This led eventually to an open and lasting schism. The final breach between Greek and Latin Christendom is usually assigned to the year 1054. Two issues were at stake: the universal supremacy of jurisdiction of the Pope, which was rejected by the Orthodox, and the doctrinal issue of the Filioque. The West had inserted a phrase into the Niceno-Constantinopolitan Creed: "I believe in the Holy Spirit... who proceeds from the Father *and the Son*".

Orthodox churches acknowledge the seven sacraments, or "mysteries" as they are termed. However, other sacramental actions are common in the liturgical praxis. Baptism is performed by immersion; chrismation (confirmation) is administered by the priest immediately after baptism, and children can partake of communion from infancy. The bread and the wine in the eucharist are considered to become, at the consecration, the true and real body and blood of Christ. The Orthodox communicate after careful preparation and confession. Services are in principle held in national languages, but in Greece, Russia, Bulgaria and other places, an old liturgical language is used, not the modern vernacular.

The veneration of icons plays a notable part in Orthodox worship, both public and private. Prayers to the Mother of God and the saints are common in liturgical texts. Monasteries have been highly influential throughout Orthodox history. From the 6th century onwards bishops have been drawn from the ranks of the monastic clergy. Parish priests, on the other hand, are generally married. The Orthodox Church has never insisted upon the celibacy of the clergy.

The Patriarchate of Constantinople has from the start firmly supported the ecumenical movement. It appealed as early as 1920 in an Encyclical Letter to "all the churches of Christ" for "closer intercourse and mutual cooperation", and it became a founding member of the WCC. The Ecumenical Patriarchate has had a permanent representative in the WCC since 1955, the Russian Orthodox Church since 1962. Both representatives participated regularly in the annual conferences of representatives of world confessional families. The Orthodox churches mentioned above have a total membership of over 100 million.

Oriental Orthodox Churches

These churches have histories which go back to the Nestorian and Monophysite controversies over the one or two natures of Christ during the 4th and 5th centuries. Two Ecumenical Councils — Ephesus in 431 and Chalcedon in

451 — dealt with these christological disputes. The Oriental churches constitute a group of communities, peoples and nations which in terms of race, language and culture, display a wide diversity. They are present not only in the Middle East but also on the African continent (Ethiopia) and in South India. The Oriental Orthodox churches are not in communion with the Eastern Orthodox but are generally held to belong to the family of Eastern churches. Recently they affirmed a major convergence in their christological doctrine. They are also referred to as Ancient Oriental, Lesser Eastern, and Pre- or Ante-Chalcedonian churches. The First Pan-Orthodox Conference, held in Rhodes in 1961, discussed the relations between the Eastern Orthodox and the Oriental Orthodox churches.

The Syrian Orthodox Church has its centre in the Patriarchate of Antioch (now Damascus, Syria). It is spread over Syria, Iraq, Lebanon, Jordan, Turkey and other countries of the Middle East. The Syrian Orthodox Church in India is situated in the state of Kerala in India. The Coptic Orthodox Church in Egypt has gone through a series of persecutions. Outside Egypt there are Coptic dioceses in Jerusalem, in the Sudan, and in South Africa. The Ethiopian Orthodox Church, having lived for many centuries under the influence of the Coptic Church, has been autonomous and autocephalous since 1959. Considerable segments of the Armenian Church are spread all over the world from the Middle East to the Far East, from Canada to Australia and from Europe to Transcaucasia, its homeland being Armenia, part of which is under Soviet rule and part under the Turks. These five churches together have an estimated membership of 23 million.

Anglican Church

The Church of England separated from Rome in the 16th century after Henry VIII's quarrel with the papacy over the question of his divorce from Catherine of Aragon. The Act of Supremacy in 1534 rejected the authority of the Pope. The establishment of a new national church was completed by the Act of Uniformity during the reign of Elizabeth I, and by the issue of Archbishop Cranmer's *Book of Common Prayer* in 1549 and the publication of the King James Authorized Version of the Bible in 1611.

Both the beliefs and organization of the Church of England represent a blend of Protestant and Roman Catholic traditions and teachings. The Protestant principles of the Reformation were introduced through a gradual process. Doctrine and ritual were laid down in the *Thirty-nine Articles* of faith, finally promulgated in 1571, and in the revised *Book of Common Prayer* of 1559. The Bible was the final authority and was available to all men and women. Ritual was simplified, the sacraments reduced in number. The cult of the Virgin and the Saints and the insistance on the celibacy of the clergy were rejected. Services were held in English instead of Latin.

On the other hand, Anglicanism laid great stress on the continuity of its faith. It maintained all the creeds and doctrines of the early church, and its bishops are claimed to be ordained in direct succession from the first apostles. This inclusiveness has left room for all shades of opinion within the Church. It absorbs both evanglicals, with their emphasis on simple faith and personal salvation, and Anglo-Catholics with their high view of the sacraments and their emphasis on ritual.

The spread of Anglicanism was due partly to migration and partly to missionary effort by the Society for the Propagation of the Gospel and the Church Missionary Society. The Anglican churches overseas are all independent national churches. The Church of England no longer exercises authority over them. They are held together by a common faith and doctrine, common liturgy and common episcopal polity.

Bishop Ralph S. Dean, secretary of the Advisory Council on Missionary Strategy, pointed out in 1968 that "the Anglican Communion is not a confessional body in the ordinary sense of the term", but that Anglican churches "are bound together chiefly by the fact that each is in communion with the see of Canterbury and with each other, that there is no specifically Anglican confession of faith, no central authoritative structure, no longer even one Book of Common Prayer, for at least eight different rites now obtain, though all partake of a common shape of the liturgy". There are some 396 dioceses in the Anglican communion. The number increases by about eight a year. They exist in all continents. The number of members, in terms of those who describe themselves as Anglicans, is about 61 million.

The Lambeth conferences, in which all bishops participate, began in 1867. The conference is presided over by the Archbishop of Canterbury. A second field of communication has been the pan-Anglican congresses. These have been held in London in 1908, in Minneapolis, USA, in 1954, and in Toronto, Canada, in 1963. The congress, though like the Lambeth conference in having no executive authority, is distinguished from it by the presence of clerical and lay representatives from all the dioceses in the communion.

Since 1971 the Anglican Consultative Council — its headquarters are in London — has met every two or three years in different parts of the world; its standing committee meets in the intervening years. The Council has no legislative powers, but fills a liaison role, consulting and recommending, and at times representing the Anglican communion. Its ecumenical functions are:

— to encourage and guide Anglican participation in the ecumenical movement and the ecumenical organizations; to cooperate with the World Council of Churches and the Christian world communions on behalf of the Anglican communion; and to make arrangements for the conduct of pan-Anglican conversations with the Roman Catholic Church, the Orthodox churches and other churches;

— to advise on matters arising out of national or regional church union negotiations or conversations and on subsequent relations with united churches.

Baptist Churches

The modern Baptist Church was founded in Holland in 1609 by John Smyth, a clergyman who had broken away from the Church of England. He maintained that the church should receive its members by baptism after they had consciously acknowledged their faith and, since a child is unable to do this, he opposed infant baptism. Some of his followers established a Baptist church in London in 1612, its pastor being Thomas Helwys, who believed in religious toleration for all men and women, including atheists and pagans as well as Christians.

The spread of Baptist churches was greatly influenced by the revival movements during the following two centuries. In 1891 the General and the Particular Baptists were united in the Baptist Union of Great Britain and Ireland.

The Baptists are the largest denomination in the USA. There are significant Baptist communities in the Soviet Union, Romania, Sweden, in the Federal Republic of Germany and the German Democratic Republic. But it is a world church, and Baptists witness in many other countries of the world as well.

Interpreting the New Testament, Baptists stress that the church as the body of Christ is a communion of the faithful who have made personally and voluntarily a decision for Christ, and because of their personal confession of faith become, through baptism, members of Christ's church. Baptists recognize only the Bible (no creed) as binding authority. Under the guidance of the Holy Spirit each church may interpret the scriptures and design the life of its community. The pronounced congregational constitution does not allow for a centralized church structure but promotes unions and conventions of individual churches.

The Baptist World Alliance is a voluntary association among Baptists in unions and conventions of churches, with a total membership, in 1975, of 33,758,075. There are several millions of other Baptists who belong to churches which are not members of the Alliance. The preamble of its constitution reads: "The Baptist World Alliance, extending over every part of the world, exists as an expression of the essential oneness of Baptist people in the Lord Jesus Christ, to impart inspiration to the brotherhood, and to promote the spirit of fellowship, service and cooperation among its members; but this Alliance may in no way interfere with the independence of the churches or assume the administrative functions of existing organizations.".

The First Baptist World Congress was held in London in 1905. The Thirteenth Congress took place in Stockholm in 1975. An executive committee governs the Alliance between congresses. A large part of the budget of the Baptist World Alliance comes from the over thirteen million member Southern Baptist Convention (USA), whose only official ecumenical relationship on a membership basis is with the Alliance. The Southern Baptist Convention was organized in Augusta, Georgia, in 1845. It holds to a more conservative Calvinistic theology than Baptists in the north. Regional sub-organizations of the Alliance exist in North America and in Europe. The Alliance, with headquarters in Washington DC, has study commissions working on various concerns, themes and programmes.

Christian Church (Disciples of Christ)

Early in the 19th century several groups separated themselves from the Presbyterian Church in North America, because of their preference for the form of the church during New Testament times. Now that they were in a new country, these groups desired to overcome the old church divisions, and soon called themselves "Christians", "Christian Churches", "the Church of Christ" or "Christian Disciples".

Groups around Burton W. Stone, Thomas and Alexander Campbell joined together in one church: Christian Churches (Disciples of Christ). Soon sister churches were established in England, Australia and New Zealand. Missionary churches were founded, in particular in some countries of Africa and in the Pacific.

Christian Churches follow a congregational pattern of churches polity which they regard as being in accordance with New Testament teaching. One of the major goals is to align all church practice and belief with the scriptures. Nothing is to be accepted as an article of faith or as a condition of communion but "what is expressly taught and enjoined... in the word of God," which is "the perfect constitution for the worship, discipline and government of the New Testament church". The Bible is the best source of information about God, far better than creeds or statements of dogma. The Disciples of Christ affirm their belief in the trinity, the virgin birth, the vicarious atonement, the necessity of spiritual birth, and the need for believer's baptism by immersion.. The Christian Church (Disciples of Christ) in the USA, with 1,200,000 members, is the largest church within the family of Christian Churches. It has been greatly active in the ecumenical movement. Already in 1910 a Council of Christian Unity was created which participated in the early Faith and Order movement. From 1961 onwards the ecumenical journal *Midstream* has been published regularly.

The World Convention of the Churches of Christ (Disciples) was started in 1930 in the United States. Each convention elects an executive committee to which the executive secretary is responsible. Between conventions work is carried on through committees on study, finance, programme and interfaith relations.

The preamble to the constitution of the World Convention says: "The World Convention of Churches of Christ exists in order more fully to show the essential oneness of the churches in the Lord Jesus Christ; impart inspiration to the world brotherhood; cultivate the spirit of fellowship; promote unity among the churches; and to cooperate with Christians everywhere towards the unity of the church upon the basis of the New Testament scriptures. The World Convention may in no way interfere with the independence of churches or assume the administrative functions of existing ongoing organizations or institutions among us."

The Disciples Ecumenical Consultative Council was created at Nairobi in 1975 during the Fifth Assembly of the WCC. It helds its First International Conference at Kingston, Jamaica, in October 1979. Its charter is ecumenical. It intends to nurture and to challenge the Disciples of Christ, from the beginning an ecumenical movement, to commit themselves to the church's ecumenical future with intelligence and firmness. The theme "Your Kingdom Come: Mission and Unity in a Global Perspective" of the Commission on World Mission and Evangelism of the World Council of Churches in Melbourne, Australia, was chosen deliberately by the First Conference.

The Christian Churches have a membership of approximately 1,350,000.

Lutheran Churches
The teaching of Martin Luther found early expression in several confessions and fomulations which were brought together in the *Book of Concord* of 1580. In these the scriptures are affirmed to be the sole rule of faith, to which all the creeds and other traditional statements of belief are subordinated. The principal Lutheran tenet is justification by faith alone. Redemption consists in the justification of human beings by faith in Christ, by reason of which, though in fact they were great sinners before, they are now accounted righteous in the sight of God without any initiative on their part. In the later 16th and early 17th centuries Lutheran doctrines were elaborated in a scholastic mould which gave them a severely intellectual cast. Against this scholarly "Orthodoxy" the Pietism of the later 17th century strongly reacted.

The worship varies from country to country, but its principal feature is always the sermon set in the framework of the vernacular liturgy. Lutheranism has favoured a sound elementary and secondary religious education as well as theological and biblical studies. There is only one order of clergy, examined and provided for by the government in certain places. Both clergy and laity are organized in synods.

Apart from Germany, where Lutheranism had been accepted by the majority of the population before the end of the 16th century, it became the official religion also in Scandinavian countries. The Evangelical Church in Germany (EKD) embracing Lutherans, Calvinists and "United" was formally constituted in 1948. The varied backgrounds of the Lutherans who came to the USA, together with different dates of their arrival, led to a proliferation of Lutheran bodies in this country. Gradually, and particularly during this century, there have been mergers among American Lutheran communities.

Most Lutheran churches of the world were loosely affiliated in 1923 in the Lutheran World Convention, which in 1947 developed into the Lutheran World Federation. In its doctrinal basis the LWF "acknowledges the holy scriptures of the Old and New Testament as the only source and infallible norm of all church doctrine and practice, and sees in the three ecumenical creeds and in the confessions of the Lutheran Church, especially in the Unaltered Augsburg Confession and Luther's Small Catechism, a pure exposition of the word of God."

Lutheranism and the LWF programme continue to emphasize the theological contributions Lutherans can make to the entire ecumenical movement. This includes official dialogue with Anglican, Methodist, Orthodox, Reformed and Roman Catholic churches. The Institute for Ecumenical Research in Strasbourg, France, sponsored by the Lutheran Foundation for Interconfessional Research, contributes to the fulfilment by the Lutheran churches of their ecumenical responsibility in the area of theological research. The LWF has today 97 member churches representing 54 million faithful. There are a further 16 million Lutherans not represented in the LWF.

Mennonites

The community is the oldest Protestant Free Church. The Mennonites are followers of Menno Simons (1496-1561). At one time parish priest in Dutch Friesland, he renounced his connections with the Roman Catholic Church in 1536 and joined the Anabaptists, then suffering severe persecution after the attempted kingdom of the saints in Munster. For twenty-five years he shepherded and reorganized the stricken communities in Holland and neighbouring territories. His views put stress on believers' baptism, a connectional type of church organization with an emphasis on the responsibilities and the rights of the local congregation, a rejection of Christian participation in the magistracy, and on non-resistance.

The common ground for the different Mennonite communities later became the rejection of church organization, infant baptism and the doctrine of real presence in the eucharist. Every congregation is independent and the Lord's Supper is administered by elders chosen by the community. Both men and women may preach. Most Mennonites refuse military service, the taking of the oath and any public office. On the other hand, they recognize no common doctrine so that some of them are practically Unitarian in their views while others hold the doctrine of the Trinity.

Originally the movement had a strong sense of mission, which suffered considerably during the many decades of persistent persecution resulting in the withdrawal of the group into isolated areas in various countries. One of the characteristics that the Mennonites share with the Quakers, the Church of the Brethren, and some other groups, is their peace witness, which led them during the two World Wars to accept alternative service, and to do relief work in war-stricken countries under the auspices of the Mennonite Central Committee. The general conference of the Mennonite Church united with the Federal Council of the Churches of Christ in America in 1908, but reluctantly withdrew in 1917 because of the positive attitude to war which seemed to characterize so many American Christians at that time.

There are about 600,000 baptized Mennonites in the world. Smaller communities live in Holland, the Federal Republic of Germany, the German Democratic Republic, the USSR, Canada and Mexico. The largest community is in the United States. The Dutch and German communities were founding members of the WCC in 1948. American Mennonitism is yet to arrive at an agreement on the question of joining the World Council.

The First Mennonite World Conference was held at Basel in 1925. The Tenth World Conference was held at Wichita, Kansas, in 1978. Among the aims of the conference are mission and evangelism, diakonia and worldwide service, Christian and theological education. The first part of Article I of the constitution of the Mennonite World Conference states: "The purpose of the Conference is to bring together in fellowship the Mennonites, Brethren in Christ, and related bodies of the world. By its activities, under the leadership of the Holy Spirit, it seeks to deepen faith and hope, to stimulate and aid the church in its ministry to the world, and to promote the kingdom of God in greater obedience to the Lord Jesus Christ." The general council meets at least once between assemblies and during the assembly sessions.

Methodist Church

Methodism is the form of Christian belief and practice adopted by the followers of John and Charles Wesley who tried to bring a greater spiritual enthusiasm to the life of the Church of England in the 18th century. Their efforts were successful, but proved inacceptable to the Anglican clergy, so that a separate church was ultimately established.

From his high church days, John Wesley carried over the optimistic Arminian view that salvation was possible for all human beings, in contrast to the Calvinistic ideas of election and predestination that were accepted by most Non-Conformists. He also stressed the important effect of faith on character, and that perfection in love was possible in this life.

The Methodist Church considers itself part of the church universal, believing in the priesthood of all believers and following in organization the principles laid down by Wesley for the pastoral oversight of the societies of Methodists which had grown up as a result of his preaching. The weekly class-meeting for "fellowship in Christian experience" has from the beginning been a valuable institution. By tradition Methodism has an active concern for both evangelism and social welfare, and by means of its centralized organization it is able to make coordinated efforts in this direction.

The Methodist faith became as popular in the USA as in Great Britain, but later there were secessions and splinter movements. American Methodism became primarily espiscopal, without claiming episcopal orders in a Roman Catholic sense. Movements towards reunion began in the late 19th century and gathered momentum in the 20th. Serious discussions began in England in 1955 for reunion with the Anglican Church, but the proposals agreed on by the Methodist conference were rejected for a second time by the Church of England in 1972.

The first World Methodist Conference — then called the Ecumenical Methodist Conference — was held in 1881 in London, England. Conferences were then held every ten years until World War II. At the first meeting after the war in 1947, it was decided in principle to establish a permanent structure, and since 1951, when a new constitution was adopted, the Council has met every five years. The Council is composed of approximately 500 persons elected to serve for a five-year period. From the Council the executive committee is named, with at least one member from each member church.

The headquarters of the World Methodist Council are in Lake Junaluska, North Carolina. The Council also maintains an office in Geneva, responsible among other things for day-to-day liaison with the WCC and a number of Christian world communions.

Among the purposes and activities of the Council, the following may be specially mentioned:
— It has regular programme committees on evangelism, ecumenical conversations; social and international affairs; worship and liturgy; theological education; youth; family life; publishing and communication; and exchange of ministers.
— Two important affiliated organizations — the World Federation of Methodist Women and the World Methodist Historical Society — function as supporting bodies of the Council.
— The Oxford Institute of Methodist Theological Studies meets every four years, bringing theologians from around the world to deal with specific theological themes.
— The Council is engaged in bilateral dialogues with the Roman Catholic Church and, since early in the last quinquennium, with the Lutheran World Federation. Steps have been taken to seek bilateral conversations with the Orthodox.

The Fourteenth World Methodist Conference in Honolulu in July 1981 marked the centennial of the first World (Ecumenical) Methodist Conference. There are at present 62 member churches, active in 90 countries around the globe. They have some 20 million communicant members and total membership of some 50 million people.

Old Catholic Churches

Old Catholics are a group of national churches which at various times separated from Rome. The term "Old Catholic" was adopted to mean original Catholicism. Old Catholic Christians are composed of three sections: (1) the Church of Utrecht which originated in 1724 when its chapter maintained its ancient right to elect the Archbishop of Utrecht, against opposition from Rome; (2)

the German, Austrian and Swiss Catholic Churches which refused to accept the dogmas of the Infallibility and the universal ordinary jurisdiction of the Pope, as defined by the Vatican Council of 1870; (3) smaller groups of Slav origin. National church movements among the Poles in the USA (1897) and the Croats (1924) have resulted in the establishment of the National Polish Church with four bishoprics in America and one in Poland, and of the Yugoslav Old Catholic Church. The Philippine Independent Church established sacramental communion with Old Catholics in 1965.

The doctrinal basis of the Old Catholic Churches is the Declaration of Utrecht (1889). The Old Catholics recognize the same seven Ecumenical Councils as the Eastern Orthodox Churches, and those doctrines accepted by the church before the Great Schism of 1054. They admit seven sacraments and recognize apostolic succession. They also believe in the real presence in the eucharist, but deny transubstantiation, forbid private masses, and permit the reception of the eucharist under one or both elements. Bishops, as well as the rest of the clergy, are permitted to marry. All services are in the vernacular. From the start, Anglicans have been close to Old Catholics. They participated in an international conference of theologians, convened at Bonn by Old Catholics in 1874, to discuss the reunion of churches outside Rome. Old Catholics recognized Anglican ordinations in 1925. Since 1932 they are in full communion with the Church of England. Old Catholic-Orthodox dialogues have taken place since 1931. After the Second Vatican Council the Old Catholic Churches have been in conversation with the Roman Catholic Church. A limited agreement on church communion was reached in 1974.

An international Old Catholic congress has met regularly since 1890. The international Old Catholic bishops' conference is the main instrument for the maintaining of the ties of the communion. It does not only decide on internal church matters but serves to promote relationships with various other churches. The president of the conference is the Archbishop of Utrecht. Old Catholics number over 400,000.

Pentecostal Churches

The Pentecostal movement began in the first years of the 20th century among believers who sought a baptism in the Holy Spirit accompanied by speaking in tongues along the lines recorded in Acts. The movement spread rapidly. It received its greatest impetus in the British Isles between 1925 and 1935 under the fervent preaching of the Welsh evangelists, Stephen and George Jeffreys. It attained its greatest dimensions in North America, South America, especially Brazil and Chile, and in Scandinavia. A total world membership of nearly six million is estimated.

Pentecostal Christians are characterized by a distinctive emphasis on sanctification that includes a conversion process in which an adult makes a decision or has a conversion experience; a cleansing from sin, or justification; and a renewal of the gifts of Pentecost consequent to baptism, especially the climatic charismata of glossolalia and faith healing. The Bible is the sole doctrinal authority. Some of the Pentecostal churches celebrate the Lord's Supper, but allow a free interpretation of its significance. Many practise foot-washing as part of the divine ordinances. Good works, as part of the spirit-filled life and as a preparation for the coming of the Lord, are urged on all Pentecostalists. They include visiting the sick, strengthening the weak, encouraging the faint-hearted, and pointing out the way of salvation. The Pentecostal ethos prescribes a strict abstinence from indulgence in worldly pleasures and the support of the Church through tithes. Members are discouraged from participating in war, destroying property, or injuring human life.

Worship is informal rather than ritualistic or liturgical, and freedom is encouraged. Government is generally along the lines of congregational polity, although in some instances the organization of the church includes district conferences, annual conferences, and a general conference. Missionary work is vigorously carried on at home and in many foreign countries under the guidance of local or denominational missionary boards.

Differences between the various Pentecostal churches made it difficult to establish an international community. The First Pentecostal World Conference was held at Zurich in 1947. During the Second World Conference at Paris in 1949 the idea of a permanent world organization was rejected. The conferences at London, 1952, and at Stockholm, 1955, showed a greater openness to other churches. Two small Pentecostal churches in Chile joined the WCC in 1961. The large Evangelical Pentecostal Church "Brazil for Christ" joined the Council in 1969. Since 1972 conversations with the Roman Catholic Church (the Secretariat for Promoting Christian Unity) have taken place.

Presbyterian and Reformed Churches

The term is sometimes taken to include all the Protestant churches which have accepted the principles of the Reformation, but in a narrower and more accurate sense it is used specifically of the Calvinist bodies, as contrasted especially with the Lutherans. All adhere, with some variations, to a form of ecclesiastical polity wherein the Church is governed by presbyters. Its proponents in the 16th and 17th centuries did not regard it as an innovation but as a rediscovery of the apostolic model found in the New Testament. According to Calvin the Primitive Church had four different offices: pastor, doctor or teacher, deacon, and presbyter or elder. He recognized, however, that other offices might be adopted. Synods consist of members of several presbyteries within a large area. The general assembly is the supreme legislative and administrative body.

The primary presupposition of the Reformed churches is that the risen Christ is the only head of the church. He rules his people by his word and Spirit. Thus there is no stress on a special elite group which has received through direct revelation or by the laying on of hands extraordinary powers of authority. Doctrines are traditionally Calvinistic. Worship is simple, orderly and dignified, with an emphasis upon the hearing and preaching of the word of God. Few churches have weekly celebration of the eucharist; monthly celebration is not uncommon. The level of education required for the Presbyterian minister is traditionally high.

Churches in Holland, France, Switzerland, Hungary and other European countries carry the name "Reformed". In Anglo-Saxon countries the name "Presbyterian" is more common. There are large Presbyterian churches in South Africa, New Zealand, Australia, Indonesia and Korea. After the Roman Catholic Church, the Reformed churches are the most widely spread throughout the world.

Twenty-one Reformed and Presbyterian churches meeting in London in 1875 officially constituted "The Alliance of the Reformed Churches throughout the World Holding the Presbyterian System". At that time, it was mainly a grouping of European and North American churches. In 1949 the International Congregational Council was formally established. At Nairobi, Kenya, in 1970, the two organizations, Reformed and Congregational, came together in the new World Alliance of Reformed Churches. At the time of this merger the Alliance had 114 member churches in 70 countries. Today it has a total of 147 member churches with approximately 70,000,000 members. Nearly forty of the WARC member churches are at present engaged in union negotations. Leaders of the Reformed family of churches were among the pioneers of the WCC.

The constitution underlines that the Alliance is much more a family of churches than a confessional institution. Subscription to "any narrow and exclusive definition of faith and order" is not listed among the conditions for membership. Churches belong to the Alliance because they see in it an instrument of common witness and service. Point 9 of the purpose of the Alliance (constitution, article III) reads as follows: "To facilitate the contribution to the ecumenical movement of the experiences and insights which churches within this Alliance have been given in their history, and to share with churches of other traditions within that movement, and particularly in the World Council of Churches, in the discovery of forms of church life and practice which will enable the people of God more fully to understand and express God's will for his people."

Regional needs and growing membership have given rise to area organizations within the Alliance. Two areas are structured — the European, and the Caribbean and North American. The central offices of the WARC are located in the Ecumenical Centre in Geneva. Besides the General Secretariat, the secretariats of the two departments on theology, and cooperation and witness are also housed here.

Religious Society of Friends

The community of Quakers, later called the Religious Society of Friends, originated about 1650 under the leadership of George Fox and other voluntary itinerant preachers. Within a short time their message spread throughout Great Britain and Ireland, Northern Europe, the British colonies on the American seabord, and to the West Indies. Because of their rejection of compulsory church attendance, their refusal to take up military service, and their deliberate disregard of minor social conventions, such as deference to superiors and judicial oaths, the Quakers met vigorous opposition nearly everywhere. In 1682 William Penn founded the Quaker community in Pennsylvania.

The central doctrine of the Society of Friends is the "Inner Light". Its possession consists chiefly in the sense of the divine and direct working of Christ in the soul, by which human beings are freed from sin, united to Christ and enabled to perform good works. Among its visible effects are a moral character, simplicity, purity and truthfulness. From the paramount importance given to the Inner Light derive the rejection of the sacraments, the ministry and all set authority of church, creed, or Bible. The Friends have thus retained their emphasis on continuing first-hand religious experience. A belief in spiritual baptism and spiritual communion is maintained. The Friends' devotion to social and educational work

— and especially in the 20th century to international relief — has earned them very widespread respect.

Though there is no formal ministry, the Society recognizes certain officers with specific duties, including "elders" responsible for the holding and due conduct of meetings for worship, and "overseers" responsible for the pastoral care of the congregation. The early simple organizations consisting of local meetings were grouped into progressively larger units called respectively monthly, quarterly, and yearly meetings. They are largely autonomous. Larger groupings of yearly meetings came into existence in America in 1902: the Friends General Conference and the Five Years Meeting of Friends. The First Friends World Conference was held in 1920; the Fourth World Conference in 1967.

The Friends World Committee for Consultation, which started its activities in 1937, has met every three years. As its name indicates the Committee has no executive power over its constituent yearly meetings. Its aim is to promote deeper understanding between Friends in various nations, and to engage in dialogue with people of other Christian communities and also of other faiths. The Committee further endeavours to strengthen the spiritual life of Quaker groups throughout the world and their efforts to work for peace. In 1948 the Friends World Committee was recognized by the Economic and Social Council of the United Nations as a non-governmental organization with consultative status. It represented the Society at the Second Vatican Council.

United Churches

The search for the unification of churches has been an integral aspect of the ecumenical movement which proceeded quite independently of its varied organizational forms. Little causal connection can be drawn between, for instance, Life and Work, Faith and Order, or the WCC on the one hand, and the unions which have been achieved. Between 1925 and 1945 19 united churches have been formed, involving 57 churches. More than 60 churches have taken a leap of faith into "organic" union since World War II. Some churches have already gone through more than one union. That this movement is worldwide is indicated by the fact that the unions took place on all six continents and included a great number of countries.

Among most of the churches which have already joined, or will be joining, doctrinal issues do not appear to be all-important. There are some exceptions of highly confessional churches involved in union. Where doctrinal differences do exist among church people negotiating for union, such differences do not follow denominational lines. They are differences which exist within all the churches. The Church of South India, which in 1947 brought together Anglican, Methodist and Reformed traditions, was certainly the most celebrated of the "early" church unions, though far from unique. During one five-year period from 1965-1970, united churches were ushered in in Zambia, Jamaica and Grand Cayman, Madagascar, Papua New Guinea and the Solomon Islands, Belgium, North India, Pakistan and Zaïre. These have been a source of genuine ecumenical hope — and a good deal of surprise.

During the past decade fewer unions have been consummated than in the previous ten years. One of the unions that have taken place involved the Protestant Church of Belgium, which underwent its second union in ten years in 1978.

The year 1977 saw the birth of the Uniting Church in Australia, a church that includes 2,000,000 Christians. These are hardly insignificant achievements.

The two major issues are the unification of ministries and the order of the united church. The first is highlighted in negotiations like the one in Great Britain between Anglicans and Methodists, where the proposed "Service of Reconciliation" between ministries and memberships has been a crucial issue. The other was devised in the course of the discussions in North India. Nevertheless bishops of the united church have received into their jurisdiction ministers of the uniting churches with the laying on of hands and prayer. A related issue in the discussion of ministry, which has sometimes impeded church union in some parts of the world, is that of the ordination of women. Negotiations are under way in a few places between churches which have ordained women presbyters and those who refuse ordination to women.

Advanced negotiations aimed at church union are currently taking place in several countries. These negotiations often reveal a willingness to learn from past efforts. There is a positive desire that the new church should be as healthy as possible at the time of birth. Many ecumenically committed Christians have wanted to set organic union as the final goal, and they are disappointed when the new churches have to struggle for unity after union.

Such negotiations are not easy. But many of the current negotiations seem to point to the existence of a genuine basis for unity. United churches must always be uniting churches, constantly seeking a deeper and broader unity in Christ. Present developments are indeed encouraging. A more recent development in India, for instance, is the setting up of a joint council by the Church of South India, the Church of North India and the Mar Thoma Church. Representatives of the three churches, working through the joint council have reached a great measure of agreement on matters of faith, ministry and sacraments. The goal is organic-cum-conciliar union, and negotiations have reached the point where the Council has asked all three churches to suggest a possible name for the United Church which would do justice to their separate past, distinctive emphases at present and common future.

A fourth consultation of united and uniting churches took place in Colombo, Sri Lanka, in November 1981. The theme was "Growing Towards Consensus and Commitment". Much of the discussion centred around a series of "case studies" that focused on particular problems or issues as they have appeared in the life of selected united and uniting churches. The consultation benefited from the presence of observers representing the Roman Catholic Secretariat for Promoting Christian Unity and the Orthodox Task Force of the WCC. Earlier consultations took place at Bossey (1967), Limuru (1970) and Toronto (1975).

For further reading

Ehrenström, Nils and Gassmann, Günther, *Confessions in Dialogue: a Survey of Bilateral Conversations Among World Confessional Families 1959-1974*, 3rd, revised and enlarged edition, Geneva, WCC, 1975.

Empie, Paul C., "Dilemmas of World Confessional Groups with Respect to Engagement in Mission and Unity", *International Review of Missions*, Vol. LV, No. 218, 1966, pp. 157-170.

Fey, Harold E., "Confessional Families and the Ecumenical Movement", in *A History of the Ecumenical Movement*, Vol. 2, 1948-1968, Philadelphia, Westminster Press, 1970, pp. 115-142.

"Growing Towards Consensus and Commitment", report of the Fourth Consultation of United and Uniting Churches, Colombo, Sri Lanka, *Faith and Order Paper No. 110,* Geneva, WCC, 1981.

Ishida, Yoshiro, Meyer, Harding and Perret, Edmond, *The History and Theological Concerns of World Confessional Families*, LWF Report, August 1979.

Mudge, Lewis S., "World Confessionalism and Ecumenical Strategy", *The Ecumenical Review*, Vol. XI, No. 4, July 1959, pp. 379-393.

Puglisi, James F., *A Workbook of Bibliographies for the Study of Interchurch Dialogues*, Rome, Centro Pro Unione, 1978.

A Continuing Bibliography for the Study of Interchurch Dialogues (1980), Centro Pro Unione Bulletin, No. 17, spring 1980.

Schmidt-Clausen, Kurt, "The World Confessional Families and the Ecumenical Movement", *Lutheran World*, Vol. X, No. 1, 1963, pp. 35-44.

Africa

ALGERIA

PROTESTANT CHURCH OF
ALGERIA * (Eglise protestante d'Algérie)
31 rue Reda Houhou, El-Djazaïr, Tel:
662216. 500 members — 8 local com-
munities — 3 pastors. Publication: Let-
tres Circulaires (in French, English and
German). WCC (1974), AACC, MECC,
WARC. President: Rev. Dr Hugh G.
Johnson — Secretary: Mr Ruben
Bayemi.

Until 1962, when Algeria became an
independent nation, the Reformed
Church in Algeria was part of the
Reformed Church of France and as such
had no separate history. In the main, it
was not a missionary church either. The
Church's main preoccupation was to give
pastoral care to French Protestants who
had settled down in the country. The
parent churches of this Algerian Christian
community were the Reformed Church of
France and the United Methodist
Church. In 1962, the Protestant Church
of Algeria became an independent
church; at that time a great many of its
pastors and laypeople went back to
France.

The Church has now become an international community of Christians from
thirty different nations and 25 different
traditions. Among them are many who
have come from European countries to
spend a few years in the country. At
Christmas, Easter and Pentecost services
Bible selections are read in 15 different
languages. Mission work has now become
the responsibility of the Church. There are
missions in Menas in the Aurès and in
Raisinville at Mostaganem as in the
Cashbah of Algiers, where the work is carried out in collaboration with other missionary groups.

During the Christian holidays the
Church is entitled to a religious radio
broadcast.

BENIN

PROTESTANT METHODIST CHURCH
IN THE PEOPLE'S REPUBLIC OF
BENIN (Eglise protestante méthodiste en
République populaire du Bénin)
B.P. 34, 54 avenue Sékou Touré, Cotonou
— Tel: 312520. 56,000 members — 330
parishes — 21 pastors. WCC (1972),
AACC, WMC. President: Rev. Harry Y.
Henry — Secretary: Rev. Samuel J.
Dossou.

The Church was founded in 1843 by a
missionary, Thomas Birch Freeman, of the
Methodist Missionary Society in London.
Freeman also undertook missionary work
in Ghana, western Nigeria and Togo. He
employed liberated slaves from the
Americas who were already Christians. The
first evangelist and pastor was a liberated
slave from Brazil. The Church grew slowly,
but now has seven synods and three fields
of mission which are under the direction of
the general synod. The three fields are
north Benin, the Atacora and the Borgou
regions.

The Church plays an active role in the
social life of the nation. It is interested in
the socio-economic development of the
country through rural agricultural action,
urban and industrial mission, family planning, the promotion of health and the
quality of life, and dialogue with people of
Islamic faith. It has sponsored the translation of the whole Bible into the national
language, Gun Allada.

Among the primary concerns of the
Church during the 1980s are a more comprehensive theological formation of
pastors and evangelists at the joint
theological college where ministers from
the Ivory Coast, Benin and Togo are
trained, eventual consecration of women
ministers, continued Christian education
of the people of God and the elaboration
of a catechism and improvement of the
places of worship.

CAMEROON

AFRICAN PROTESTANT CHURCH*
(Eglise protestante africaine)
B.P. 26, Lolodorf. 8,400 members — 29 parishes — 10 pastors — 5 evangelists. WCC (1968), FEMEC, AACC. General Secretary: Rev. Samuel Salinzouer.

The Church had its beginnings in the American Presbyterian Mission. For linguistic reasons it organized itself as an independent group among the Ngumba tribe 45 years ago.

It operates 15 primary schools and a rural centre. The Church receives no regular financial help from outside, but benefits from the assistance of other churches, members of the Federation of Evangelical Churches and Missions in the Cameroon, for the training of its ministers.

The APC participates in union negotiations with other churches in the nation.

EVANGELICAL CHURCH OF CAMEROON (Eglise évangélique du Cameroun)
B.P. 89, Douala — Tel: 423611 — Cable: Evangelicam. 500,000 members — 1,700 parishes — 216 ordained pastors — 591 evangelists. WCC (1958), FEMEC, AACC, CEVAA. Rev. Dr Jean Kotto — Secretary: Rev. Charles E. Njike.

The Church was born out of the work the Baptist Missionary Society (London), the Basel Missionary Society, and the Society of Evangelical Missions in Paris. It became autonomous in 1957. The Church has grown very rapidly, particularly in the region of Bamileke, due to a vigorous evangelical campaign and an awakening of Christian communities. In 1962, 8,000 people accepted to follow a catechetical course in order to be enrolled in the Church.

After its independence the ECC developed a strong sense of unity. Three regions, the south, Bamileke and Bamoun, with their different cultures, mentality and languages, became a peaceful religious and cultural community.

The Church was a founding member of the All Africa Conference of Churches in 1963. It also manifested its ecumenical orientation by accepting missionaries of the Netherlands Reformed Church, while the Society of Evangelical Missions in Paris continued to send helpers.

A Commission of Christian and Theological Education was created in 1961 to stimulate contextual theological reflection and to examine new methods of evangelism. A new catechism was elaborated — its title is: Suis-moi (Follow me) — and a new worship form for children, a biblical curriculum for primary schools and a programme for religious instruction in colleges have been designed.

The ECC maintains fraternal relations with several churches in France, Switzerland, the Netherlands and the Federal Republic of Germany, and with many French-speaking churches in Africa.

PRESBYTERIAN CHURCH IN CAMEROON
B.P. 19, Buea (S.W. Province) — Tel: 32.42.36. 177,000 members — 1,029 congregations — 133 pastors. WCC (1961), AACC, WARC. Moderator: Rt Rev. J.C. Kangsen.

This Church became autonomous in 1957. English Baptists had first come to this part of West Africa in 1845. In 1884, the country came under German protection and it was agreed, at a conference of European missionary societies, that the Basle Mission should take over the work of the English Baptists. This was done in 1886. The First World War had a tragic effect on the work. The administration of the country passed into British hands and the German and Swiss missionaries were recalled. However, a small group of faithful people continued the work, making the Church a truly indigenous one. In 1925, European missionaries began returning to the country. The Second World War again disrupted church life, which was however followed by a period of intensive activity and growth. A new constitution was drawn up and adopted, which marked the Church's independence. It consists of three parts: basic principles, organization worship and life.

The Church runs two general hospitals, one rehabilitation centre and four health centres. In the educational field it has 160 primary schools, five secondary schools, one teacher training college and a theological college where most of the pastors are trained. In the rural areas two rural training centres (for farmers) and one handicraft centre (for carving and weaving) are maintained. There are two church centres, a home-making centre for women and two youth centres. The headquarters include departments of communication, women's work, lay training and evangelism and youth. Presbook, a book distributing agency, has been established by the Church.

PRESBYTERIAN CHURCH
OF CAMEROON (Eglise presbytérienne camerounaise)
B.P. 519 Yaoundé — Tel: 32.42.36, 22.15.98 — Cable: Eprecam. 200,000 members — 360 parishes — 222 pastors. Publications: Nimfasan (in Bulu), Ndonol (in Bassa). WCC (1963), FEMEC, WARC. General Secretary: Rev. Dr Ambadiang de Mendeng.

The Cameroon Presbyterian Church traces its history to a mission established on the island of Corisco in 1847 by the Presbyterian Church, USA. This work was extended to Rio Muni and Gabon, and finally, in 1879, to Cameroon itself, where a mission was set up at Batanga on the coast. Working inland from there, the missionaries established contacts with the Fang tribes in both Cameroon and Gabon, and later, after 1892, the Boulou tribes. In 1884, Cameroon was annexed by the imperial German government, but this did not affect the work of the American mission. However, the First World War brought problems for the mission. When the war

began, the mission had 56 Americans in eight mission stations, and administered a seminary, a technical school and a printing press. But, while hostilities continued in Cameroon (1914-1916), the position of the Americans was complicated by the fact that their country was still neutral.

At the outbreak of the Second World War, the Church had an estimated membership of 100,000, cared for by some 90 ministers. In the post-war years, with the end of the missionary period in sight, it became the accepted policy to send workers to train abroad, notably in America, France and Switzerland. On 11 December 1957, the Cameroon Presbyterian Church received its independence. It is now organized in four synods and 16 presbyteries.

The Church maintains 16 colleges, 35 primary schools, 20 health development centres, two leprosy hospitals, a farm school in Libamba, and three agricultural centres. It participates actively in the work of FEMEC which sponsors the Protestant Theological Faculty in Yaoundé, a multimedia centre and a centre for evangelization. The church also has its own theological school in Bibia Lolodorf and its own printing press.

The primary concerns for the 1980s involve a new emphasis on evangelization and an evaluation and restructuring of the various tasks of the Church. The Church maintains close relations with the United Presbyterian Church in the USA and the Presbyterian Church in Canada.

UNION OF BAPTIST CHURCHES OF CAMEROON (Union des Eglises baptistes au Cameroun)
B.P. 6007, New Bell, Douala — Tel: 42.41.06. 37,000 members — 214 parishes — 46 pastors. Publication: Echos de l'UEBC (monthly, in French). WCC (1961), FEMEC, AACC, CEVAA, BWA. President: Rev. Paul Mbende — General Secretary: Rev. Emmanuel Mbenda.

The Church was born of the work of the Baptist Missionary Society in London. After the labours of Alfred Saker and others, the Baptist Missionary Society of Berlin, and still later the Society of Evangelical Missions in Paris, took over. The UBCC became autonomous in 1957. From that year onwards the Church has assumed all its responsibilities in the fields of evangelization, education and social work. Its activities extend to all parts of the nation. It is engaged in confessional and ecumenical activities on national, continental and international levels. Moreover, it is in continuous dialogue with its Muslim neighbours, in particular in the north of Cameroon.

The UBCC is committed to a deeper African expression of Christian theology because it believes that the gospel can and should be appropriated in specific cultural contexts. There is an equal interest in the theology of development. Confronted with glaring disparities between the rich and the poor in Cameroon, the Church cannot but voice its concern for social justice the struggle for human rights.

It is not accidental that the Church has a socio-medical centre in Ndiki (Somo), a college on the outskirts of Douala, several centres for women and an animation and information centre for young people in Nkondjock. It encourages the training of doctors and teachers and hopes to create an experimental agricultural centre in Bourha (north Cameroon). Above all, the intensification of evangelization in the north of the country (in the region of Dibom and Mbang, where pioneer villages are created) is a major goal. The Church is grateful for the assistance of Baptist churches in Europe through the European Baptist Mission.

CENTRAL AFRICA

CHURCH OF THE PROVINCE OF CENTRAL AFRICA

P.O. Box 769, Gabarone, Botswana — Tel: 53779 — Cable: Anglican Gabarone. 590,000 members — 10 diocesan synods.

Publication: Epifania. WCC (1956), BoCC, CCZ, AACC. Archbishop: Most Rev. W.P. Khotso Makhulu.

The Province covers Botswana, Malawi, Zambia and Zimbabwe. It was inaugurated in 1955. In 1882 William Johnson and Charles Janson reached Lake Nyasa (now Lake Malawi). Twelve days later Janson died. His companion carried on the work for 46 years, operating from Likoma Island on Lake Nyasa. In the 1950s the new diocese of south west Tanganyika and the northern half of the diocese of Lebombo were formed out of the work of the eastern lakeshore. When Malawi became independent in 1964, the diocese of Nyasaland changed its name to the diocese of Malawi.

The Church of Zimbabwe dates from the first missionary journey of Bishop Knight-Bruce of Bloemfontein. Regular work began in 1811 when the diocese of Mashonaland was created. This diocese became part of the Church of the Province of South Africa, and included part of Botswana and Mozambique, as well as the whole of Rhodesia, until the formation of the diocese of Matabeleland in 1953. The countries forming the present province are different from one another, and face different problems. Zimbabwe is relatively industrialized, while Malawi is almost entirely rural. Zambia produces much of the world's copper. Botswana's main industry has been, until recently, cattle ranching. But there are diamond, copper and nickel mines now. Malawi and Zimbabwe are predominantly Christian, while in Botswana and Zambia Christianity is a minority religion.

The constitution of the province is similar to that of other provinces in other parts of Africa, but, unlike most of them, it has a floating archbishopric. A recent development has been the creation of territorial councils in countries where there are more than one diocese. The Zambian Anglican council has extensive administrative and financial powers; the Anglican council in Malawi controls pension and trust funds; the Zimbabwe Anglican council is purely consultative.

The major task for the Church in Zimbabwe is to be involved in reconciliation, reconstruction and development after years of fighting for independence. It is important for the Church in all four countries to develop indigenous leadership and to move towards financial independence.

CONGO (People's Republic of the)

EVANGELICAL CHURCH OF THE CONGO (Eglise évangélique du Congo)
B.P. 3205, Bacongo-Brazzaville — Tel: 81.43.64 — Telex: Evangélique Bacongo-Brazzaville. 100,730 members — 99 parishes — 87 pastors. Publication: Mwendo (in French and Kikongo). WCC (1963), AACC. President: Rev. Jean Mboungou.

The Church was established in 1909, through the work of the Mission Covenant Church of Sweden. It became autonomous in 1961. It is the largest Christian community after the Roman Catholic Church in the Congo. Because of its charismatic approach and revivalist enthusiasm, the use of African musical instruments in the liturgy and its dynamic evangelisitc campaigns, it has had an impact on society. The ECC is greatly interested in the improvement of medical services, the practice of preventive medicine, and the raising of economic standards. It concentrates on a variety of youth programmes and maintains various Sunday and Bible schools. Evangelization continues to be high priority, especially in the north and among rural people. The unity of the church of Christ is a primary concern. The Church is supported by missionary societies in Sweden, Norway, Denmark and Finland.

EAST AFRICA

PRESBYTERIAN CHURCH OF EAST AFRICA
P.O. Box 48268, Nairobi, Kenya — Tel: 555122/5555230 — Cable: Presbyter Nairobi. 160,000 members — 101 parishes — 118 pastors. WCC (1957), NCCK, AACC. Moderator: Rt Rev. John G. Gatu — General Secretary: Rev. Bernhard Muindi.

The Presbyterian Church of East Africa grew out of the work of the Church of Scotland. In 1891, the first missionaries arrived at a place called Kibwezi, some eighty miles from Mombasa. It was later decided to transfer from Kibwezi to Kikuyu, and it was from that centre that the Presbyterian Church spread out.

The first Kikuyu convert was baptized in 1907. Statistics show that in 1910 there were 53 Christians. The number rose to 5,369 by 1929. Shortly after, there was a division in the Church arising from disagreements on the question of female circumcision: some felt that the practice was medically wrong and therefore the Church should discourage it; others, who felt that the issue had nothing to do with the Church, broke away to form their own schools and churches.

From 1908, the Church of Scotland began to take a greater interest in the many Scots scattered all over Kenya as settlers and government officials. For a long time the two wings, European and African, were one Church but they separated in 1936. In 1956, they came together again and formed one general assembly. Since 1935, the Church's pastors have been trained at St Paul's United Theological College along with Methodists and Anglicans. The Church has a law training centre at Kikuyu.

The PCEA has been playing an important role in Kenya. It pioneered in education and medical work. It founded the first hospital in the country. It now maintains three hospitals and several health centres, two schools for deaf children, a home for old people and a home for destitute children. It runs many schools. The Church participates in nation-building and operates several projects such as community centres, rural development projects, and centres for weaving, homecraft and secretarial training for girls.

In spite of its meagre resources and paucity of personnel, the Church faces the future with confidence. Among its primary concerns for the 1980s are seeking a still greater role in the political life of society; the better training of pastors and lay people; the reaching of the unreached tribes with the gospel; the preparation of youth for the future; and the search for ways and means to make the Church self-supporting.

The PCEA maintains relations with the Church of Scotland, the United Church of Canada, the United Presbyterian Church in the USA and the Presbyterian Church in Ireland.

EQUATORIAL GUINEA

EVANGELICAL CHURCH OF EQUATORIAL GUINEA* (Iglesia Evangélica de Guinea Ecuatorial)
Apartado 25, Ebebiyin, Rio Muni. 8,000 members — 15 congregations — 68 preaching stations — 5 ministers — 70 elders. WCC (1972), WARC. Secretary: Rev. Pablo Mba Nchama.

A group of American missionaries, after working in Liberia and Gabon, established themselves on the island of Corisco in the Gulf of Guinea in 1850. From there they crossed to the mainland where they set up their first congregation at Benito. The Presbytery of Rio Muni celebrated its centenary in 1960. In 1900, Rio Muni was ceded by the French to Spain. This led to the establishment of the Roman Catholic Church and to an inevitable change in the Church's circumstances. Its educational and medical work had to be stopped.

In 1924, all missionaries had to be withdrawn from the country. But a new period of growth began with the establish-

ment of the Spanish Republic and lasted till the outbreak of the Spanish Civil War in 1936. In 1952, the Spanish government closed all Protestant churches, and only allowed those which had been in existence prior to the establishment of the Franco regime to re-open.

In 1960, some twenty delegates met for the last time as a presbytery of the synod of New Jersey of the United Presbyterian Church, USA, accepted a new constitution, and became the Evangelical Church of Equatorial Guinea.

Since the independence of Equatorial Guinea in 1968 the Church, with other Christian churches, has been under great pressure in the country's atmosphere of militant atheism.

ETHIOPIA

ETHIOPIAN EVANGELICAL CHURCH MEKANE YESUS (Ethiopia Wongelawit Betakiristian Mekane Yesus)
P.O. Box 2087, Addis Ababa — Tel: 15.84.00 — Cable: ECMY, Addis Ababa. 521,800 members — 7 synods — 2,000 congregations — 260 pastors — 530 evangelists. Publications: ECMY Information (in Amharic and English). WCC (1979), CCCE, AACC, LWF. President: Emmanuel Abraham.

This autonomous church body, the first after the ancient Ethiopian Orthodox Church to be officially recognized by the government, was constituted in January 1959. The Church takes its name from its first congregation in Addis Ababa, Mekane Yesus, meaning the place of Jesus. It is a product of missionary work which began late in the 19th century. Ethiopian evangelists from northern Ethiopia and missionaries from Sweden, Germany and the United States had laboured in western Ethiopia and in Addis Ababa and won some converts before they were expelled by the Italians who overran Ethiopia from 1936 to 1941. But the number of followers grew steadily. During the 1950s more missionaries came from Norway, Finland, Denmark, Iceland and the United States and worked in the southern, central and northern parts of Ethiopia. A good many people responded, in rural as well as urban areas.

The Church today has two seminaries and a dozen Bible schools where ministers are trained. Pastors and evangelists are given annual refresher courses during which they discuss current theological developments, ways of dealing with contemporary questions and of better equipping members of the congregations. Voluntary preachers are given courses for several weeks. Once a year all communicant members attend a spiritual conference for a few days.

The Ethiopian Evangelical Church sees its task as an endeavour for 'integrated human development' where spiritual and material needs are seen and met together. It is engaged in education at all levels, and lays particular stress on mass education. There are more than 1,800 literacy schools established and run by the Church. The literacy schools are now being transferred to the farmers' associations. The Church is also engaged in health services, especially in the countryside. Some hospitals have been transferred to the government. There are more than thirty clinics. Great stress is laid on preventive care through education and vaccination given to people in the hospitals, the clinics and by mobile health teams. The Church has welcomed the socio-economic change brought about by the Ethiopian revolution. Dedication to the service of the whole human person requires involvement in development projects such as construction of schools and clinics, agricultural and vocational training centres, homes for the disabled and the aged, and roads and bridges.

At the ninth general assembly it was decided that Church members should gradually increase their contributions in order to become more independent of foreign aid. Since 1976 several courses on responsible stewardship have been conducted. However, the schools, the hospitals, health centres and other institutions still need the support of cooperating overseas churches and missions.

ETHIOPIAN ORTHODOX CHURCH

Ethiopian Orthodox Church Patriarchate Head Office, P.O. Box 1283, Addis Ababa — Tel: 110099, 111989, 116507. 14,000,000 members — 20,000 parishes — 18 bishops — 250,000 priests. Publications: Zena Bete Christian (weekly), Dimste Tewahido (bi-monthly), Maedot (quarterly), all in Amharic, Tensae (in Amharic and English). WCC (1948), AACC, MECC, CPC. Patriarch: His Holiness Abuna Tekle Haimanot — General Secretary: Ato Mersie Hazen Abebwe.

Christianity was introduced into Ethiopia in the 4th century by St Frumentius and Edesius of Tyre. At the end of the 5th century the arrival of the 'nine Roman (i.e. Byzantine) saints', probably from Syria, strengthened the Christian faith. It is not certain whether these 'saints' were Monophysites or Chalcedonians. After a brief period of prosperity the Abyssinian Church declined, as Islam began to spread in Africa. When c. 640 the old patriarchate of Alexandria was transferred to Cairo, the Church was made entirely dependent on it and its Monophysite patriarch. Little is known of its history during the next few centuries. When, in 1268, the old dynasty was restored, the Church entered upon another period of vitality, owing to the influence of the Abuna, Takla Hâmanôt, who combined great austerity of life with energy and ambition.

At the end of the 13th century, repeated efforts were made to restore the country to communion with Rome. Many popes sent letters and missionaries to Ethiopia. The success of a Dominican mission was short-lived, owing to the hostility of the Negus, and the religious were martyred. During the Mohammedan invasions (1520-51) there were renewed attempts when reunion was demanded as the price of military help given by the Portuguese. Under Julius III Jesuit missionaries were sent into the country. In 1625 a Catholic patriarch,

Alphonsus Mendez, was sent from Rome, and Catholicism was declared the official religion. In 1632 the union, however, came to an end and the Jesuit missionaries were banished. From 1838 more sustained Catholic missionary efforts were made once again. When in 1936 the country was opened again to the West by the Italian conquest, the Monophysite patriarch was confirmed in his office. Since 1950 the Ethiopian Church has been virtually autocephalous.

The canon of the scriptures of the Church contains certain apocryphal books such as Enoch and the Ascension of Isaiah. The literary language, Ge'ez, has for centuries been used in public worship. The Church has two kinds of clergy: the regular priests who administer the sacraments, and the learned lay clerks who are entrusted with the chant of the Church offices and the teaching in the schools. The priests may be either secular, in which case they can be married men, or regular. The Church maintains special relations with the Ethiopian Orthodox Church in North and South America, Great Britain, Sudan and Djibouti.

GABON

EVANGELICAL CHURCH OF GABON
(Eglise évangélique du Gabon)
B.P. 10080, Libreville (Baraka) — Tel: 72.41.92 — Cable: Evangab. 120,000 members — 3 regional synods — 30 parishes — 60 pastors and evangelists. Publication: Ensemble (quarterly, in French). WCC (1961), AACC, CEVAA. President: Rev. Samual Nang Essono — Secretary: Rev. Emile Ntetome.

The American Board of Commissioners for Foreign Missions started work in Gabon in 1842 and continued until 1870. Among the 35 missionaries were John Leighton, William Walker and Albert Bushnell. The first convert from Corisco, named Ibia, was consecrated as pastor in

1870. The Board of Foreign Missions of the Presbyterian Church in the USA started its mission in the country in 1870, and withdrew in 1913. Among its 66 missionaries were Albert Bushnell, William Walker, Robert H. Nassau and Arthur W. Marling. Both missions faced much resistance and many difficulties. Several missionaries succumbed to tropical diseases. The work among the Fang people was more successful than the mission among the Mpongwe people. Only slowly did both missionary societies penetrate into other remote regions.

In 1877 contacts were made with the Society of Evangelical Missions in Paris, which started its work in 1889. It sent 138 missionaries up to 1961. They also had to face various difficulties, and ten missionaries died at an early age in the country. The mission among the Fang people was more successful in their case also.

In 1961, when the Church became independent, the ECG had 45,000 members, 19 parishes, 49 primary schools with 3,579 pupils, a college with 117 students, a teacher college with 59 students and two dispensaries. There are now 126 primary schools, three colleges and six teacher colleges with a total of 680 teachers.

Among the one million inhabitants of Gabon 30 per cent are Roman Catholic, 12 per cent belong to the ECG, six per cent to the Evangelical Church of South Gabon and three per cent to the Evangelical Pentecostal Church.

The Church government is presbyterial-synodical. The national synod is composed of an equal number of pastors and lay delegates, elected by the regional synods. A national council is responsible for the ongoing activities of the ECG.

The exodus from the rural areas and the problem of increasing urbanization (in particular in Libreville) present a serious challenge to the Church. The struggle against secular tendencies of corruption and indifference calls for new strategies of evangelism. A new college for the formation of pastors, evangelists, teachers and youth workers was established two years ago. An experimental agricultural development project has also been launched.

The Church has close fraternal relations with the Evangelical Church of Togo and the Cameroon, the Protestant Methodist Church of Benin and the Union of Baptist Churches in Cameroon in cooperation with which were founded the Theological School of Ndoungue and the Protestant Theological Faculty of Yaounde.

GHANA

EVANGELICAL PRESBYTERIAN CHURCH, GHANA

P.O. Box 18, Ho, Volta Region — Tel: 755. 200,000 members — 75 pastoral districts — 700 congregations — 142 pastors. WCC (1963), AACC, WARC. Moderator: Rt Rev. Prof. N.K. Dzobo — Synod Clerk: Rev. Albert Y. Wurapa.

The Evangelical Presbyterian Church in Ghana has its roots in the north German mission of Bremen. This mission was organized in 1836, with the object of sending workers to the slave coast. Its early history is one of set-backs — fatal sickness among the missionaries, little response to the gospel and tribal opposition to the work. The Church's growth and progress owe much to the statesmanlike work of Franz Michael Zahn (1862-1900), to Schlegel's translation of the Bible into the Ewe language, and to the education of some twenty young Africans in Germany before the First World War. Despite the internment of the German missionaries during the war and the change from German to English, the Church made steady advances. At the request of the British government, Scottish missionaries began work in the Church after the First World War. They withdrew in 1930, only to be recalled during the Second World War. In 1945, the Scottish mission made it clear they could not indefinitely continue this work and, at their request, the then colonial government of the Gold Coast admitted missionaries of the former Evangelical and Reformed Church of America (now part of the United Church of Christ).

From the beginning, the Church has considered educational, agricultural, medical and technical projects a normal part of its work. It is at present taking part in union negotiations with Methodists and other Presbyterians. It depends largely on its elders for the day-to-day work. The Church has to fight a constant battle against polygamy, idolatry and the sects. The Overseas Board for World Ministries of the United Church of Christ was instrumental in establishing the EP Church Seminary, Mawuli Secondary School, Worawora Hospital (which is now a government hospital), and the Adidome EP Church hospital.

METHODIST CHURCH, GHANA

P.O. Box 403, Accra — Tel: 28120 — Cable: Methodist Accra. 274,500 members — 8 synods — 264 pastors. WCC (1960), AACC, CCG, WMC. President of the Conference: Rt Rev. Samuel B. Essamuah — Secretary of the Conference: Rev. Jacob S.A. Stephens.

The conference of the Methodist Church, Ghana came into being in July 1961. Formerly it had been an overseas district of British Methodism. The first Methodist missionary landed at Cape Coast on 1 January 1835, and began work amongst the Fantes, some of whom were already Christians. Of the 21 missionaries who went to the Gold Coast during the first eight years of the Church's life, the climate claimed the lives of 11, before they had served less than a year. Thomas Birch Freeman was the great pioneer of missionary expansion; arriving at Cape Coast in 1838 he spent the whole of his ministry on the west coast of Africa and died in Accra in 1890. Early this century the Church was established in Ashanti. In the northern region evangelism began in the period 1910-1915 but colonial government policy prevented the development of this work at that time. In 1955 missionary work was established especially in the western section of the northern and upper regions; today the Church has an agricultural project at

Wa and a mobile clinic unit at Lawra. At present the connexion consists of 52 circuits in five districts — Cape Coast, Accra, Kumasi, Sekondi, and Winneba — together with the northern Ghana mission.

The Church is heavily involved in educational work. It has the management of more than 1,700 primary and middle schools, with a total enrolment of over 200,000 children. In addition there are seven secondary schools with an enrolment of more than 4,600, including Wesley Girls' High School, founded in 1836, the oldest girls' school in West Africa, under the care of the conference. There are two teacher training colleges for which the Church is responsible with 800 students; Wesley College in Kumasi, one of the largest training colleges in the country. Ministers are prepared jointly with Presbyterian ministers and Anglican priests at Trinity College, Legon, near the University of Ghana, Accra. The Women's Training Centre and the Freeman Lay Training Centre are both in Kumasi. A small deaconess order has been formed.

The Methodist Church is in dialogue with the Anglican diocese of Accra, the Presbyterian Church of Ghana, the Evangelical Presbyterian Church and some other groups over the question of church union. There is practical cooperation with these churches in many fields and the Christian council is also very active.

PRESBYTERIAN CHURCH OF GHANA

P.O. Box 1800, Accra — Tel: 62511. 261,240 members — 805 congregations — 158 ministers — 3,824 elders. WCC (1952) CCG, AACC, WARC. Secretary: Rev. S.K. Aboa.

The Presbyterian Church of Ghana represents the harmonious blending of several traditions, primarily through the Basle Mission and the Scottish Mission. The Basle Mission is itself a blending of the German Evangelical tradition of Luther and the Swiss Reformed one of Calvin and Zwingli.

It was in 1828 that the first four Basle missionaries set foot in Ghana, settling first at Christiansborg in Accra, but soon moving to Akropong. Of the early missionaries, eight out of nine had died by 1839 and Basle seriously considered abandoning the mission. But by 1854, with the assistance of Christians from the West Indies, Akropong was firmly established: baptisms had taken place, a seminary had been established and the Twi language reduced to writing. By the end of the century, the mission had established six further head stations and achieved its long-cherished goal of working among the Ashanti people.

In 1917, because of a government decree the Basle missionaries had to leave, and the Church of Scotland responded to a call for help. That was why the Reformed Church in Ghana adopted the Presbyterian organizational pattern.

In the 1940s, still with the help of men from the Basle and Scottish missions, the Church extended its work to the northern parts of the country, until then largely closed to Presbyterianism.

KENYA

AFRICAN CHRISTIAN CHURCH AND SCHOOLS

P.O. Box 1365, Thika — Tel: 47 Gatura Via Thika Post Office. 50,000 members — 46 congregations — 26 pastors. WCC (1975), NCCK, AACC. General Secretary: Rev. Samuel Mugo Mwangi.

This Church had its beginnings in the work of the Africa Inland Mission from 1905 onwards. A conflict arose in 1947 when Kikuyu pastors and elders urged the missionaries to provide for institutions of higher education, besides the existing elementary schools. As the request was refused, the ACCS proclaimed its independence in 1948. All its elementary and secondary schools were later recognized officially and partly taken over by the government.

Although differing in educational policy, the Church has maintained the traditions of its parent mission in matters of faith, church order and rules of conduct. Originally confined to the Agikuyu tribe, it is now extended to five of the eight provinces in Kenya. There are plans to transfer the headquarters to Thika. Since 1954 the ACCS has been a member of the Christian Council of Kenya; it has sponsored students at St Paul's United Theological College, and has invited the help of four missionaries from the Canadian Baptist Overseas Mission Board.

A primary concern of the Church is a still more vigorous evangelistic campaign, in particular among the Somali-Boran people in the north-eastern province of Kenya. It also plans to establish an educational institution in Thika, a Bible college with qualified staff, and dispensary and water project in the dry areas of Ember in the eastern province. The Church is financially independent, but it can realize its new projects only with financial aid from abroad.

The structure of the ACCS is essentially democratic. Each local church sends three delegates to the parish council, from which one member is elected as representative to the general council. The general council elects a 'dignitary' or general secretary, and a 'vice-dignitary' or vice general secretary. The Church's youth fellowship and the women's action each send five delegates to the general council.

AFRICAN CHURCH OF THE HOLY SPIRIT*

P.O. Box 183, Kakamega, Kenya. 20,000 members — 53 congregations — 53 pastors — 17 parish leaders. WCC (1975), NCCK, AACC. Executive Secretary: Rev. Peter Angode Ihaji.

In 1927 this Church separated from the Friends African Mission, which is known as the East African Yearly Meetings of Friends. The pioneer of the community in the Kakamega district of Kenya was Mr Chilson who taught fellow human beings to pray and to confess their sins. They were baptized by him in the Holy Spirit by the laying on of hands. Converts spoke in tongues. In 1933, the ACHS established

itself, in the following years facing great hardship and persecution. Leaders of the Church were appointed by the Holy Spirit to organize meetings in various places. The first leader was Solomon Ahindukha, who died in 1952. Kefa Ayub Maburu succeeded him and became the high priest of the Church. In 1957, the ACHS was registered as a religious community under the government constitution.

This community is now found among the tribes of Abaluhya, Kalenjin, Embu, Meru, Akamba, Kikuyu, Waguria, Luo, Waganda and Wagishu. Branches of the Church are to be found in Iliva, Kanyamkago, South Nyanza, Cheptuyet, Nandi District, Kianjuki, Embu, Kiabio, Meru, Eldoret Molo, Nakuru, Nairobi, Kampala, Kigumba and Bumbo Sililwa (Uganda), Bethel/Mugumu, Musoma (Tanzania).

Members are identified by a cross on their clothes, and beards and turbans. Drums are used to accompany singing, with clapping of hands. Sunday services in the villages, monthly services (on the 20th of every month), quarterly meetings, and a yearly meeting (at the Church's headquarters) are held. Sunday services start with the singing of hymns, the reciting of Psalms 1:1-6 and 23:1-6 and the collecting of alms. One of the Church's elders drives out the evil spirits while the congregation kneels. The pastor preaches a sermon, which is followed by prayers and hymns. The order of service may be changed under the guidance of the Holy Spirit who inspires prophecies and dreams. It is believed that the Holy Spirit alone can heal all cases of sickness.

The Church participates actively in the programmes of the National Christian Council of Kenya.

AFRICAN ISRAEL CHURCH, NINEVEH

P.O. Box 13, Jebrock via Vihiga. 100,000 members — 250 parishes — 2,000 churches — 250 pastors. WCC (1975), NCCK, AACC. General Secretary: Mr Henry Asige Ajega.

David Zakayo Kivuli who founded the AJCN in 1942 and was its high priest, was born in 1896 in Gimarakwa at Nyangori in north Nyanza, now the Kakamega district. He went to school at the Nyangori Mission which belongs to the Pentecostal Assemblies of Canada in western Kenya. On 6 February 1932, he received full inner conviction that he was a sinner, and after twelve days he had the experience of receiving the Spirit. He was blind for 17 days.

On regaining his sight, he started to speak in tongues, and people were amazed. Later he prayed for the sick, and for childless women that they might have children. Some of his prayers were answered. The people for whom he prayed joined him, believing that he was a man of God.

In 1941, a group of Kivuli's followers went with him up a hill near his home. They spent a long time praying. It was very dry and hot but Kivuli prayed and water came out from the rock. The people with him drank the water. Among his followers were also people of the Pentecostal Church at Nyangori. Kivuli left this Church because he wanted people to confess their sins openly in public, which was contrary to missionary teaching. He was allowed to leave and start his own church; if after two years the attempt was a failure, he could return to the Nyangori Church.

Followers are found today in every large town in Kenya, but the majority are members of two tribes, the Luo and the Lyhya. A large church, called the 'ark', was built at Kivuli's home in Gimarakwa in 1958. After his death the high priestess Mama Rabecca Kivuli became the spiritual head of the Church. Besides a pastor, every church has a teacher or elder.

The AICN holds the trinitarian doctrine, and believes in the second coming of Jesus Christ and his final judgment. It practises infant baptism and the baptism of adults by the Spirit. Baptism with water is not practised. Friday is celebrated as the holy day when the Church remembers Jesus' death on the cross and his forgiveness of sins. Long sessions of prayer and meditation take place on that day. Sunday is also a holy day, celebrated by processions.

In the realm of Christian ethics, members practise monogamy, abstinence from alcohol and tobacco, and simple styles of dress. In the beginning the AICN faced many difficulties as an independent church in Kenya. Now it operates twenty primary shools and fifty nursery schools. Various women's groups are responsible for education in home economics and handcraft.

Ever since it became a member of the WCC at the Nairobi Assembly in 1975, the AICN has been eager to participate in various African and international ecumenical meetings in order to share widely in the gifts of the Holy Spirit.

CHURCH OF THE PROVINCE OF KENYA

P.O. Box 40502, Nairobi — Tel: 22265 — Cable: 'Oikoumene' Nairobi. 1,021,900 members — 1,400 parishes — 200 priests. Publication: Target (in English and Swahili). WCC (1971), NCCK, AACC. Archbishop: Most Rev. Manesses Kuria — Provincial Secretary: Ven. John Kago.

In 1969, the provincial synod of East Africa which met in Dodoma decided to divide the Province of Tanzania. The Province of Kenya was inaugurated in 1970, when the Most Rev. Testo Habakkuk Olang was enthroned in All Saints' Cathedral in Nairobi.

The Church has seven dioceses: Maseno North, Maseno South, Mombasa, Mount Kenya East, Mout Kenya South, Nairobi and Nakuru.

Theological education is provided at St Paul's United Theological College in Limuru and at Trinity College in Nairobi.

METHODIST CHURCH IN KENYA

P.O. Box 7633, Nairobi — Tel: 22265 — Cable: Oikoumene, Nairobi. 53,000 members — 400 parishes — 49 ministers (including 8 probationers). WCC (1968),

NCCK, AACC. Presiding Bishop: Most Rev. Johana M. Mbogori.

When this Church became autonomous in 1967, membership stood at about 8,000. The recent growth rate has been some 10 per cent per annum. There is a great need for more ministers. The Miathene Circuit, for example, will soon have sixty churches; it is served by three ministers and 130 local preachers.

The British Methodist Church entered Kenya in 1862 through the work of the then United Methodist Church. Today the work is concentrated in six main areas: Meru (north of Mount Kenya), Tana River, the coast, Nairobi, Kisii and northern Kenya.

The Church sponsors over a hundred schools, two hospitals, two agricultural training centres, and ten village polytechnics. It also shares with other churches in St Paul's United Theological College at Limuru.

LESOTHO

LESOTHO EVANGELICAL CHURCH

P.O. Box MS 260, Maseru 100, Lesotho — Tel: 3942. 207,000 members — 56 congregations — 470 preaching stations — 36 ministers — 2,896 elders. WCC (1965), CCL, AACC, WARC. Executive Secretary: Rev. John Monaheng Diaho.

The Paris Evangelical Missionary Society was invited in 1833 by King Moshesh I of the Basuto people to send missionaries to work among his people. Their work led to the formation of the Evangelical Church which became autonomous in 1964. The Evangelical Church, the second largest Christian community in Lesotho, is a founder member of the country's Christian Council which was established in 1964.

The Church runs a theological college and a Bible school, a girls' training college, a hospital and a literature centre. One of the main problems is a shortage of candidates for the ministry: the Church, with a membership of well over 200,000 people, has only 36 ordained pastors.

LIBERIA

LUTHERAN CHURCH IN LIBERIA

P.O. Box 1046, Monrovia — Tel: 261984. 25,000 members — 20 parishes — 150 congregations — 25 pastors. Publications: Loma (weekly), Kpelle Messenger (monthly), Drumbeat (in English). WCC (1972), AACC, LWF. Bishop Roland J. Payne.

This Church developed out of the work of missionaries sent from North America by antecedent bodies of the Lutheran Church in America. The mission advanced very slowly in the early years; but recently the Church has been growing very rapidly. Its membership has more than doubled during the last fifteen years. Members are mainly Kpelle and Loma people who speak their own languages. The Kpelle occupy the interior region; the Loma live still further inland, near the Guinea border. Most of the members are engaged in subsistence farming, but over the years many have found employment in the Monrovia area or elsewhere in industry. The Roman Catholic Church has the largest membership; among the Protestants, Baptists, United Methodists and the Lutherans have about the same strength. The Protestant Episcopal Church comes next in membership.

Organized in 1947, after 87 years under missionary status, the LCL became fully autonomous in 1965 and elected one of its pastors as bishop. Its organization combines congregational and synodical features, the revised constitution (1972) providing for a balance of local responsibility and common action. Church headquarters in Monrovia include conference and boarding facilities. The LCL's urban ministry in the capital is becoming increasingly important. The aim is to make the central administration and the congregations self-supporting by 1982, with expected income from farmlands and forests making up for diminishing overseas subsidies.

An indigenous church leadership, long overdue, is in the making. Future pastors are being educated in the newly opened Gbarnga School of Theology, a joint venture (1976) with the Methodists and the Episcopalians, located about 140 miles from Monrovia. Deacons are prepared in the LCL Lay Training Centre (1968) in Salayea, Lofa County, which offers a two-year course. Ordained deacons are authorized to administer the sacraments in the absence of a pastor. The Church operates one senior high school, three junior high schools, one elementary school and two literacy centres for the Kpelle and Loma languages. The New Testament has been translated into these two tribal languages. An Old Testament translation is in preparation. The LCL also operates two hospitals, Phebe and Curran Lutheran Hospital, making an important contribution to the country's health service.

Although the Church faces shortage of funds and personnel, evangelism is high on its agenda. The youth programme has been intensified; young people are taking keen interest in the activities of the Church.

The LCL maintains relations with the Lutheran Church in America, the Lutheran Church of Bavaria, the Church of Sweden Mission and the Danish Evangelical Mission.

PRESBYTERY OF LIBERIA IN WEST AFRICA*
c/o City Hall, Monrovia. 1,200 members — 12 congregations — 10 ministers — 40 elders. WCC (1969), NCCL, AACC, WARC. Stated Clerk: Rev. Ellen A. Sandimani.

During the 17th and 18th centuries, many Africans were taken to America. They were often the first "non-Christian" people from overseas encountered by Americans, and so Africa understandably became the first overseas mission field for churches in the United States. In 1831, the Western Foreign Missionary Society was formed and chose Central Africa as its field of work.

In 1837, the board of foreign missions was set up by the Presbyterian Church in the USA. It took over the work in Liberia. For some time the policy was to send only African missionaries to Liberia; this was abandoned later. One of the African missionaries was a signatory of the Monrovian Declaration of Independence in 1847. The last missionaries sent from the United States came in 1887. In 1894, the board of foreign missions voted to continue financial aid on a diminishing scale until the Presbytery of West Africa in Liberia would become fully independent.

In 1944, the Presbytery decided to start a mission station in the hinterland. The station, with a mission school, was opened in 1945. Women have played an important part in the work of the Church in Liberia, and many of them have been ordained as evangelists.

MADAGASCAR

CHURCH OF JESUS CHRIST IN MADAGASCAR (Fiangonan' I Jesoa Kristy Eto Madagasikara).
"Ifanomezantsoa", Analakely, B.P. 623, Antananarivo — Tel: 268.45 — Cable: Fijekrima. 1,250,000 members — 76 regional synods — 3,000 parishes 12 synodal presidents — 925 pastors. Publication: Vaovao FJKM (in Malagasy and French). WCC (1969), CCM, AACC, WARC. President: Rev. Joseph J. Ramambasoa — General Secretary: Rev. Paul A. Ramino.

The three Protestant churches in the northern half of Madagascar, after eighteen years of negotiations, have now been united and constitute the Church of Jesus Christ in Madagascar. They had a common origin. For more than half a century there had been only one mission working in this island. The first missionaries sent by the London Missionary Society landed in the country in 1818. Between 1820 and 1835 schools were opened, the first church was founded, and the entire Bible was translated into Malagasy. Later on, however, up to 1861, missionaries were unwelcome, and Malagasy Christians were severely persecuted. In 1862, under a more liberal reign, LMS missionaries were allowed back in Tananarive. When they came they found an indigenous church which was still very active.

In 1864 a small group of Quakers came to work in cooperation with the LMS. They finally constituted a "Friends Church" south-west of the capital. The Society of Evangelical Missions (Paris) did not arrive until after the French conquest of the country in 1896. It is interesting to note that the Madagascar union negotiations were begun by missionaries but led to completion by Malagasy church leaders.

The CJCM is the largest Protestant church in the country. There are also two million Roman Catholics and 750,000 other Christians. Five and a half million of the population are animists.

The Church is actively engaged in solving political and socio-economic problems of the society. It has a strong ecumenical outlook. Among the current concerns are putting church property to greater use, improving ministers' salaries and pension funds, the creation of a Protestant theological faculty and the improvement of Protestant schools.

MALAGASY LUTHERAN CHURCH
(Fiangonana Loterana Malagasy)
B.P. 538, Antananarivo. 464,000 members — 2,897 congregations — 566 pastors. WCC (1966), CCM, AACC, LWF. President: Rev. Ranaivojaona-Razafimantsoa.

In 1966, when the Malagasy Lutherans celebrated their hundredth anniversary, they remembered their long history and their partnership with Norwegians and Americans. The Norwegian Missionary Society began work in southern Madagascar in 1866. The field was ripe. The work of the London Missionary Society, begun in

1818 with the encouragement of the Malagasy King Kadama I, was also encouraging. The Bible had been translated into Malagasy, and the Christians who had endured the period of persecution were now spreading the good news throughout the island. In 1888, a Norwegian-American missionary couple arrived in Fort Dauphin and were welcomed by government officials as the first Protestant missionaries to the southern tip of the country.

The Church consists today of seven regional synods with a general synod which coordinates the work. The general synod meets every three years and is the chief authority in matters of doctrine, discipline, institutions and evangelization. Administration is in the hands of the president and the executive committee assisted by a general secretary.

Since its mission beginnings, the MLC has been in the vanguard in the fields of evangelization, education, medical and social work, and development. Its traditional parish programme of Sunday schools and youth and women's work is supplemented by innovative ways of reaching people. A nationwide indigenous revival movement with emphasis on healing had its beginnings in MLC congregations. The "messengers" usually begin work in new areas where they stay for two years before returning home. The Church attempts to integrate this general movement into its life by a process of careful selection, training, and supervision.

Nearly 50,000 students are enrolled in the 111 primary and 32 secondary schools of the Church. Nine of the latter include teacher training programmes and four prepare students for university exams. The Church conducts a Bible school in Morondova on the west coast. A school for the blind in Antsirabé has rendered over fifty years of service; another for the deaf and dumb was founded in 1953. These two up-to-date institutions are the only ones of their kind in the country.

The Church's medical programme, begun in the early years of mission work, was greatly handicapped during the French occupation. Following the Second World War, permission was granted to build a hospital which has developed into the medical centre at Manambaro. Another hospital at Ejeda, surrounded by a network of child-care clinics, emphasizes preventive medicine. Two leprosaria, in Morondova and Antsirabé, have a long history of service. They employ modern methods of treatment, and also provide an educational programme for adults and children.

Since Madagascar became independent in 1960, the Church, with government help, has initiated 29 development projects. Among other pioneering efforts are a farm school at Tombontsoa (1960), a rural assistance centre at Manatantely (1973), and a centre for agricultural research at Manakara (1974). In 1976, the Church's second development workshop was held at Antsirabé. Plans are projected for farms which will act as training centres in each of the seven regional synods, an overall health and medical programme, a programme of assistance for the handicapped, and an intensive leadership training programme for technicians, teachers, and pastors. The latter will include the restructuring of the theological education programme to meet the pressing need to relate the gospel of Jesus Christ to all people.

colonial administration. The Church undertook educational, social and medical work and was supported by two English missionary societies, the Church Missionary Society and the Society for the Propagation of the Gospel. As the Church grew, indigenous pastors were trained and ordained to the ministry.

The total population of Mauritius is about one million. There are 600,000 Hindus, 250,000 Christians, 150,000 Muslims and small minorities of Buddhist and Bahai believers. The Roman Catholic Church is predominant, because the French colonial power had encouraged and supported the Church. Mauritius is a microcosm of different cultures and faiths, eastern and western, Asian, African and European.

The Anglican Church embraces the different cultures and strives to be relevant to the society, in spite of its minority position. It maintains a theological college and centres for the care of old people and blind and unwanted children, and two secondary schools. Besides its commitment to mission and evangelism, it seeks to be involved in interfaith dialogue.

MAURITIUS

CHURCH OF THE PROVINCE OF THE INDIAN OCEAN
Bishop's House, Phoenix, Mauritius — Tel: 865158. 65,000 members — 371 parishes — 93 priests. Publications: Anglican Herald (in English and French), Diocesan Magazine, Seychelles (in English). WCC (1975), ACC. Archbishop of the Province of the Indian Ocean and Bishop of Mauritius: Most Rev. Trevor Huddleston.

The Anglican Church in Mauritius started as the 'Church of England in Mauritius' after Great Britain took over the country from France in 1810. At first its ministers were civil chaplains serving the

MOZAMBIQUE

PRESBYTERIAN CHURCH OF MOZAMBIQUE* (Igreja Presbiteriana de Moçambique)
Caixa Postal 21, Maputo — Tel: 23139/22445. 15,000 members — 17 parishes — 23 pastors. WCC (1981), AACC, CCM, WARC, CEVAA. President of the Synodal Council: Isaias Funzamo.

The Presbyterian Church of Mozambique dates from 1887 when the mission of the Free Church of the canton of Vaud in Switzerland, now part of the Swiss mission, decided to extend its work to include the Tsongas of Mozambique. In 1948 the Church assumed its own financial responsibilities. In 1962, at a meeting of representatives of the Church and the

Swiss mission, the autonomy of the Church was officially recognized, and the status of missionaries serving the Church was clarified. An important synod of the Church was held at Lourenço Marques in 1963. Five new pastors were ordained, and a new constitution was adopted.

The synod discussed the important problem of making the sacrament of the Lord's supper available to its scattered membership. It adopted a solution which stresses the collegiate character of its pastoral ministry. The consistory of each congregation, under the direction of its minister, can now arrange for elders in pairs to conduct communion services, on dates already announced, in many of the places of worship which the pastor is unable to visit regularly.

From 1972-1974 the Church suffered greatly at the hands of the Portuguese authorities. Many Presbyterian church leaders were imprisoned in 1972; the Church's president, the Rev. Zedequias Manganhela, and one of its elders were killed in the infamous Machava concentration camp.

The PCM, together with the Anglican and Methodist Churches, ranks among the larger Protestant churches of the country. The Roman Catholic Church is the largest Christian community. Animists form the majority followed by Muslims. The new state ideology has resulted in far-reaching changes in Mozambique society.

Evangelization has always been accompanied by social work (hospitals, schools, farms, etc.). The PCM has had a profound influence on the cultural, social and political life of the people. It continues to search for new forms of 'Christian presence' within society by equipping its faithful with a mature biblical faith. The training of the laity and the education of youth through various programmes are priorities on the Church's agenda.

NIGERIA

CHURCH OF THE LORD (ALADURA)
(Ijo Enia Olluwa (Aladura)
Anthony Village, Ikorodu Road, P.O. Box 308, Ikeja, Lagos State — Tel: 01.964749. 1,103,340 members — 35 dioceses — 550 parishes — 520 bishops and pastors. WCC (1975), CAN, AACC. Primate: Dr E.O.A. Adejobi — General Secretary: Archdeacon S. Olu. Ajayi, Private Mail Bag 1063, Yaba, Lagos State.

The Church of the Lord is spread over the whole west African coast — from Kano in northern Nigeria, over 500 miles inland from Lagos, through Ghana and Liberia to Sierra Leone. The independent Church was founded in 1930 by the late Dr Josiah Olunowo Oshitelu in Ogere. He preached the gospel of repentance and regeneration from town to town — Ibadan, Ijebu-Ode, Abeokuta and even in Sabongida Orra in the Ishan division of the present Bendel State. His first converts were baptized at Abeokuta in 1931, and right from the beginning he started training Christians for active ministry. In 1937, he founded the Holy Mount Tabborrar festival which has become an annual event in the church during August. In spite of opposition from other Christian churches and resistance from traditional African religions, the Church grew steadily. In 1947 the Church was extended through the apostle E.O.A. Adejobi to Sierra Leone on the west coast of Africa. Many politicians and public servants are today members of the Church.

The Church is one of the first three pentecostal churches in Nigeria which have brought considerable revival among African Christians. It introduced a good deal of African culture and many African customs into its liturgy and church life. The Church subjects itself to the guidance of the Holy Spirit. It practises an evangelical ministry and has an ecumenical outlook; it accepts all who believe and proclaim Jesus Christ as Lord as brothers and sisters. Its major concerns for the 1980s include intensive evangelization, development of its seminary in order to train more efficient church workers, and social contributions to the society at large.

CHURCH OF THE PROVINCE OF NIGERIA

Bishopcourt, Bodija Estate, P.O. Box 3075, Ibadan. 802,830 members — 19 dioceses — 19 bishops — 1,119 priests and deacons. Publication: Provincial Magazine (in English). WCC (1980), AACC, CCN. Archbishop of Nigeria: Most Rev. T.O. Olufosoye — Secretary, Provincial Synod, P.O. Box 1666, Ibadan.

Nigeria's first link with the Church Missionary Society was through a slave boy, Ajayi, who was baptized in 1825 and later became the first African bishop.

Henry Townsend, a CMS missionary, entered Nigeria through Badagry in 1842. Later he came with a stronger missionary team to Nigeria in 1845. The work of evangelization progressed so well that in 1852 the Church Missionary Society Yoruba mission was founded. The Church Missionary Society Niger mission started its work at Onitsha in 1857. By 1957, there were five dioceses in West Africa. Two of them were in Nigeria — the diocese of Lagos (1919) and the diocese of Niger (1920). These two, together with the other three dioceses — Sierra Leone (1852), Accra (1909) and Gambia (1935) — formed the Province of West Africa. Since then, the Church has witnessed a rapid growth. The number of dioceses in Nigeria rose to 16. Steps were taken in 1979 to form the Province of Nigeria. Roman Catholics, Methodists and Baptists in Nigeria claim an equally large following.

The attendance at divine services everywhere is impressive. The Church is committed to evangelization in various areas where old beliefs erode, to fight against the increasing indifference to religion, and to meet the aggressive Islamic challenge.

Every diocese is self-supporting and has development programmes. Existing schools of theological education, classes for the training of members of tent-making ministries, and lay training centres need to be further strengthened. The Province has an office in Lagos from where the affairs of missionaries are administered, and a transit lodge for Christians of all denominations.

METHODIST CHURCH NIGERIA

21/22 Marina, P.O. Box 2011, Lagos — Tel: 01.631853, 01.632386, 01.635058 — Cable: Methodist, Lagos. 300,000 members — 12 dioceses — 71 circuits — 1,650 societies (churches) — 20 bishops — 340 ministers. Publication: Remembrancer (in English). WCC (1963), CCN, AACC, WMC. Patriarch: His Pre-eminence Bolaji — Secretary of Conference: Rt Rev. Rogers O. Uwadi.

In 1962 the conference of the Methodist Church Nigeria was established under the leadership of its Nigerian president. It was formed from the western Nigeria district, whose history began with the establishment of a mission at Abeokuta in 1842, and the eastern Nigeria district, which was the first scene of the labours of the Primitive Methodists, who in 1893 extended to the mainland the mission they had established on the island of Fernando Po.

The present Church is spread over all the regions of Nigeria and is divided into twelve districts with a total of 71 circuits. The conference has under its care 15 medical institutions of varying size, including the leprosy settlement at Uzuakoli, for which it receives financial help from the government. In the realm of education, the Church also makes an important contribution: it manages 522 day schools and 18 secondary schools, and also helps to provide teachers for Nigeria through the work of 15 teacher-training colleges — the most famous of which is Wesley College, Ibadan, founded more than sixty years ago. Ministers are trained at one or the other of the joint theological colleges — Emmanual College in the west and Trinity College in the east.

In 1974, a ministerial retreat reflected on matters relating to the constitution, liturgy, hymns, worship, structure and indigenization of the Church. In 1976, a patriarchal form of church government was introduced providing for a patriarch, archbishops and bishops in the Methodist Church of Nigeria.

United Methodist work in Nigeria, an outgrowth of the former Evangelical United Brethren Church under the auspices of the Sudan United Mission, is limited to the autonomous Muri Church of Christ in the Congola State, one of the least developed regions of Nigeria. Eighteen small tribal groups participate in the Muri Church. They are among the many minorities which, in the north, are dominated by the Hausas and Fulanis who are Muslim.

The MCN is putting greater emphasis on the evangelization of Muslims, the nurture of its own members to make them more committed Christians, and also on making provision for the unemployed and the neglected, and on more intensive work among youth.

NIGERIAN BAPTIST CONVENTION

Baptist Building, P.M.B. 5113, Ibadan — Tel: 412146, 412267, 412308. 300,000 members — 650 organized churches — 377 ordained ministers — 305 unordained ministers. Publication: The Nigerian Baptist. WCC (1971). President: Rev. Dr Osadolor Imasogie, P.O. Box 30, Ogbomosho — General Secretary: Rev. Dr S.T. Ola Akande.

Christian mission began in Nigeria in 1850 when Thomas J. Bowen, a missionary of the Southern Baptist Convention, entered the country. There was little progress during the first forty years because of health conditions, slave trade, and tribal war. After 1890 there was slow, steady growth. In the 20th century the membership of the Church rapidly increased. The NBC was formed at Ibadan in 1914. The Convention is divided into 12 state conferences, each conference made up of several associations of churches. An average of 5-20 churches form an association. The president, who presides over the annual sessions of the Convention and the executive committee, is elected for three years, and can be re-elected for a second term.

Primary education in Nigeria is financed chiefly by the government, with mission agencies providing necessary supervision of schools allocated to them. The Convention provides a religious curriculum for a great number of schools. The Nigerian Baptist Theological Seminary, which started in 1897, is now housed in a new building in Ogbomosho. Theological courses are arranged in such a way as to meet the needs of students with different levels of education. There are also four training schools for pastors with lower academic qualifications. The Convention has three large hospitals, two of which have a school of nursing. The Baptist building, opened in Ibadan in 1950, accommodates a dental clinic, a library and a book store. The Church has a printing press equipped with modern machinery. The departments of Sunday school, of youth work and student ministries, of lay training and of mass media are active. There is a strong women's missionary union. The Convention carries on missionary work in Sierra Leone.

PRESBYTERIAN CHURCH OF NIGERIA

26/29 Ehere Road, Ogbor Hill, P.O. Box 2635, Aba, Imo State — Cable: Presbyter ABA. 500,000 members — 8 presbyteries — 67 parishes — 439 congregations — 100 pastors. Publications: The Presbyterian Magazine, Synod Monthly Bulletin, Desk Diary and Church Almanac (in English, Igbo and Efik languages). WCC (1961), CCN, AACC, WARC. Moderator: Rt Rev. Dr Inya Okata Agha Ude, Yaba, 394 Murtala Mohamed Way, Box 251, Ebuta-Metta, Lagos — Synod Clerk: Very Rev. Akanu Alu Otu.

Nigeria became independent in 1960. In the same year the Presbyterian Church of Nigeria emerged as an independent church. The work goes back to 1846, when a group of Scottish and Jamaican missionaries, led by Hope Masterton Waddell, arrived at Calabar. The Jamaicans were former slaves who were making a 'freedom's offering' after emancipation in the West Indies. The first observance of the Lord's Supper took place at Duke Town, Calabar in 1847. The first Efik translation of the New Testament, by the Rev. Hugh Soldie, was published in 1861. The Church of Scotland's mission presbytery was dissolved in 1945 and the Presbyterian Church of Biafra was constituted. This Church was autonomous, but educational and medical work remained under the guidance of the Church of Scotland's mission board. In 1952, the Church was renamed the Presbyterian Church of Eastern Nigeria, and with the country's independence the word 'Eastern' was dropped. During the Nigerian civil war the Church suffered much. Church buildings have been rebuilt but the psychological and spiritual strain of the war years has not entirely disappeared.

Because of the discipline of the PCN, this Christian community has remained relatively small, as many Nigerians continue to practise polygamy. Church members are encouraged to play an active role in politics and to influence the government with Christian values. The Church is noted for the place women have been given in its affairs. There is a teaching centre for church sisters. The first woman minister was licensed to preach in January 1981 and was ordained in February 1982. Since each minister has the oversight of some 25 congregations, the duties are largely administrative and concerned with the celebration of the sacraments. The normal weekly services are for the most part conducted by the elders.

Primary concerns of the PCN in the coming years are the training of more ministers and evangelists (male and female), construction of maternity buildings, the promotion of Christian Girls in Training (CGIT), the development of the Presbyterian Young Peoples' Association of Nigeria (PYPAN) and boys and girls brigades. Successful fund-raising is also a major concern because the Church needs many new buildings for its activities.

Special relations are maintained with the Church of Scotland, the Presbyterian Church in Canada, the United Presbyterian Church in the USA, the Netherlands Reformed Church and some churches in the FRG.

RWANDA

PRESBYTERIAN CHURCH OF RWANDA (Eglise presbytérienne au Rwanda)
B.P. 56, Kigali — Tel: 2929. 52,000 members — 41 parishes — 32 pastors (another 11 in training) — 129 evangelists. WCC (1981), PCR, AACC, WARC. President: Michel Twagirayesu — Secretary: Rev. Edouard Gafaringa.

The gospel was first preached in Rwanda at the end of the 19th century by Protestant missionaries from the German Bethel Mission who came to Rwanda from Tanzania. After the First World War, they were replaced by missionaries from Belgium, Britain, Denmark and Switzerland. The Presbyterian Church of Rwanda is the only Reformed church in this part of Central Africa. It resulted from the work of representatives of the Belgian Protestant Mission.

Until 1957, the Church consisted of three parishes or missionary stations. The Church became independent in February 1959 as the Evangelical Presbyterian Church in Rwanda, but later changed its name to the Presbyterian Church of Rwanda. It wished to emphasize in a spirit of ecumenism that all churches are evangelical and did not wish to claim the title exclusively for itself. A large part of the pastoral and missionary work of the Church is carried out by evangelists and catechists.

The Presbyterian Church of Rwanda maintains close relationships with the Reformed churches in Belgium, the Netherlands (Gereformeerde Church) and in French-speaking Switzerland. The Church was a founding member of the Protestant Council of Rwanda in which it participates actively.

SIERRA LEONE

METHODIST CHURCH SIERRA LEONE

4 Kingharman Road, P.O. Box 64, Freetown — Tel: 40816 — Cable: Methodist Freetown. 25,420 members — 27 circuits — 21 pastors — 4 sector ministers — 11 probationers — 5 retired ministers. Publications: Almanac, Diary and Bulletin (in English). WCC (1967), SLUCC, AACC, WMC. President of Conference: Rev. Nelson H. Charles — Secretary of Conference: Rev. S.L. Wallace.

The Church was part of the British conference, and became autonomous in 1967. The conference undertook to continue in partnership in the gospel. The work had started in 1792 when the missionary society of the Wesleyan Methodist Church sent missionaries at the request of the converted settlers from Nova Scotia who, on arrival in the country, had formed themselves into religious classes. A few people served as local preachers and class leaders. Personnel from the Methodist Church in Great Britain and Ireland developed the missionary work in the provinces. There are now three district synods within one conference.

Church membership is widely representative of all sections of the nation. There is a strong lay leadership, with increasing participation by women in responsible positions. An indigenous liturgy has developed over the past thirty years among the Mende speaking members. Traditional marriage customs are still practised in the Mende family structure.

There is an increasing political awareness throughout the connexion. Several lay persons hold high offices in government. Many are in the civil service, the judiciary and in medical services.

The Church continues to make a valuable contribution to children's education through the management of many primary schools and ten secondary schools. It also participates in the national adult literary programme. The MCSL is greatly concerned about unemployment problems, heavy migration to urban areas and the consequent growth of slums, and the urgent need for low-cost housing, safe water supply and sanitation.

The Church maintains the Nixon Memorial Methodist Hospital with financial aid from the Methodist Church in Great Britain. The hospital runs a nurses' training programme in cooperation with the Roman Catholic hospital, and a community health project. The Lassa fever research project has made considerable progress. In the ophthalmology ward of the hospital many blind have received successful treatment.

The Tikonko Agricultural Extension Centre teaches new skills to farmers. Through the joint theological hall and a lay training centre the Church continues to prepare its members for the on-going mission and outreach of the Christian community in Sierra Leone. It maintains relations with several Methodist churches in West Africa, Gambia, Ghana, Benin, Togo, Nigeria and the Ivory Coast.

SOUTH AFRICA

CHURCH OF THE PROVINCE OF SOUTH AFRICA

Bishopscourt, Claremont 7700, Cape Province — Tel: 021.71-2531 — Also: P.O. Box 4849, Johannesburg 2000 — Tel: 011.28-2251/5 — Telex: 8-6519. 2,200,000 members — 731 parishes — 17 dioceses — 1,210 bishops and priests. Publications: Seek-Church Newspaper, Yearbook and Clerical Directory. WCC (1948), SACC, AACC, ACC. Archbishop: Most Rev. P.W.R. Russell — Provincial Executive Officer: Rev. Canon M.J.D. Carmichall, P.O. Box 4849, Johannesburg 2000.

The first bishop, Robert Gray, was sent out to be Bishop of Cape Town in 1847. His diocese included the Cape, the Free State, Natal and the Island of St Helena. By 1870 he had formed and organized several dioceses into a self-governing Province of the Anglican Communion. In 1955 the Dioceses of Mashonaland, Matabele and the southern half of Botswana left from the Church of the Province of South Africa when the Church of the Province of Central Africa was formed. The Province is now composed of 17 dioceses in the Republic of South Africa, the "Independent Homelands" of Transkei, Bophuthatswana and Vendaland, Namibia, the neighbouring territories of Lesotho, Swaziland, Mozambique and the Island of St Helena with Ascension Island. It is likely that the name of the Church will be changed in 1982 to the Church of the Province of Southern Africa. The Church forms the fifth largest Christian community after the Dutch Reformed Churches, the Independent African Churches, the Methodist Church of South Africa and the Roman Catholic Church.

The Church works in several countries, and in each it has its own characteristics. In the Republic of South Africa the dominating factor is the policy of apartheid. Lesotho and Swaziland are independent African countries, Lesotho being the poorer of the two. In Mozambique there is a Marxist government which has curtailed the freedom of the Church. In Namibia the border war between the South African army and SWAPO has put a great strain on the Church's work in Ovamboland. The racial composition of the CPSA is about one-fifth white, one-fifth so-called coloured, about 6,000 Indian and the rest African.

The main priorities in the years ahead are renewal and evangelism, total opposition to apartheid in Church and society, unity between its people across barriers of work, class, status, race, political views and national boundaries, and a ministry relevant to the emerging society. The major programmes are leadership training and providing for experience overseas for potential African leaders with a view to developing African leadership in the Church, theological training to ensure a sufficient number of theological teachers for the four seminaries and for theological education by extension, extensive diocesan schemes of the training of the laity.

EVANGELICAL LUTHERAN CHURCH IN SOUTHERN AFRICA

P.O. Box 32413, Braamfontein 2017 — Tel: 011.39-1968/9 — Telex: 86519. 515,349 members — 1,571 congregations — 326 parishes — 5 dioceses — 5 bishops — 407 pastors — 222 evangelists — 579 lay workers. Publications: ELCSA News, ELCSA Almanac. WCC (1976), SACC, AACC, LWF, ALICE. Presiding Bishop: D.P. Rapoo, P.O. Box 536, Rustenburg 0300 — General Secretary: M.D. Assur.

Behind the ELCSA lies a missionary legacy spanning over 140 years. In 1834, the Berlin mission began work in the Orange Free State. In 1911, the congregations of this mission were grouped into five regional synods and the beginnings of self-government foreshadowed a coming church. Other Lutheran missions from Germany and North America also came on the scene. It was a diverse and confusing situation, and in 1917 the first steps towards cooperation were taken by Lutherans — steps which laid the basis for the Federation of Evangelical Lutheran Churches in Southern Africa. The ELCSA was organized as an autonomous church in 1975.

The languages used are English, Afrikaans, and a variety of African dialects. Membership is both rural and urban. Most of the members live in the eastern half of South Africa, including Natal (Zululand), Transvaal, Orange Free State, and various parts of Cape Province. Because of apartheid, those employed in cities and towns must commute from all-black "locations", some of which are very large.

The diocese comprises circuits headed by deans; the circuits comprise parishes; the parishes, congregations. Each parish has a pastor or lay preacher, plus other workers, including one or more evangelists and deaconesses. The synod of the diocese is held every two years. Pastors are educated in Umpumulo Theological College and Marang Theological College. Other workers are educated in various schools and institutions operated by the Church. There are also health and welfare programmes, urban missions, and literature and communications projects. The ELCSA maintains relationships with the Evangelical Lutheran Churches in Namibia, Zimbabwe and the Federal Republic of Germany, the churches in Norway and Sweden, the Evangelical Church in Berlin and the American Lutheran Church.

METHODIST CHURCH OF SOUTHERN AFRICA

P.O. Box 2256, Durban 4000 — Tel: 379407 — Cable: Bollington. 354,236 members — 5,064 congregations — 302 circuits — 10 synods — 646 pastors. Publications: Dimension (monthly, English), Minutes of the Conference (English). WCC (1948), SACC, AACC, WMC. President of Conference (elected annually, holding office from October to October) — Ecumenical Affairs Convener: Rev. Dr D.G.L. Cragg, 2 Gilbert Street, Grahamstown 6140.

The British garrison at the Cape of Good Hope after 1806 included Methodist laymen who worked among the soldiers. Missionaries of the Wesleyan Methodist Missionary Society in England arrived in 1916, and work was eventually established in most parts of the present Republic of South Africa. The Wesleyan Methodist Church of SA became an affiliated conference of the Methodist Church in Great Britain in 1883, and it achieved independence in 1926. After the incorporation of the Primitive Methodist Missions and the Transvaal and Swaziland District of the British Conference in 1932, it was renamed the Methodist Church of South Africa. The name was later changed to the Methodist Church of Southern Africa in 1978, in view of the changing political geography of the sub-continent. There have been schisms from time to time, the largest and most recent being in 1978 when the government of Transkei banned the MCSA and the "United Methodist Church of SA" was formed.

According to census figures the Methodist Church (of which MCSA is by far the largest) ranks after the family of Dutch Reformed Churches and the rapidly growing African Independent Churches in a population that is predominantly Christian by confession.

The life of the MCSA reflects the strains and tensions of an apartheid society. Although it has a long tradition of opposition to segregation and racial injustice, its influence upon successive white governments has been minimal and much of its structure and organization reflected the social separation of the races. In spite of this, the conference and synods have long since been non-racial, and more recently there has been a sustained and deliberate endeavour to remove all traces of racism both from the constitution and the work of the Church. One expression of this is the endeavour to redefine circuits on a geographical rather than a racial basis. At the same time there is a growing awareness of the need for Africanization.

The Methodist Church is a member of the Church unity commission, but the unity movement has not made much progress at the local level.

Propaganda attacks on radio and TV and the activities of the government-subsidized Christian League of South Africa have contributed to dissatisfaction among some white laymen with the social and political stance of the conference. On the other hand, some younger black people regard the stance as too conservative.

The Methodist Church has to work out the implications of obedience to Jesus Christ as Lord and Saviour in the rapidly-changing social, political and economic context of Southern Africa. Major concerns will be on an evangelism which emphasizes both personal conversion and commitment to social justice, the promotion of non-racialism in the leadership and work of the Church, ministry to members in opposing political camps and, in particular, to the victims of apartheid, and a Christian critique of all political and social programmes.

An ad hoc commission appointed by the president of the conference has initiated an in-depth examination of the life of the Church. An assembly of 1,000 Methodists entitled "Obedience '81" was held at the University of the Witwatersrand in July 1981 to consider the role of the Church in the 1980s.

It is hoped to have the covenant of the church unity commission which involves, *inter alia*, the mutual recognition of the membership and ministries of the Anglican, Congregational, Methodist and Presbyterian Churches, before the 1982 conference.

MORAVIAN CHURCH IN SOUTH AFRICA

P. Bag 524, P.O. Cedarville, East Griqualand — Tel: 2204. 26,400 members — 127 parishes — 21 pastors — 6 evangelists WCC (1961), SACC, AACC. Rt Rev. Dr S. Nielsen.

Moravian mission started in South Africa when Georg Schmidt reached Cape Town in 1737 and began evangelization among the Hottentots. Subsequent missionaries were sent by the Moravian Church in Herrnhut, but faced various difficulties because of changes in the colonial government and the Boer War (1899-1902). Evangelization among the Kaffirs resulted in the construction of two flourishing villages, Shiloh and Goshen, which were both destroyed during an uprising of the population, and afterwards rebuilt. In 1857 a Moravian membership of 7,037 was recorded. Activities developed in the east and in west South Africa. Both started various ministries, like teaching, schooling relief and welfare.

Throughout the 19th and 20th centuries Moravians fought against intemperance and heathen feasts, African rites of circumcision, polygamy enhancing the wealth of the husband, superstition and the practices of witch doctors. To combat these influences the Church relied on Christian education, on prayer groups and organizations among men and women and young people, often sponsored by native Christians themselves.

Plans were made in 1909 to open a theological school at Shiloh, but a two-year theological course was established only in 1929. Since the Second World War the two Moravian provinces have been consciously drawing closer together. Fraternal visits were arranged. A joint theological seminary was opened in 1951 at Fairview. Instruction is given in Afrikaans and in English. During the fifties work in the gold fields was undertaken jointly. South Africa east provided leaders for the Xhosa-speaking congregations, while South Africa west started work at Langa among the Africans in Cape Town.

In 1956 the feasibility of union between the two provinces was discussed. At the synod of the Unitas Fratrum in 1967 the MCSA became an independent province. It has still close relations with the mother organization in Germany.

PRESBYTERIAN CHURCH OF AFRICA

P.O. Box 36043, Ntokozweni 4066, Durban, Natal — Tel: 032152.66. 2,000,000 members — 288 pastors — 116 evangelists — 55 lay youth organizers. WCC (1981), SACC, WARC, AACC. Synod chief clerk: Rev. Samson A. Khumalo.

The Presbyterian Church of Africa was founded in 1898 by the Rev. James Phambani Mzimba who broke away from the Free Church of Scotland, because of a misunderstanding between black and white clergy. Initially it had only two presbyteries and four ordained ministers, but within eighteen months it grew to four presbyteries and 50 ministers. Fifteen candidates were sent for ministerial education in the USA in 1915. Candidates for the ministry were later trained at Fort Hare University College; now they go to the Federated Theological Seminary of Southern Africa. It has consistently stressed that all ministers must be trained before ordination.

In 1973, the general synod of the PCA accepted that there is no scriptural ground for remaining exclusively black, and decided that its independent community should not remain isolated from other parts of the body of Christ. There are now eight presbyteries: six in South Africa, one in Zimbabwe and one in Malawi.

The Church has a strong leadership, without being clergy-dominated. Its task is seen as belonging to the whole people of God, though it has a sense of its own charismatic gifts. Among the younger ministers, many are today carrying out a tent-making ministry, pursuing other professions along with their pastoral work. Since the Church was all black, it has always had limited funds, and has grown completely without any outside help. It runs several projects without outside assistance, related to agricultural and community development, scholarships, work for the needy, etc.

PRESBYTERIAN CHURCH OF SOUTHERN AFRICA

P.O. Box 72057, Parkview, 2122 Johannesburg — Tel: 643.3151 — Cable: Presbytery. 75,000 members — 220 congregations — 200 pastors. Publication: "What's Going On Here" (Occasional Newsletter). WCC (1948), SACC, AACC, WARC, CUC (SA). Moderator changes every year — General Secretary: I.C. Aitken.

The Presbyterian Church of Southern Africa originated in the early years of the 19th century when missionaries began ministering to the soldiers of Scottish regiments stationed at Cape Town. Its earliest church, St Andrew's, was opened for worship in 1829. As the British settlement grew, congregations were formed in other parts of South Africa, and in 1897 a general assembly was constituted. This consisted of 23 congregations of members of European origin and ten of members of African origin. Today this Church has approximately 220 congregations/parishes throughout South Africa, Zimbabwe and Zambia, with one in Namibia. Of the approximately 75,000 members, two-thirds are white, the remainder being mostly black, though there is a small but growing work among the Indian community and

among the so-called coloured people of South Africa. At presbytery and general assembly level, men and women of all races sit and debate together. Compared to the other churches in the country, the Presbyterian Church of Southern Africa is a small church. The Dutch Reformed Churches, for instance, have over two million members.

Because the members of the Church are drawn from a variety of cultural and social backgrounds, it is difficult to describe the relationship of the Church to culture and society in simple terms. The white members of the church generally have a Scottish cultural background, though this is not as marked today as it was in an earlier period in the Church's life. The black members of the Church come from a variety of South African tribal backgrounds. There has been very little cultural interchange between the members. The Church, in its official comments on the political situation in the country, is generally critical of the policies of the government. The membership of the Church, on the other hand, reflects the wide variety of political divergence within the country.

The primary concerns of the Church in the 1980s revolve around the issues of race, reconciliation and Church unity. It seeks to be an agent of reconciliation among the races in South Africa. It also seeks to maintain better and deeper contacts between its own members of different races, and to express its mind on the racial issues which are constantly before the people.

The Church is involved in negotiations with two other Presbyterian churches, as well as with the United Congregational Church in Southern Africa, with a view to possible unity. It is also engaged with the Anglican and Methodist churches in the Church Unity Commission. Other issues in the life of the Church at the present moment include the effect of the charismatic renewal, the need for training leadership in the Church (particularly among the black membership), and the preparation of all members of the church for change in the society.

The significant programmes and activities in the Church at the present moment include the following: (a) lay leadership training conferences; (b) the Presbyterian Educational Fund — providing bursaries for university and school education for under-privileged people; (c) the development of centres of concern, to aid the development of the domestic workers; (d) the need to develop lines of communication within the Church. The Church maintains particular relations with the Church of Scotland, the United Presbyterian Church of the USA, Presbyterian Church of the United States and the Presbyterian Church of New Zealand.

REFORMED PRESBYTERIAN CHURCH IN SOUTHERN AFRICA

48 Eagle Street, Umtata, Transkei. 52,000 members — 81 parishes — 770 preaching stations — 46 ministers — 1,551 elders. WCC (1954), SACC, AACC, WARC. General Secretary: Rev. G.T. Vika.

The Reformed Presbyterian Church in Southern Africa, formerly Bantu Presbyterian Church of South Africa, was born out of the mission work of the various Scottish churches. The Church became autonomous in 1923. Educational and medical work remained necessarily in the hands of the mission board; but the oversight of congregations passed to the presbyteries. Although educational and medical work has now been taken over by the government, the Church still continues a pastoral ministry in these institutions.

In the Church's scattered congregations, the elders play a vital role in the conduct of worship. Since the Church's establishment, there has been a steady growth in the number of congregations, membership and income. The number of black ministers has increased, and that of missionaries has come down.

The Church is involved in union negotiations with the Presbyterian Church of Southern Africa, the Tsonga Presbyterian Church and the United Congregational Church of Southern Africa. In addition to these union negotiations, the Church is engaged in union negotiations with the Church of the Province of South Africa,

the Methodist Church of Southern Africa, the United Congregational Church of Southern Africa, the Presbyterian Church of Southern Africa and the Tsonga Presbyterian Church of South Africa.

UNITED CONGREGATIONAL CHURCH OF SOUTHERN AFRICA

P.O. Box 31083, Braamfontein, Transvaal — Tel: 396729. 117,000 members — 260 congregations — 2,400 preaching stations — 180 ministers. Publication: Christian Leader. WCC (1968), SACC, AACC, WARC. Secretary: Rev. Joseph Wing.

South African Congregationalism had two main sources. The London Missionary Society began work in 1799, and within fifty years had over thirty stations among the African and coloured peoples. In 1848, under pressure to extend northwards, it began a process of disengagement which was completed in a further thirty years or so.

The first purely European church was formed in 1813, but it was not until the 1850s, when the help of the Colonial Missionary Society was invoked, that the number of these churches began to grow substantially. A voluntary union of all these churches came into being in 1859, which led to the formation in 1877 of the Congregational Union of South Africa, embracing African, Coloured and European churches. Work and mission were extended into Rhodesia (Zimbabwe) at the end of the 19th century.

In 1967, the Congregational Union of South Africa united with the Bantu Congregational Church and the churches of the London Missionary Society (now the Congregational Council for World Mission) to form the United Congregational Church of Southern Africa. Further union negotiations are being held with the Presbyterian Church of Southern Africa.

The two church publications, *Presbyterian Leader* and *The Congregationalist* were merged to become the *Christian Leader,* with a circulation of some 23,000 copies.

The UCCSA operates several primary schools, secondary boarding schools, a teacher training college, a maternity centre and two dispensaries.

SUDAN

CHURCH OF THE PROVINCE OF THE SUDAN

P.O. Box 110, Juba. 1,000,000 members — 130 priests. Publication: News Letter (monthly). WCC (1977), SCC, MECC, AACC. Archbishop: Most Rev. Elinana J. Ngalamu — Provincial Secretary: Rev. John Lasu Kanyikwa.

In 1974, the diocese of Sudan, formerly part of the Jerusalem Archbishopric, reverted to the sole jurisdiction of the Archbishop of Canterbury as an extra-provincial diocese while awaiting the setting up of the new province of Sudan. The province, consisting of four dioceses — Juba, Omdurman, Rumbek and Yambio — was inaugurated in 1976.

Theological education is provided at Bishop Gwynne College, Mundi, via Juba, Equatoria.

PRESBYTERIAN CHURCH IN THE SUDAN*

P.O. Box 40, Malakal — Tel: 22260. 67,000 members — 9 parishes — 180 congregations — 23 ministers. WCC (1965), SCC, AACC. General Secretary: Rev. Thomas Maluit.

The Presbyterian Church in the Sudan is the fruit of missionary activity in Sudan by Presbyterian and Reformed Churches in the USA. It achieved autonomy in 1956. Christian believers in the Upper Nile had first been organized into a presbytery of the Nile which has since become the Coptic Evangelical Church (in Egypt). The Presbytery of the Upper Nile became the independent, autonomous Church of Christ in the Upper Nile, partly in order to include members of the Reformed Church in America who served as missionaries in the Upper Nile. In 1963, non-Sudanese members of the Church were removed from the church roll and given an associate relationship in the Church, which functions as a single presbytery.

The Church has been struggling for its very existence and for the liberty to carry on its task of making Christ known. The government expelled missionaries on the ground that they are foreigners; the Sudanese Christians today witness to their Lord in difficult circumstances.

Following the end of the long civil war, the Presbyterian Church in the Sudan became actively involved in the resettlement of refugees in the southern province, and set up a Bible and vocational training centre in Dolieb Hill near Malakal. Among its concerns at present are the communication of the gospel to people in remote rural areas, literacy campaigns and community development.

The PCS is the third largest church in the country after the Roman Catholic Church and the Episcopal Church. It maintains close relations with the United Presbyterian Church and the Reformed Church in the USA and the Basel Mission and the Presbyterian Church of East Africa.

TANZANIA

CHURCH OF THE PROVINCE OF TANZANIA

P.O. Box 899, Dodoma. 647,000 members — 9 dioceses — 1,800 parishes — 270 priests. Publications: 'Sauti Ya Jimbo' (quarterly, in Swahili), Target and Lengo (bi-weekly, in English and Swahili). WCC (1971), AACC. Archbishop: Most Rev. Musa Kahura-nanga, P.O. Box 13, Kasulu — Provincial Secretary: Rev. Martin H.K. Mbwana.

Following the provincial synod's decision at Dodoma in 1969 to divide the province of East Africa into the province of

Kenya and the province of Tanzania, the province of Tanzania was inaugurated in 1970, and the Bishop of Dar-es-Salaam, the Rt Rev. John Sepeku, was enthroned as the first Archbishop in the cathedral church of St Nicholas and African Martyrs, Ilala, Dar-es-Salaam. He retired as Archbishop in 1978. His successor is the Most Rev. Musa Kahura-nanga (Bishop of Western Tanganyika).

Theological education is provided at St Mark's Theological College in Dar-es-Salaam and at St Philip's Theological College in Kongwa.

EVANGELICAL LUTHERAN CHURCH IN TANZANIA (Kanisa la Kiinjili la Kilutheri Tanzania)

P.O. Box 3033, Arusha — Tel: 3221 — Cable: Luthang, Arusha — Telex: 42054 Luthang. 874,000 members — 14 synods/dioceses — 1,969 parishes, congregations, preaching places. Publication: Uhuru na Amani (in Swahili). WCC (1967), CCT, AACC, LWF. Rt Rev. Sebastian Kolowa Mkuu, Box 10, Lushoto — General Secretary: Mr Joel Ngeiyamu.

The Church was officially inaugurated in 1963. It now comprises eight dioceses and five synods in Tanzania and one synod in Kenya. Between 1886 and 1900 several missionaries from Lutheran church missionary societies in Germany came to Tanganyika to start work in the Usambara mountains, the coastal areas of Dar-es-Salaam, the southern highlands, the northern, central and western areas of the country. In spite of hardships faced from the beginning, and the interruption of activities during World Wars I and II, the gospel work continued and expanded. Seven antecedent Lutheran churches were the result of European and American missionary effort. The formation of the ELCT as a nationwide church coincided with the early years of Tanganyika's emergence as a new nation, just prior to its becoming Tanzania.

Lutherans are the largest Christian denomination in the country after Roman Catholics. Muslims form 32 per cent of the population while those of indigenous religions form 33 per cent.

The main language used in the Church is Swahili, though local dialects are also used. The general assembly meets every two years; it is the Church's highest authority. Its chief officer, the presiding bishop (president), is elected for a four-year term.

The Church had in the past followed western models; in recent years it has encouraged the revival African culture, especially in composing church songs and hymns. From the beginning it has assisted the government in the running of schools and hospitals; 70 per cent of the people have passed through church schools.

Major programmes of the Church are in the area of training pastors, evangelists, deacons and parish workers for evangelistic work. The gospel is not only proclaimed in Tanzania; missionary work is undertaken in Zaïre and Burundi and soon it will be extended to Mozambique. The Church has a theological college at Makumira, a medical training centre, a radio recording studio and several Bible schools. The ELCT has close relationships with the Church of Sweden and the Evangelical Lutheran Church in Denmark, Finland, Bavaria and Hanover.

TOGO

EVANGELICAL CHURCH OF TOGO
(Eglise évangélique du Togo)

1 rue Maréchal Foch, B.P. 2, Lomé — Tel: 214669 — Telex: 5327 Congat. 91,640 members —293 congregations — 57 pastors. Publication: Dutifafa na mi. WCC (1960), AACC, CEVAA. Moderator: Rev. Eli Kofi Ayiyi — Synod Secretary: Rev. Béné Touleassi.

The Church is the fruit of the work of the Norddeutsche Missionsgesellschaft which started its activities in the western region of Togo — which is today the Volta region of Ghana. The Church was established at the end of the 19th century. All missionaries except one had to abandon their work during the First World War. When the last missionary left the country in 1921, the Church had 22,000 members. Under the leadership of its first African president, the churches of the English- and French-speaking Togos were united in one synod in 1922, when it became an independent church. The Société des missions évangéliques de Paris assisted the Church from 1929 onwards in its relations with the colonial government, church schools, formation of catechists and the evangelization of northern Togo. From 1959 onwards the Church accepted full responsibility for all ongoing tasks. Its aim is to help each church member to appropriate the salvation of God in Jesus Christ in all aspects of daily life.

The Church is engaged in new forms of evangelism. It is hoped that these will lead to the realization of the liberation and the identity which God offers in his Son including liberation from physical illness. Each church member is being urged to become a witness of the gospel by discovering that he or she belongs to the Church of the poor.

UGANDA

CHURCH OF THE PROVINCE OF UGANDA, RWANDA, BURUNDI AND BOGA-ZAIRE
Primatial and Provincial Headquarters: P.O. Box 14123, Kampala, Uganda. 3,520,000 members — 6,700 parishes — 380 priests. Publication: The New Century (monthly, in English). WCC (1961), UJCC, AACC. Archbishop: Most Rev. Silvanus G. Wani — Provincial Secretary: Mr A. Gidudu.

A long history of devoted missionary work and Christian expansion led to the formation, in 1961, of the Church of Uganda, Rwanda and Burundi. The Archbishop of Canterbury inaugurated the province on

16 April 1961. Boga-Zaire was added in 1972. The province consists of twenty-three dioceses, ten of which formerly comprised the old diocese of Uganda, seven comprised the diocese of the Upper Nile and six are in Rwanda, Burundi and Boga-Zaire.

The francophone council was formed in 1976 to enable consultation to take place between the French-speaking dioceses of Rwanda, Burundi and Zaire and the Church of Uganda, Rwanda, Burundi and Boga-Zaire, with the intention of working towards the creation of a new province. In 1980 this new province was inaugurated, comprising the dioceses of Boga-Zaire, Bujumbura, Bukavu, Butare, Buye and Kigali.

Theological education is provided at Bishop Tucker Theological College, Mukono; Bishop Balya College, Fort-Portal; Canon Barham Divinity College, Kabale; Ngora Diocesan Training Centre, Ngora; Namungongo Martyr's Seminary, Lugogo; Aduku Diocesan Theological College, Lira; Kabwohe College, Mbarara; and Ringili College, Arua.

WEST AFRICA

CHURCH OF THE PROVINCE OF WEST AFRICA
Bishopscourt, P.O. Box 128, Freetown, Sierra Leone. 327,000 members — 800 parishes — 760 priests. WCC (1953), AACC. Archbishop: Most Rev. Moses Nathaniel Christopher Omobiala Scott.

In 1951, with the consent of the Archbishop of Canterbury and according to articles submitted by him after consultation with the dioceses concerned, the diocesan bishops of five West African dioceses holding mission from the see of Canterbury 'solemnly decreed and declared' that their dioceses were united in the Province of West Africa. It was to be "a Province of the Catholic Church in full communion with the Church of England and with the Anglican communion of churches".

The synod of the three houses met for the first time in November 1957, following the Crowther centenary celebrations of the Niger mission. The synod then made arrangements to prepare its constitution and canons. At its second meeting in Lagos in 1962 the constitution was finally passed, and received the approval of the Archbishop of Canterbury.

According to the articles, the provincial synod of the Church of the Province has the power to divide the Church into separate provinces related to one another within the Church, to admit new dioceses, and to authorize the creation of missionary dioceses or missionary areas. In 1952 the former diocese of Lagos was divided into the four dioceses of Lagos, Ibadan, Ondo-Benin and the missionary diocese of Northern Nigeria. The diocese of the Niger Delta was separated from the diocese on the Niger which was further divided by the creation of the diocese of Owerri. In 1962, a new diocese of Benin was created, taking part of its territory from the diocese on the Niger and part from the diocese of Ondo-Benin (now the diocese of Ondo). In 1967 the diocese of Ekiti was formed out of part of Ondo diocese, and in 1970 the diocese of Enugu was formed out of part of the diocese on the Niger.

In 1972, the diocese of Aba was formed out of part of the diocese of the Niger Delta. In 1973 the Archdeaconry of Kumasi was formally inaugurated as a diocese and two further dioceses were formed in 1974 in Nigeria, Kwara, from parts of Ibadan and Ondo dioceses, and Ilesha from Ibadan diocese. Two further dioceses were inaugurated in 1976 from parts of Lagos diocese, Ijebu and Egba-Egbado. In 1977, the diocese of Asaba was inaugurated from part of Benin diocese, and the diocese of Liberia was received as an associate diocese of the Province.

In 1979, the new Province of Nigeria was inaugurated comprising the dioceses of Aba, Asaba, Benin, Egba-Egbado, Ekiti, Enugu, Ibadan, Ijebu, Ilesha, Kwara, Lagos, the Diocese on the Niger, the Niger Delta, Northern Nigeria, Ondo and Owerri.

The dioceses of Accra, Kumasi, Liberia, Gambia and the Rio Pongas and Sierra Leone continue in the Province of West Africa.

Theological education is provided at Trinity College, Legon, Ghana and at Cuttington Divinity School in Suacoco, Monrovia, Liberia.

ZAIRE

CHURCH OF CHRIST IN ZAIRE (COMMUNITY OF DISCIPLES)
(Eglise du Christ au Zaïre — 10-Communauté des Disciples) B.P. 178, Mbandaka — Tel: 31.062.2225 — Telex: 21742 ECZ, Kinshasa. 301,420 members — 65 districts — 155 pastors (of whom 49 ordained) — 67 evangelists — 942 catechists. Publications: Bulletin d'Information des Disciples (BID — in French, Lonkundo and Lingala). WCC (1965), AACC. General Secretary: Rev. Dr Elonda Efefe — Ecumenical Correspondent: Rev. Ikedji Kesenge.

In 1897, Ellsworth E. Farris and Harry N. Biddle sailed from Boston to the Upper Congo. They had instructions from the Foreign Christian Missionary Society to explore areas near stations of the American Baptist Missionary Union, which by that time had become over-extended and was willing to consider transferring some of the work in the equator region to the FCMS. Farris and Biddle selected Bolenge as the most suitable site. On his way home in 1898 Biddle died. The work opened at Bolenge when Farris was joined by Dr and Mrs Royal J. Dye in 1899.

In 1964, the Community of Disciples became independent, although the United Christian Missionary Society (with offices in Indianapolis, USA) continued to support it financially. The Society helped with the construction of houses for the population of Mbandaka. In 1979 the United Evangelical Mission of Germany (offices in Wuppertal) agreed to support the mission of the Community of Disciples.

New laws were proclaimed in 1971 by President Mobutu covering the official recognition of religious bodies within Zaire. Only the Roman Catholic Church, the Church of Christ in Zaire and the Kimbanguist community were officially recognized. A year later, the Jewish community, the Muslims and the Greek Orthodox Church were also given government recognition. All Protestant churches and mission agencies were required to be associated with and to work through the Church of Christ in Zaire or close their work within the territory.

The Roman Catholic Church has a membership of 11,753,000; Protestant churches 8,878,000; the Kimbanguist Church 3,500,000; and the Muslim community 500,000. In the provinces of the equator the Community of Disciples is the largest church after the Roman Catholic Church.

The Church sponsors agricultural development projects in Bolenge and Ikengo, the raising of cattle, and the training of young people. It is in the process of building up a medical centre, a social centre for women in Mbandaka, a housing settlement and a large school in the same city, and a plant for the making of bricks. All these projects are indispensable, if Christians are to struggle against poverty, hunger, malnutrition, poor housing, disease and high infant mortality in the nation. The whole work is related to the gospel of reconciliation and salvation.

The Community of Disciples makes serious efforts to preserve African culture and art in liturgical celebrations. A small choir will sing African hymns in the FRG and the USA in 1982. The Church also sponsors religious services on radio and television.

Feuille episcopale (in French), Feuille episcopale (in Swahili and Kiluba). WCC (1973), AACC, BWA. Bishop Kitobo Kabwe-ka-Leza, Cabinet épiscopale ECZ-CEBA, B.P. 10.110, Kinshasa 1.

The Church was founded as an autonomous African community before the independence of Zaire, at Lubumbashi, in December 1956, by a Swiss missionary E. Clemann, with the help of Kabwe-ka-Leza and his friends. It cooperates with all other churches in Zaire and elsewhere in Africa.

The Church has an episcopal structure. The general episcopal conference meets every five years; the extraordinary episcopal conference meets annually. The episcopal cabinet is responsible for the ongoing work. A regional council meets as the need arises. Each episcopal communion has a council to discuss local problems.

Besides the bishop, three are three auxiliary bishops and an episcopal assistant. Auxiliary bishops and episcopal delegates are nominated by the bishop and approved by the general episcopal conference. Male and female candidates for the ministry are accepted by the episcopal cabinet. Ministers are educated at the Higher Theological Institute. They are ordained by the bishop or by his delegates. The Church insists on a thorough biblical and theological training. There are various social, diaconal, educational and medical activities which are promoted under the leadership of one or two pastors, the bishop or a lay person. The Church receives regularly voluntary workers from abroad. It is a founding member of the Church of Christ in Zaire and maintains close relations with churches in Denmark, Belgium, France, Switzerland and the European Association of Baptist Churches.

CHURCH OF CHRIST IN ZAIRE — EPISCOPAL BAPTIST COMMUNITY OF AFRICA*
(Eglise du Christ au Zaïre — Communauté épiscopale baptiste en Afrique)
B.P. 7112, Lubumbashi 4 — Tel: 5317 — Cable: CEBA. 58,000 members — 108 parishes — 110 pastors. Publications:

CHURCH OF CHRIST IN ZAIRE — 52d COMMUNITY OF LIGHT (Eglise du Christ au Zaïre — 52e communauté lumière)
B.P. 10498, Kinshasa I. 180,000 members — 100 parishes — 4 bishops — 120 pastors. WCC (1973), AACC. Patriarch Kayuwa Tshibumbu Wa Kapinga.

This Church celebrated its 50th anniversary in 1981. The origin of the Church can be traced to 1918 when, in the village of Kafinga, the father of the present Patriarch, Pastor Kayuwa, dedicated his life to the service of the Lord. The CCZ is an independent Christian community proclaiming the gospel of Christ and evangelizing people in order that the whole human being may be liberated. Sunday is considered the holy day instituted by God in the fourth commandment (Exod. 20:8). On Wednesday many gatherings take place — prayer sessions, Bible studies, etc. The first Friday of each month is reserved for a spiritual meeting of all the members of the congregation.

The Church is an integral part of the cultural and religious life of the society. It organizes various meetings for youth and women, vacation schools, evangelistic campaigns, literacy courses for adults, Sunday schools, and is involved in health centres and in common transportation. It also sponsors projects of agricultural development and cattle breeding. The Church maintains close relations with other Christian communities in Zaire, and abroad with the disciples of Christ. It became a member of the AACC in 1969.

CHURCH OF CHRIST IN ZAIRE (MENNONITE COMMUNITY) (Eglise du Christ au Zaïre — Communauté mennonite)

B.P. 18, Tshikapa. 40,000 members — 121 places of worship — 384 Sunday schools — 63 ordained pastors — 103 lay preachers — 172 deacons — 231 catechists. WCC (1973), AACC. General Secretary: Rev. Kabangy Djeke Shapasa.

Before the formation of the Congo Inland Mission in 1912, the Mission Board of the Mennonite Church (organized in 1883) and the Central Illinois Amish Mennonite Conference (organized in 1899) had sent missionaries to the Congo. The United Mennonite Board of Missions was organized in 1911 and incorporated as the Congo Inland Mission in 1912. The name was changed to the Africa Inter-Mennonite Mission, Inc. in 1970. Missionaries of the Swedish Baptist Mission joined the Congo Inland Mission in 1914.

American Mennonite missions have been at work principally in three provinces: Bandundu, Western Kasai and Eastern Kasai. In 1948, the Mennonite community, like other churches, began receiving financial support from the government for the operation of schools. Thousands of children were educated and the Church sponsored Bible translations and literacy programmes.

The Evangelical Mennonite Church of the Congo was established in 1960. At the time of the struggle for independence from colonial rule, Mennonite missionaries had to leave the country. After independence the Mennonite community became stronger; today it continues its extensive school programme. At present it operates two Bible schools and a theological school also.

CHURCH OF CHRIST IN ZAIRE (PRESBYTERIAN COMMUNITY) (Eglise du Christ au Zaïre — Communauté presbytérienne)

B.P. 117, Kananga. 150,000 members — 941 congregations — 252 pastors — 1,176 elders. WCC (1972), CCZ, AACC, WARC. General Secretary: Dr Tshihamba M.L.

The Presbyterian Community within the Church of Christ in Zaire, which was originally known as the Presbyterian Church in the Congo, has grown out of the work begun by the American Presbyterian Congo Mission which entered the field in 1891 by opening a station at Luebo. Church organization began with the ordination of pastors, even before congregations were organized. Originally these pastors served regional churches, and in order to have sessions which could function with the pastors, teaching evangelists of outstanding ability were elected as elders and put in charge of groups of villages in which the evangelists worked. With the ordination of these elders, presbyteries were organized and met several times a year.

By 1930, several organized congregations had called their own pastors and elected elders from among their own members; they had also chosen deacons to see to the material side of the Church's affairs. Continued work on the Book of Church Order and the organization of the presbyteries into a synod marked the steady growth of the Church, and in 1959 the Mission was relieved of supervision of the Church and the synod became autonomous. The next year, the synod received its "personnalité civile" or incorporation as a legally responsible body in the eyes of the government.

In 1971 and 1972, by presidential decrees, all but three of the more than 1,300 religious groups in the country were asked to re-apply for permission to function. The three exempted were: the Roman Catholic Church, the Church of Christ in Zaire, which has within it a number of Protestant churches including the Presbyterian Community, and the Kimbanguist Church.

CHURCH OF CHRIST IN ZAIRE — 23 EVANGELICAL COMMUNITY (Eglise du Christ au Zaïre — 23 Communauté évangélique)

B.P. 36, Luozi. 33,750 members — 50 parishes — 48 pastors. Publication: Minsamu Mia Yenge (Messages of Peace, in Kikongo and French). WCC (1961), AACC. President: Rev. K. Lukombo Ntontolo.

The Church was born out of the Svenska Missionförbundet which was founded in 1878 in Stockholm as an outcome of a revival movement in Sweden. Carl Johan Engvall was the first missionary to reach the Congo. Soon after it was agreed that the Swedish Missionary Society should work in cooperation with the Livingstone Inland Mission. Later some stations of the American Baptist Missionary Union were transferred to the Swedish mission. The Church became autonomous in 1961.

The work of the Evangelical Community is mainly rooted in the countryside and communication and transportation present problems. In recent years evangelistic campaigns have been undertaken also in larger cities of the country. The Church sponsors various primary and secondary schools, three hospitals and several dispensaries. It also has a printing press, a library and a museum. Three doctors and about fifty medical assistants take care of 20,000 sick people every year. The schools and hospitals were established before the government took over responsibility for schooling and medical care. The Church works in close relationship with the state authorities.

Besides evangelization, the principal concerns in the 1980s are further involvement in education, medical work and women's programmes. The Church continues to maintain its relations with the Swedish Missionary Society and also has close contacts with the Evangelical Church of the Congo.

CHURCH OF CHRIST ON EARTH BY THE PROPHET SIMON KIMBANGU (Eglise du Christ sur la terre par le Prophète Simon Kimbangu)

B.P. 7069, Kinshasa I — Tel: 68944, 68851, 69217 — Telex: 21315 Kimbang Kinshasa. 5,000,000 members. WCC (1969), AACC. Spiritual Head: His Eminence Joseph Diangienda-Kuntima.

When the Kimbanguist movement began in 1921, it was regarded by the colonial authorities as a political time-bomb. Extreme repressive measures were adopted against the movement by the government. For the most part these met the approval of European Christians — Catholic and Protestant alike. Simon Kimbangu's prophetic career lasted only for a few months; he was imprisoned as a dissident for the remaining thirty years of his life. In 1951 a military court sentenced him to death. The sentence was commuted by King Albert I of Belgium into detention for life. Kimbangu was deported to Lubumbashi (200 km from his home) where he died. Nearly 100,000 of his followers were exiled between 1921 and 1957. These measures served only to the strengthen the movement. It spread rapidly. Even though no triumphalist claims have ever been overtly made by the Kimbanguist leaders, such claims were often attributed to them because of the official status granted to the movement, on a basis of complete equality with Roman Catholic and Protestant churches. They insisted on being identified as Kimbanguists rather than as Protestants.

The Church was officially established in 1959. A theological faculty was opened in Kinshasa in 1970. The Kimbanguist Church is governed by an international council and an international executive council. There are Kimbanguist communities in Zaire, Congo, the Central African Republic Angola and Burundi. There are active communities in Paris and Brussels. Eighty-seven per cent of the members are from the main line churches (Roman Catholic, Reformed, etc.). *Esssence of Kimbanguist Theology* contains the Church's theological statement. It recognizes four sacraments: baptism, eucharist, marriage and ordination. The eucharist is celebrated three times a year at Christmas, Easter and 12 October. The Church adheres to the Nicence Creed. From 1976-1981 the largest church building in Africa, seating 37,000, was built; it was inaugurated at Easter 1981. The social involvement of the Kimbanguist Church has been impressive; its educational programme is exceptional; and women are accorded an equality in the Church that liberal western institutions seldom achieve. Like every movement which is being shaped into an organization, the Kimbanguist Church has also been caught up in an inevitable process of institutionalization. Yet it remains the deep desire and longing of the Church that the charismatic element break through again and again. Spiritual retreats have been declared necessary for all church members, particularly for theological students; they last up to five days and include prayer, singing, the Bible meditation, fasting and confessing of sins (called purification).

Mr Bena-Silu is the first Kimbanguist to be elected as member of the WCC Central Committee and Executive Committee. He was elected in 1975.

ZAMBIA

UNITED CHURCH OF ZAMBIA

P.O. Box 50122, Nationalist Road at Burma Road, Lusaka — Tel: 250641 — Cable: Unichurch. 100,000 members — 648 parishes — 92 pastors. WCC (1966), CCZ, AACC, WARC, WMC. President: Rev. Doyce M. Musunsa — General Secretary: Rev. Joel Chisanga.

The United Church of Central Africa in Rhodesia, now part of the United Church of Zambia, owes its beginnings to the work of the London Missionary Society, the Church of Scotland Mission, the Union Church of the Copperbelt and the Copperbelt Free Churches. It was the London Missionary Society which sent David Livingstone and many others in the last quarter of the 19th century.

In the Copperbelt of Northern Rhodesia, mining commenced early in the 1920s. Christians from various areas went to work in the mining towns, and interdenominational worship began in both the African and European housing areas. Helped by the fact that they were already cooperating in education and welfare, the Church of Scotland, the Methodist Missionary Society, and the London Missionary Society came together in African areas to form the Union Church of the Copperbelt. Shortly after this, the congregations of the European areas came together in the Copperbelt Free Church Council.

By 1945, the way had been prepared for the union of the London Missionary Society and the Church of Scotland Mission in Northern Rhodesia. These congregations, along with the Union Church of the Copperbelt, joined to form the Church of Central Africa in Rhodesia. In 1958, the act of union took place. In 1965, the Church united with the Methodist Church and the church of Barotseland to form the United Church of Zambia.

The UCZ maintains good relations with the Methodist Church in Great Britain, the Church of Scotland, the United Church of Canada, the United Presbyterian Church and the United Church Board for World Ministries in the USA.

Asia

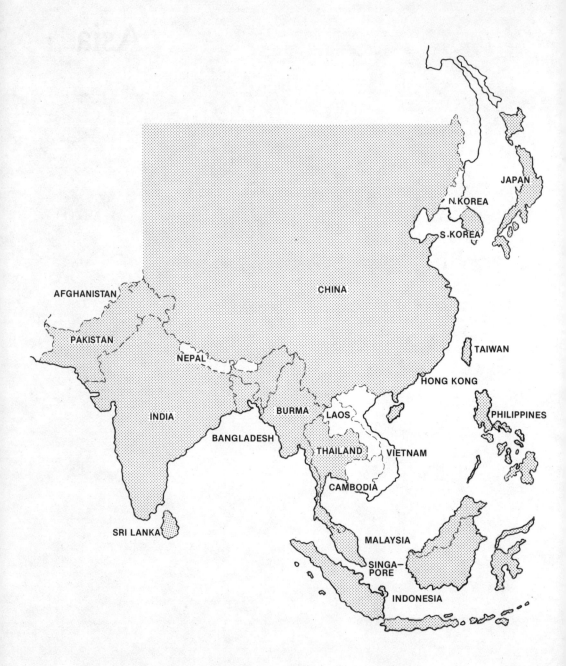

AFGHANISTAN

PAKISTAN

NEPAL

CHINA

N.KOREA

S.KOREA

JAPAN

TAIWAN

HONG KONG

INDIA

BANGLADESH

BURMA

LAOS

THAILAND

VIETNAM

CAMBODIA

PHILIPPINES

SRI LANKA

MALAYSIA

SINGA-
PORE

INDONESIA

BANGLADESH

BANGLADESH BAPTIST SANGHA

Sadarghat, P. O. Box 1108, Dacca I — Tel: 234644. 26,500 members — 8 districts — 192 churches — 74 ministers and missionaries. Publication: 'Sangha' (in Bengali). WCC (1976), NCCB, CCA, ABF, BWA. President: Mr M.S Adhikary — Executive Secretary: Rev. R.N. Baroi.

A first convert, Krishna Pal, from the Church at Serampore founded by William Cary, came to Dacca and preached the gospel. Most of the churches were established in Dinajpur, Jessore, Khulna, Barisal and Faridpur districts from 1800 to 1850. Later Australian and New Zealand members of Baptist Missionary Societies started work in East Bengal (now Bangladesh). The Church was one community with headquarters in Calcutta until India was divided into Pakistan and India in 1948. In 1971 the Church took the title: Bangladesh Baptist Sangha. It is the largest Christian community in the country; there are several other smaller denominations, among which are the Church of Bangladesh (12,150), the Garo Baptist Union (16,000), the Sylhet Presbyterian Synod (9,500) and the Evangelical Christian Church (12,350).

Some of the best educational institutions belong to the Church. The BBS medical institutions meet the needs of a considerable section of the population. Nurses trained in these institutions work in several government hospitals. The Church has very little political influence but it is active in the cultural realm.

Islamic leaders often urge the government to control Christian activities.

The BBS faces difficulties in the 1980s because of the 'Foreign Donation Ordinance' of the government. All medical, relief, educational and missionary institutions have to be registered, their projects approved and their accounts audited by the government. Foreign missionary personnel is reduced to a minimum and no new missionaries are allowed to enter the country.

Since Bangladesh is one of the poorest nations in the world, the Church's main emphasis is on improving economic and medical conditions, wherever possible. Its economic development board is very active. Its hospital Chandraghona is one of the best in the country and its leprosy centre the only place where reconstructive surgery is carried on. There is also a boarding school for blind girls and a training centre for blind women. The Church is steadily growing. It tries to maintain relations with the Baptist Missionary Society in London and the Liebenzeller Mission in the Federal Republic of Germany.

CHURCH OF BANGLADESH*

St Thomas Church, 54 Johnson Road, Dacca 1 — Tel: 234650. 12,400 members — 36 parishes — 18 bishops and priests. Publications: Bishop's News Letter (twice a year) in English, Kapot in Bengali. WCC (1975), CCA, NCCB. The Bishop of Dacca: Barnabas Dwijen Mondal.

The Church was founded over a hundred years ago, as a result of the work of the Church Missionary Society, the Oxford Mission to Calcutta and the English Presbyterian Society. When Bangladesh became an independent state, the Diocese of Dacca of the Church of Pakistan was constitutionally organized as an autonomous church under the name of the Church of Bangladesh. It is the second largest Protestant church in the country, after the Bangladesh Baptist Sangha. The Roman Catholics number 250,000.

Like other Christian communities, the Church of Bangladesh is closer to the Hindu community than to the large Muslim population. Christians are often thought of as a product of the former British rule, and they have little influence in society. Most of the faithful come from the poor classes of farming people with large families and very limited resources. There is much unemployment and poverty.

The Church of Bangladesh has a few child care and primary schooling programmes. It is also engaged in small self-help development activities.

The Church maintains particular relations with the Church of North India, the Church of Pakistan, the United Reformed Church, UK, the Church of Scotland, the Reformed Church in the Netherlands, the Episcopal Church, USA, and the Anglican Church in Australia.

BURMA

BURMA BAPTIST CONVENTION
143 St John's Road, Rangoon — Tel: 72419 and 73238 — Cable: Burbaptist. 372,250 members — 2,855 congregations — 821 ordained pastors. Publications: Myitta Taman Magazine (in Burmese). WCC (1957), BuCC, CCA, BWA. General Secretary: Rev. Victor San Lone.

The kingdoms of Ava and Pegu, later united under British rule as Burma, received their first missionaries from the Roman Catholic Church when a Barnabite mission arrived in 1722. In 1807 English Baptists opened a mission, but the first permanent Baptist mission came in 1813 from America under Adoniram Judson. During his life-time — he died in 1850 — 63 congregations were established; 163 workers, both national and foreign, ministered to the needs of over 7,000 Baptists. Christianity has been particularly well received by the Karens, a hill tribe with a tradition that they had once possessed and then lost the knowledge of the true God and that foreigners would help them recover it.

In 1865, the Baptist churches in Burma organized themselves under the name Burma Baptist Missionary Convention. In 1954 the name was changed to Burma Baptist Convention. In 1958, the BBC took over responsibilities for mission from the American Baptist Foreign Mission Society. The Convention today represents all Baptists in the nation. During the last two decades its relation to the Kachin Baptist Convention has been strengthened.

Christians, including Roman Catholics, represent 4.3 per cent of the total population of 32.5 million people. The Baptists are the largest denomination in Burma.

Eighty per cent of the congregations are located in rural areas, where people are engaged in agriculture, forestry and mining. Most local churches support themselves. In the years ahead the BBC hopes to develop backward areas through several church programmes, to lead the faithful to a fuller and more mature Christian life and to encourage leadership training at every level of church life.

CHURCH OF THE PROVINCE OF BURMA (Myanma Nainggan Krityam Athindaw)
Bishopscourt, 140 Pyidaungsu Yeiktha Road, Dagon P.O., Rangoon 11191 — Tel: 72668 — Cable: Bishopscourt. 45,000 members — 300 parishes — 125 priests. Publication: Newsletter (in Burmese). WCC (1971), BuCC, CCA, ACC. The Most Rev. Gregory Hla Gyaw, Archbishop of Burma.

The Church was established on the west coast by army chaplains around 1825. It was only in 1853 that the first missionaries arrived. The diocese of Calcutta had pastoral and administrative oversight of the Church in Burma. In 1877 the diocese of Rangoon was inaugurated. Since the Second World War, missions which were not already operating in Burma have not been allowed to enter the country. The last of the missionaries were asked to leave in 1966. The early emphasis on a trained leadership, lay and ordained, as well as on an educated laity generally, has proved an invaluable asset to the Church. A new Province of Burma was formed in 1970 with four dioceses: Rangoon, Mandalay, Pa'an and Akyab.

The Church is not involved in social work as this field is the total responsibility of the government. In times of national catastrophe the Church provides aid for relief. Primary concerns of the Church are evangelism, improvement of teaching programmes and the training of clergy evangelists. The Church of the Province of Burma is actively involved in the Burma Council of Churches (so constituted in 1974, formerly the Burma Christian Council) with Baptists, Methodists, Presbyterians, Lutherans and the Salvation Army.

HONG KONG

CHURCH OF CHRIST IN CHINA, THE HONG KONG COUNCIL

Morrison Memorial Centre, 191 Prince Edward Road, Kowloon — Tel: 3.803346 — Cable: Churchinch, Hong Kong. 40,000 members — 33 parishes — 40 pastors. WCC (1967), HKCC, CCA, CWM, WARC, WMC. General Secretary: Rev. Peter Wong.

After the establishment of the People's Republic of China, the Hong Kong Council became an independent unit of the Church of Christ, of which it had originally been a district in the Kwangtung synod. (The Church of Christ in China was founded on the mainland in 1927 when some fifteen denominations and missions — over half of them Presbyterians — united.)

Conditions in the densely populated territory of Hong Kong necessitate emphasis on educational, social and medical work, and so the Hong Kong Council operates 53 schools with about 1,000 teachers and 40,000 pupils. In higher education, the Church is involved in Chung Chi College, one of the three colleges that make up the Chinese University. The famous Nethersole Hospital offers a wide range of services. A new United Christian Hospital at Kwun Tong near Kowloon has been constructed. Attached to this hospital is a task force on community health.

The Hong Kong Council of the Church of Christ in China shares in the work of the Hong Kong Christian Service.

INDIA

INDIA

BENGAL-ORISSA-BIHAR BAPTIST CONVENTION*

Sepoy Bazar, Midnapore, West Bengal — Tel: 437. 6,050 members — 63 parishes — 50 pastors. WCC (1965), BeCC, BiCC. Executive Secretary: Rev. S.K. Bepari.

In 1836 Free Will Baptists started missionary work in this part of India which spread to the western section of Bengal, the southern part of Bihar and the northeastern part of Orissa. These states were and remain the cradle of orthodox Hinduism in spite of a century and a half of missionary enterprise. In 1911 the Free Will Baptists handed their work over to the American Baptist Mission. Recently, owing to many changes, the major work has become the responsibility of indigenous leadership under the Christian Service Society. The headquarters are in Midnapore, West Bengal. The Church runs five high schools, two junior high schools, a hospital and a technical school. After the Roman Catholics the Baptists are the largest single denomination in this area.

The Church is keenly aware of the particular cultural context in which it evangelizes. It is concerned over the social conditions of the local community, the improvement of housing, health, hygiene and education. It is the Church's conviction that the gospel addresses itself to the whole human being, physically and spiritually. A continuous education of the congregation is of crucial importance. Stewardship is greatly encouraged. Annual refresher courses are given to pastors and members of congregations. Spiritual needs are met by agencies like the Bible Society and radio evangelism and in open air witness and home visitation by a team of church workers. Film evangelism is promoted. Much work is still supported by the Board of International Ministries of the American Baptist Churches in the USA.

CHURCH OF NORTH INDIA

"Wesley Lodge", 16 Pandit Pant Marg, New Delhi 110 001 — Tel: 386513 — Cable: Synod, New Delhi. 1,063,000 members — 23 dioceses — 1,200 pastorates — 23 bishops — 954 presbyters. Publication: The North India Churchman (in English). WCC (1972), NCCI, CCA, WARC. Moderator: Most Rev. Dr R.S. Bhandare — General Secretary: Rev. Pritam B. Santram.

The series of consultations, with a view to church union in North India, began in 1929. Two bodies, the Round Table Conference and the Joint Council, were formed in order to make a preliminary study. Eventually, on the "basis of negotiation" prepared by the Round Table Conference in 1939 and revised in 1940, a plan of church union was drawn up. A negotiating committee was constituted in 1951 by the church bodies concerned — which were the United Church of North India, the Anglican Church of India, Pakistan, Burma and Ceylon, the Methodist Church of Southern Asia, the British and Australian Methodist Churches and the Council of the Baptist Churches in Northern India. In 1957, the Church of the Brethren and the Disciples of Christ also joined in the negotiations. The plan reached its fourth and final edition in 1965 and, on that basis, the Church of North India was inaugurated in 1970 in Nagpur. However, at the last moment, the Methodist Church in Southern Asia decided not to join the union.

The Church in India must make its witness in a context of many faiths. It is a minority church which still enjoys the freedom to worship and witness. Christianity in India was for centuries associated with colonial domination, though in actual fact Christianity in India dates back to the days when one of Christ's disciples, Thomas, is said to have arrived in India, bringing the good news to the sub-continent.

One of the primary concerns of the Church is to bring about unity among churches. A joint council of the Church of North India, the Church of South India and the Mar Thoma Syrian Church is working towards conciliar union. In 1981 they moved a step further in their ecumenical endeavours in expressing their "organic oneness".

Major programmes of the CNI include church life, expression and witness of faith, development, education, medical and health care, relief and social care for the orphaned, widowed, aged and disabled. All these programmes are meant for the community at large.

CHURCH OF SOUTH INDIA

P.O. Box No. 4906, Cathedral, Madras 600 086 — Tel: 811266. 1,471,000 members — 1,228 parishes — 8,715 congregations — 20 dioceses — 1,214 bishops and priests. Publication: South India Churchman. WCC (1948), NCCI, CCA. Moderator: Most Rev. I. Jesudason, Bishop's House, LMS Compound, Trivandrum 695001, Kerala State — General Secretary: Rev. M. Azariah.

The Church of South India was inaugurated in 1947, after thirty years of union negotiations between the South India United Church — the combined body of Presbyterians and Congregationalists — the Anglican dioceses in South India and the South Indian districts of the Methodist communion. Out of the twenty dioceses, one is in Jaffna, Sri Lanka. The basis of the constitution is the Lambeth Quadrilateral, the historical episcopate being accepted in a constitutional form. From the beginning all ordinations have been by bishops.

Resolutions of the Lambeth Conference of 1968 and the Anglican Consultative Council of 1971 advised Anglican churches and provinces to re-examine their relation to the CSI with a view to entering into full communion with that Church. The main limitation which remains in establishing closer relations with the CSI is the presence of a small number of presbyters who are not episcopally ordained. Men and women with specialized qualifications are still welcomed for the work in the Church.

Primary concerns are evangelism and social justice. The Church is engaged in a consultation on priorities for the mission of the Church both at diocesan and synod levels. A synod consultation to this effect was held at Madras in October 1981. Major programmes and activities of the CSI are: evangelism, stewardship, healing and educational ministries, technical and vocational training, rural and urban development, Christian nurture of the congregation, theological education and training of pastors.

MALANKARA ORTHODOX SYRIAN CHURCH (Malankara Orthodox Suriyani Sabha)

Catholicate Palace, Devalokam, Kottayam-686038, Kerala — Tel: 8500 — Cable: Devalokam, Kottayam. 1,600,000 members — 15 dioceses — 130 congregations — 1,130 churches — 15 bishops — 950 priests — 62 deacons. Publications: Malankara Sabha and 'Orthodox Youth' (both in Malayalam). WCC (1948), CCA, OOCC. His Holiness Moran Mar Baselius Mar Thoma Mathews I, Catholicos of the East and Malankara Metropolitan — Secretary for Interchurch Relations: Bishop Paulos Mar Gregorios, Orthodox Theological Seminary, 686001 Kerala.

The history of the Indian Orthodox Church dates back to 52 A.D. when the apostle St Thomas, according to an old tradition, landed in Cranganore, Kerala. During a twenty-year stay he converted the Brahmins and others and was martyred on St Thomas Mount, Madras.

The connection with the Roman Catholic church began in 1599. The synod of Diamper ended it officially in 1653 with the "vow at Curved Cross" (Coonen Cross) when a large number of people, holding a long rope tied to a cross at Mattancherry, Cochin, vowed that they and the succeeding generations of church members would have no connection with the Pope of Rome and the Roman Catholic faith.

The next association was with the Syrian Church of Antioch, from which Mar Gregorios was sent to regularize the ordination of Mar Thoma I in 1665. The Syrian Church began to demand increasing authority over the Indian Church. In 1886, a council was called by Patriarch Peter II at Mulanthuruthy to claim ownership of the temporal wealth of the Indian Church also. The dispute ended in 1912 when Patriarch Abdul Masiah established the Catholicate in India and announced that the Catholicate of Edessa (East Syria), defunct for years, was now re-established in India. A dissident group wanted the powers of the Patriarch of Antioch to continue in India. The resulting feud ended in 1958 with the decision of the supreme court to recognize the Indian Catholicos, the Malankara Metropolitan, on all matters of dispute including the validity of the constitution and canon.

The members of the MOSC live within the social setting of the people of other Christian traditions as well as of other faiths and ideologies. As a Christian community it is part of the nation's history for more than nineteen centuries. It has always sought its Eastern Orthodox ecclesiastical identity, while being rooted in its Indian heritage. A founding member of the WCC, it seeks to maintain healthy relations with all churches in both East and West.

The Church has hospitals, schools and colleges where service is rendered to people, irrespective of caste and creed. The Orthodox Theological Seminary turns out annually about twenty students with a four-year theological training. A federated faculty for post-graduate studies, in which the MOSC, the Mar Thoma and the CSI seminaries participate, has been inaugurated. The seminary is also planning to introduce a programme of religious education for lay persons by extension. A missionary training centre trains young men and women for specific missionary vocations. A committee has been appointed to study the improvement of worship and music.

The MOSC has parishes in Malaysia, the Gulf countries, in the USA, UK and Germany. It has particular relations with sister churches in Syria, Egypt, Ethiopia and Armenia.

MAR THOMA SYRIAN CHURCH OF MALABAR (Malankara Mar Thoma Suriani Sabha)
Poolatheen, Tiruvalla, Kerala 689 101 — Tel: 2449. 500,000 members — 7 dioceses — 790 parishes — 6 bishops — 440 priests. Publication: Malankara Sabha Tharaka (in Malayalam). WCC (1948), NCCI, CCA. Metropolitan: Most Rev. Dr Alexander Mar Thoma — Secretary: Rev. C.G. Alexander.

According to tradition the Church was founded by St Thomas in A.D. 52. During the 14th and 15th centuries the Mar Thoma Church had friendly relations with the Church in Antioch. When at the beginning of the 17th century the Portuguese established their power in India the Church was forced to accept the jurisdiction of the pope in Rome. But in 1653 the Church declared itself independent.

In the beginning of the 19th century India came under British rule. British missionaries established educational institutions and assisted the Syrian Church in the founding of a theological seminary. The Bible was translated into Malayalam in 1829. Abraham Malpan and other committed Christians initiated a movement for reformation in the Church. They insisted on reordering the life and practice of the Church in the light of the scriptures, and spearheaded a movement of reform which got rid of the corrupt observances and ceremonies which had crept into the Church. The reformed section of the old church became known as the Mar Thoma Syrian Church of Malabar, or simply the Mar Thoma Church.

While retaining the traditional characteristics of the ancient Eastern Church, it has kept very close relations with Christian churches in other parts of the world. The Church is in full communion with the Anglican Church. Particular relations are maintained with the Episcopal Church in the USA and the Uniting Church of Australia. The Joint Council of the Church of North India, the Church of South India and the Mar Thoma Church are currently forging ahead towards the goal of conciliar unity.

The Mar Thoma Church, professing the biblical faith and awakened to missionary responsibility, has been engaged in active evangelism, and the promotion of general education, technical training and medical work. It participates actively in the political life of society. It is involved in the ecumenical movement and has always stood for church unity and active cooperation with other churches. It has maintained good relations with Hindus, Muslims and other religious groups. The members form one of the most literate communities in the country and they have contributed to the social and cultural advancement of the nation.

Issues like poverty, unemployment, injustice and violence have been taken up for special study and action. The church has a particular concern for Harijans, and has worked for their uplift. It runs orphanages and homes for the poor, supported by church members from their own resources. A school for the blind and a school for the mentally retarded are being established. The care for the aged is taken up as a special programme.

SAMAVESAM OF TELUGU BAPTIST CHURCHES
C.A.M. Highschool Compound, Nelore 3 AP, South India — Cable: Ambaptist. 340,000 members — 1,880 parishes — 110 pastors. WCC (1965), NCCI, CCA, BWA. General Secretary: Rev. K.C. George.

The STBC is a registered organization consisting of 515 independent Baptist churches. American Baptists started missionary work in South India among the Telugu speaking people in 1836. In 1887 the existing churches were organized into the Convention of Telugu Baptist Churches. In 1962 it became the Samavesam of Telugu Baptist Churches with a unanimously adopted constitution. From then on, funds of the American Baptist Foreign Mission Society were channelled through the Samavesam.

The theological training of pastors and evangelists began in Ramapatnam in 1874. Students are now educated at Andhra

Christian Theological College in the Vijayawada-Guntur area. Bible training has been maintained in Ramapatnam. There are over a thousand Sunday schools with an enrolment of over 40,000 children.

Strongly favouring interdenominational cooperation, the STBC is active in the Andhra Christian Council and the National Christian Council of India. The Nagarjunasagar Christian Centre is a joint project with the Andhra Evangelical Lutheran Church. The Samavesam also participates actively in the retreat and training centre programme of the Andhra Christian Council in training voluntary church workers. It is involved in the work of the Henry Martin Institute of Islamic Studies in Jabalpore and the Christian Medical College in Vellore. It supports the Student Christian Movement and the United Mission Tuberculosis Sanatorium in Arogyavaram.

UNITED EVANGELICAL LUTHERAN CHURCHES IN INDIA

'Luther House', Gurukul Campus, Thumbuswamy Road, Kilpauk, Madras 600010 — Tel: 664266. 1,500,000 members — 3,000 congregations. Publication: Indian Lutheran (in English). WCC (1948), NCCI, CCA, LWF. Executive Secretary: Rev. Dr K. Rajaratnam.

Nearly three out of ten of Asia's Lutherans live in India, where Protestant missions began work in 1706. India's Lutheran churches, established by German, Danish, Swedish, Norwegian, and American mission societies and boards, extend from the far north to the southern tip along the eastern part of India.

In 1853 the first Evangelical Lutheran synod was held at Guntur, Andhra Pradesh. In 1905 a Lutheran general conference was held in Kodaikanal with representatives from five missions. The first all-India Lutheran conference was held in 1908, and was represented by nine missions. In 1928 the constitution of the Federation of Evangelical Churches in India was presented. The common liturgy was approved in 1935. In 1947, a convention at Ranchi proposed the forming of a United Lutheran Church in India. Lutheranism found new meaning by changing the constitution of the FELCI so that it became the United Evangelical Lutheran Churches in India in 1975.

The following nine churches belong to UELCI: Andhra Evangelical Lutheran Church; Arcot Lutheran Church; Evangelical Lutheran Church in Madhya Pradesh; Gossner Evangelical Lutheran Church; India Evangelical Lutheran Church; Jeypore Evangelical Lutheran Church; Northern Evangelical Lutheran Church; South Andhra Lutheran Church; and Tamil Evangelical Lutheran Church.

Through the UELCI the nine member churches participate collectively in the WCC and the CCA, but they are individual members of the LWF.

Lutherans in India were pioneers in composing indigenous lyrics to Indian tunes.

Primary concerns for the 1980s include developing programmes sponsored by the Division of Social Action; awareness building on the need to fight poverty, hunger and unemployment; self-reliance in matters of theology, publications and finance; effective participation in the Indian ecumenical movement; global partnership as a task of each Christian community; and improvement of the training of ministers at Gurukul Theological College and Research Institute.

The UELCI maintains close relations with the American Lutheran Church, the Lutheran Church in America, the Lutheran Church Missouri Synod, VELKD, Hermannsburg, Santal Mission, Gossner Mission and the Danish Missionary Society.

INDONESIA

BATAK CHRISTIAN COMMUNITY CHURCH* (Gereja Punguan Kristen Batak)

Jln. HOS. Cokroaminoto 96, Jakarta Pusat — Tel: 343884 — Cable: Gereja PKB Jakarta. 15,000 members — 1 synod/

diocese — 35 congregations — 16 pastors — 5 evangelists. WCC (1975), CCI, LWF. Ephorus/Bishop: Rev. L.H. Sinaga — Secretary: Mr J.P.L. Tobing.

The Church was established in 1927, and acknowledged by the government as a church in 1933. Besides its congregations in the Jakarta area in Java, it has branched out to Palembang (south Sumatra), and Tapanuli (north Sumatra), where it continues to evangelize the Maya-Maya people.

The BCCC is organized into five districts. With the approval of the governing body, the central synod, each congregation chooses its own pastor. Congregations unable to support themselves cooperate with other congregations in ways coordinated by the central synod.

All congregations are visited at least annually by members of the general synod, who survey their progress and provide guidance. Financially weak and underdeveloped congregations are helped in this way. Lack of pastors and evangelists is still a great problem for the Church.

The Church's doctrinal basis derives from Luther's small catechism, and its forms of worship and other practices are in keeping with the Lutheran legacy. It maintains particular relations with the Joint Evangelical Mission in Wuppertal, Federal Republic of Germany, and the Lutheran Church of Australia.

BATAK PROTESTANT CHRISTIAN CHURCH (Huria Kristen Batak Protestan) Pearaja-Tarutung, North Sumatera. 1,160,000 members — 1,702 congregations — 310 ordained pastors — many workers in education, youth, health and community services. WCC (1948), CCI, CCA, LWF. General Secretary: Rev. F.H. Sianipar.

Although the Church became independent in 1930, the German missionaries continued in leadership until 1940, when they were interned by the Dutch government after the Nazi attack on the Netherlands. This left the Church with neither money nor leadership. The period of the Japanese occupation (1942-1945) was particularly difficult when the members were forced to conform to Shinto practices and to work on Sundays. The teaching of religion in schools was prohibited, church meetings were controlled, and houses of worship often used as stables.

A confession of faith was adopted by the BPCC synod in 1951. The ecumenical creeds, the Reformation confessions and more recent ones like the Barmen Theological Declaration (1934) were the foundations on which the Church built its own confession. Until recently, animism and Islam were the main temptations. New ones are now evident, and the Church's confession of faith names them, e.g. Adventists, Pentecostals, nationalistic Christianity, and syncretism. Other Batak churches have either adopted this confession or produced similar ones.

The Nommensen University, opened in 1954, was built in response to the felt need for higher education in the new nation. Its main campus in Pematang Siantar houses a theological faculty and a school of education; its second campus in Medan houses the agriculture and economic departments and the schools of technology and business administration. The university has links with the Luther Seminary in south Australia and plays an important part in APAS, the Lutheran-initiated Asian Programme for Advanced Study.

The majority of the members are rural people, engaged in small farming and living in villages, some of which still preserve the traditional multi-purpose houses. Other members are city-dwellers, with large numbers in Pemantang-Siantar, Medan, and elsewhere in Sumatera, as well as in Jakarta, other parts of Java and various places in Kilamantan (Borneo). As Christians and as Bataks, they are making an impact on Indonesian life. The church language is Batak. Most of the BPCC congregations are self-supporting.

The Church's long involvement in health and community services includes the hospital in Balige, near Lake Toba, with its deaconess centre and training programme. A growing number of Batak deaconesses, serving as nurses and community workers, are replacing the initial group of sisters from the house of deaconesses in Kaiserswerth, Germany. The Christian Publishing House in Jakarta, developed in cooperation with other churches, serves Indonesian Christianity. Since 1968, the BPCC and the Lutheran Church in America have developed mutually helpful relations.

CHRISTIAN CHURCH IN CENTRAL SULAWESI (Gereja Kristen Sulawesi Tengah)
Tentena, Poso, Central Sulawesi. 100,000 members. WCC (1948), CCI. President: Rev. J.P. Lagarense.

The great majority of the population of central Sulawesi belongs to this Church which became independent in 1947. It has a presbyterial-synodical order.

Among the priorities are the encouragement of wider participation of members in the life of the Church and the promotion of youth programmes and of community development projects.

CHRISTIAN CHURCH OF EAST JAVA
(Gereja Kristen Jawi Wetan)
Jln. Supriadi 18, Tilpun 5846, Malang, East Java — Tel: 0341.25946. 123,850 members — 101 congregations — 112 pastors. Publication: Duta (in Indonesian). WCC (1948), CCI, CCA, WARC. General Secretary: Rev. Suharto, SH — Moderator: Rev. Sardjonan.

The Christian Church of East Java is a church of the Javanese people and still uses Javanese in its services and Sunday school instruction. Though the Church was only organized in 1921, its beginnings can be traced to 1840 when the first Javanese convert was baptized. This first convert was introduced to the Christian faith through the witness of two laymen, an Indo-Russian farmer and a German watchmaker. The watchmaker had twice been imprisoned, because missionary activities were then prohibited.

The first Dutch missionaries came in 1860, when the ban on missionary work among the Javanese was lifted. Their leadership of the existing Christian community so decisively moulded its life and mission that the Christian Church in East Java can rightly be regarded as a daughter Church of the Netherlands Reformed Church.

The Church has been a missionary church from the beginning. In 1956, the population of East Java was 21 million, 85 per cent Islamic. In 1955 the Church took a radically new approach to its evangelistic task, which until then had been carried out largely through traditional methods. This new approach has involved training lay people to equip them for a more conscious, and intensive personal witness. A number of 'mature' congregations became responsible for at least three neighbouring Christian communities.

Unity among churches in Indonesia, whether such churches are members of the National Council of Churches or not, is a primary concern for the years ahead.

The CCEJ maintains particular relations with the Netherlands Reformed Church and the United Presbyterian Church in the USA.

CHRISTIAN CHURCHES OF JAVA
(Gereja-Gereja Kristen Java)
Jln Dr Sumardi 5, Salatiga, Mid Java. 121,500 members — 174 congregations — 136 ministers — 580 preachers. WCC (1950), CCI, WARC. Executive Secretary: Mr Hadi Purnomo SH.

The Church came into being in 1949 as the result of a union of the Christian Javanese Church in south central Java (founded in 1931 through the missionary work of the Reformed Churches in the Netherlands) and the Christian Javanese Church of North Central Java (founded in 1937 through the work of the Salatiga mission, sponsored by the "Waisen- und Missionsanstalt" of Germany). It ack-

Protestant Christian
Batak Church

Christian Protestant
Church in Indonesia

Indonesian Christian Church

Karo Batak Protestant Church

Simalungun Protestant
Christian Church

Kalimantan
Evangelical
Church

Protestant Eva
Church in Min

Nias Protestant
Christian Church

Christian Churches
of Java

Christian Church
of East Java

Toraja Church

Christian Ch
Central Sul

Batak Christian Community Church

Indonesian Christian Church

Pasundan Christian Church

Protestant Church in Indonesia

Protestant Christian Church
in Bali

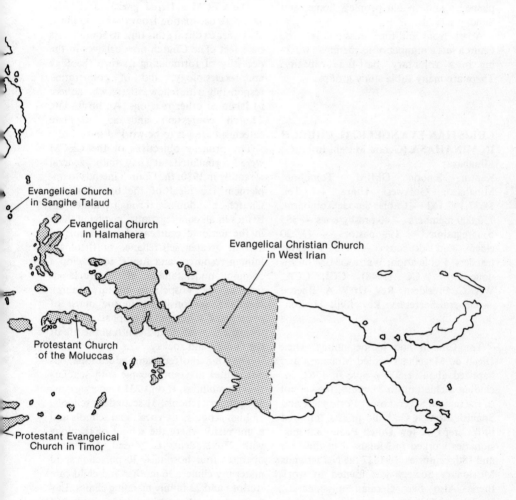

Evangelical Church
in Sangihe Talaud

Evangelical Church
in Halmahera

Evangelical Christian Church
in West Irian

Protestant Church
of the Moluccas

Protestant Evangelical
Church in Timor

nowledges the Apostles' Creed and the Heidelberg Catechism. In government it is presbyterian.

The CCJ carries on missionary work among Javanese transmigrants in Sumatra and in central Java through a number of agencies. These include schools for education at all stages, teacher training schools and hostels for students; general hospitals and maternity hospitals; a bookshop; orphanages and an old people's home; and Sunday schools.

Apart from full-time missionaries, the Church has a number of its members working in a voluntary, part-time capacity. There are many Bible study groups.

CHRISTIAN EVANGELICAL CHURCH IN MINAHASA (Gereja Masehi Injili Minahasa)

Kantor Sinode GMIM, Tomohon, Minahasa, Gulawesi Utara — Tel: 36.37.107.162 — Cable: Sinode Tomohon. 730,000 members — 40 presbyteries — 555 congregations — 199 pastors — 13,220 elders and deacons — 155 religious teachers. Publication: Warta GMIM (in Indonesian). WCC (1948), CCI, CCA, WARC. President: Rev. Dr W.A. Roeroe — General Secretary: Rev. Kelly H. Rondo.

The Church had its beginnings when Diego de Magelhaes visited Minahasa and baptized about 1,500 people in 1563, including a chieftain in Manado, the capital of the region. Several other Portuguese and Spanish Roman Catholic priests followed in his steps. A few Dutch Protestant missionaries worked in Minahasa in the 17th and 18th centuries. In 1827 the Netherlands Missionary Society was invited to work there. Also two German missionaries, Riedel and Schwarz, started a mission in 1831. A teacher training school was opened as early as 1851. Assistant pastors were trained but not allowed to administer the sacraments. By 1880 the Christian community had grown to 80,000 members which was about 80 per cent of the Minahasa population. In 1876 the Church

became a part of the colonial state church, the Church of the Indies. It was later called the Protestant Church in Indonesia. In the first synod meeting at Tomohon in 1934, the Church was proclaimed independent and took its present title. Besides a few Dutch pastors there were only twenty indigenous 'assistant pastors'. Most congregations were being cared for by 'teacher-preachers' of the teachers training school.

The CECM suffered greatly under the Japanese occupation from 1942-1945 but it also learned during this time to stand on its own feet. The Church now believes in the necessity of formulating its own theology and ecclesiology, and of cooperating responsibly with fellow citizens who adhere to Islam or other religions. An up-to-date Church confession and an adequate catechism are yet to be worked out.

The primary objectives of the CECM were formulated at its ninth general assembly in 1980; the Church intends to implement the ideal of the one Christian Church in Indonesia through planned activities in all congregations, involving them in the national ecumenical movement; to aim at greater self-reliance in theology, human resources and funds; to develop a common understanding of the proclamation of the gospel; to nurture church members' responsibility in the midst of society and state; and to emphasize the active role of women and youth in the life of the church and society.

The Church offers many educational opportunities to young people with scholarship possibilities. It runs 231 kindergartens, 367 primary schools, 51 secondary schools, 15 high schools, six vocational schools and a university where the school of theology with 250 students is housed. It further operates four hospitals, 30 polyclinics, 12 maternity clinics, 36 mother and child care stations and 22 family planning clinics. Lay training courses are regularly conducted which concentrate on social justice and stewardship education and participation in village cooperatives.

Particular relations exist between the CECM and the Protestant Church in Sabah, Malaysia, the Japan Overseas Christian Medical Cooperative Service, the

Netherlands Reformed Church and the Reformed Churches in the Netherlands, the Church of the Brethren in the USA, the Covenant Church in the USA and the Disciples of Christ, the United Presbyterian Church in the USA, the Basel Mission and the Evangelical Mission in South West Germany.

CHRISTIAN EVANGELICAL CHURCH IN SANGIHE-TALAUD (Gereja Masehi Injili Sangihe-Talaud)

Kantor GMIST, Tahuna, Sangir Talaud, Sulut — Cable: Sinode GMIST Tahuna. 190,000 members — 326 parishes — 111 pastors. Publication: Church Letter (in Indonesian). WCC (1974), CCI, CCA, WARC. Chairman of the synod: Rev. S. Kanalung — Secretary of the synod: Rev. S.S. Londo.

The territory of the Church consists of about 70 small islands, with a population of 240,000. It is situated to the north of Sulawesi and to the south of the Philippines. In this area Roman Catholics, Adventists, Pentecostalists and Muslims are minority communities. In 1563 the king of Siau was baptized and became a Roman Catholic. Portuguese missionaries stayed on the island until 1677. During the Dutch period the Church grew slowly through the work of missionaries sent first by the Far East India company and from 1856 onwards by the Netherlands Reformed Mission Board. The Evangelical Church faced difficult periods during which education stagnated and people relapsed into animism. When the Japanese armed forces landed on the islands in 1942, all foreign missionaries were put in prison and several of them murdered.

The Church achieved autonomy in 1947. It continues, however, to rely in part on the help of the Board of Foreign Missions of the Netherlands Reformed Church. From 1967, the Church has employed a missionary in the southern islands of the Philippines, who works together with the Philippine church.

The Christian Evangelical Church is active in the field of health and education. It has almost 200 elementary schools, four high schools, two theological teachers' college, three polyclinics and a hospital. Its primary concerns for the 1980s are raising the educational standards of its ministers, the construction of a synod office building and a large meeting place, the securing of pension for its retired pastors and the raising of living standards of the population. The Church maintains relations with the mission boards of the Netherlands Reformed Church and the Reformed Churches in the Netherlands, the Swiss East Asia Mission and the Presbyterian Church in New Zealand.

CHRISTIAN PROTESTANT CHURCH IN INDONESIA (Gereja Kristen Protestan Indonesia)

Kantur Pusat/Head Office, Jalan Kapt. M.H. Sitorus 13, Pematangsiantar, SU — Tel: 22664 — Cable: GKPI Pusat. 177,980 members — 622 parishes — 100 pastors. Publication: Suara GKPI (The Voice of GKPI, in Indonesian). WCC (1977), CCI, CCA, LWF. Bishop: Rt Rev. Dr A. Lumbantobing — General Secretary: Rev. R.M.G. Marbun.

The congregations of this Church are located in north, central, and south Sumatra, as well as in Java. The official language is Indonesian, but for purposes of evangelization and mission, various Batak and other dialects are used. The members are mainly farmers, but many, in towns and cities, are in the civil service, educational service and business.

This Church emerged out of a reform movement in the Batak Protestant Christian Church and became an independent body in 1964 under its present name. It is headed by a bishop who, with the general secretary, forms the CPCI leadership; they are responsible to the general synod of the Church. The Church's central legislative body of 25 comprises eight pastors and 17 lay people. Each congregation is headed by a lay teacher-preacher. Congregations are grouped into "ressorts" or circuits headed by a pastor.

Church headquarters in Pematangsiantar are centrally located for the Batak country. Pastors of the Church are educated in various places, including Nommensen University and Jakarta Theological Seminary.

The CPCI traces its roots back to the work of Dr I.L. Nommensen (the apostle to the Bataks) and to the Rhenish Mission, now called the Vereinigte Evangelische Mission (VEM-United Evangelical Mission). In 1975, the Church became a partner within the VEM; in the same year it was accepted also as a member of the LWF. Because of certain issues (mainly concerned with property matters) between the CPCI and the BPCC, membership in the Council of Churches in Indonesia (CCI) was delayed for several years. It was only in 1976 that the CCI, in its eighth general assembly, unanimously voted to accept the CPCI as a full member.

Special projects of the Church include a health centre, two rice-planting estates, complete with medical clinics, for resettling landless people, a small orphanage, a home for retired Bible women and, in Medan, a 500-watt radio station for evangelism.

The Church maintains close relations with the Lutheran Church of Australia, the Lutheran Church in America, the Overseas Missionary Fellowship, the Christian Missionary Society and the Norwegian Christian Mission.

EVANGELICAL CHRISTIAN CHURCH IN HALMAHERA

Synod Office, Tobelo, Halmahera, Maluku Utara. 97,000 members — 283 congregations — 126 pastors — 76 evangelists. WCC (1979), CCI, WARC. General Secretary: Rev. O.R. Djawa.

This Church in the North Moluccas grew out of the missionary work of the Netherlands Reformed Church. It became a self-governing Church of presbyterian tradition in 1949. The ECCH is a founding member of the Council of Churches in Indonesia and of the Moluccan Regional Council. It supports the work of Ujung

Pandang Seminary and is a member of the Indonesian Christian Schools' organization. Since 1974 it has operated its own theological college at Ternate.

EVANGELICAL CHRISTIAN CHURCH IN WEST IRIAN (Gereja Kristen Injili di Irian Jaya)

Jln Argapura/Kotakpos 14, Jayapura, Irian Jaya. 360,000 members — 800 congregations — 77 ministers — 900 evangelists. WCC (1967), CCI, CCA, WARC. President: Rev. W. Maloali.

The ECCWI is the fruit of missionary work of the Netherlands Reformed Church. It became autonomous in 1956 and its first synod met at the end of the same year.

West Irian was formerly West New Guinea, a Dutch colony. As a result of an agreement signed in New York in 1962, the western half of New Guinea, now called West Irian, became part of Indonesia.

The Church plays an important role in the educational system of the whole country. Sixty per cent of the schools are under its care. Lack of funds and personnel continues to be a major problem. The Church is involved in mission work in the hinterland among the people of the high mountain regions. In this work, it is assisted by Dutch and German missionaries.

INDONESIAN CHRISTIAN CHURCH (Gereja Kristen Indonesia)

Jln. Panglima Polim I/51A, Kebayoran Baru, Jakarta — Tel: 712040. 71,170 members — 103 congregations — 132 pastors. Publications: Pelita and Maria and Marta (in Indonesian). WCC (1965), CCI, CCA, WARC. General Secretary: Rev. Dr J.H. Wirakotan.

The Indonesian Christian Church is essentially a Chinese church. It was formed in 1962 by the coming together of the

Christian Church of West Java, the Christian Church of Central Java and the Christian Church of East Java. Each of the constituent churches forms a synod of the united Church. Each synod has still its own constitution and keeps a certain autonomy within the united Church. For the whole united Church, there is a general assembly, as well as a Moderamen (executive committee) of no less than six persons elected for four years.

The Gereja Kristen Indonesia is entirely autonomous. While recognizing the essential interdependence of the churches, particularly those of the same confession, it is responsible to no other church for the conduct of its own life, including the training, ordination and maintenance of its ministers, the enlisting, development and activity of its lay forces, the propagation of the Christian message, relations with other churches and the disposal of funds. The Church is in regular contact with the Netherlands Reformed Church and the Reformed Churches in the Netherlands.

INDONESIAN CHRISTIAN CHURCH
(Huria Kristen Indonesia)
Kantor Pucuk Pimpinan (Centre), Jalan Marihat 109-111, Pematangsiantar, Sumatera — Tel: 23238. 516,525 members — 540 congregations — 80 pastors — 561 teacher-preachers. WCC (1974), CCI, CCA, LWF. President: Rev. Ludin Manurung — General Secretary: Rev. Eli Sihotang.

The HKI was formed in 1927, asserting self-government, and independence from the control of the Rhenish mission. At issue were the ordination of Batak ministers, the indigenous role in regional and local church affairs, and the Batak role in national identity. Soon after the Indonesian proclamation of independence in 1946 the Church changed its original name "Huria Kristen Batak" to "Huria Kristen Indonesia". The HKI adopted a synodal form of policy, headed by a president. Since 1964 it has used Nommensen University for the education of pastors, teachers, and others.

The congregations are located mostly in Sumatra, where the language is Batak Toba. The majority of members live in rural areas. They are small farmers who also raise cattle, water buffalo, pigs and chickens. Others live in towns and cities, including Jakarta, working as civil servants, policemen, soldiers, retailers, etc.

Since 1970, the Church has had connections with the Lutheran Church in America. With expatriate assistance, it conducts a programme in theological education by extension in which the Gereja Kristen Protestan Simalungun, the Batak Nias Kristen Protestan on the island of Nias and other churches participate. In 1982 a theological education programme for teacher-preachers is being started. Some of the newly trained church members will be sent as evangelists to the frontiers. A third programme is the family discussion group, undertaken in rural and urban places.

The HKI is also involved in development projects. In 1976, an agricultural smallholders' rice-growing project was initiated with outside aid. As the invested money is repaid, the revolving fund will help launch new projects for more people.

KALIMANTAN EVANGELICAL CHURCH (Gereja Kalimantan Evangelis)
Jalan Jenderal Sudirman 8, Kotak Pos No. 86, Banjarmasin, Kalimantan Selatan — Tel: 4856 — Cable: Synode Unum GKE. 162,000 members — 55 parishes — 147 pastors. Publication: Berita GKE (in Indonesian). WCC (1948), CCA, CCI, WARC. President: Rev. E. Masal — General Secretary: Rev. E. Mihing.

During the period of 1835-1950 the Rhenish Missionary Society carried on the work of evangelization, but it was slow because of the Dajaks who held tenaciously to their traditional beliefs and practices, and because of Muslim opposition. By 1925 there were only 5,400 Christians, after 90 years of mission. From 1925-1935 the Basel Missionary Society took over from the

Rhenish Missionary Society, but they also faced many difficulties. It transferred the work back to the Rhenish Missionary Society in 1935. In that year the Church became an independent body under the name Gereja Dayak Evangelis, with a synod organization of its own. The young Church endured great hardship under the Japanese occupation, when a number of missionaries were arrested and killed. In 1950 the Church adopted the name Kalimantan Evangelical Church. This title symbolizes the fact that the entire island, occupied by other tribes besides the Dayak tribes, is the Church's mission field.

The membership of the Church in relation to other Christian confessions is about 11 per cent; in relation to the total population it is 0,12 per cent. The Church is involved in cultural and social matters of the island and has assisted the government in the 'transmigration' and reallocation of people. Its primary concerns include financial self-support and theological independence; it seeks to strive, with other churches which are members of the CCI, towards church unity and to equip church members for Christian service. It is committed to train church leaders in order that they may become fully aware of their calling in relation to the challenges of the socio-political and cultural situation in the country.

KARO BATAK PROTESTANT CHURCH (Gereja Batak Karo Protestan)
Jln. Kapt. Pala Banun, 90 Kabanjahe, North Sumatra — Tel: 0628.20466 — Telex: Synode Ka. 135,000 members — 419 congregations — 113 pastors — 50 evangelists. WCC (1969), CCI, CCA, WARC. Moderator: Rev. A. Ginting Suka — General Secretary: Rev. E.P. Gintings.

The Church was founded in 1890 by the Netherlands Zendelings Genootschap (Netherlands Missionary Society). The first missionary was H.C. Kruyt, who settled at Buluhawar, a small village in the mountain area. The first baptism was in 1892. In 1940, when the Church celebrated its 50th

anniversary, the total membership was 5,000. In 1941, the Karo Batak synod was formed and two Karo Batak candidates were ordained to the pastoral ministry.

The Japanese occupation from 1942 to 1945 compelled the Church to become entirely independent, both financially and spiritually. It went on growing and when the 75th anniversary was celebrated in 1965, church membership had increased to 25,000. The total Karo population is 450,000 and there is therefore ample opportunity for the Church to do evangelistic work. It works in close cooperation with the Regional Council of Churches in Sumatra, especially in the field of evangelism, and maintains fraternal relations with the Netherlands Reformed Church and the Presbyterian Churches in Australia and New Zealand.

NIAS PROTESTANT CHRISTIAN CHURCH (Banua Niha Keriso Protestan)
Gunungsitoli, Nias, North Sumatera. 250,000 members — 450 congregations — 75 pastors. WCC (1972), CCI, CCA. General Secretary: Rev. H.S. Harefa.

The NPCC grew out of the missionary work of the Rhenish Mission which started in 1865. The Church became independent in 1936. It has a presbyterial-synodical structure.

The majority of the Nias population belongs to the NPCC. There are minority communities of Roman Catholics, Pentecostals and Muslims. Pastors are trained in Indonesian theological schools. Great emphasis is put on lay leadership because the Church is scattered over a vast region and there is a shortage of ministers.

PASUNDAN CHRISTIAN CHURCH (Gereja Kristen Pasundan)
Jalan Pasirkaliki 121-123, P.O. Box 178, Bandung, West Java — Tel: 022.614803. 21,000 members — 38 congregations — 30 pastors. Publication: Surat Bulanan

(monthly, in Indonesian). WCC (1960), CCI, CCA, WARC. President: Rev. Arifin Dani, Jalan Bratayudha 40, Bandung, West Java — General Secretary: Rev. Weinata Sairin.

When Jakarta (then Batavia) was founded in 1619, it had already a Christian congregation, administered by the Rev. Husebos. The evangelization of the Sundanese people, however, did not take place until the middle of the 19th century. The Sundanese Protestant Church of West Java came into existence in 1861. The missionary work in one of Indonesia's strongest Muslim regions grew out of the witness and dedication of Christian lay people. It was not the result of organized efforts by western missionary societies. A Dutch judge, F.L. Anthing, started a fruitful work of evangelization, with the help of Javanese and Sundanese evangelists whom he trained in his home. The mission spread to the wider area of Jakarta and Banten and Bogor. The Netherlands Missionary Society started work in the Priangan area which spread later to the whole of West Java. Several congregations were established from 1852 onwards.

From the beginning the work has encountered strong Muslim opposition. In spite of Islamic resistance, individual Muslims were converted to Christianity. During the Second World War, the relations with the Netherlands Missionary Society were totally cut off. During the last few years there were revival movements in the Church. Near Tjirevon and in a village near Tasikmalaja (South-East of Bandung) new congregations of former Muslims have been formed.

The structure of the Church is presbyterial-synodical. Congregations are fully autonomous. Several congregations together live in the fellowship of a district. Each congregation is guided by its pastor, and the elders and deacons who are appointed for four years. The four districts are Jakarta, Priangan, Bogor and Cirebon. Synod meetings are held every two years. An executive committee of the synod is responsible for ongoing activities. Among the problems the church still has to solve

are ministerial training, lay education, and preparation for real dialogue in depth with Islam. The Netherlands Reformed Church and the Basle Mission continue to support this Christian community.

PROTESTANT CHRISTIAN CHURCH IN BALI* (Gereja Kristen Protestan Di Bali)

P.O. Box 72, Jalan Debes 6, Denpasar, Bali — Tel: 2914 — Cable: Bali Church, Denpasar. 6,000 members — 47 congregations — 25 pastors. Publication: Warta GKPB (in Indonesian). WCC (1976), CCI, CCA, WARC. Moderator: Rev. Dr I.W. Mastra — General Secretary: Rev. K. Suyaga Ayub.

Although in the thirties the government of the Dutch East Indies did not give its consent to the appointment of an overseas missionary in Bali, the Christian Church of East Java, without official approval, sent one of their ministers to Bali. Through the Christian Church of East Java the mission of the Netherlands Reformed Church also participated in the work. Already in the thirties some congregations emerged. During the Second World War the congregations grew and new ones were formed so that they are now spread over a great part of the island of Bali. Although from the beginning no important decisions were taken without the consent of the delegates from the congregations, the Church did not consider itself fully independent until 1948 when the first synod met.

Significant developments took place after 1950. The Church contextualized the gospel in the local culture of Bali through architecture, symbols and teaching. Through traditional decoration, woodcarving, painting, dancing and music, the Church is also engaged in the development programme of the government. Two Balinese pastors are now working in Europe and five pastors in other parts of Indonesia.

The PCCB sponsors a meditation centre, Dhyana Pura, which is visited by church members from far and near. It also maintains a second centre, Maha Bhoga Marga, which trains Christians in farming, poultry, fishing and programmes of self-support. The Church has close ties with the Netherlands Reformed Church, the Evangelical Mission in South-West Germany and the Uniting Church in Australia.

PROTESTANT CHURCH IN INDONESIA (Gereja Protestan di Indonesia)
Jln. Medan Merdeka Timur 10, Jakarta — Tel: 342895. 2,287,000 members — 2,896 congregations — 9 synods — 1,920 pastors. Publication: Berita GPI (in Indonesian). WCC (1948), CCI, WARC. Chairman: Rev. D.J. Lumenta.

The Protestant Church in Indonesia is the former East Indian State Church, a continuation of the church of the period of the East India Company in the 17th and 18th centuries. In 1835 Calvinist and Lutheran congregations came together in Batavia (Jakarta) to become the Protestant Church in the Netherlands East Indies. A board of moderators was responsible for the conduct of its affairs throughout the archipelago. Its status as a corporate body covering all churches of Calvinist tradition was recognized by the government in 1927. The PCI is now composed of the following Churches: Gereja Masehi Injili Minahasa (1934), Gereja Protestan Maluku (1935), Gereja Masehi Injili di Timor (1947), Gereja Protestan di Indonesia Barat (1948), Gereja Protestan di Gorontalo (1964), Gereja Protestan di Donggala-Palu (1964), Gereja Protestan di Buol-Tolitoli (1964), Gereja Kristen Luwuk-Banggai (1976). The general assembly meets every three years. The Church has an impact on the cultural, social and political life of the nation.

Men and women are ordained to the eldership and the diaconate. The Church operates schools at all levels, and has recently opened a Christian University in Minahasa. The university includes a faculty of theology. The regional churches are active in medical work and care of orphans and the elderly.

The major concern of the PCI is to strive for closer ties between the regional churches, and for the unity of the Church throughout Indonesia. The general synod, meeting in Kawangkoan in July 1980, presented to the Council of Churches in Indonesia a draft constitution of the 'Gereja Kristen yang Esa' in Indonesia.

PROTESTANT CHURCH OF THE MOLUCCAS (Gereja Protestan Maluku)
Jalan Imam Bonjol 2, Ambon — Tel: 2248.3043 — Cable: BPGPM. 575,000 members — 27 dioceses — 720 parishes — 438 pastors (345 men, 93 women). Publication: Bulletin Informasi GPM (in Indonesian). WCC (1948), CCI, CCA, WARC. Moderator: Rev. Dr Arnold Nicolaas Radjawane — General Secretary: Rev. A.J. Soplantila.

The Moluccas are the "spice islands" towards which Colombus thought he was sailing when he discovered America in 1492. The islands cover a land-water area as large as the Philippines. The Christian faith was preached there early. Francis Xavier found Christians in the island when he visited Ambon in 1546.

The Dutch East India Company and the Netherlands Indies government gave the inhabitants of the Moluccas some military and minor government positions, but they did little to improve the economic and social conditions of the people. The Church suffered much during the Japanese occupation. A quarter of the ministers on the island of Ambon were killed and the population of several villages massacred. More than fifty church buildings and local church offices were destroyed. Another serious blow to the Church was the revolt of the Republic of the South Moluccas in 1950 during the quelling of which the Indonesian government employed twelve divisions of troops. All churches in Ambon were destroyed and another 75 churches in Ceram burned or wrecked. A grave refugee problem was created which was only solved after many years. It took a long time to get places of worship and congregational buildings restored.

Today the economic and social conditions are steadily improving, and the Church is looking confidently into the future.

PROTESTANT EVANGELICAL CHURCH IN TIMOR (Gereja Masehi Injili di Timor)
Jenderal A. Yani 35, Kupang-NTT — Tel: 22039 — Cable: GMIT Kupang. 700,000 members — 1,324 congregations — 321 pastors. Publication: Berita GMIT (in Indonesian). WCC (1948), CCI, CCA, WARC. President: Rev. Th.A. Messakt.

The first Dutch pastor came to Timor in 1612. There was no continuous ministry until 1821, partly owing to the scarce commercial interest of the Netherlands East India Company in the islands. The Church slowly grew and spread to the islands of Roti and Sawu. The Netherlands Missionary Society was active in Timor from 1821 to 1863. The Indian Church (Indische Kerk) took over the administration from 1863 to 1942. Only after the 1930s did the PECT grow and spread to the interior regions of Timor and Alor. Due to mass Christianization the Church faced the problem of an insufficient number of leaders to minister to the needs of the people. The Church became autonomous in 1947. By that year it had gained a membership of 224,000 in 315 congregations served by 80 ministers. The territory of the PECT now includes all of the Nusa Tenggara Timor province, except the Sumba and Sumbawa islands. At the national level the PECT is the third largest church after the Batak Church and the Protestant Church in Minahasa.

The Church still faces the problem that there has been little economic and cultural development in the region. A good deal of education is needed to assist Christians in the transition from a traditional society into the modern period caused by rapid social change. The whole Church needs to be responsibly involved in community development through schools, health centres, orphanages, literature and vocational training centres. The Church attempts to motivate lay people to be active in various church ministries in order that the priesthood of all believers becomes real. The primary concerns for the 1980s are to increase the number of qualified leaders through lay and community training, to promote study and research for development and to provide education in rural and urban ministry. The unity of the church in Indonesia is another primary aim of the PECT.

It maintains special relations with the Netherlands Reformed Church, the United Presbyterian Church in the USA, the Uniting Church in Australia and the Presbyterian Church in Ireland.

SIMALUNGUN PROTESTANT CHRISTIAN CHURCH (Gereja Kristen Protestan Simalungun)
Jln. Jend. Sudirman 14, Kotak Pos 2, Pematangsiantar, Sumatera — Tel: 23676 — Cable: GKPS. 141,000 members — 350 parishes — 54 pastors — 13 evangelists — 15 women Bible teachers. Publication: Ambilan pakon Barita GKPS (edited in the local language). WCC (1973), CCI, CCA, LWF. Ephorus: Rev. A. Munthe — General Secretary: Rev. H.M. Girsang.

This Church, autonomous since 1963, has congregations mainly in northern Sumatra, among the approximately 300,000 people who speak Simalungun, a Batak dialect, and in Java, where the Church has followed its people. About 70 per cent of the members are farmers; others are engaged in various occupations in urban centres like Pematangsiantar, Medan, Tebingtinggi, and the nation's capital, Jakarta. The church organization combines congregational and synodical features similar to those of the Huria Kristen Batak Protestan (HKBP), the 'mother church'. An ephorus (presiding bishop) and a general secretary, elected for a specific term, head the church.

Church headquarters in Pematangsiantar are conveniently near Nommensen University, where the church's pastors and many of its school teachers are trained; other students attend Jakarta Theological Seminary and the seminary in Jogjakarta. The Church maintains many elementary and secondary schools. Its agricultural training centre outside Pematangsiantar offers short courses in rice growing, poultry raising, cattle breeding, and other areas of rural economy. Its medical clinic, 'Bethesda', in Saribu Dolok, helps to relate health services to community needs. The Church has contributed to the supply of drinking water to people, and has a service programme for the unemployed.

The Church traces its beginning to two events: Ludwig Nommensen's arrival in the Batak country in 1864 and the recognition secured by the Simalungun people on linguistic and cultural grounds in 1903. In 1940, their congregations became a separate district within the HKBP. Under the name HKBP-Simalungun, it was granted far-reaching independence by the HKBP, and in 1963 it withdrew amicably and formed a separate church.

A translation of the entire Bible, begun about 1957, was completed in 1969, the work not of expatriates but of Simalungun scholars. Among the Simalungun people are some 5,000 Roman Catholics and several thousand Muslims. Some of the population are still animists. The Church continues to work among them. A strong missionary motivation animates the community. The Church has close ties with the Lutheran Church in America and the Lutheran Church in Australia.

TORAJA CHURCH (Gereja Toraja)
Jln Taman Bahagia 43, Rantepao, South Sulawesi. 181,000 members — 390 congregations — 231 preaching stations — 80 ministers. WCC (1967), CCI. Secretary: Rev. Y. Tandilolo.

This Church in the Rantepao area of the island of Sulawesi (formerly Celebes) grew out of the efforts of missionaries sent by the Gereformeerde Zendingsbond of the Reformed Churches in the Netherlands in 1913. Early on in its history, schools and

teacher training colleges were established, and a hospital was built in 1930. Immediately after World War II, the Church became autonomous. The membership figure of 75,000 in 1947 almost doubled by 1954.

In the late fifties and early sixties, the TC endured persecution at the hands of the fanatical Darul Islam movement. Christian villages were attacked, houses and churches burnt, and people tortured and killed. The government restored order in 1964.

Faced with limitless opportunities, the TC needs more personnel to do justice to the demands of witness and service.

JAPAN

ANGLICAN EPISCOPAL CHURCH IN JAPAN (Nippon Sei Ko Kai)
4-21 Higashi 1 — Chome Shibuya-Ku, Tokyo 150 — Tel: 400.2314 — Cable: Seikokai. 55,570 members — 324 parishes — 11 dioceses — 11 bishops — 348 pastors and active church workers. Publication: The Seiko Kai Shimbun (in Japanese). WCC (1948), NCCJ, CCA, ACC. Primate: The Rt Rev. Titus Yoshio Nakamichi — General Secretary: Rev. Joshua S. Kominami.

The Church was founded in 1859 when the first missionary from the Episcopal Church in the USA came to the country. It was legally established in 1887, and became an official province of the Anglican Church in 1930. From 1978 onwards it has been financially independent. It continues to receive missionaries from overseas partner churches and also to send missionaries to overseas partners. All bishops and other church leaders are Japanese. The Church is the third largest Christian community, after the Roman Catholic Church and the United Church of Christ.

The concern for a more effective mission remains crucial for the Church. In order to render a faithful witness, internal organizational structures are being constantly renewed, and there is a continuing emphasis on better stewardship. A major programme is called "Asu no kyokai o kizuku Kai", the building up of the church of tomorrow. The programme is also designed to help Christians seek for renewal in their own lives. This is a difficult task because there is always a tendency to feel small and powerless in a growing secular, non-Christian climate.

JAPANESE ORTHODOX CHURCH
(Nippon Haristosu Seikyoukai)
No. 1-3, 4 Chome, Surugadai, Kanda, Chiyoda-Ku, Tokyo. 25,000 members — 100 parishes — 3 dioceses — 2 bishops — 30 priests. Publications: Seikyo-jiho (monthly), 2 diocesan papers (in Japanese). WCC (1973). Archbishop: His Eminence Metropolitan Theodosius.

In 1861 a young Russian missionary priest-monk, St Nicholas Kassathin (canonized in 1977), brought the light of Orthodoxy to Hakodate in Japan. After baptizing Takuma Sawabe, a Shinto believer who became the first Orthodox Christian, St Nicholas converted almost 20,000 people within a few years. Thus Orthodoxy spread from Hakodate through Sendai to Tokyo, from Tokyo to the Kansai area to Kyoto, Osaka and Kobe in western Japan, and then to Kyushu. St Nicholas translated the major prayer books of the Orthodox Church into Japanese. He was also active in building churches — the cathedral is now a national landmark in Japan. It was dedicated to the resurrection of the Lord but is affectionately called Nicholai-do, which means the prayer house of St Nicholas.

He died in 1912. Metropolitan Sergei Tikhomiroff succeeded him. During his time, the Church suffered from political and economic problems, as well as internal and external difficulties stemming from canonical problems with the Russian Orthodox Church after the Russian Revolution. Metropolitan Sergei was responsible for the maintenance of the cathedral during the Second World War,

and for its restoration after an earthquake shortly after the war.

The Church faced the problem of making Orthodoxy indigenous in Japan. Metropolitan Theodosius was consecrated (before autonomy was granted in 1970), thereby providing a native Japanese hierarchy. Financial-economic independence was attained through regular contributions from members. The problem of the canonicity of the Japanese Orthodox Church was solved in 1970 when Patriarch Alexis granted it autonomy. There are now three dioceses: the eastern diocese of Sendai, the archdiocese of Tokyo, and the western diocese of Kyoto. They publish newsletters containing articles on religion, diocesan announcements and teachings of Orthodoxy.

The Orthodox Church is the third largest church in Japan, after the Protestant and Roman Catholic Churches. The Church participates actively in collecting donations for welfare activities. A major concern is to intensify mutual fellowship among the local Orthodox parishes. Programmes for training people in stewardship and in providing assistance for the growth of the Church receive particular attention.

KOREAN CHRISTIAN CHURCH IN JAPAN*
Japan Christian Centre, Room 52, 2-3-18 Nishi-Waseda, Shinjuku-Ku, Tokyo 160 — Tel: 03.202.5398 — Cable: Korepan. 2,340 members — 46 parishes — 40 pastors. Publications: Gospel News (in Japanese and Korean), Arirang (in English), Todai (in Japanese), Koge (in Japanese and Korean). WCC (1963), NCCJ, CCA, WARC. Moderator: Rev. Chang Eun Yun, 2-2-24 Higashi, Shorinji-cho, Sakai-shi 590 — General Secretary: Rev. Kim Kun Shik.

In 1978, the Korean Christian Church in Japan celebrated seventy years of evangelical witness among Koreans in Japan. The work, begun by the YMCA in 1906, was carried on in various forms up to the time of the Pacific War, when the Chosen Christian Church, as it was then known, bowing to government pressure, was amalgamated with the United Church of Christ in Japan. Soon after the end of the Second World War, the Church was reorganized under the present name. It is a self-governing denomination having special fraternal relations with the Methodist Church and Presbyterian Churches in Korea and the Presbyterian Church in Canada.

Over 80 per cent of the present Korean minority consists of Japan-born Koreans and their children. Their parents were forced to migrate to Japan because of economic or political reasons. While nearly 1.5 million Koreans returned to their country, about half a million chose to remain in Japan.

The KCCJ understands its particular calling in terms of evangelism and pastoral care of Koreans in Japan. The Church adopted in 1973 a basic mission policy which clearly sets out its position in terms of evanglism, education and service. It has embarked on an ambitious programme of education through nursery schools, kindergartens, "prep" schools and adult education groups, aimed at making Koreans in Japan aware of their identity and their cultural heritage. This is carried on directly by church-sponsored schools, and indirectly through church-related institutions.

In 1971 the Korean Christian Centre was set up. It is a social service centre, located in an area of Korean concentration, and its aim is to act as a focal point for community outreach; it addressed itself to the problem of discrimination in education and employment to which the Korean minority in Japan is still subjected.

The Research-Action Institute for the Koreans in Japan (RAIK) came into being following a National Christian Council of Japan Consultation on Korean Issues held in June 1972. It was formed in 1974 and has been an effective agency in promoting the Korean struggle for basic civil and human rights as well as self-identity and self-determination.

KCCJ congregations are scattered over Japan, from Hokkaido to Okinawa. They are divided into four districts roughly centring on Tokyo, Nagoya, Osaka and Kita-Kyushu. The Church as a whole is governed by a general assembly which meets every two years.

UNITED CHURCH OF CHRIST IN JAPAN (Nippon Kirisuto Kyodan)

31 Japan Christian Center, 2-3-18 Nishi Waseda, Shinjuku-ku, Tokyo 160 — Tel: 03.202.0541 — Cable: Japankyodan. 191,830 members — 16 districts — 1,668 congregations — 1,722 pastors — 693 others. Publications: The Kyodan Times (in Japanese), Kyodan News Letter (in English). WCC (1948), NCCJ, CCA, WARC. Moderator: Rev. Toshio Ushiroku — General Secretary: Rev. John M. Nakajima.

Protestant Christianity in Japan began with the work of foreign missionaries who came to the country in 1858. They were missionaries of the American Presbyterian and Reformed Churches. The first Protestant church, the Nihon Kirisuto Kyokai (Presbyterian-Reformed), was established in Yokohama in 1872. At the 1890 synod meeting, the Confession of the Church of Christ in Japan was adopted. Later other missionaries arrived from Europe and North America. With the promulgation of the religious organizations law, all Protestant churches had to become united. Unity was achieved at the Fujimicho Church in 1941.

At the end of the war, the religious laws were abolished, and the Episcopal, Lutheran and parts of the Baptist and Holiness Churches, with the Salvation Army, withdrew from the United Church. The majority of the ministers of the Nihon Kirisuto Kyokai wanted the United Church to become a federal union, but this proposal was rejected. In 1951, 39 congregations withdrew from the United Church and re-established the Nihon Kirisuto Kyokai. Its confession, published in 1953, is based on the confession of 1890.

The UCCJ is the largest Protestant church in Japan. Christians form only one per cent of the total population. Japan's major religions are Shinto and Buddhism. There are also in the country various syncretistic communities representing 'new religions'.

As the Tokyo district does not at present participate in the general assembly of the UCCJ, the work of the Kyodan executive committee is considerably hampered. At the 21st general assembly it was decided that the Church must continue to fight discrimination against the Buraku people, and the Buraku centre in Osaka has now begun its activities. There has been progress in establishing official relations with the Korean Christian Church in Japan. Relationships with overseas churches have grown steadily — with the three sister churches in Korea, the Presbyterian Church in Taiwan, and the Evangelical Church in Germany.

KOREA

KOREAN METHODIST CHURCH
Methodist Building, KPO Box 285, Seoul. 675,760 members — 2,291 parishes — 2,000 ministers. WCC (1948), NCCK, CCA, WMC. Bishop Chi Kil Kim.

The KMC is a product of foreign mission endeavour beginning in the late 19th century. The Church will celebrate its centenary in 1984. In 1930 the Church became fully autonomous, retaining affiliation with denominational bodies in America which later merged into what is now the United Methodist Church. From the time it became autonomous, the entire leadership of the Church has been national. Women have been ordained in the Church since 1930. In spite of difficulties during the Japanese occupation of the country from 1905-1945 and the devastating Korean war which followed the tragic division of the country in 1945, the Church has continued to thrive. It is now administratively divided into five annual conferences (of Seoul, Jungbu, Dongbu, Nambu and Samnam). The national office includes boards of

laity, Christian education and missions, evangelism and social responsibility as well as a general affairs office which is responsible for all property related matters.

The Christian population of Korea comprises about 15-20 per cent of the total population — depending on how many of the fringe sects are included. Catholic believers number well over one million. Buddhism claims the largest number of adherents, though many are only nominal believers. The total number of Presbyterians in Korea is now close to three million but these are divided into a number of different Presbyterian denominations, with different degrees of relationship with one another. Methodists rank third in membership among separate Protestant denominations in Korea.

In the last decade, Korea has been transformed from a predominantly rural society to an overwhelmingly urban and highly industrialized society. The consequent changes in traditional and family ties have created problems which the Church is only beginning to wrestle with. Creative programmes in urban and industrial missions have developed, but they are now faltering because of intense government pressure. A strongly authoritarian government in Korea presents a serious challenge to the Church and at times threatens to divide the Church. Numerous Christians have paid dearly for challenging government activity.

The Korean Methodist Church is presently going through a very rapid growth phase. Thousands of class meetings — these meetings were a hallmark of early Methodism — are held every Friday all over the nation. Ten families gather together to form one class meeting and they study the class meeting textbooks, led by the class meeting leader. The board of education publishes more than 20,000 copies of the leaders' textbooks annually.

The Church has substantial plans to embark on the development of a training centre as part of its centennial celebration in order to help realize the goal of transforming quantitative growth into Christ-centred qualitative growth. The Church has begun a massive local fund-raising campaign to achieve this end and is formulating plans to invite participation from overseas churches.

PRESBYTERIAN CHURCH IN THE REPUBLIC OF KOREA (Hankuk Kidokyo Changno Kyohwae)

P.O. Box 147 Kwanghwamoon, Seoul 110 — Tel: 763.7934 — Cable: Keypresby, Seoul. 230,280 members — 871 congregations — 530 pastors. Publications: PROK News (in English, four times per year), Whaebo (in Korean, monthly). WCC (1960), NCCK, CCA, WARC. General Secretary: Rev. Park Jay Bong.

The Korean Jesus Presbyterian Church was established in 1907, as a result of the work of missionaries from Australia, Canada and the United States labouring together with Korean Christians. A theological dispute raised by conservative sections in the Church, centring in particular on the authority of the scriptures, led to the establishment of the Presbyterian Church in the Republic of Korea in 1954.

There are five main Presbyterian denominations in Korea. The largest is the Hap Tong denomination (well over one million members); the second is the Presbyterian Church in Korea (PCK or Tong Hap, also over one million members). The PROK is the third. The two other mainline Presbyterian churches have about 190,000 and 17,500 members. The Roman Catholic Church has more members than the PROK but fewer than the PCK. Among other Christian denominations, the Methodists are the largest, with over 600,000 members, followed by the Korean Evangelicals with 374,500 members and the Assemblies of God with 336,750 members. The Baptist Church is slightly smaller than the PROK. There are other and smaller denominations in the country. Buddhist believers outnumber the total number of Christians in Korea, while the number of Confucian believers is about half that of Buddhists.

The Presbyterian Church in the Republic of Korea is opposed to a self-absolutizing conservative theology, and endeavours to create an indigenous theology. It is a strong promoter of the ecumenical movement, and committed to build a wider fellowship within and outside Korea, and to share in the history of other churches in the country and abroad. It actively participates in social and political programmes, and in the prophetic ministry of proclaiming and upholding the cause of social justice, human rights and freedom. This stance, in the present Korean situation, has meant much suffering and testing, but the Church moves forward with active faith in the Lord. Within its own community it is dealing with the development of a pension system and a minimum salary system, and attempting to narrow the gap between rich and poor congregations and promote democratization within the Church.

PRESBYTERIAN CHURCH OF KOREA (TONG-HAP) (Taehan Jesu-kyo Changno-hoi — Tong-hap)

Christian Building, 136-46 Yun-Ji Dong, Chongro-ku, Seoul — Tel: 763.8315, 7915. 1,115,550 members — 3,713 churches — 34 presbyteries — 2,416 ministers. Publication: Kidok Kongbo in Korea (weekly, in Korean). WCC (1948), NCCK, CCA, WARC. Dr H. Paul Ko, Busan Youngnak Presbyterian Church, 22-1 ka, Bumin-Dong, Busan, Korea 600 — General Secretary: Rev. Eui-ho Lee.

The history of the Presbyterian Church in Korea dates from the coming of Horace Underwood, the first Presbyterian missionary, in 1885. For a time, during the first half of the century, the Church grew rapidly. Among the reasons for this rapid growth are the religious mentality of the people, the fact that the two great traditional religions, Buddhism and Confucianism, had lost much of their vitality and influence and the desire of the Korean people, emerging from a long period of isolation, to have some contact with Western civilization. From 1936, it was a difficult period for the Korean Church. The Japanese government's 'Japanization movement' continued with increasing pressure until the end of the Second World War.

The precipitate emancipation from Japanese colonial rule, however, threw church and people into a state of confusion. Unprepared as the church was to meet the new situation with wisdom and power, conflicts and divisions arose inevitably. Several splits and divisions took place between 1951 and 1959.

But the Presbyterian Church of Korea remains one of the main Presbyterian churches in Korea. It maintains relations with the Presbyterian Church US, the United Presbyterian Church in the USA, the Presbyterian Church of Canada, the United Reformed Church of England and the Uniting Church in Australia.

MALAYSIA

METHODIST CHURCH IN MALAYSIA
8th Floor, Wisma Methodist, Lorong Davidson, Kuala Lumpur 05-05 — Tel: 03.202797. 71,000 members — 302 parishes — 222 pastors. WCC (1977), CCM, CCA, WMC. Bishop C.N. Fang.

The general conference of the MCM is composed of five annual conferences formed on linguistic and cultural bases. In Peninsula Malaysia there are the Trinity annual conference (English-speaking), the Chinese annual conference (Chinese-speaking), and the Tamil annual conference (Tamil-speaking). In Sarawak, there are the Sarawak Chinese annual conference (Chinese-speaking) and the Sarawak Iban annual conference (Iban-speaking). This is due to the Church's complex social composition and particular needs.

Methodist work began in Malaysia with the arrival of William F. Oldham in Singapore in 1885. The work of the mission grew in several directions. Singapore and Malaysia Methodists formed the Southeastern Asia central conference,

along with the Methodists in Indonesia, and Burma in 1950. This general conference was an integral part of the general conference of the Methodist Church (USA).

In 1968, the general conference granted an enabling act for the annual conferences to constitute the affiliated autonomous Methodist Church in Malaysia and Singapore. In 1977 the Methodist Church in Malaysia and Singapore separated into two churches following national boundaries. Now each Church has its own bishop. The MCM is no more a mission of the United Methodist Church in the USA. It is now a community of those who are committed to give according to their ability.

PROTESTANT CHURCH IN SABAH*
(Gorija do Protestant sid Sabah)
P.O. Box 69, Kudat, Sabah, Malaysia. 13,000 members — 7 parishes — 150 places of worship — 61 pastors — 200 lay preachers. WCC (1975), CCM, CCA.

The Church is constituted of congregations formed by the Basel Mission Society amongst the Rungus and adherent tribes.

It accepts the holy scriptures of the Old and New Testament as the only basis of faith, and the Apostles' Creed.

All people who believe in God — that is God the Father the Creator of the universe, and God the Son Jesus Christ the Saviour and Mediator of humankind, and God the Holy Spirit the Comforter and Strengthener, Originator of the faith and of the Church — and who confess their sins and put aside all superstition and former beliefs in spirits, ghosts and gods, can receive baptism and become members of this Church.

Church members take an active part in the daily life of the community and of government, as long as their rules do not oppose Christian principles.

PAKISTAN

CHURCH OF PAKISTAN
Lal Kothi, Barah Patthar, Sialkof-2 — Tel: 53790. 400,000 members — 8 dioceses — 8 bishops — 600 pastors. WCC (1971), NCCP, CCA, WARC, WMC. Moderator: Rt Rev. J. S. Qadir Bakhsh.

The history of the churches in Pakistan is part of the history of Christianity in the Indian sub-continent. Their beginnings can be traced to the work of several Christian missions from the 16th century onwards. Pakistan came into existence when British rule ended on the Indian sub-continent in 1947. The predominantly Muslim areas in the West and the East became a separate state, with over a thousand miles of Indian territory in between. The eastern province broke away in 1971.

The Church of Pakistan (1970) is the result of a union of churches of Anglican, Lutheran, Methodist and Scottish Presbyterian traditions. Its membership accounts for one-third of the Christians in the nation (half the Christians are Roman Catholic, many from Goa). The United Presbyterian Church which had been involved in the negotiations did not join. The organizational plan is the diocesan pattern, (combining Anglican, Methodist and Presbyterian patterns of polity), with the Church being administered through four dioceses. This number had recently been expanded to eight, with a bishop presiding over each. The COP is one of two in the world where Anglicans and Methodists have united — the other being in India — but the only one in which Lutherans have united.

About 3 per cent of the population is Christian; over 96 per cent is Muslim. Islamic religion is predominant. Some political leaders continue to favour the Islamic way of life for the country, though efforts are maintained to secure full rights for religious minorities, including participation in political parties. Christian scholars, teachers, social workers and lawyers are appreciated for their contributions, but face problems of identity and full participation in the social and political life. There is no legal bar to evangelistic work, but the propagation of the gospel is not always welcomed.

Like other developing countries, Pakistan has a low per capita income. Planned development has been attempted, though with indifferent success. Christians are among the poorest in the nation. In rural areas most of them are landless labourers. The COP conducts a broad programme of Christian education, many types of social development projects — including housing, land reforms and medical care — especially for the poorest of the poor. Missionary visas are granted only to replace those missionaries who live in the country.

Outstanding institutions include Forman Christian College, Murray College, United Christian Hospital, Gujranwala Theological Seminary and Karachi Theological Seminary. Most of the educational institutions like colleges and schools have been nationalized and now operate under the control and direction of the government. The Church of Pakistan has initiated some significant steps to continue its role in education in the light of the policy of nationalization.

UNITED PRESBYTERIAN CHURCH OF PAKISTAN
Naushran Virkan, District Gujranwala. 100,000 members — 180 congregations — 12 preaching stations — 158 ministers — 1,260 elders. WCC (1961), NCCP, CCA, WARC. Secretary: Rev. Bahadur Khan.

In August 1947, the Indian sub-continent was divided into two separate and independent states, India and Pakistan. With a population of one hundred million Muslims, Pakistan emerged as one of the most powerful Islamic states. Soon after partition, it was evident that the newly established boundary was so divisive that the Punjab mission, established over a century ago, could no longer administer the work in the two countries. In April 1949, therefore, two separate missions were formed, one the Punjab mission in India, the other the Pakistan mission.

The division was particularly difficult for the Pakistan mission. In rural areas the Christian community was very poor. There was much anxiety over what policy the new state would adopt towards the Christian minority. Out of this has grown a strong tie among the Protestant denominations working in Pakistan.

The United Presbyterian Church of Pakistan came into being in 1961, as an autonomous Presbyterian church, after a long history as a synod of the United Presbyterian Church of North America and, later, of the United Presbyterian Church in the USA. The constitution adopted by the Church is a modification of that of the United Presbyterian Church of North America, with the addition of provisions for an executive committee and a permanent juridical commission.

PHILIPPINES

EVANGELICAL METHODIST CHURCH IN THE PHILIPPINES (Iglesia Evangélica Metodista en las Islas Filipinas) 640 Penalosa, Tondo, Metro-Manila — Tel: 21.67.76. 120,000 members — 132 congregations — 3 bishops — 135 pastors. Publication: Ang Ilaw (in Filipino and English). WCC (1972), NCCP, CCA, WMC. General Superintendent: Bishop George F. Castro, 1240 General Luna Street, Ermita, Metro-Manila.

The Evangelical Methodist Church in the Philippines is the first Protestant indigenous church in the Philippines. Its organization grew out of the nationalistic aspirations of some Filipino Methodists who wanted to establish a self-governing, self-sustaining and self-propagating church.

Nicholas Zamora was the first Filipino to be ordained minister. Owing to a series of differences with the American Methodist missionaries on the role of the Filipinos in the running of church affairs, he joined the nationalist movement and, as its head, proclaimed in 1909 the Church independent of the mother church. There were about 3,000 members.

The early leaders were simple people. Consequently, their ways and methods of evangelism were attuned to the temper of the ordinary Filipinos. This mainly accounted for their success in building up the Church; in 17 years (1926), the membership had grown to about 20,000.

Till 1948, the Church's policy was patterned after that of the Methodist Church. Its rituals and services followed those of the Methodist Church. In 1948, the Church amended its discipline and lodged the power to run the Church with a supreme consistory of elders. This body, composed of 13 members (11 elders and two laymen), is elected quadrennially by the general conference. From the ministerial members of the supreme consistory of elders the general conference in turn elects a general superintendent, secretary, evangelist and treasurer. Other members are assigned by the general superintendent as heads of the ministries (finance, Christian education, justice, men's organization, women's organization, youth organization and sacred music). The Church is composed of eight districts each headed by a district superintendent appointed by the general superintendent.

The Church stands solidly against any discrimination (particularly racial), drug addiction and divorce. Each member is urged to evangelize one person in 1981, two in 1982 and three in 1983, etc. It continues to conduct a nationwide seminar on Christian stewardship and through its community development programme aims to develop cottage industries for the unemployed.

PHILIPPINE INDEPENDENT CHURCH (Iglesia Filipina Independiente) 1500 Taft Avenue, Ermita, P.O. Box 2065, Manila 2801 — Tel: 505724. 4,500,000 members — 33 dioceses — 726 parishes — 2,218 village chapels — 44 bishops — 688 priests — 50 deacons — 470 lay readers.

Publication: Aglipayan Review (in English). WCC (1958), NCCP, PICOPUI, CCA, CCEA. Supreme Bishop: Most Rev. Macario V. Ga.

Catholic missionary work started in the Philippines in 1565 when five Augustinian missionaries arrived with the conquering Spanish army. Muslim missionaries had already been at work for two centuries. By the early 17th century the Augustinians had been joined by Franciscans, Jesuits, Dominicans and Recollects. Within a few years they could claim that most of the population had been baptized. The Church soon became an integral part of the colonial government.

There were instances of protests and revolts against the corruption of the Spanish friars in the 17th and 18th centuries, but it was the 19th century that saw the emergence of organized struggles within the Filipino church. In 1841, Apolinario de la Cruz became the first martyr, executed as a subversive. The Spanish-American war of 1898 enabled the revolutionaries to proclaim an independent republic. But the Treaty of Paris, without consulting the Filipinos, ceded the country to the USA. The Filipinos revolted and were eventually suppressed, but the political upheavals inevitably affected the church. The 1898 revolutionary government had expelled the religious orders, confiscated their lands, and appointed Gregorio Aglipay — the only clerical member of the revolutionary congress — as head of the Philippine Church. As the Vatican refused to appoint Filipino bishops, the Philippine Independent Church was born in 1902, with Aglipay taking the leadership.

Partly because of the appeal of nationalism, the Church drew some two million former Roman Catholics into its membership. But in 1906 the supreme court ruled that all the churches they were using should be returned to the Roman Church. This seriously weakened the new denomination. Under the theological leadership of Isabelo de los Reyes, the PIC adopted a Unitarian stance, but after his death in 1938 it returned to a more Catholic position and entered in 1961 into intercommunion with the Philippine Episcopal Church with which it now shares a seminary.

Out of the total population of 49 million people, 78 per cent are Roman Catholic, nine per cent belong to the PIC, five per cent to other Protestant churches, six per cent to Islam and two per cent to other faiths. There was a strong ecumenical emphasis from the beginnings of Protestantism in the country. The establishment of the Union Theological Seminary in 1907 was influential in the forming of the United Church of Christ in the Philippines in 1948. But the strong nationalism of many Filipino Christians has also hampered the ecumenical movement.

The PIC has now one college in Manila, three theological seminaries, 14 primary and secondary schools, and many kindergartens. It is much involved in problems of population control, drug addiction, health and sanitation, and public welfare. Better Christian education and stewardship, the training of more qualified priests and more aggressive campaigns against all forms of poverty are high on its agenda.

The Church maintains relations with Anglican Churches in Australia, New Zealand, Japan, Pakistan, Burma, Ceylon, the Provinces of East Africa, Uganda, Rwanda and Burundi, South Africa and West Indies; Old Catholic Churches in Europe; the Lusitanian Church; and the Polish National Catholic Church of America.

UNITED CHURCH OF CHRIST IN THE PHILIPPINES

P.O. Box 718, Manila 2801 — Tel: 99.59.91 — Cable: 'Unichurch' Quezon City. 300,000 members — 2,000 parishes — 5 bishops — 525 ordained ministers. Publication: United Church Letter. WCC (1948), NCCP, CCA, WARC, WMC. Bishop Estanislao Q. Abainza.

The United Church, the largest and most widespread Protestant group in the Philippines, came into being in 1948, uniting in one church the United Evangelical Church of the Philippines (a 1929 union of Presbyterian, Congregational, and United Brethren Churches with the small United Church of Manila), the Philippine Methodist Church and the Evangelical Church in the Philippines (a 1944 union of various Evangelical churches).

It seeks to preserve the heritage of faith brought into the union by the constituent churches, respecting the cardinal beliefs expressed in their various statements of faith. There is no common credal formula, but all affirm the basic belief: "Jesus Christ, the Son of the living God, our Lord and Saviour". Its government is largely presbyterian, with area overseers called bishops. Bishops have mainly a spiritual and pastoral oversight of the Church. Government is locally by congregations or congregational councils, regionally by district annual conferences, and nationally by general assembly, which meets quadrennially.

The UCCP has 16 church-related educational institutions, six hospitals, and four clinics all over the country from Luzon to Mindanao. Its programmes involve evangelism and stewardship, mission (among the cultural communities), Christian nurture, theological education, social concerns, lay ministries, emergency assistance and rehabilitation, children's, youth and student work. These programmes and concerns are implemented throughout the four jurisdictions.

The Church is self-supporting save for some assembly promotional projects which are partly supported by contributions from churches abroad. The Church has made a standing invitation to other churches to discuss closer cooperation or organic union. It has 21 missionaries working in various parts of the world.

The Church has special working relationships with the United Presbyterian Church in the USA, the United Church of Christ, Christian Church (Disciples) and the United Methodist Church in the USA.

SINGAPORE

METHODIST CHURCH IN SINGAPORE*
10 Mount Sophia, Singapore 0922 — Tel: 337.5155 — Cable: Methodist. 14,830 members — 33 congregations — 1 bishop — 49 pastors. Publications: Methodist Message (in English), Chinese Annual Conference News (in Chinese). WCC (1977), NCCS, CCA, WMC. Bishop Kao Jih Chung.

The Methodist Church was planted in Singapore in 1885 when two missionaries, James M. Thoburn and William F. Oldham, arrived in the island to launch mission work. Both men later became bishops. Bishop Thoburn was the first to exercise supervision in this area. Bishop Oldham was responsible for the early expansion of the work, particularly through establishing the first of the large number of Methodist schools in Singapore and the peninsula. Later other missionaries from England and America, and local pastors contributed to the growth and spread of the work.

Singapore became the nerve centre of the Methodist Church in South-East Asia. From here the Methodist Church spread to Malaysia, Indonesia, the Philippines and Sarawak. Gradually, the Church grew in these other areas, and because of geographical factors, developed its own centres of administration. After the Second World War the Central Conference of Southeast Asia was formed. It was composed of Singapore, Burma, Malaysia and Indonesia. One by one these became established autonomous churches, first Burma, then Indonesia, followed by the five annual conferences of Singapore and Malaysia in 1968.

In 1976 Singapore and Malaysia formed separate national and autonomous Methodist Churches. The Methodist Church in Singapore is composed of three annual conferences, i.e. the Chinese annual conference (CAC), the Emmanuel Tamil annual conference (ETAC) and the Trinity annual conference (TRAC). There are eight schools and one junior college, with a total enrolment of 12,723 pupils and teachers. Although teachers' salaries are paid by the government, the Church is encouraged to provide moral and religious education in the schools. The government has now decided to make religious knowledge a compulsory subject in all secondary schools. The Church is concentrating on outreach in the housing estates and among students. At Trinity Theological College ministers of several denominations are educated. The many linguistic, cultural and ethnic differences among Christians are constant challenges in ecumenical endeavours.

According to the 1980 census, out of the 1,982,000 people who represent the population over ten years of age, 203,500 are Christians (10.3%). Of these 112,500 are Protestants, Methodists numbering 14,830 at the end of 1981 — the largest Protestant Church in Singapore. Buddhists and Taoists form a large percentage. The majority of Indians are Hindus. Practically all Malays are Muslims.

The Church has made a significant contribution to the nation and the society. The 1980 census revealed that among those who get a university education, over 35 per cent are Christians. Many national and community leaders are Christians. There are a large number of officers in the military who are Christian. The Church faces a strong challenge and a great opportunity in helping to train teachers of religious knowledge for schools in the island.

The MCS maintains close relations with the United Methodist Church in the USA, the Methodist Church in the UK and the Methodist Churches in Indonesia and Malaysia.

SRI LANKA

CHURCH OF SRI LANKA
Bishop's House, 358/2 Bauddhalko Mawatha, Colombo 7. 78,000 members — 155 parishes — 100 priests. WCC (1948), NCCSL, CCA. Rt Rev. Swithin Fernando, Bishop of Colombo.

In 1930 the Anglican Church in India separated from the Church of England and became the independent Church of India, Burma and Ceylon, still within the worldwide fellowship of the Anglican communion. In spite of the fact that Sri Lanka is close to India, it is very conscious of having a history and a culture of its own. The Anglican diocese of Colombo did not join the Church of South India. The mission of the American Board (Congregational Christian) in the north of Ceylon was part of the old South India United Church and did therefore join the Church of South India as the diocese of Jaffna.

It was evident from the beginning that, if Sri Lanka as a whole was to have a united church, it must work in its own way and produce its own independent scheme. The first step towards union was taken in 1934. In 1941, an official committee, representing all the churches that were members of the National Christian Council of Ceylon, was formed.

The movement towards church union in Sri Lanka — involving the Anglican dioceses of Colombo and Kurunagala, the Methodist Church, the Baptist Church, the Jaffna diocese of the Church of South India, and the churches of the presbytery of Lanka — is still active in spite of a decade of delays resulting from various legal disputes.

A scheme of church union in Ceylon was published as early as 1955. By 1972, the five churches involved had taken official votes favouring the union, and thanksgiving services anticipating the union were held. In the summer of 1972, however, several members of the Anglican diocese of Colombo challenged the decision of their church in civil court on the ground that the resolution to unite had failed to get two-thirds majority in the whole house of clergy (even though more than three-quarters of the clergy who were present had voted in favour of union). This case was finally dismissed by the district court of Colombo in May 1980, but a notice of appeal has been given and is pending. Efforts are being made to expedite the proceedings. Lawsuits brought by individual Baptists and Methodists opposed to union have already been dropped.

Another step towards union was taken in May 1981 when the consultative conference of heads of churches and their advisors (the group now responsible for church union activity) approved a resolution that makes provisions for those opposed to union. The resolution states that the Church of Sri Lanka "shall provide for any of our members to exercise their freedom of worship and practice thereof as existing at the date of union and for any of our Ministers to exercise their ministry of the word and sacrament as at the date of union and to receive their emoluments and other benefits including pensions in terms not less favourable than at the date of union while in active full-time service in the Church of Sri Lanka or on retirement."

This resolution has now been sent to the churches for their approval. The Methodist synod of clergy and the Kurunagala synod have already accepted the resolution and have passed it on for further action. The Church still retains the title of the Church of Sri Lanka. The proposed dioceses of the United Church are Colombo, Kurunagala, Jaffna, Galle and Badulla.

METHODIST CHURCH IN SRI LANKA

Methodist Headquarters, Colombo 3 — Tel: 24599. 28,000 members — 146 parishes — 48 pastors. WCC (1950), NCCSL, CCA, WMC. President: Rev. P. Basil Rajasingam.

The MCSL is the result of British mission efforts. The first missionaries arrived in 1814. They built the first church in the town of Colombo in 1816. Historically, this church in the Pettah was the first Methodist Church in the whole of Asia.

In 1960 the state took over all the schools established and run by the Methodist Church except two — Wesley College a school for boys, and Methodist College, a girls' school, both in Colombo. The Church supports clubs for underprivileged children; creches for children aged one to five; a family planning clinic; a pre-school; and the Harvard Vocational Training Centre, which was started in 1979 for the rehabilitation of boys aged 8-14 years who

have dropped out of school. The Harvard Women's Hostel and Harvard Settlement (for men) are both residential institutions.

Membership of the Methodist Church in Sri Lanka is about 14,000 with a church community of twice that number.

A development commission initiates, promotes and coordinates the development activities of the various circuits. The university has started a department of Christian civilization, and a number of Buddhist clergy are following the university courses.

More full-time workers are needed due to retirements and dearth of new recruits.

TAIWAN

PRESBYTERIAN CHURCH IN TAIWAN (Tai-Oan Ki-Tok Tiu-Lo Kau-Hoe)

89-5 Chang Chun Road, Taipei 104 — Tel: 511.5286.9 — Cable: Prestaiwan Taipei. 161,820 members — 1,005 congregations — 818 pastors. Publication: Taiwan Church News (in Chinese). WCC (1951), CCA, WARC, CWM. Moderator changes every year — General Secretary: Rev. C.M. Kao — Acting Secretary: Rev. C.C. Shang.

The Church began with the work of English and Canadian Presbyterian missionaries in the south of the island in 1865 and in the north in 1872. After the Japanese occupation in 1895, mission bodies were refused entry into the country. This resulted in the development of a single Protestant Church, without the complications of denominational diversity. Following the Second World War, English and Canadian missionaries returned to Taiwan, and other mission boards were also allowed to enter. After the Communist takeover of mainland China in 1949, many Christians fled to Taiwan and a large number of missionaries were redeployed to work there. In 1951 the synods of the north and the south came together in one general assembly of the Presbyterian Church. Whereas during the early post-war years the Church was preoccupied with issues of survival and recovery, the years 1955-1965 were characterized by rapid growth. The Church doubled its membership and the number of local congregations. Following the year 1965 the Church has carried out three five-year programmes — the New Century Movement, the Faithful Servant Movement and the Self-Support and Mutual Aid Movement. In 1978 the Church launched the Ten Plus One Movement, focused on evangelism and witness, with the goal of doubling the communicant membership in eight years.

The Roman Catholic Church has a membership of 279,000. The total Protestant constituency is estimated at 305,000. Presbyterians make up about 53 per cent of the Protestant membership. They represent 0.92 per cent of the total population of Taiwan, which now is about 17,500,000. The Presbyterian Church has fraternal church relationships with churches in Korea and Japan, the Hong Kong Council of the Church of Christ in China and the Evangelical Church of Berlin-Brandenburg.

The Church has made significant contributions to Taiwanese society. Through preaching, healing, and other forms of ministry it continues to work towards indigenization of the faith, and to make it a part of the life of the common person. It has sought to uphold human rights and to stress the meaning and value of human life in the midst of rapid social change. Its outlook is ecumenical, and the Church is open to dialogue with people of other faiths.

A primary concern in the 1980s is the Ten Plus One Movement. Among its major programmes and activities are: lay training and relevant theological programmes, medical ministries, women's work, Christian literature programmes, promotion of youth work among university students, discipleship seminars, crisis and family counselling, and community development especially among tribal people.

THAILAND

CHURCH OF CHRIST IN THAILAND
14 Pramuan Road, Bangkok 5 — Tel: 234.7991, 234.7992, 234.0098, 235.5086 — Cable: CCTOFFICE, Bangkok. 30,900 members — 14 districts — 208 congregations — 80 worship groups — 98 ordained ministers — 70 religious teachers — 32 evangelists. Publication: Church News (in Thai). WCC (1948), CCA, WARC. Moderator: Mr Vibual Pattarathammas — General Secretary: Rev. Samran Kuangwaen.

French Roman Catholic priests began work in Siam in 1662, and by 1688 had established a seminary and a number of chapels. European Protestant missions began work in 1828. American Congregationalists and Baptist and Presbyterian missionaries followed from 1831 onwards, the Presbyterians developing the major work. The Church of Christ in Thailand was organized in 1934. In 1957 the Presbyterian mission was integrated into the CCT, and turned over all its property. The work of the British Churches of Christ, which had begun in 1903 and was continued by the Christian Church (Disciples of Christ) from 1951, was integrated into the CCT in 1962. There are fraternal workers in the Church from Korea, Philippines, India, Germany (Marburg Mission), Britain and the USA, representing Baptist, Disciples, Lutheran, Presbyterian and United (Church of South India and United Church of Christ in the Philippines) traditions. There are Thai, Chinese, Karen and English language congregations.

The Church represents 90 per cent of the total Protestant constituency. The Roman Catholic Church has an estimated membership of 189,000. The Evangelical Fellowship of Thailand, the Seventh Day and the Southern Baptist Mission are very small Christian groups, with respectively 14,000, 4,580 and 1,650 members.

The Church runs a seminary, now called the McGilvray Faculty of Theology of Payap College, seven church hospitals, one leprosy hospital and research centre, a number of schools and a cooperative farm. The College has done much to capture and to pass on to future generations the riches of Thai music. Handicraft work has been revitalized under the social development and services department. This department also works in slum areas, among labourers, and attempts to expand its rural life programme.

The Church is further involved in dialogue, through a coordinating committee, consisting of Roman Catholics, Buddhists, Muslims and Sikhs. Its primary concern is that of evangelism, but the number of Christian leaders, responsible for this task, is still woefully inadequate. The CCT hopes to become a self-supporting church over the next 20 years. Congregations are asked to pay 10 per cent of the pastor's salary for the first year; the District and the CCT pay 45 per cent. Each year the congregation is expected to contribute a little more so that it develops its own tasks and structures. The CCT has been involved, with the support of the WCC, in difficult refugee work in Thailand.

Caribbean and
Central America

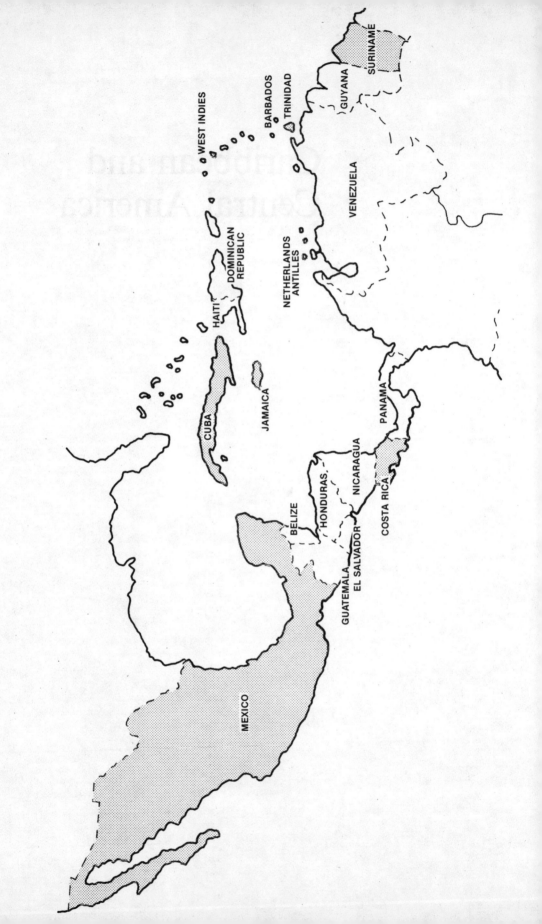

COSTA RICA

EVANGELICAL METHODIST CHURCH OF COSTA RICA* (Iglesia Evangélica Metodista de Costa Rica) Apdo. 5481, San José — Tel: 232052 and 228258. 6,000 members — 23 churches — 42 preaching points — 19 pastors. WCC (1975), UNELAM, WMC. President: Rev. Luis Fernando Palomo B.

In the years 1886 and 1891 Costa Rica was visited by Franciso G. Penzotti, a Methodist evangelist and American Bible Society agent. Mr Penzotti's work of preaching and Bible distribution laid the foundations for later evangelical advance. However, no definite organizational work of American Methodism emerged during this period.

In 1917 the Interdenominational Committee on the Survey and Occupation of Latin America expressed the judgment that the Methodist Episcopal Board was the appropriate agency to take up work in Costa Rica. George A. Miller, then superintendent of the Panama mission and later bishop, made a brief exploratory visit to Costa Rica, accompanied by Eduardo Zapata of Mexico. Follow-up work began in 1918, led by Sidney W. Edwards. In 1921 Panama and Costa Rica were included as districts of the Central American mission conference. The Central America provisional annual conference was organized in 1940. In 1961 Costa Rica and Panama became provisional annual conferences.

From the time of the Latin America Methodist Consultation in Buenos Aires in early 1962, the movement for autonomy among the Methodist churches of the area was greatly accelerated. With the churches in Panama and Costa Rica becoming autonomous in 1973, the last vestiges of the Latin America central conference disappeared.

The highest elected authority of the Evangelical Methodist Church of Costa Rica is the president. Programme planning and implementation are carried out through three general councils of the church: programme, administration and ministry. The assembly (conference) meets biennially, and between its sessions policy coordination is vested in the "junta general" (executive committee).

The Church has several institutions serving the community: a grade and high schools, a book store, a kindergarten, and an experimental farm that does effective work in agricultural extension.

CUBA

METHODIST CHURCH IN CUBA* (Iglesia Metodista en Cuba) Calle 58, No. 4305, Havana — Tel: 32.0770. 10,000 members — 106 congregations — 8 district superintendents — 50 pastors (one quarter are women). WCC (1968), WMC. Bishop: Armando Rodriguez Borges.

The origins of Cuban Methodism can be traced to Cuban expatriates in Florida before the Spanish-American war. In 1873 Methodist work began among Cubans in Key West. Ten years later, two Cubans were sent as missionaries, Enrique B. Someillan and Aurelio Silvera. The first church was organized in Havana in 1888, with 194 members. The Spanish-American war interrupted this flourishing work, and it was not reorganized until 1899. The Cuba mission was organized in 1907; a mission conference took place in 1919; and the Cuba annual conference in 1923.

At the Methodist unification in 1939, the conference became a unit of the southeastern jurisdiction. In 1964 the general conference of the Methodist Church passed an enabling act to allow the Cuban Methodist Church to become autonomous. Autonomy was declared in 1968 and Bishop Rodriguez was elected to the episcopacy — a position in which he continues.

The MCC's future became uncertain when most of the elders left the country in 1962; only two ordained ministers remained. But the Church revived, and it has sent one of its pastors as a missionary to Guyana, and is helping start Methodist work in Colombia. When the trained leadership left Cuba in 1962, women kept the church alive, and they were given the status of lay preachers. Gradually more men received training and began to take responsibility. Since 1969 the MCC has been self-supporting. There are well-organized activities in the areas of evangelism, Christian education and leadership development.

Together with Methodists in the Caribbean, Central America and Mexico, the church participates in studies and projects of evangelistic work in countries in the region where there is no work of the Methodist Church.

PRESBYTERIAN-REFORMED CHURCH IN CUBA* (Iglesia Presbiteriana-Reformada en Cuba)

Apartado 154, Matanzas — Tel: 2190 (Matanzas), 61.1558 (Havana). 8,000 members — 29 parishes — 21 pastors. Publications: Heraldo Cristiano, Su Voz Jupnecu (in Spanish). WCC (1967), CEC, CCC, WARC, CPC. General Secretary: Rev. Dr Sergio Arce.

The first Presbyterian missionaries arrived in Cuba from Tampa and other places in Florida in 1890. The first congregation was organized in 1900. After 1902, many North American missionaries worked in the island. In the course of the next sixty years the Presbyterian Church extended its work into three provinces: Havana, Matanzas and Las Villas. In 1967 the PRCC was established as an autonomous church with its own form of government. It was no longer dependent on the United Presbyterian Church in the USA.

Although a minority, Cuban Presbyterianism has been involved in the history of the nation. It supported the struggle against Spanish colonialism, the nationalist cause during the phase of the neo-colonial Republic under North American aegis and the Cuban revolution which started in 1959.

The PRCC has also been in the forefront of ecumenical endeavours. At present, both the president and the executive secretary of the Ecumenical Council of Cuba are Presbyterians; so are the director of the Ecumenical Study Centre and the instructor of the United Seminary in Matanzas, the national advisor of the Student Christian Movement, the president of the Latin American Union of Ecumenical Youth and the first vice-president of the Christian Peace Conference.

The main concerns of the Church in the decade ahead are in the areas of contributing to theological reflection, training of leaders for the Church, the promotion of a social conscience in the socialist society and the preparation of a new curriculum for Christian education. These are sought to be realized through (a) the Las Villas centre for national activities, for children and youth camps; (b) development programmes for training lay people; (c) strong support of the theological development of the United Seminary of Matanzas seeking to increase the number of qualified professors and students; and (c) the sustaining of the work of the Ecumenical Council of Cuba.

In 1977 the Church produced a new confession of faith.

JAMAICA

MORAVIAN CHURCH IN JAMAICA

3 Hector Street, Kingston 5 — Tel: 809.928.1861 — Cable: Unitas — Telex: c/o Cadec, Jamaica. 25,000 members — 52 congregations — 17 pastors. Publication: Jamaica Moravian (in English). WCC (1969), JCC, CCC. President: Rev. Robert W.M. Cuthbert, Box 500, Kingston 10.

In Jamaica the Church began in 1754 when three missionaries from England, Zacharias Caries, Thomas Shallcross and Gottlieb Haberecht, arrived in the island to minister to the enslaved negro community.

The Moravian Church has always been interested in community development. Before the abolition of slavery the Church pioneered in the field of primary education and skills training. After the abolition of slavery, it led the way in land settlement, public water supply and teacher training education for women. The Moravians introduced Irish potatoes which became a major agricultural crop in a large part of the island. Road construction, farmer cooperatives, parent-teacher associations, savings banks and community councils — all these were the result of Moravian initiative. The Church continues to play an important role in education, with an emphasis on responsible citizenship, though this is now primarily the responsibility of the government. In recent years Moravians have ventured into new areas of skills development, especially in the urban areas where unemployment is high. Under the direction of Unitas, the newly formed development arm of the Church, there has been a revitalization of people-based efforts. Underdeveloped land resources are recovered, a school for baking pastries has been converted into a productive centre, and a medical clinic has been set up offering health care to many underprivileged people.

The primary concern for the 1980s is to develop among local people a sense of self-sufficiency and to join in the battle against unemployment. Internationally, the Church pays much attention to the debate on disarmament and the lessening of world tension in order that more resources may be made available for the feeding of the hungry and a meaningful existence for the marginalized. The Moravian Church participates in the training of men and women for full-time ministry at the United Theological College of the West Indies. It also seeks to set up counselling facilities in family life education and home management. Greater emphasis is now being placed on stewardship and training for evangelism, in order that members of the Church may share more fully in the Church's total witness.

UNITED CHURCH OF JAMAICA AND GRAND CAYMAN

12 Carlton Crescent, P.O. Box 359, Kingston 10. 13,450 members — 148 congregations — 66 pastors. Publication: In Touch. WCC (1967), JCC, CCC, WARC. General Secretary: Rev. S.H. Smellie.

The Church was formed in 1965 by the union of the Presbyterian Church of Jamaica and Grand Cayman and the Congregational Union of Jamaica. The Presbyterian Church came into being as a result of the work of the Scottish Missionary Society which sent three missionaries to Kingston in 1800. It was not until 1824, though, that work was undertaken on a large scale on the great sugar estates. The early missionaries were ministers of the United Secession Church. With emancipation in 1838, some 300,000 people were freed. Ten years later, the first synod was held in Falmouth. As early as 1841 the decision was taken to embark on a mission to Calabar, which continued until the independent Church in Nigeria came into being. The Church also undertook work in Rajputana, and evangelized among East Indians in Jamaica.

Congregational churches were formed through the activities of the London Missionary Society from 1834. The first church was established five years later. The Congregational Union of Jamaica was formed in 1877. With practically no financial or manpower resources, a serious crisis soon arose. Apeals were made to the Congregational Union of England and Wales and to the International Congregational Council, which resulted in the Colonial Missionary Society taking over responsibility for financial support and the provision of ministers from Britain. The churches began to grow again and in more recent years moved rapidly towards independence.

The UCJGC is the sixth largest domination in the island, coming after the Anglican Church, the Roman Catholic Church, the Baptists, the Seventh Day Adventists, and the Methodists.

Several members of the United Church have been members of parliament. On the social level, the Church has pioneered vocational training, children's homes, and a rehabilitation home for older prisoners. It has been in the forefront in the fight against social evils like gambling, promiscuity and economic injustices. It is deeply concerned about the plight of the less fortunate, especially in the cities, and is embarking on a special ministry to the urban poor. The Church is active in education, and sponsors six high schools.

Church growth is a major concern. The United Church is seeking to increase membership by 10 per cent and its giving by 20 per cent each year. It is also committed to missions at home and abroad and is seeking to persuade young people to enter full-time ministry and to go overseas in the service of Christ. A significant activity in the life of the Church is a youth movement, which centres in an annual youth camp at Clarendon College. Through this camp a number of young people have committed their lives to Christ, and serve the Church in various capacities.

The UCJGC maintains special relations with Presbyterian Churches in Scotland, Ireland, the USA and the United Church of Canada.

NETHERLANDS ANTILLES

UNITED PROTESTANT CHURCH*
(Iglesia Protestant Uni)
Fortkerk, Fort Amsterdam, Curaçao. 11,280 members — 8 congregations — 7 pastors. WCC (1962), CCN, WMC. President: Rev. R.F. Snow.

From the 17th century most missionary work in the Netherlands Antilles was undertaken by Roman Catholics. Brethren communities were mainly responsible for early Protestant missionary work.

The UPC consists of the Protestant Church of Aruba, the United Protestant Church of Bonaire and the United Protestant Church of Curaçao. All congregations in the UPC are autonomous, and carry

their own responsibilities, among others in Christian education and ordination of ministers. Most congregations were formed at least one hundred years ago. The Fortkerk in Curaçao is already four hundred years old.

Relations with other churches in the Netherlands Antilles are good. Close relations with churches in Holland, in particular with the Netherlands Reformed Church, are maintained.

TRINIDAD

PRESBYTERIAN CHURCH OF TRINIDAD AND GRENADA
Paradise Hill, San Fernando, Trinidad, W.I. — Tel: 652.4829 — Cable: Trinipress. 40,000 members — 33 congregations — 100 preaching stations — 40 ministers — 310 elders. WCC (1961), CCT, CCC, WARC. General Secretary: Rev. Rawle Sukhu.

In 1868, a missionary named John Morton was sent by the Presbyterian Church of the Maritime Provinces of Canada to begin the Canadian mission to East Indian indentured labourers on the sugar-cane estates of Trinidad. He was joined a few years later by Kenneth Grant, and the two men lived to see the Church firmly established in those parts of the country where Indians had settled on crown land or continued to work on estates. The missionaries and those who took over from them became proficient in the Hindi language, but today Hindi has been replaced by the language of the majority, English.

By 1868, other denominations had already won most of the native population to Christ, so that the Presbyterian Church is almost entirely an East Indian church. The great contribution made by the Church to the development of education in the country is recognized both by government and the general public. Theological education was started on a private tutorship basis long before the theological college was established in 1892. This college served the

Church adequately until the rising standard of general education made it imperative for candidates for ministry to go abroad. The Church operates 73 primary schools and five secondary schools.

Since national independence in 1962, the Presbyterian Church, with its long-standing tradition of democratic government, has been making a marked impact on the total life of the nation. The Church maintains particular relations with the Presbyterian Churches in Australia and New Zealand.

WEST INDIES

CHURCH OF THE PROVINCE OF THE WEST INDIES

Bishop's House, Box 128, Saint Vincent, West Indies — Tel: (809 45) 61895 — Cable: Archbishop Saint Vincent — Telex: Saint Vincent 7500 (code 321 or 0399). 1,780,000 members — 9 synods — 9 dioceses — 12 bishops. WCC (1948), CCC, ACC. Archbishop of the West Indies: Most Rev. G.C.M. Woodroffe.

The Anglican Church came to the West Indies with the original British settlers in the 17th century, the clergy for the most part being state chaplains to the officials and planters. The Bishop of London (Dr Beilby Porteus), under whose jurisdiction the Anglican work in foreign lands fell, was instrumental in forming the Incorporated Society for the Conversion, Religious Instruction and Education of the Negroes which sent out catechists and teachers to the West Indies. Schools were also started with financial support from the Church Missionary Society in England.

A significant stage in the advance of the Church came with the creation of the first dioceses and the appointment of the first bishops — to the dioceses of Jamaica (which included the Bahamas and the settlement in the Bay of Honduras) and to the diocese of Barbados (including the Leeward Islands, the Windward Islands,

Trinidad, Tobago and Guyana). In the course of the century the area was divided into eight dioceses. Venezuela was added in 1975. The Province of the West Indies came into being in 1883. The provincial synod became fully representative in 1959. The Anglican Church ranks second in terms of membership; the first is the very large Roman Catholic Church.

The Anglican Church is concerned to be the leaven which will nourish the multi-national, multi-political peoples of the Caribbean. The region is made up of several independent nations which are sorely dependent on multinationals and big companies from North America and Europe. In the Church there is a growing concern for justice and peace.

THE METHODIST CHURCH IN THE CARIBBEAN AND THE AMERICAS

P.O. Box 8, St John's, Antigua — Tel: 21234 — Cable: Methicon Antigua, W.I. 69,630 members — 686 congregations — 8 synods — 149 bishops and pastors. Publications: Annual Minutes of the Conference, Annual Supplement to the Discipline. WCC (1967), CCC, WMC. President: Rev. C. Donald Henry — Secretary of the Conference: Rev. Eric St.C. Clarke.

This Church was formally inaugurated in 1967, at the Methodist Conference Centre in Belmont, St John's, Antigua. At that time the Church comprised six former overseas districts of the British Methodist Conference, namely, Guyana, Honduras, Jamaica with the sub-districts of Haiti, Leeward Islands, Panama and Costa Rica, and the South Caribbean districts. This number increased to eight in 1968, by the addition of the Bahamas and the elevation of Haiti to district status. Beginning with the witness and preaching of the Hon. Nathaniel Gilbert, Speaker of the House of Assembly in Antigua, in 1760, the work grew into a mission field of the Methodist Missionary Society of London. John Baxter became the leader of the Island Methodists and was appointed by the Baltimore Conference of 1784 as an elder. In 1786 Dr Coke arrived in Antigua with three British ministers who were stationed in Antigua, St Kitts and St Vincent. The Church now covers an area where, besides English, French, Spanish, Dutch, French creole, papiamento and Guyami (the language of the Guyami Indians of Panama) are spoken.

Close ties have been maintained with British Methodism through its overseas department, and both churches have a continuing interest in partnership in mission. In 1976, the conference passed provisional legislation for a concordat with the United Methodist Church (USA) for the purpose of bringing the two churches together into a closer relationship. Significant outreach projects in Jamaica, Haiti and Panama are jointly supported by the two churches.

The Church is a founding member of the Caribbean Conference of Churches, and is an active participant in both CADEC (Christian Action for Development in the Caribbean) and ARC (Agency for the Renewal of the Church) — the development and renewal arms respectively of the CCC. The Church works with the objectives of releasing a new spiritual dynamic in the territories, increasing the witness and the service of the Church, and mobilizing its resources to work for Christian unity. A task force has been appointed to examine new forms of ministry — ministerial and lay — which will be relevant for the 1980s. The Church continues to give urgent attention to education at all levels, especially in areas in which governments are unable to provide trained persons and facilities.

MORAVIAN CHURCH, EASTERN WEST INDIES PROVINCE

Cashew Hill, P.O. Box 504, Antigua, W.I. — Tel: 23469. 28,630 members — 44 congregations — 2 bishops — 20 pastors. Publication: Information — a Newsletter of the Province. WCC (1971), CCC.

Chairman of the Provincial Elders' Conference: Rev. Neville C. Brown.

In 1731, Nicholas von Zinzendorf attended the coronation of Christian VI of Denmark, where he met a negro slave, Anthony Ulrich, from St Thomas Danish West Indies, who had come to the coronation with his master. Zinzendorf invited Anthony to his estate in Herrnhut, to give Moravians an eye-witness account of the terrible conditions of the slaves on the plantations. The result was that Leonard Dober, a potter, and David Nitschmann, a carpenter, travelled from Herrnhut and reached St Thomas in December 1732. Through their work, the Moravian Church in the Eastern West Indies was established.

During the first century of its life, the Church was administered by a mission board of Herrnhut. In 1879 a synodal province of the Moravian Church, Eastern West Indies, was constituted. The Church was nevertheless greatly dependent on the continental provinces until 1967, when it was granted full autonomy.

The membership of the Moravian Church is about the same as that of other mainline churches such as the Anglicans and the Methodists. In some islands, church members hold high positions in the government. Others are deeply involved in the social life of the communities through membership in various service clubs and organizations.

The Moravian Church will celebrate its 250th anniversary in 1982. A primary concern today is to deepen the spiritual life of members. To this effect a programme for the training of mature people who are unable to go to the seminary has been started. After the successful completion of a two-year course of studies, these persons will be ordained and employed as supplementary ministers.

The Moravian Church in the Eastern West Indies is greatly concerned about the threat to peace posed by the world powers in their context for supremacy in the Caribbean.

Europe

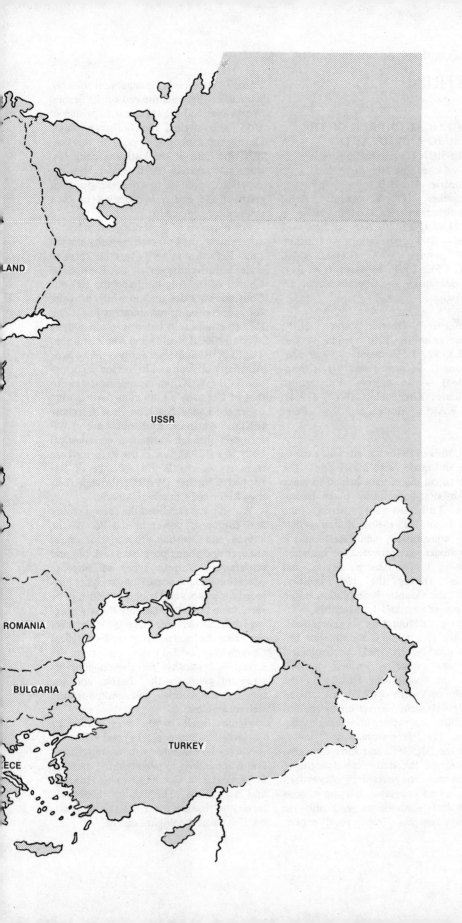

AUSTRIA

EVANGELICAL CHURCH OF THE AUGSBURG AND HELVETIC CONFESSION (Evangelische Kirche Augsburgischen and Helvetischen Bekenntnisses A.u.H.B.)

Evangelischer Oberkirchenrat A.B., Severin Schreibergasse 3, 1180 Vienna — Tel: 0222.47.15.23. 402,300 members — 7 dioceses — 200 congregations — 1 bishop — 250 pastors. WCC (1948), AMC, EC-CA, CEC, LWF. Moderator: Rt Rev. Oskar Sakrausky — Oberkirchenrat Dr Hans Fischer.

Evangelischer Oberkirchenrat H.B., Dorotheergasse 16, 1010 Vienna — Tel: 0222.52.83.93. 7,530 members — 9 congregations (5 Reformed and 4 Lutheran-Reformed) — 16 pastors. Publication: Reformiertes Kirchenblatt. WCC (1961), CEC, WARC. Moderator: Rev. Peter Karner.

The Lutheran Reformation came early to Austria and made rapid initial gains. The Turkish threat might have helped to make the Habsburg temporarily more lenient towards Lutherans in Austria than elsewhere. In the 1570s, church orders (liturgy, constitution, guidelines) on the Saxony model were provided for Lutheran parishes in Lower Austria, Styria, and Carinthia. During the 17th century, however, the Counter-Reformation began to make headway, and Lutheranism in effect went underground for six generations. During the 19th century, the situation improved steadily. In 1821, a theological school was authorized, which in 1927 became the Evangelical Faculty in the University of Vienna. In 1861, a Lutheran church government was set up by the imperial court; its structure underlies the present one. The "Free from Rome" movement in the later 19th and early 20th century increased the numerical strength of Lutheranism considerably. Accessions through mixed marriages and conversions from Roman Catholicism, and also via Lutheran refugees from south-eastern Europe (Yugoslavia, Hungary, Romania), particularly between the end of the Second World War and the Hungarian uprising of 1956, also swelled the Lutheran ranks. During the tempestuous years of this century, the faith of the Lutheran congregations was severely tested (under Nazi occupation), and it led to a deepening of their spiritual life and a broadening of their ecumenical contacts.

For purposes of legal recognition by the government, the Lutheran majority and the small Reformed minority together form an ecclesiastical entity called the Evangelical Church of the Augsburg and the Helvetic Confessions, a designation which provides for cooperation in certain areas but leaves the two groups fully independent in matters of confessional identity and administration. The ECAHC dual legal entity is the basis of Austrian Lutheran and Reformed participation in the WCC, an arrangement akin to that of Germany's Lutherans participating under the Evangelical Church in Germany (EKD). Austrian Lutherans are LWF members through their own ecclesiastical body, the ECAC, just as the Reformed are members of the World Alliance of Reformed Churches (WARC) through their own Reformed Church of Austria.

Worship has remained the central reality and source of power in the life of the church, and Christian education for school children and young people is a task of great importance. Various types of ongoing education and missionary outreach are provided for pastors and laity. Problems, to be sure, have persisted, notably those springing from indifference. Since 1961, the edict regarding the legal rights of the Evangelical Church has provided public support for the Evangelical Faculty, for the religious instruction given by the church, and for military chaplaincies and church-related welfare services.

Finding itself in the very centre of Europe, the Church makes great efforts to promote the dialogue with various Christian communities in neighbouring nations, in particular in Czechoslovakia, Hungary and Yugoslavia. Through its theological faculty in Vienna it contributes to the ongoing European theological debate.

The Reformed part of the Church has particularly strong ecumenical interests. It has been engaged in conversations with the Roman Catholic Church in Austria since the autumn of 1980, and it supports actively the WCC Programme to Combat Racism. It is engaged in tackling the national problems of minority groups, and in the whole energy debate (construction of nuclear plants), in the struggle for peace and the right to work. It has sponsored various theological publications and participates actively in radio and television work.

OLD CATHOLIC CHURCH IN AUSTRIA (Alt-Katholische Kirche Oesterreichs)

Schottenring 17, 1010 Vienna — Tel: 348394. 25,000 members — 13 parishes — 16 priests. Publications: Altkatholische Kirchenzeitung, Jahrbuch der Altkatholischen Kirche Oesterreichs (both in German). WCC (1967), AMC. Bishop: Nikolaus Hummel.

The Church separated from the Roman Catholic Church after the definition of Infallibility and the Universal Primate of Jurisdiction of the Pope as a dogma in 1870. The OCCA became in 1877 an established church, through the recognition of the Austrian Imperial government, although it did not permit the consecration of a bishop or recognize the validity of marriages performed by Old Catholic priests. Neither did it allow the church tax paid by Old Catholics to be used for the clergy, as was done in the case of all other denominations. Consequently, Old Catholics, mostly working-class people, were constantly in financial straits. They also had trouble in getting priests. After the disintegration of the Austro-Hungarian Empire in 1918, only three parishes remained. Nine more were established later. The first bishop was consecrated by the Archbishop of Utrecht and other bishops during the International Old Catholic Congress at Berne in 1925. The church suffered much during the period 1933-1945, and flourished again from the foundation of the Second Republic of Austria onwards.

The Church struggles in a context of increasing religious indifference, and tries to activate its members as responsible Christians. A new canon law was established at the end of 1981, upholding the Catholic orders of bishops, priests and deacons but also inaugurating new offices, especially for women. The 23rd International Old-Catholic Congress is being organized by the Church in 1982 in Vienna. Some 500 delegates from all Old Catholic Churches will participate.

BELGIUM

UNITED PROTESTANT CHURCH OF BELGIUM (Verenigde Protestantse Kerk in België — Eglise protestante unie de Belgique)

5 rue du Champ de Mars, 1050 Bruxelles — Tel: 02.511.44.71 and 513.58.49 — Cable: Synprobel. 35,000 members — 104 parishes — 101 pastors. Publications: Paix et Liberté (in French), De Stem (in Dutch), Info (in French and Dutch). WCC (1948), CEC, CEPPLE, WARC, WMC. President: Dr A. Pieters.

This Church traces its history to the Reformation which had a great influence in the country. Political forces and the Counter-Reformation did not lead to its elimination. However, was only after the independence of Belgium in 1830 that Protestantism found the necessary freedom for its development. New churches were now added to those which had survived difficult times. This was a result of evangelization by the Reformed Churches in Switzerland, France and the Netherlands.

From 1925 onwards two different strands developed in Belgian Protestantism. There were churches which desired to stay outside the ecumenical movement; others participated in the worldwide movement and in the Federation of Protestant Churches in Belgium. From 1962 onwards four churches realized an organic church union in two stages. In 1969 the Evangelical Protestant Church of Belgium united with the Belgian Conference of the United Methodist Church to form the Protestant Church of Belgium. In 1971 this Church started union negotiations with the Reformed Church of Belgium (founded in 1837 as the Belgian Christian Missionary Church, mainly working in Wallonia, the French-speaking part of Belgium) leading in 1979 to the formation of the United Protestant Church of Belgium. Roman Catholicism is the dominant religion of the nation. There are in the country a few Orthodox churches, and an increasing number of migrant workers adhering to Islam.

The UPCB is a minority church, but it contributes to the social and religious life of the people in several ways. It has created two organizations which work towards the integration of refugees and migrants into society. It administers several old people's homes. Programmes of evangelization have been developed. The Church sponsors radio and television work and maintains the missionary enterprise of the Presbyterian Church in Rwanda. It is concerned about questions of development of third world countries. A considerable number of African students, in particular from Zaire, are enrolled in the Theological Faculty of Brussels. From 1960 onwards relations with the Roman Catholic Church have improved and deepened, and there is today an atmosphere of confidence and cooperation.

As a new united Church representing different traditions, the UPCB faces new challenges. It benefits from its close ties with the Netherlands Reformed Church, the Reformed Churches in the Netherlands and the United Methodist Church in the USA.

BULGARIA

BULGARIAN ORTHODOX CHURCH
Bulgarian Patriarchate, The Holy Synod, 4 Oborishte Street, P.O. Box 376, 1090 Sofia — Tel: 87.56.11. 8,000,000 members, —

13 dioceses (two of which are overseas) — 3,700 churches and chapels — 2,600 parishes — 120 monasteries — 1,800 priests — 400 monks and nuns. Publications: 'Tsarkoven Vestnik' (Church Gazette, in Bulgarian), 'Duchovna Cultura' (Spiritual Culture, in Bulgarian), periodicals of the Theological Institute (in Bulgarian, with summaries in foreign languages). WCC (1961), CEC, CPC. His Holiness Patriarch Maxim of Bulgaria, Chairman of the Department for Ecumenical Relations: Metropolitan Pankraty of Stora Zagora.

Christianity came to Bulgaria in 864-5, with the baptism of Prince Boris. The canonical foundations of the local Bulgarian church were laid in 870. It began as an autonomous archdiocese under the jurisdiction of the Patriarchate of Constantinople. Under Tsar Simeon I (893-927), the Bulgarian kingdom attained great cultural brilliance; it was the period when a range of rich Christian literature was produced in Slavonic. During his reign the Bulgarian Church became autocephalous, its head assuming the title Patriarch, with its seat first at Preslav, and then from 971, at Ochrid.

Following the defeat of Bulgaria by the Byzantines in 1018, the Bulgarian Patriarchate was suppressed, but it was restored during the years 1235-1393. Its seat during that period was in Trnovo. During the Turkish domination the Bulgarian Church became more and more subject to Constantinople, and it completely lost its independence as Archbishopric of Ochrid in 1767. Struggling for national and cultural identity and political independence, the Bulgarians created an autonomous exarchate in 1870, but it was not recognized by the Patriarchate of Constantinople. In 1945 the Patriarch of Constantinople rescinded by official synodical act the schism proclaimed in 1872 and declared the exarchate autocephalous. In 1953, Cyril, Metroplitan of Plovdiv, was elected Patriarch of Bulgaria. The restored Patriarchate has gradually entered into canonical and eucharistic communion with all Eastern Orthodox churches.

The BOC has been separate from the state since 1947. The constitution of the people's Republic of Bulgaria (1947 and 1971) and the special law on religious confessions (1949) regulate "the legal status, questions of material support and the right of self-government of the various religious communities". The Church has taken active part in the common struggle to make real the evangelical legacy of human fellowship and peace by participating in various interconfessional, international, interchurch, ecumenical and pan-Orthodox conferences and consultations.

Other churches in Bulgaria are the Roman Catholics of Western rite (50,000), the Roman Catholics of the Eastern rite (10,000) and the Armenian Apostolic Church (20,000). Protestants number 16,000, Jews about 6,000. Islam has about 800,000 followers.

The holy synod of the BOC has the supreme clerical, judicial and administrative power. There is also a supreme church council at the holy synod which deals with economic and financial matters. The Church has eleven dioceses in the country itself. For the Orthodox Bulgarians in America, Canada and Australia it has two more dioceses with seats in New York and in Akron. The Bulgarian parishes in Istanbul, Budapest, Vienna and Bucharest are also under the jurisdiction of the BOC.

The theological seminary of St John of Rile in Gara Cherepish and the theological academy St Klement of Ochrid in Sofia together have 400 students. The theological academy publishes a yearbook of theological studies. A central historical and archeological church museum (1923) houses valuable monuments of Bulgarian Christian art and iconography. The Institute for Church History and Archives (1974) studies, processes and publishes literature on the history of the Church, its present mission and ecumenical activities. The most famous monasteries are the Rila Monastery (10th century), the Bachkovo Monastery (11th century) and the Troyan Monastery (17th century).

A new Bulgarian edition of the Bible will be ready in 1982, and will be used by all Christians in the nation. Religious educa-tion is given in each local church, the teaching predominantly carried out by the parish priest and through the distribution of sermons and catechetical literature. Besides Sunday sermons, lectures and talks are given once a week on particular subjects, either by the priest or by a lay member of the community. Through teaching, the celebration of the divine liturgy and the care of souls, each congregation is built up and becomes an integral part of the Body of Christ.

About 80 per cent of the population belong to the BOC. The Church is recognized as being "the traditional confession of the Bulgarian people". The state legislation continues to provide favourable conditions for good relationships among the different confessions, for developing local ecumenism and for the cooperation among various Christian traditions.

CZECHOSLOVAKIA

CZECHOSLOVAK HUSSITE CHURCH
(Ceskoslovenská Církev Husitská)
V.V. Kujbyseva 5, 166 26 Prague 6-Dejvice
— Tel: 320041. 500,000 members — 5 dioceses — 343 parishes — 5 bishops — 296 priests. Publications: Cesky Zapas (weekly); Theologicka revue (bimonthly). WCC (1963), ECCCS, CEC, CPC. Patriarch: Rt Rev. Dr Miroslav Novak.

Czechoslovakia became an independent state in October 1918 after the collapse of the Habsburg monarchy which ruled Bohemia and Slovakia for 300 years. Spiritually the Czechoslovak Hussite Church was born in 1919 when some Roman Catholic priests read the mass in Czech instead of Latin (translated by Karel Farsky). Under Farsky's leadership the Church was founded on 8 January 1920 in Prague during a meeting of progressive Catholic priests, after the Pope had rejected all proposals for reform. There was the influence of Catholic modernism, but the strongest impulse came from the

Hussite tradition. Most of the church buildings were named after John Huss. The Church has a Huss Czechoslovak faculty. Its liturgy is basically the Hussite mass, with communion of both elements and the singing of the Hussite Lord's Prayer.

The dioceses are led by a diocesan council and a bishop. The Church as a whole is governed by the Central Council and the Patriarch. The highest authority is the general synod, composed of clergy and lay persons, which meets every ten years. The Czechoslovak Hussite church is the largest non-Catholic Church representing 3.3 per cent of the population.

Its members take an active part in the cultural, social and political life of the society. There is regular participation in the ecumenical fellowship with other churches. The sixth general synod was held in August 1981. It concentrated on various issues of a theological, socio-ethical, liturgical, pastoral, organizational and legal nature. It made some corrections in the liturgy of Karel Farsky, called for a spiritual revival through a programme of intensive Bible studies and sought to promote the knowledge of the foundations of faith of the Czechoslovak Hussite Church.

EVANGELICAL CHURCH OF CZECH BRETHREN (Ceskobratrská Církev Evangelická)
Jungmannova 9, Prague 1 — Tel: 247101.2 — Telex: Evangrada, Prague. 240,000 members — 272 parishes — 387 preaching stations — 13 seniors — 246 pastors (including 31 women) — 15 lay preachers. WCC (1948), ECCCS, WARC, CEC. Moderator: Rev. Miloslav Hajek, DD — General Secretary: Rev. Jiri Otter, DD.

The present Evangelical Church of Czech Brethren resulted from the union of the former Czech churches of the Helvetic and Augsburg Confession. Its history begins, however, with the 14th century religious awakening through the work of John Huss. In 1457, the small Unitas Fratrum came into existence. Through constant struggle for legal recognition, the Protestants and Brethren finally won complete religious freedom granted by the Habsburg rulers in 1609. Some years later, however, the Battle of the White Mountain in 1620 once again meant for them the loss of freedom. Although they constituted nine-tenths of the population, Protestants and Brethren were outlawed in their own homeland. They had either to leave the country or accept the Catholic faith. The most notable of the exiles was J.A. Comenius, the last bishop or senior of the Unitas Fratrum. In 1781, Kaiser Joseph II, by a royal patent of toleration, granted them a measure of religious liberty. But they had to belong either to the Lutheran or to the Reformed Church. Only in 1918 was union reached on the basis of a common return to the Hussite and Brethren Reformation. All non-Catholic churches, with 1.8 million members, represent only eight per cent of the total population. The ECCB is the largest Czech evangelical church.

The congregations of the ECCB have a presbyterian order and the whole Church is organized on synodical principles. The synod meets every two years and its 101 members are elected by the seniorate meetings. Within the boundaries of the state constitution the Church can carry on its work in all religious spheres, including church publications. It published recently a new hymn book (110,000 copies) and a choir book (29,000 copies), and took an important part in publishing a new ecumenical translation of the Bible, which came out in 1979. A new catechism is planned. Some ten new students start their studies every year at the Comenius Theological Faculty in Prague.

The Church is deeply concerned about the spiritual life of its members, theological reflection on the unity of the Church (continuing the ecumenical work of J. L. Hromadka), on the role of conscience, on holy communion for children and the significance of ordination. Its major programmes for the 1980s include postgraduate theological training of pastors, courses for lay preachers and other lay workers, the deepening of the Church's fellowship through spiritual courses and retreats, and modernization of church buildings. The

200th anniversary of the Edict of Toleration was celebrated in 1981. The ECCB has close ties with the Church of Scotland, the United Reformed Church in Great Britain, the EKD and Evangelical Churches in Baden, Rhineland and Saxony.

ORTHODOX CHURCH OF CZECHOSLOVAKIA (Pravoslavaná Církev v CSSR)

V. Jame 6, Prague 1 — Tel: 227934. 150,000 members — 4 dioceses — 150 parishes — 3 bishops — 126 priests. Publications: "The Voice of Orthodoxy" (in Czech), "Heritage of St Cyril and St Methodius" (in Slovak and Ukrainian). WCC (1966), ECCCS, CEC, CPC. His Eminence Dorotej, Metropolitan of Prague and All Czechoslovakia — Chancellor: Archpriest Dr Jaroslav Suvarsky.

The OCC owes much to the missionary work of the Slavonic apostles Cyril and Methodius in the 9th century. They founded a Slavonic-Byzantine church in the country which was gradually replaced by the Roman Catholic Church. Several Czechs accepted the Orthodox faith in the 19th century, and by 1910 the number had risen to about a thousand. After the First World War, 11 congregations, with about 10,000 members, attached themselves to the Czech Orthodox Church. An autonomous diocese was established under the jurisdiction of the Serbian Orthodox Church in Prague as a result of the labours of Bishop Gorazd (Pavlik), who was executed by the National Socialists in 1942. Ten congregations grew up in East Slovakia with about 10,000 members, and by 1939 the church in Bohemia, Moravia and Slovakia had about 35,000 members.

The post-war task of reconstituting the OCC, which had been liquidated by the National Socialists in 1942, was accomplished with the help of the Russian Orthodox Church; 30,000 Orthodox Czechs returned from Volhynia in the USSR to their mother country in 1947, and in 1950 the full assembly of the Uniate Church in Presov declared itself for a return to Orthodoxy. The Greek Catholic Uniate Church was allowed to operate again in 1968; since then there has been a gradual normalization and consolidation of relations within the East Slovakian Orthodox Church. Among the 150,000 members of the OCC are Czechs, Slovaks, Ukrainians, Russians and others.

The OCC became autocephalous in 1951, though this status is not yet recognized by the Ecumenical Patriarchate. The holy synod consists of all the bishops and is responsible for canonical matters. The metropolitan council is responsible for administration and finance. It is elected by the full assembly of the Church and consists of all the bishops, four priests and eight laymen. It has a printing press and a finance department. Priests are educated at the Orthodox Faculty of Theology in Presov. The essential task of the Orthodox Church is understood as confirming members in the faith, and promoting a cultural and national consciousness among the people.

REFORMED CHRISTIAN CHURCH IN SLOVAKIA (Ref. krest. církev na Slovensku)

Kalininova 14 IV/26, 04001 Kosice. 130,000 members — 304 parishes — 165 pastors. WCC (1948), ECCCS, WARC. Bishop Dr Emerich Varga.

Until 1918 the Reformed Christian Church of Slovakia formed part of the Reformed Church of Hungary. The Reformed Church of Hungary was already firmly established by the year 1567. The Counter-Reformation of the 17th century, backed by the militant might of the Habsburgs, brought severe measures against the Reformed congregations right down to the end of the 18th century. Legal toleration was secured for congregations by the 1781 Edict of Tolerance issued by Kaiser Joseph II. Unlike the rich and powerful Roman Catholic Church, which also enjoyed special state privileges, the Reformed Church has always been a minority Church. This unequal position was remedied only in 1948.

The organization of the Reformed communities is closely associated with the name of Meliusz Juhasz Péter, Bishop of

Debreçen in 1567; it kept closely to the two Reformed Confessions, the Heidelberg Catechism and the Second Helvetic Confession.

From the 16th century onwards, Sunday afternoon services have been devoted to teaching. In view of increasing secularization, the synod tries hard to ensure that teaching in new and contemporary forms remains an essential ingredient in the life of congregations, using the Heidelberg Catechism and the Second Helvetic Confession in alternate years.

More than three quarters of the congregations are Hungarian-speaking; the rest are mainly Slovak-speaking.

SILESIAN EVANGELICAL CHURCH OF THE AUGSBURG CONFESSION
(Slezská Církev Evangelická AV) Na Nivach 7, 73701 Cesky Tesin — Tel: 566.56. 48,000 members — 19 parishes — 2 deputy bishops — 20 priests. Publications: Pritel lidu-Przyjaciel Ludu (monthly in Czech), Evanglicky kalendar-Ewangelicki Kalendarz (yearly in Czech and Polish). WCC (1955), ECCCS, LWF, CEC, CPC. Bishop: D. Vladislav Kiedron.

The origin of the Church goes back to the Reformation. Students studying in Wittenberg brought the tenets of of Lutheranism to Silesia. The Duke of Silesia favoured the Reformation. After the Thirty Years War and the Counter-Reformation the Church continued to exist illegally in the mountains of Beskyden. It endured two centuries of repression. Even in modern times, true religious liberty was slow to come to this Church. During the 20th century it passed through five stages of identity: up to 1918 it was part of the Evangelical Church of the Augsburg Confession in Austria; in 1918-20 it was part of the Lutheran Church in the new Poland; in 1920-38 it was autonomous within the new Czecholslovakian Republic; in 1939 it was again under the Lutheran Church in Poland; from 1940 to 1945 it was part of the Evangelical Union Church in Breslau. After the war, it finally became officially

recognized in 1948 as an equal among the other churches in the CSSR.

Overarching these changes is the painful course of Eastern Europe's political history and its impact upon church life. In the local congregations, the practice of Christian faith has persisted, and worship, preaching, religious instruction, confirmation and a motivation for mission have continued. In recent years, future pastors have been educated in Slovak-speaking Bratislava on Czechoslovakia's southern border. The Church is in great need of new candidates for the ministry, as many pastors have retired. Fellowship with Lutheran believers in Slovakia, Poland, Hungary, Yugoslavia and the German Democratic Republic, and with the Scandinavian churches, has given the Church a new lease of life. The worship languages are Czech and Polish, a reminder of the stormy political past.

SLOVAK EVANGELICAL CHURCH OF THE AUGSBURG CONFESSION IN THE CSSR (Slovenská evangelická církev a.v. v CSSR)
Palisady 46, Bratislava 801 00 — Tel: 332842. 300,000 members — 384 parishes — 3 bishops — 350 pastors. Publications: Cirkevné Listy (monthly), Evanj. posolspod Tatier (bi-weekly), Sluzba Slova (monthly). WCC (1948), LWF, CEC, CPC. Presiding Bishop: Prof. Dr Jan Michalko.

The first Christian church in Slovakia was built in 830 in Nitra. The evangelization of the people was carried on by the Slavic apostles Cyril and Methodius from Saloniki from 863 onwards. Reforming efforts in Slovakia, then part of Hungary, were supported by the Hussites. They prepared the soil for Luther's Reformation, which was eagerly accepted. The Counter Reformation struck heavily and caused many losses. More than 800 churches were confiscated. Many pastors were persecuted and killed. In 1781 King Joseph II issued the Edict of Tolerance. Within a few years a hundred new churches were built. Until 1918 the Church was part of the Hungarian Lutheran Church. After the First World War it took the title of the Lutheran Church A.C. in Slovakia, with two bishops, and a theological faculty in Bratislava. A new state constitution, after the Second World War, guaranteed the Slovak Lutherans the same status as the Roman Catholic Church. Many churches were renovated and new parishes built up. Each congregation is governed by a presbytery or council of elders, and the Church as a whole is guided by a general convention. The Church has had to work out its relation with the government, upholding the place of the gospel in a society controlled by a Marxist ideology.

The Slovak Evangelical Church draws on a rich spiritual legacy of Christian works, including a hymnal which contains over 1,300 hymns. This hymnal is to be revised during the next three years. The Church has published two editions of the new Bible translation, altogether 70,000 copies. The Church's long established emphasis on quality education has benefitted the nation as a whole, and has remained a positive force in the cultural and spiritual life of its members. As early as the 1920s, women were admitted to the study of theology. By 1964, there were 15 ordained women; in 1971 the first woman was assigned to a full pastorate. The Church is engaged in a major programme of education of lay preachers. For this purpose it has published a new Postil containing sermons for all Sundays throughout the year. A church museum is being set up in Modra. For the 500th anniversary of Martin Luther's birth, a collection of his most important writings will be published. The theological faculty in Bratislava serves also Baptists, Methodists, Adventists and members of the Church of Brothers.

The Slovak Evangelical Church maintains close relationships with immigrant Christians of the Slovak Lutheran Church in Yugoslavia and the Slovak Synod Sion in the USA. It is a founding member of the WCC, LWF, CEC and CPC and continues to be involved closely in all ecumenical movements.

DENMARK

BAPTIST UNION OF DENMARK
(Danske Baptistsamfund)
Laerdalsgade 5, 2300 Copenhagen S — Tel: 01.59.07.08. 6,400 members — 42 congregations — 39 pastors. Publication: Baptist (weekly, in Danish). WCC (1948), EAD, NEI, EBF. Rev. Erik Christensen, Principal, Baptist Theological Seminary, 4340 Tølløse — General Secretary: Rev. Gunnar Kristensen.

The Baptist movement in Denmark began in the 19th century, a century marked both by national disasters following the Napoleonic wars, and by strong national, political and spiritual movements. Reformation in the 16th century had left Denmark with a Lutheran state church which was the clerical counterpart of an authoritarian monarchy and would not allow other forms of religion. Pietism later created a tradition of conventicles, small groups of lay people meeting for Bible study under the supervision of the clergy.

After 1830, one of these conventicles in Copenhagen developed traditional Baptist beliefs on the brotherhood of believers, Bible, and baptism, independently of Baptists elsewhere. An emissary from the Baptist church in Hamburg, a Danish Jew who had been baptized there, found this group, and after some hesitation they formed a Baptist church in Copenhagen in 1839, the first free church congregation in the Scandinavian countries.

Until the free constitution in 1849 accorded religious liberty, the Copenhagen Baptist church and sister churches formed in other parts of the country had to put up with severe persecution by state and clerical authorities. On account of persistent discrimination many Baptists emigrated to the USA during the following decades. Relations with Baptists from Germany, England, Danish Baptists in the USA, and later the American Baptist Convention and Southern Baptist Convention, helped the Baptist movement develop into mature Baptist churches.

Relations have now been established with other free churches and with large parts of the Lutheran church, through the Evangelical Alliance and later through the Ecumenical Council. Today relations among most local churches — from Roman Catholics to Pentecostals — are cordial. This is due both to the influence of the ecumenical movement and to a recognition of the pluralistic form of modern society. The Baptist Union has been a member of the WCC from the beginning.

Numerically the Baptist Union is small. But the denomination is a very active one. Baptists conduct worship services in seventy church buildings (each of them will normally have the same number of participants at the Lord's Supper as the local parish church); they own 45 other buildings; they support 40 pastors, and 20 missionaries serving the Baptist Unions of Burundi and Rwanda. The denomination's Sunday school work is the oldest in the country, and young people's unions and children's clubs are active. Children and young people play a very important role in church life. The Baptists maintain a theological seminary, a folk high school, a high school, and a small publishing house.

A matter of concern is that the average age of baptism is going up, perhaps because of the influence of the pluralistic society. Atheistic thinking as well as new religious movements, often of Hindu origin, have been gaining ground. The rising unemployment expecially among young people points to the economic disparities in society and challenges the churches to rethink their role.

CHURCH OF DENMARK (Evangelisk-Lutherske Folkekirke in Danmark) Nørregade 11, 1165 Copenhagen K — Tel: 01.133508. 4,517,000 members — 2,313 parishes — 1,965 pastors. Publication: Church News of Denmark. WCC (1948), ECD, LWF, CEC. Rt Rev. Bishop Ole Bertelsen — Secretary on Inter-Church Relations: Rev. Elisabeth Lidell.

Christianity came to Denmark around 825, when Ansgar, a Benedictine monk from France, became the apostle to the north. He gained the confidence of the Danish king Harald Klak. The influence of the Roman popes was rather restricted. The 1520s brought the Lutheran Reformation. In 1537, Johannes Bugenhagen crowned the new king and consecrated the seven new superintendents who replaced the former bishops, thus breaking the apostolic succession. Renewal came to the Church in various ways. Despite this rich legacy, the Danish Church, though a national church (still today 94 per cent of the 5.1 million inhabitants are its members), has tended to experience renewal on an individual basis. Pietism, like liberalism, accentuated religious freedom. During recent decades a number of voluntary organizations have emerged, and they understand their role as instruments of the Church. Congregations are actively involved in the work of these organizations. In the critical period of German occupation (1940-45), especially in the resistance movement, it became clear how closely the Church and the people were bound together.

Organizationally, the Church is episcopal. Bishops, once royally appointed, are now named by the crown from a slate of three elected by the congregational councils and pastors of a given diocese. The Church is also congregationally organized. Since 1903, elected congregational councils have managed the affairs of the local churches. Outreach overseas includes the work of the Danish Missionary Society (1821) in South India, Yemen, Syria, Tanzania, Taiwan and Japan. The Lutheran Missionary Society of Denmark (1868) fosters church renewal at home and assists Moravian missions in Surinam and Tanzania. The Danish United Sudan Mission (1913) works in Cameroon and eastern Nigeria. Eleven missionary societies cooperate in the Danish Missionary Council. Danchurchaid (1922), which works for inter-church aid, development and other forms of assistance overseas, is one of the oldest church agencies of its kind.

FINLAND

EVANGELICAL-LUTHERAN CHURCH OF FINLAND (Suomen evankelis-luterilainen kirkko)

Satamakatu 11, 00160 Helsinki 16 — Tel: 90.18 021 Telex: 12-2357 infic sf. 4,780,000 members — 8 dioceses — 590 parishes — 8 bishops — 1,234 pastors. Publication: Kirkon nelivuotiskertomus (church's four-year report). WCC (1948), LWF, CEC. Archbishop Mikko Juva — Secretary General for the Committee for Foreign Affairs: Dr Jouko Martikainen.

The Christian faith spread to Finland in the 11th century. Orthodox Christianity established itself in the Eastern regions, but the rest of Finland — by far the largest part — fell within the Roman Catholic sphere of influence. The Reformation was carried through peacefully in this area — then ruled by Sweden. The Church comprises 90.4 per cent of the population. Although the state itself is denominationally neutral, it accords to the Lutheran and Orthodox Churches a special position.

Finnish society has become increasingly secularized and the Church is not directly involved in political activity. The Church and the state together appointed a committee during the 1970s to study the development of relations between the ecclesiastical and the secular authorities. No major changes are anticipated, but the aim is to increase the Church's independence.

The question of the ordination of women has been discussed at length but has not received the three-fourths majority vote in the synod due to different views in conservative and liberal wings. Since the early 1970s discussions on socio-ethical questions have broadened, e.g. in relation to Namibia which is linked through a long history of Finnish missionaries, to the nation.

Parishes are very independent in their activities. Congregations are large, with a considerable number of employees. Only one parish employee out of four is a pastor. This means that parishes can offer specialized services.

A comprehensive educational programme has been drawn up, and its implementation has now reached the personnel training stage. Confirmation classes are attended by over 90 per cent of the country's over-15s each year. As the result of a special campaign conducted in 150 parishes in 1980, a large number of new small groups, led by lay persons, have been formed. Most of the revival movements which sprang up in the 19th century are well integrated into the work of the Church, but some still pursue their own activities in a lively manner. Their summer festivals attract a total of about 140,000 participants each year.

FRANCE

EVANGELICAL CHURCH OF THE AUGSBURG CONFESSION OF ALSACE AND LORRAINE (Eglise de la Confession d'Augsbourg d'Alsace et de Lorraine)

1A quai St Thomas, 6708 Strasbourg, Cedex — Tel: 88.234586. 225,000 members — 206 parishes — 246 pastors. Publication: "Jalons" (in French and German). WCC (1948), LWF, DEFAP, CEVAA, CEC, FPF. President: Pasteur André Appel.

During the 16th century the Reformation took root in Alsace. The message of Martin Luther was communicated by the Strasbourg Reformer Martin Bucer, and a number of towns and territories of Alsace adopted the Lutheran Reformation. In the beginning of the 19th century the autonomous and independent churches were united by the 'Articles organiques' promulgated by Napoleon I in 1802. These articles provided a constitution which is still in force today. The united churches adopted the name Evangelical Church of the Augsburg Confession of Alsace and Lorraine because, like many other churches of the Lutheran Reformation, the confession of Augsburg (1530) was recognized as their confession of faith and the norm for the interpretation of the scriptures and the revelation of Jesus Christ. During the 19th century the Church faced a serious conflict: liberalism, dominating until 1850, confronted pietist awakening and Lutheran confessionalism. The Church today knows various theological tendencies, like confessionalism, pietism, liberalism, charismatic renewal.

The Church of the Augsburg Confession represents about one-third of French Protestantism. It represents approximately five per cent of the population of Alsace. Its influence on society is relatively significant, though the influence of Roman Catholicism is preponderant.

In the 1980s the Church's concern is to discover its specific Protestant role in the complex structures of society. Its activities centre around the worship and the formation of the people of God. New educational programmes are in preparation. Among its numerous activities may be mentioned its clinics and old age homes in Strasbourg, Mulhouse, Colmar and Ingwiller. Its institution "Sonnenhof" for the mentally retarded in Bischwiller is nationally known.

EVANGELICAL LUTHERAN CHURCH OF FRANCE (Eglise évangélique luthérienne de France)

24 rue des Archives, 75004 Paris — Tel: 81. 915750. 15,000 members — 70 parishes — 51 pastors. Publications: Positions luthériennes (four times a year), Fraternité Evangélique and L'ami chrétien (both monthly). WCC (1948), DEFAP, LWF. President: Rev. Paul Steffen.

This Church is made up of two inspectorates or districts. There are the Paris inspectorate, which includes congregations in Lyon and Nice, and the Montbéliard inspectorate, divided into five consistories or circuits. At present, the Church has a shortage of pastors and in the Montbéliard inspectorate several parishes are currently vacant.

Historically, the two geographic parts of the ELCF have sprung from different roots and were first brought together in 1802.

During the 16th century, the Montbéliard region — then part of the duchy of Württemberg — accepted the Lutheran Reformation under the initial leadership of Guillaume Farel (who was Calvin's predecessor in Geneva). The church order of 1560 introduced compulsory education and urged that book learning be undergirded with genuine piety. Developments in Montbéliard generally paralleled those in Strasbourg and surrounding Alsace.

In Paris, there was a significant Lutheran influence during the 1520s and 1530s, but the first permanent Lutheran congregation was that meeting in the chapel of the Swedish embassy (1626). Later another began meeting in the Danish. In 1809, the first more conventional congregation was organized. From 1853 to 1870, the Paris inspectorate was part of the church in Alsace and was largely supported from there.

The present situation has necessitated the training and use of lay assistants in the teaching and preaching task of the Church. In the environment of Montbéliard, for example, extensive industrialization (including the Peugeot automobile works founded years ago by a Lutheran entrepreneur) has changed the social composition drastically. Some 150 years ago, it is said, this region, lying north of Basel and Besançon, was almost entirely Protestant; today only one person in six is Protestant. The Church finds itself challenged to develop further its involvement in industrial mission, to train new kinds of leaders for Bible study and for counselling and practical services to meet emerging social problems and family needs. The Montbéliard inspectorate maintains a conference centre in nearby Glay.

The members of the Paris inspectorate are scattered among the ten million people of metropolitan Paris. Like other French churches, it is entirely dependent on voluntary contributions. Its small numbers make it difficult to respond to the vast missionary challenge.

The Church sees its problem not only as one of survival but also as one of resisting the temptation to retreat into a ghetto. This threatened isolation has been met in part by a concern for others. The Church has now become a member of CEVAA which consists of 23 francophone churches in Africa, Madagascar, Europe, and the Pacific islands and has also joined in a global partnership of Reformed, Lutheran, and other confessions.

REFORMED CHURCH OF ALSACE AND LORRAINE (Eglise réformée d'Alsace et de Lorraine)

2 rue du Bouclier, 67000 Strasbourg — Tel: (88) 321617. 45,000 members — 55 congregations — 66 pastors. Publication: Feuille synodale (irregular, in French). WCC (1948), DEFAP, CEVAA, CEPPLE, CEC, WARC. President: Rev. Christian Schmidt.

Of the congregations which now make up this Church, 16 were already in existence at the close of the 16th century. John Calvin himself helped to organize the French-speaking Reformed Church in Strasbourg in 1538. Since then, the Reformed Christians in Alsace and Moselle have been faced with many difficulties. The Church's 55 congregations are dispersed throughout the three departments of Haut-Rhin, Bas-Rhin, and Moselle. They are a minority within the Protestant population of these regions, and an even smaller minority within the largely Catholic population. In 1916 the Church counted more than 77,000 members of which many were forced to immigrate to Germany after the First World War.

Three problems remain unresolved: (1) The dispersion of local congregations appears in two distinct forms. On the one hand, small groups of families are dispersed over a relatively wide area. On the other hand, there is a 'social and religious' dispersion, characteristic of congregations in the urban and industrial zones. (2) More than half of the heads of the families earn their living as workers in the mining, iron-ore, chemical and textile industries. Very few belong to the middle and leisured class, and these few are concentrated mainly in the prosperous districts of Strasbourg, Mulhouse and Metz. The

large proportion of mixed households (Catholic and Protestant), more than half in fact, makes any discussion of genuine mission and openness even more difficult. (3) There is no separation between church and state in Alsace and Lorraine. The state pays the clergy. The question is whether the Reformed Church would welcome a separation of church and state and assume its own financial responsibilities.

All these have led to a new preoccupation with questions of renewal, the task and the meaning of ministry, theological training, permanent religious instruction of adults, youth and children, formation of lay people for evangelistic witness and relevant service, and the rediscovery of the diaconal ministry. Consistories have a new awareness of population movements and are conscious of the need to take up new tasks. The Church participates actively in the national ecumenical and missionary organizations in France, and maintains good relations with the Roman Catholic bishoprics in Strasbourg and Metz.

REFORMED CHURCH OF FRANCE (Eglise réformée de France)

47 rue de Clichy, 75009 Paris — Tel: 1.874.9092. 400,000 members — 500 parishes — 600 pastors. Publications: Bulletin information, Evangélisation (in French). WCC (1948), DEFAP, CEVAA, CEC, WARC. President: Rev. J.P. Monsarrat — General Secretary: Jacques Terme.

Organized from 1520 onwards, this Church united in 1559 around a confession of faith known as the Confession of La Rochelle, adopted a Discipline, and spread throughout France the 'Geneva style' of worship. Its main inspiration was John Calvin, and the ministers were Geneva-trained. The Reformed Church met with strong opposition from the Roman Catholic hierarchy which was linked by temporal ties with the royal power and the great families. For some 250 years, Reformed Christians in France were subjected to persecution. In 1598, they were given the status of a religious minority by the Edict of Nantes. This Edict only gave them a grudging toleration; down to its Revocation in 1685, it served as a means of limiting the spread of the Protestant communities. The Church had some respite during the century of the Enlightenment. It achieved a measure of recognition, was re-established by Napoleon, reorganized by outstanding leaders and reawakened by preaching and conversion. But the Reformed Churches dwindled away in the 19th century owing to conflicts between the orthodox and the liberal movements, between 'believers' and 'multitudinists', between the congregationalists and the synodalists. Missionary zeal and ecumenical searching brought the churches together in 1938 in a unity which still seeks fuller expression. The Reformed Church of France represents two per cent of the total population.

French Protestantism was semi-rural and semi-urban, grouped in almost precise demographic territories. This situation is changing; rural Christians are today a more scattered minority and have great difficulty to adapt themselves to diaspora conditions. Urban Reformed Christians are not much better off, facing similar difficulties in gathering together, in particular in the suburbs of the large cities. It is no exaggeration to say that 50 per cent of the French Protestants live in a situation of accentuated dissemination. The consequences are that the traditional image of the church's life in parishes — with the Sunday morning worship, youth meetings, catechetical instruction, and gatherings for prayer and Bible study — is in the process of disappearing. Zones of Protestantism grouped together are becoming increasingly rare. There is a chronic shortage of pastors; there are 50 vacant posts now. The Church is giving a great deal of thought to the question of lay ministries and of ministry in general.

Some parishes have become more and more introverted. Others have opened up to the international Christian community, taking mission, development aid and other ecumenical concerns seriously. The Church is in regular contact with several churches in Latin America.

German Churches
FEDERAL REPUBLIC OF GERMANY

BREMEN EVANGELICAL CHURCH
(Bremische Evangelische Kirche)
Franziuseck 2-4, Postfach 106929, 2800 Bremen 1 — Tel: 0421.50971. 400,000 members — 69 congregations — 148 pastors. Publication: Bremer Kirchenzeitung. WCC (1948), EKD, CEC. President: Eckart Ranft — Secretary: Rev. Wolf-Udo Smidt.

The Church grew out of the Reformation as early as 1525. Around 1600, during the so-called Second Reformation, the Protestant population of Bremen turned slowly to the Reformed confession. Soon after 1800 most of the congregations of the church became united. Today the Bremen Evangelical Church is one of the few churches in the whole of Germany with United, Lutheran and Reformed congregations. After the First World War the senate of Bremen agreed to a complete separation of church and state. Since 1920 the Church has had its own constitution which provides for a maximum of autonomy for each local congregation.

The Roman Catholic Church has nearly 60,000 members. The Evangelical-Methodist Church, the Baptist Church and other Christian communities are small in number, though not in influence. The Protestant churches and the Roman Catholic Church participate in the Ecumenical Working Group of Bremen which functions as a regional council of churches. The Church faces a decrease in membership because of increasing secularization and religious indifference. The arms race, world peace, ecological problems and justice in an international perspective will receive a good deal of its attention in the coming years. The Church has few general programmes because of the highly structured autonomy of the congregations. It maintains particular relations with the Presbyterian Church of Ghana and the Evangelical Church of Togo.

Evangelical
Lutheran Church
of North Elbian

Evangelical Church
of Greifswald

Evangelical Lutheran
Church of Mecklenburg

**GERMAN DEMOCRATIC
REPUBLIC**

Evangelical
Lutheran
Church in
Oldenburg

Evangelical Church
of Bremen

Evangelical-Reformed
Church in
Northwestern Germany

Evangelical
Lutheran Church
of Hanover

Evangelical
Lutheran Church
of Schaumburg-Lippe

Evangelical
Church
in Brunswick

Evangelical Church
in Berlin-Brandenburg
(Berlin-West)

Evangelical Church
in Berlin-Brandenburg

Evangelical Church
of Westphalia

Church
of Lippe

Evangelical
Church
of Anhalt

Evangelical Church
of the Province
of Saxony

Evangelical
Church of the
Goerlitz Region

Evangelical Church
of the Rhineland

Evangelical Church
of Hesse
Electorate-Waldeck

Evangelical
Church in
Hesse and Nassau

Evangelical Lutheran
Church in Thuringia

Evangelical Lutheran
Church of Saxony

United Protestant
Evangelical Christian
Church of the Palatinate

**FEDERAL REPUBLIC
OF GERMANY**

Evangelical Lutheran
Church in Bavaria

Evangelical Church
in Württemberg

Evangelical Church
in Baden

CATHOLIC DIOCESE OF THE OLD-CATHOLICS IN GERMANY
(Katholisches Bistum der Alt-Katholiken in Deutschland)
Gregor-Mendel-Strasse 28, 5300 Bonn 1 — Tel: 0228.232285. 28,000 members — 53 parishes — 62 priests — 9 deacons. Publications: Alt-Katholische Kirchenzeitung (monthly), Alt-Katholisches Jahrbuch (both in German). WCC (1948), ACKBD, CEC. Bischof: Dr Josef Brinkhues.

The chief organizer of the Old Catholic movement in Germany was Johann Friedrich von Schulte, who began, immediately after the Vatican Council, to organize a meeting of professors of various universities to protest against the new dogmas. A meeting was held in Neurenberg on 25-26 August 1870. It drew up a formal manifesto in which it declared that the Vatican Council was not a true ecumenical council, because it was neither free nor morally unanimous. After the opponents to the Council were excommunicated, a bishopric was established in Germany which chose the university professor, Dr Josef Hubert Reinkens, ordained as priest in 1848, as its first bishop. He was consecrated by Bishop Heykamp of Deventer in the Netherlands. It was through his skill and under his guidance that the German Old Catholic Church was consolidated and that such reforms as the liturgical use of German and the introduction of clerical marriage were carried through with success. A first Old Catholic Congress was held from 22 to 24 September 1871 in Munich, to which representatives from Austria, Switzerland and the Netherlands were invited. The second Old Catholic Congress took place a year later at Cologne, 22-24 September 1872. Many other congresses have been held.

Since 1931 intercommunion is practised with the Anglican churches, and more recently with the Philippine Independent Church, the Spanish Reformed Episcopal Church and the Lusitanian Catholic-Apostolic Evangelical Church of Portugal. The dialogue with the Orthodox churches continues. A pastoral agreement with the Roman Catholic Church is in preparation.

The CDOCG continues to work for unity among Christians by witnessing to the truth of the gospel and by emphasizing the need for deep reform of the Church. It supports an Anglican-Franciscan mission in Tanzania and a (former Anglican) medical programme in Zambia.

CHURCH OF LIPPE (Lippische Landeskirche)
Leopoldstrasse 27, Postfach 132, 4930 Detmold — Tel: 05231.23033. 280,000 members — 66 parishes — 130 pastors. Publication: Informationen aus der Lippischen Landeskirche. WCC (1948), EKD, GMC, AK, RBBRD, WARC. Landessuperintendent: Dr Ako Haarbeck.

The Hansa city of Lemgo opened itself to the Reformation in 1533. But only after the Religious Peace of Augsburg in 1555 did the synod of Cappel (1556) openly embrace the Lutheran Reformation. In 1571, the consistory of the Church of Lippe was established. The Roman Catholic bishop of Paderborn tried to win the Church back to the Catholic communion; but Count Simon VI helped confirm the Reformation in the spirit of Melanchthon's theology. From then onwards the Lutheran and Reformed confessional streams developed in the Church. After 1684 the Reformed constitution was suppressed, and the Lutheran church constitution officially recognized. This situation remained unchanged until 1918 when the Church found a new form. In 1931 a new presbyterial-synodical constitution was given to the Church of Lippe which has proved adequate till today. A similar constitution with regard to membership in the EKD in the FRG was adoped in 1970.

The Church of Lippe has taken another step towards unity by consenting to the Agreement of Leuenberg in 1973. Its relationship to the state, in particular to North Rhine-Westphalia, was laid down in the Accord of Detmold in 1958. In spite of limited financial resources, the Church continues to support diaconal institutions (e.g. the evangelical deaconesses home and the nursing home 'Eben-Ezer') and various kinds of work among men, women and youth.

At the present time the Church finds itself in a difficult situation, which in itself is a reason for rejoicing: the number of theological students has risen so steeply that in the coming years there will not be a sufficient number of pastoral charges for new ministers. It is being explored whether other employment can be found for them. Because of financial limitations it will be very difficult to create a number of new posts.

The small Church of Lippe attaches great importance to a renewed partnership with Presbyterian churches in Ghana and Togo. This solidarity, a result of the missionary efforts of the last century, is now being cultivated through an exchange of delegates, theological ideas, etc. The Church of Lippe continues to stress the missionary structure of the congregation and is engaged in the search for world peace. In Eastern Europe it maintains a particular relation with the Evangelical Church of Anhalt in the GDR and the Reformed Church in Hungary.

EUROPEAN CONTINENTAL PROVINCE OF THE MORAVIAN CHURCH (DISTRICT BAD BOLL)

(Europäisch-Festländische Brüder-Unität — Distrikt Bad Boll)
Badwasen 6, 7325 Bad Boll — Tel: 07164.2047. 15,435 members, district Bad Boll (FRG, the Netherlands, Switzerland, Denmark, Sweden) — 16 congregations — 32 pastors (including three members of the Board and two retired bishops). Publications: Moravian Daily Texts (in 33 languages), Der Brüderbote (in German), Unitas Fratrum (in German), De Herrnhuter (in Dutch). WCC (1948), CEC, affiliated with EKD. President: Rev. Roland Baudert — Secretary: Rev. Hans Beat Motel.

(For the early history of the Moravian community see the European Continental Province of the Moravian Church (District Herrnhut) in the German Democratic Republic.)

Besides the Moravian Church in the FRG and the GDR there are 16 other Moravian communities in Europe, Africa, North and South America (in 28 countries). The Synod of 1931 was an assembly of Europeans and North Americans representing four unity provinces, convened to discuss the mission fields. In 1981 an assembly of 17 unity provinces took place reviewing the political, racial and religious tensions in the world and praying for a new spirit of peace, love and understanding.

The future concerns of the Bad Boll district of the Unitas Fratrum relate to racism, peace, disarmament, a simple lifestyle and the furthering of the ecumenical movement through christocentric theology, a variety of liturgies and openness to Christians elsewhere.

The main activities are focused on the pastoral care of Moravians in the diaspora and of guests at home (Bad Boll and Königsfeld-Switzerland), children, youth and student work, boarding schools in the FRG and Switzerland, pastoral care of the Surinam people in the Netherlands, of the mentally retarded in Ramallah (West Jordan), aid to sister churches in Tanzania, South Africa, Surinam, Labrador, and missionary and educational work among the Tibetans of North India. The ecumenical emphasis in the work of the Moravian Church in all the countries mentioned above is widely recognized.

EUROPEAN CONTINENTAL PROVINCE OF THE MORAVIAN CHURCH (DISTRICT HERRNHUT)

(Europäisch-Festländische Brüder-Unität — Distrikt Herrnhut)
Vogtshof, Zittauer Strasse 20, 8709 Herrnhut — Tel: 259. 2,900 members — 10 congregations — 21 pastors. Publication: Moravian Daily Texts (since 1731). WCC (1971), AGCK, CEC. Rev. Christian Müller.

The Unitas Fratrum, founded in 1457, had its origin in the Reformation of Jan Hus. Its members were scattered during the Thirty Years War, and fled in 1722 to Saxony to find refuge in Herrnhut, a community established by Count Zinzendorf (1700-1760), one of the leaders of German Pietism. Reacting to the unbelieving rationalism and the barren Protestant orthodoxy of this time, Zinzendorf proclaimed a "religion of the heart", based on an intimate fellowship with the Saviour who, conceived as creator, sustainer and redeemer of the world, dominated his theology. Originally he meant to realize his religious ideals within the framework of the different Protestant churches, but he was forced by circumstances to build a separate organization, though he continued to maintain close relationship with Lutheranism. His emphasis on the place of feeling in religion infused new life into Protestant orthodoxy and profoundly influenced 19th century German theology. He was also a forerunner of the 20th century ecumenical movement. Zinzendorf travelled widely through Europe and the United States and spent his last years in pastoral work at Herrnhut. The first missionaries from the Church went to the Caribbean in 1732; afterwards there were missions to the Eskimos in Alaska, the Indians in North America and the Hottentots in South Africa. The many mission fields developed into provinces of the Moravian Church.

Other Moravian congregations after Herrnhut were established in Germany in Niesky, Kleinwelka near Bautzen, Gnadau near Magdeburg, Neudietendorf near Erfurt and Ebersdorf near Lobenstein. Still other congregations developed in Berlin, Dresden, Zwicknau and Forst. In 1954 two districts of the European Continental Province of the Moravian Church came into being, the district of Bad Boll consisting of the congregations in the FRG, Holland, Switzerland, Denmark and Sweden.

The Moravian Daily Texts are published annually — 350,000 copies in 33 languages. In 1980, the 250th edition of the Moravian Text Book was commemorated. The GDR television made a telecast in connection with the event. Newsletters from Herrnhut are circulated among all Moravian communities in the world. Diaconal homes offer care for the sick, disabled, mentally disturbed and old people. In 1977 a new rehabilitation centre "Johannes Amos Comenius" was started at Herrnhut. Many thousands of visitors come every year to Moravian hostels. The Herrnhut archives occupy a special position in the Unitas Fratrum as the official repository of historical documents relating to the entire unity.

A main concern for the 1980s is evangelization in a socialist society where many people have turned away from the church and are indifferent to religion. The Church also will continue to participate fully in the Federation of Christian Churches in the GDR in order to promote the ecumenical movement in the nation and abroad.

EVANGELICAL CHURCH IN BADEN
(Evangelische Landeskirche in Baden) Blumenstrasse 1, Postfach 2269, 7500 Karlsruhe — Tel: 0721.1471. 1,500,000 members — 680 parishes — 30 districts — 1,000 pastors. Publications: Aufbruch (weekly), Mitteilungen (monthly) (both in German). WCC (1948), EKD, EKU, CEC. Bishop: Prof. Dr Klaus Engelhardt.

The Church was founded as a Union of Lutheran and Reformed churches in 1821. It embraces congregations in the south-west corner of the Federal Republic of Germany, in the Neckartal, along the Rhine, in the Black Forest and along the Bodensee. Almost half of the population of Baden is Roman Catholic. There are also small free churches and a few congregations belonging the Greek Orthodox Church.

The life of the Church is shaped by the diversity of the congregations. There are rural congregations, and congregations in university cities which confront the problems of an industrial society. The cooperation between different confessional groups is an important feature of the life of the Church. It faces theological questions, problems of ecumenism at the local level, issues of diaconal-pastoral work, migrant workers, development as an international social question and the dialogue with new religious movements. In the synod and in the parishes problems of peace, environment, dialogue with other religions and the elimination of racism are on the agenda.

The Church maintains particular relations with the Presbyterian Church in Ghana and the Cameroon, the Church of South India, the National Council of Churches in Indonesia and Korea, the United Church of Christ in Japan, the Moravian Church in South Africa, the Waldensian Church in Italy and the Evangelical Presbyterian Church in Portugal.

EVANGELICAL CHURCH IN BERLIN-BRANDENBURG (Berlin West)

(Evangelische Kirche in Berlin-Brandenburg — Berlin West) Bachstrasse 1-2, Berlin 21 — Tel: 030. 390911 — Telex: epzd D 181241. 1,040,000 members — 12 dioceses — 168 parishes — 527 pastors — 38 auxiliary pastors. Publications: Berliner Sonntagsblatt and Kirchliches Amtsblatt (in German). WCC (1948), EKD, ACKBD, CEC. Bishop: Dr Martin Kruse.

After 1945 the Church became an independent Christian community with its own dioceses and patterns of administration. The first bishop was Otto Dibelius. Bishop Kurt Scharf succeeded him in 1966. After the building of the Berlin wall Christians from Berlin West were refused entry into the other part of the city. Separate synods of the Evangelical Church were held in both parts of the city. In 1972 Bishop Albrecht Schönherr, who had become responsible in 1967 for the administration of the Eastern part of the Church, became the Bishop of the Evangelical Church in Berlin-Brandenburg. Two separate regional synods have been formed, but the *Landeskirche* is considered by both as one spiritual unit.

The Church is fully integrated into the cultural and social life of the city. But the membership is decreasing, owing partly to a steady population decline and partly to the fact that people are leaving the Church.

The Church continues its activities among children (800 helpers), and in hospitals and ambulant medical services (235 helpers); 605 catechists are responsible for religious education in public schools. The church is challenged by increasing conflicts, particularly in regard to the problems of youth and foreigners. It plays a role in the search for reconciliation and peace. New activities cannot be initiated because of financial limitations. However, more emphasis is laid on the stimulation of the spiritual life of the Church and the pastoral care of young families. Ecumenical cooperation and an honest confrontation with Islam are clear priorities.

Of the total West Berlin population of 1,900,000 million 1,040,000 are Protestants, 270,000 Roman Catholics and 150,000 Muslims. The Church maintains through the Berlin mission particular relations with Evangelical Lutheran churches in Southern Africa, Tanzania, Ethiopia, the Korean Christian Church, the National Council of Churches in Japan, and the Presbyterian churches in Korea and Taiwan.

EVANGELICAL CHURCH IN GERMANY (Evangelische Kirche in Deutschland)

President of the Council: Bishop D. Eduard Lohse, Herrenhäuserstrasse 2A, 3000 Hannover 21. President of the Office for Foreign Relations: Dr Heinz Joachim Held, Kirchliches Aussenamt, Friedrichstrasse 2-6, Postfach 174025, 6000 Frankfurt am Main 1 — Tel: 0611.7159.1.

At the end of 1977, the membership of the constituent churches of the Evangelical Church in Germany (EKD) totalled 26,700,000 (43,5 per cent of the population of the Federal Republic of Germany). In the 17 member churches of the EKD there are over 10,500 separate congregations, about 16,000 are pastoral charges and over

20,000 pastors, of whom about 15,500 are in active ministry. About six per cent of the active clergy are women. Altogether, the EKD and its service agencies employ about 245,000 people as pastors, preachers, deaconesses, deacons, social workers, nurses, kindergarten teachers, church musicians, churchwardens, executives and other administrative staff.

The Roman Catholic Church in the FRG has 26,800,000 members (43,6 per cent of the population). The Protestant Free Churches have about 1,200,000 members and the various Orthodox Churches and the diocese of the Old Catholics together account for around 660,000 others.

Until 1918 the present EKD member churches were closely related to the civil authorities. The territorial churches adopted their own constitutions based on the separation of church and state. The desire for closer union led in 1922 to the establishment of the German Protestant Church Alliance. Following the seizure of power by the National Socialists in 1933, it became the German Protestant Church.

Some of the territorial churches, pre-eminently the Confessing Church, tried to resist the attempts of the National Socialist rulers to turn the Church into a new state church. Their objections were clearly stated in the Barmen Declaration of 1934. This, together with the Stuttgart Confession of Guilt of 1945, provided the basis for a new ordering of the Protestant Church. In 1948 at Eisenach, the 13 Lutheran churches, two Reformed churches and 12 United churches in both parts of Germany came together to form the EKD. In 1969 eight Protestant territorial churches in the German Democratic Republic established the Federation of Evangelical Churches in the GDR. Despite their separate constitutional existence and structure, the EKD and the Federation acknowledge the unity of all Protestant Christianity in Germany.

A new kind of theological church fellowship became possible among the EKD member churches as a result of the Leuenberg Agreement (1973), a doctrinal agreement between Lutheran and Reformed Churches in Europe.

The VELKD (United Evangelical Lutheran Church in Germany) groups together since 1948 the five Lutheran EKD churches of Bavaria, Brunswick, Hanover, North Elbe and Schaumburg-Lippe. This came about after a century's efforts to unite German Lutheranism. Since 1969 the three founding VELKD churches in the GDR constitute the VELKD in their country.

The EKU (Evangelical Church of the Union) dates back to the efforts of the King of Prussia, Friedrich Wilhelm III, in 1817, to heal the divisions between Lutheranism and Calvinism in German Protestantism by establishing a Prussian Protestant Church. Out of this emerged the Protestant Church of the Old Prussion Union which was made up of the church provinces in Berlin-Brandenburg, Saxony and Pomerania, in the Rhineland and Westphalia, as well as in parts of East Germany. As the VELKD, the EKU was eventually divided into two areas after 1972, with one part in the FRG and Berlin (West) and the other in the GDR.

Founded in 1884 as a voluntary association of Reformed pastors and church members, the Reformed Alliance (Reformierter Bund) is today supported by the two Reformed churches within the EKD in Northwest Germany and Lippe, as well as by a number of Reformed congregations in the United churches.

The Arnoldhainer Conference was founded in 1967 when the EKD Council initiated theological studies on the question of intercommunion between Lutheran and Reformed Churches. Despite its minimum organization the AC serves as the counterpart to the VELKD in the dialogue within the EKD.

The EKD is led and administered by various agencies, official bodies and departments. The chief of these are the synod, the church conference, and the council. The synod has 120 members. It is elected for six years and is led by a presidium. It normally meets annually, each year in a different place. The church conference, made up of representatives of member churches, discusses the work of the EKD and its member churches. The council consists of 15 members, lay people and clergy. It is officially represented at the seat of the Federal Government in Bonn.

Among the major EKD agencies may be mentioned the Diaconal Work (Diakonisches Werk, created in 1957), Bread for the World (founded in 1959), the United Evangelical Mission, the Protestant Association for World Mission, the Churches' Development Service, the Protestant Central Agency for Development Aid, and the Joint Association for Christian Communication.

The roots of the Kirchentag, a lay conference re-established in 1949 as a "permanent organization", go back to the 19th century. Meeting every two years it emphasizes the inseparable unity of liturgical celebration and social commitment, of biblical study and the concern for political and practical issues.

The most important ecumenical organization in the FRG is the Joint Working Group of Christian Churches (ACK). In a somewhat similar way to the national Christian councils in other countries, the ACK brings together confessional churches of various traditions. It embraces the EKD, the Roman Catholic Church, and the Greek Orthodox Metropolitan, as well as the Protestant Free Churches and two Pentecostal communities. The German Evangelical Alliance plays an important part in facilitating contacts between evangelical Christians.

The EKD was a founder member of the WCC. The territorial Lutheran churches which constitute the VELKD, though represented in the WCC through the EKD, are counted direct members of the World Council.

Despite the limited nature of the authority of the EKD in relation to its member churches, as defined in the constitution, it is able to assist its member churches effectively by performing the common tasks they have entrusted to it in many fields. In addition to this, it has shared in the contemporary dialogue in society through its official statements and memoranda *(Denkschriften)*, and in this way made a distinctive contribution to the solution of problems affecting society as a whole. (e.g. the so-called *Ost-Denkschrift* in 1965).

EVANGELICAL CHURCH IN HESSEN AND NASSAU (Evangelische Kirche in Hessen und Nassau)
Paulsplatz 1, Postfach 669, 6100 Darmstadt — Tel: 06151.4051. 2,160,000 members — 7 districts — 800 congregations — 1,300 pastors. Publication: Amtsblatt der Evangelischen Kirche in Hessen und Nassau. WCC (1948), ACKBD, CEC. President: Dr Helmut Hild.

The Evangelical Church in Hessen and Nassau was established in 1947 when the three churches of Hessen, Nassau and Frankfurt came together. Already in 1934 the three churches were forced to a union under the Nazi regime. A long common history, the experience of the church struggle from 1933 to 1945 and the responsibilities of the Church in the territories of Rhine and Main have led to the union Church. It is the first Christian community of its kind in the FRG in which questions of different confessional background (the Augsburg Confession and the Barmen Declaration) have been officially settled.

Half of the population of Hessen and Nassau is Protestant, the other half Roman Catholic. The percentage of members leaving the Church is relatively small, compared to the experience of other churches.

The particular tasks of the ECHN grow out of the increasing industrialization of the Rhine-Main region, which affects also the countryside, although the smaller towns and villages still play a creative role in the life of the Christian community. A major responsibility is the pastoral care of people. The estrangement from the traditional church has made it necessary to think in terms of tasks.

Religious education of the young generation calls for careful planning. An increasing number of theological students, who will graduate in the near future, have to be placed in parishes and other church positions in the coming years. It is an open question as to whether the ECHN will be able to employ many additional young pastors.

Among the major services the Church renders are the work of the Evangelical Academy in Arnoldshain, a pedagogical centre in Schönberg, a ministry for the upbuilding of congregations and publicity. It is the only church in the Evangelical Church in Germany which publishes a quarterly, *Im Gespräch*, which is widely distributed among church members.

The ECHN maintains close relations with the Presbyterian Church in Ghana, the Waldensian Church in Italy and the Polish Ecumenical Council.

EVANGELICAL CHURCH IN RHINELAND (Evangelische Kirche im Rheinland)

Hans-Böckler-Strasse 7, Postfach 320340, 4000 Düsseldorf 30 — Tel: 0211.45621. 3,500,000 members — 46 synods — 819 congregations — 1,808 pastors. Publication: Kirchliches Amtsblatt (in German). WCC (1948), EKD, GMC. Präses: Dr Gerhard Brandt.

The history of Christianity in Rhineland dates back to the Roman Empire. Its expansion took place in the 8th century through Anglo-Saxon missionaries and under the reign of Carolingian kings. After the Reformation, Lutheran and Reformed congregations suffered much hardship and lived in diaspora. Efforts of reformation in the bishoprics of Cologne and Treves failed. Since the Council of Trent, Roman Catholicism has been predominant in the Rhineland countries. Pietism played an important role at the end of the 18th century in bringing Lutheran and Reformed Christians together.

The Evangelical Church in Rhineland was constituted in the territory which was assigned to Prussia in 1815 by the Congress of Vienna after the collapse of the Napoleon Empire. The Church inherited the presbyterian-synodal system of the 16th century. The transition from the 'church of pastors' to the 'community of collaborating Christians' became particularly visible during the struggle against National Socialism. It was not accidental that the first synod of the Confessing Church took place in Rhineland (Barmen) in 1934.

The Church seeks today to deepen contacts with the Roman Catholic Church with which it has coexisted for centuries, with free churches which separated from the 'Volkskirche', and with the Orthodox churches — the last as a result of the presence of many migrant workers in Rhineland. It maintains a relationship with the United Church of Christ in the USA through the Evangelical Church of the Union.

Among its preoccupations are the effort to be a Christian presence in society, and the attempts to tackle issues like the North-South and the East-West conflict and the problem of massive unemployment (in particular of the young generation), and to work for the integration of migrant workers in society. The Church strives after a renewal of church education, in order to prevent the withdrawal of the young generation, a renewal in worship, enriched by experiences in ecumenical encounters, and a renewal in witness and service.

EVANGELICAL CHURCH OF KURHESSEN-WALDECK (Evangelische Kirche von Kurhessen-Waldeck)

Wilhelmshöher Allee 330, 3500 Kassel — Tel: 0561.30831. 1,100,000 members — 4 dioceses — 944 parishes — 624 pastors. Publications: Amtsblatt and Blick in die Kirche (in German). WCC (1948), EKD, AK, GMC. Bishop: Dr Hans-Gernot Jung.

The Church traces its origin to the mission of Bonifacius in the 8th century. After an encounter with Philip Melanchthon in 1524, Landgrave Philip of Hessen introduced the Reformation into the Church. He was assisted by Adam Krafft and for a short time by Martin Bucer from Strasbourg. The University of Marburg was established in 1527. After the death of Landgrave Philip, the landgraviate and its churches were divided among his four sons. This division lasted for centuries, and it was only after 1945 that Hessen was politically reunited. The Evangelical Church of Kurhessen-Waldeck and the Evangelical Church in Hessen and Nassau show in their historical existence that the organizational separation of the territory into two churches has been maintained until today. A confessional contrast has been expressed by the fact that an Upper-Hessian Lutheranism around the city of Marburg acknowledged the Confessio Augustana and not the Formula of Concord. The Lower-Hessian reformed region around Kassel adopted the Confessio Augustana in the wording of the so-called Variata. It is not accidental that, because of different confessional traditions, the Evangelical Church of Kurhessen-Waldeck was among the first to subscribe to the recent Leuenberg Agreement. Its ecumenical openness goes back to the time when Waldensian and Huguenot refugees asked for asylum. Today it is in continuous dialogue with the Roman Catholic bishopric of Fulda in its territory.

Until 1918 the Church was a state church. In 1924 the Church received its own constitution. In 1934 the Evangelical Church of Hessen-Kassel and the former Principality of Waldeck-Pyrmont were united in the Evangelical Church of Kurhessen-Waldeck. It represents 60 per cent of the total population. It takes an active part in the cultural, social and political life of the society.

Its primary goal is the proclamation of the gospel of Jesus Christ. Its further emphases are pastoral care, education, mission and diaconia. The Church struggles to find the right answers to problems of political and social peace, disarmament, ecology and the human mastering of economy and technology. Particular contacts are maintained with the Evangelical Lutheran Churches in South Africa (western diocese) and Namibia, the diocese of North-Karnataka of the Church of South India, the synod of North-Brabant of the Reformed Church in the Netherlands and the Roman Catholic bishopric in the same territory of the Netherlands.

EVANGELICAL CHURCH OF THE PALATINATE (Evangelische Kirche der Pfalz)

Domplatz 5, 6720 Speyer/Rhein — Tel: 06232.1091 — Telex: 0465100. 680,000 members — 438 parishes — 387 pastors. Publications: Evangelischer Kirchenbote, Informationen (in German). WCC (1948), GMC. President: Heinrich Kron.

The Church of the Palatinate is a union church of Lutheran and Reformed Christians, established in 1818. The church constitution is presbyterial-synodical. It is one of the smaller communities among the 17 territorial churches in the FRG.

The ECP is aware of the need for missionary-diaconal renewal of its congregations living in the midst of an increasingly secularized society. This also calls for a permanent openness to ecumenical dialogue, in order to become a more faithful witness to the gospel and to join in common action with others in matters of reconciliation and peace. The Church attempts to learn from the insights and experiences of the worldwide church which today faces manifold forms of human suffering and injustice and is challenged to share in the struggle for a more equal distribution of power and wealth.

The Evangelical Church of the Palatinate regards itself consciously as a "Volkskirche". It sponsors a considerable number of institutions and runs several programmes for children, for the disabled, for the elderly. It renders pastoral services to various groups of society, prisoners, police, students, soldiers, conscientious objectors. The Church further promotes a variety of youth activities and programmes for adult education.

The ECP has close ties with the Protestant Church of Anhalt (GDR), the United Reformed Church in the UK, the Reformed Church of France, the Reformed Church in Yugoslavia and a number of churches in Africa, Asia and Latin America, through the Association of Churches and Missions in South West Germany.

EVANGELICAL CHURCH OF WESTPHALIA (Evangelische Kirche von Westfalen).
Altstädter Kirchplatz 5, Postfach 2740, 4800 Bielefeld 1 — Tel: 0521.594.1. 3,600,000 members — 1,676 congregations — 1,565 pastors. Publications: Kirchliches Amtsblatt der Evangelischen Kirche von Westfalen. WCC (1948), EKD, EKU, AK, CEC. President: Dr Heinrich Reiss.

From 1524 onwards the Reformation spread through the territory of Westphalia, particularly in the cities. Besides the Lutheran congregations, a few Reformed communities also came into being. A few churches remained Roman Catholic and others were won back by the Counter-Reformation. Lutheran secondary schools in Dortmund and Soest as well as Reformed secondary schools in Herborn, Steinfurt, Duisburg, Lingen and Hamm played an important role in the history of Protestantism. A presbyterial-synodal church order was devised in 1835.

In 1945 the ECW became an independent church and joined the Evangelical Church in Germany. There are evangelical faculties of theology at the Universities of Münster and Bochum, and a theological school in Bethel. At the eighth synod of 1979, the ecumenical concerns of the Church in the FRG and in the world were discussed in depth.

EVANGELICAL CHURCH OF WÜRTTEMBERG (Evangelische Landeskirche in Württemberg)
Gänseheidestrasse 2-4, Postfach 92, 7000 Stuttgart 1 — Tel.: 0711.2149.1. 2,500,000 members — 4 regions — 51 deaneries — 1,380 parishes — 4 district superintendents — approx. 1,500 pastors. Publications: Evangelisches Gemeindeblatt, Konsequenzen, Für Arbeit und Gesinnung, Unter Uns (all in German). WCC (1948), ACKBD, LWF, CEC. Bishop: Dr Hans von Keler.

Missionaries from Ireland and France brought the gospel to the country in the 6th century. In the Middle Ages, piety, developed through the influence of such leaders as John Tauler and Meister Eckhart, had a strong impact. It has reflected in Württemberg pietism ever since. The Reformation made its influence felt as early as 1517. Later the country lay in the path of two competing Protestant forces: the Zwinglian reform from Zürich and the Lutheran from Wittenberg. Württemberg, led by Johannes Brenz, decided for the Lutheran. The confessional development included the Württemberg Confession (1551) and the Great Church Order (1559), spelling out the ways of parish life and the relation between church and state. Doctrine, piety and Christian life were later influenced by Lutheran orthodoxy (Jacob Andreae), pietism (John Albrecht Bengel, Ludwig Hofacker), Enlightenment and liberalism (Ferdinand Bauer and David Friedrich Strauss).

The Württemberg Bible Society was founded in 1812 and the Basel Mission Society in 1815. The ECW organizational structure is synodical, and its clerical head bears the title of bishop, introduced in 1933 on the eve of the church struggle. The first Evangelical Academy was started in 1945 in Bad Boll. The efforts of Bishop Theophil Wurm (d. 1953) on behalf of a confessing Christian unity typified the ecumenical and evangelical role of Württemberg's Lutherans. Almost half of the population is Roman Catholic. The number of non-Christians, mostly Turkish Muslims in the large cities, is growing.

As 'Volkskirche' the Church continues to profit from the support of the state (collection of church taxes and the provision for religious education in public schools). Active participation in Church life is numerically on the decline, but there is perceptible increase in intensity.

Tasks for the years to come are: evangelism in an increasingly secular context, the strengthening of community with the Roman Catholic Church, social and diaconal services to the underprivileged and the disabled (migrant workers, the sick and the aged), development work with churches in other continents, the holding and bringing together of different trends in church and political life. The major activities take place within the individual parishes. The question raised during the Missionary Year 1980, and to be raised again at the 450th anniversary of the Reformation in Württemberg (1984) is: What is the challenge of evangelism for our Church, yesterday, today and tomorrow?

Partner churches are the Presbyterian Church of Cameroon, the American Lutheran Church and the Lutheran Church of America, the La Plata Evangelical Church in Brazil and the Waldensians.

EVANGELICAL LUTHERAN CHURCH IN BAVARIA (Evangelisch-Lutherische Kirche in Bayern)

Meiserstrasse 13, 8000 Munich 2 — Postfach 370240, 8000 Munich 37 — Tel: (089) 55951 — Telex: 529 674 (lkrm d). 2,650,000 members — 71 deaneries — 1,625 parishes — 6 regional bishops (Oberkirchenräte) — 1917 pastors. Publications: Amtsblatt and Nachrichten (both in German). WCC (1948), EKD, VELKD, ACKBD, LWF, CEC. Bishop: Dr Johannes Hanselmann.

To the present state of Bavaria, whose early settlers were Bavarians, Swabians and Franconians, the gospel was brought by Boniface and other missionaries in the 8th century. Slowly the faith took root and the church and its institutions became firmly implanted. The Lutheran Reformation was fully established in Nuremberg by 1524. In 1530, the city of Augsburg gave its name to the major Lutheran confession. The Religious Peace of Augsburg (1555), laying down the principle that the religion of the ruler determines the religion of his subjects *(cuius regio, eius religio),* and the rise of the Counter-Reformation returned to the Roman Catholic Church over one half of the gains made in Bavaria. Seventeenth-century theological orthodoxy, the Thirty Years' War (1618-48), Pietism and the Napoleonic era left their marks on Lutheranism.

The actual founding of the Church took place in the year 1803. About 27 per cent of Bavaria's population today is Lutheran. The Church is divided into six districts: Ansbach, Augsburg, Beyreuth, Munich, Nuremberg, Regensburg. As in the case of other churches in the Federal Republic, support for the Church comes through the income tax surcharge collected by the government's fiscal office. Voluntary offerings for special purposes are received in the congregations.

In the worship of Bavarian Lutheran churches, the liturgy and hymns are integral to the preaching of the word and the administering of the sacraments. Being a 'Volkskirche' the Church is concerned to serve its constituency in many ways. There is provision for religious services in all localities, for religious instruction in schools and Sunday schools. A particular concern is the provision of church services for tourists. The peace question and a new approach to the so-called youth religions and sectarian movements are high on the agenda. The Church continues to seek and strengthen ecumenical fellowship with other churches through a variety of programmes and activities. It maintains special relations with Evangelical Lutheran Churches in Papua-New Guinea, Tanzania and Brazil.

EVANGELICAL LUTHERAN CHURCH IN BRUNSWICK
(Evangelisch-Lutherische Landeskirche in Braunschweig)

Neuer Weg 88/90, 3340 Wolfenbüttel — Tel: 05331.8021. 558,000 members — 13 dioceses — 397 congregations — 266 pastors — 20 vicars. Publications: Amtsblatt and Kurier (both in German). WCC (1948), EKD, GMC, VELKD, LWF. Bishop: Dr Gerhard Heintze.

Following the centuries when the Roman Catholic Church, with its vast monastic properties and many churches, had become firmly established, the Reformation made gains slowly. The city of Brunswick accepted Lutheranism in 1528, the duchy of

Brunswick-Wolfenbüttel in 1568. Martin Chemnitz, called the 'second Martin' after Luther, was a leader in the second generation of reformers. Other leading theologians were Johannes Bugenhagen, Basilius Sattler, Nikolaus Selnecker, Jakob Andreae, and Nikolaus von Ansdorf. The establishment of the Julius University at Helmstedt in 1576 proved decisive for the further development of the Church. It was dissolved by Napeoleon in 1810. The Enlightenment and rationalism, not pietism and revivalism, influenced this Christian community in the 18th and 19th centuries. After the abolishment of the monarchy in Germany in 1918, the Church was governed by the bishop. It went through many trials during the national socialist period. The Church represents 72 per cent of the population; 18 per cent are Roman Catholic. There are also some free churches and several Orthodox congregations in the area. The Church maintains good ecumenical relations with the other churches and also the Jewish community in its territory. It also maintains special relations with Lutheran churches in Japan, India, Ethiopia, South Africa and Brazil through the Evangelical Luther Mission in Lower Saxony.

The Church in Brunswick participates in many cultural activities, in particular in the realm of music. The year 1980 was marked by several activities in connection with the observance of the 'missionary year'. Neighbour parishes were contacted and asked to participate in a celebration of missions at Hermannsburg. In the same year was held an assembly of youth. Preparations are now under way for a 'Landeskirchentag' in Brunswick in 1982. The theme is: 'Strengthening the Faith'.

Besides communal activities among men, women and youth, the Church faces a serious shortage of pastors, but there is hope that this problem will be solved in the eighties as more students will soon finish their theological education. The financial situation also presents a problem. Economic measures are being considered and a choice of priorities will be made.

EVANGELICAL LUTHERAN CHURCH IN OLDENBURG (Evangelisch-Lutherische Kirche in Oldenburg)

Evangelisch-lutherischer Oberkirchenrat, Postfach 1709, Philosophenweg 1, 2900 Oldenburg — Tel: 0441.7701.0. 520,180 members — 13 dioceses — 120 congregations — 220 ordained pastors — 22 pastors abroad and in military chaplaincy. Publications: Briefe an Kirchenälteste, Gesetz und Verordnungsblatt (irregular, in German). WCC (1948), EKD, ACKBD, AK, LWF. Bishop: Dr Hans Heinrich Harms.

The Christianization of this Frisian and Saxon territory began in 780. By about the year 1000, part of the organized church came under the archdiocese of Hamburg-Bremen and part under the diocese of Osnabrück. In 1050 the Duchy of Oldenburg was formed. During the ensuing era, some large and attractive church edifices — like the one in Wiefelstede — were built, and these are still greatly admired.

The Reformation era found Oldenburg opening slowly to Lutheran, then to Calvinist, and — via the city of Münster — also to Anabaptist influences. The Lutheran forces won out. In 1573, the first Lutheran church order (constitution, liturgy, doctrinal guidelines, etc.) was introduced, and Calvinists and Anabaptists were denied freedom of worship. Orthodox Lutheranism, however, generated no great response in the relatively passive parishes. When most of the duchy came under Danish rule (1667-1773), King Frederick IV, under pietist influence, tried to stimulate church life and introduced a new church order. His efforts were unsuccessful.

During the Enlightenment and under a change of political rule, still another church order was enacted. Heavily influenced by Rationalism, it completely bypassed the Lutheran confessions. The 19th century brought renewal in the church and — through the church order of 1853 — a restoration of confessional emphasis. Similarly, the church constitution of 1920 reaffirmed the confessions of the Reformation.

A specifically Lutheran commitment reasserted itself during the church struggle of the 1930s and early 1940s when a scripturally founded confession of faith was of vital importance. This kind of emphasis underlay the subsequent church constitution of 1950 — still in effect — which is itself a confessionally based and ecumenically oriented document. When the United Evangelical Lutheran Church in Germany (VELKD) was organized in 1948, Oldenburg did not join.

The Church is headed by a bishop (the title since 1934) and a superior church council (Oberkirchenrat). The synod is the Church's legislative body; it elects the bishop and council members. The pastors are educated at various universities and theological schools. With its diversified staff, the Church maintains a variety of institutions and services in the fields of Christian education, health, welfare, and pastoral care to tourists. Like its sister church in Hanover, the Church in Oldenburg has a cordial working agreement with the state of Lower Saxony (1955). One of the Church's great preoccupations is with the problem of world peace. Its present bishop is a member of the WCC Central and Executive Committees.

EVANGELICAL LUTHERAN CHURCH OF HANOVER (Evangelisch-Lutherische Landeskirche Hannovers)

Rote Reihe 6, 3000 Hannover 1 — Tel: 0511.1941. 3,651,000 members — 76 districts — 1,550 congregations — 8 superintendents — 1,776 pastors. Publications: Kirchliches Amtsblatt, Evangelische Zeitung. WCC (1948), EKD, VELKD, LWF. Bishop D. Eduard Lohse, Haarstrasse 6, 3000 Hannover 1.

The Church is the largest of the Evangelical Lutheran churches in the FRG. The urban population has grown rapidly in Lower Saxony in recent decades. Hanover ranks eighth among the cities of the Federal Republic. The general secretariat of the EKD and the offices of the VELKD are located in this city.

During the reign of Charlemagne (d.814), Anglo-Saxon missionaries assisted in the conversion of the people of Lower Saxony. Many of today's parish boundaries are from medieval times. Over 800 years ago, Loccum cloister became the land's first training centre for clergy, and daily vespers has continued unbroken as a moving reminder of an abiding Christian presence. The introduction of the Reformation began in 1527. Moderating influences kept Hanoverian Lutheranism from extreme confessionalism. Pietism gained little following. The Enlightenment proved more popular, but eventually yielded to the religious awakenings of the early 19th century. Hanover's contemporay contribution to world Lutheranism and to the modern ecumenical movement is best summed up in the dynamic career of Bishop Hanns Lilje (1899-1977), a President of the WCC from 1968-1975.

The ELCH combines episcopal, synodical and other elements in its organization. The constitution, first adopted in 1922 and most recently amended in 1965, provides for several central church organs. The bishop is the spiritual (clerical) head of the Church. He chairs the senate, the Church council, and the bishop's council which is made up of the district superintendents of the Church's eight districts. Pastors of the ELCH receive their education in Göttingen and in other universities. Additional training is provided by the Church's four seminaries for preachers which prepare theological students for the parish ministry, and by other centres, including the abbey of Loccum, where special programmes are offered. Increasing numbers of women have become vicars and pastors in recent years.

The Church maintains official relations with the Evangelical Lutheran Church in South Africa, the Ethiopian Evangelical Church Mekane Yesus, the Tamil Evangelical Lutheran Church of South India, the Evangelical Lutheran Church of France, the Evangelical Church of the Augsburg Confession in Poland, the Lutheran Church of Great Britain and Lutheran churches in several other countries.

EVANGELICAL LUTHERAN CHURCH OF SCHAUMBURG-LIPPE (Evangelisch-Lutherische Landeskirche Schaumburg-Lippe)
Landeskirchenamt, Herderstrasse 27, Postfach 1307, 3062 Bückeburg — Tel: 05722.4230. 80,000 members — 21 parishes — 2 superintendents — 37 pastors. Publication: Kirchliches Amtsblatt. WCC (1948), LWF, GMC. Bishop Dr Joachim Heubach.

Schaumburg-Lippe, a part of the old duchy of Schaumburg and since 1946 a county in Lower Saxony some 35 miles west of the city of Hanover, contains one of Germany's smallest autonomous territorial churches. About 85 per cent of the mainly rural population are members of the Lutheran Church. Besides agriculture, there is some mining and light industry in the area. In the period from the introduction of Christianity during the time of Charlemagne until the 16th century, Roman Catholicism was firmly established in this region. Despite the resistance of the ruling Catholic bishops, the Reformation had its impact. By 1559, the entire duchy had become Lutheran, and the sovereign was declared temporal head of the church. In 1614, a new church order replaced the one adapted from that of Mecklenburg. New schools, including the University of Rinteln (1620-1809), contributed to education at all levels. Protestantism weathered the storm of the Thirty Years' War. Lutheran orthodoxy was mellowed in the 18th century by a Pietism fostered by the followers of Zinzendorf.

Among the superintendents of this Church, Johann Gottfried Herder, serving in Bückeburg 1771-76, is the best known. Although the Enlightenment made its impact here as elsewhere in Germany, a renewal of Lutheranism swept through the Church during the 19th century. To this renewal the Church owes the formation of a mission society (1840), a new evangelically oriented order of worship, and an awakened Christian concern among the people. The polity of the Church has episcopal and synodical elements, with the bishop presiding over the church council.

Despite its small size, the territory of Schaumburg-Lippe in its church situation represents the world at large in miniature. Besides the few Roman Catholic and Reformed congregations, there are also now the various sectarian groups, including Jehovah's Witnesses, Latter Day Saints (Mormons), and others. In 1976, the Church was host to the synod of the United Evangelical Lutheran Church in Germany. It was the first church to join the VELKD. The Church maintains specific relations with the Lutheran Church in Hungary and the Evangelical-Lutheran Church in Southern Africa.

EVANGELICAL REFORMED CHURCH IN NORTH-WEST GERMANY (Evangelisch-reformierte Kirche in Nordwestdeutschland)
Saarstrasse 6, 2950 Leer/Ostfriesland — Tel: 0491.13031 — Cable: Landeskirchenrat, Leer. 200,000 members — 10 dioceses — 130 congregations — 1 Landessuperintendent — 10 Superintendenten — 120 pastors. Publications: Sonntagsblatt and Kirchenbote (in German). WCC (1948) EKD, RBBRD, WARC, AK. President: Rev. Hinnerk Schröder — Landessuperintendent: Dr Gerhard Nordholt.

The Church serves mainly the area of Lower Saxony, especially in East Friesland, the County of Bentheim, and the regions of Göttingen, Osnabrück and Bremerhaven. In addition, it has a number of isolated congregations.

Most of its congregations originated in Reformation times. Through the influence of the regional princes of Reformed persuasion and the work of John à Lasco (at Emden 1540-1549), these congregations were led to adopt the Reformed faith. Reformed congregations in the County of Lingen were influenced by the Netherlands House of Orange at the end of the 17th century. In 1882, 114 of these congregations united to form the Church. Other congregations subsequently attached themselves to it, for example congregations of

Huguenot origin. In 1925 the Church adopted its present form of government. Church headquarters have been located in Leer (Ostfriesland) since 1955.

The Church is governed on Presbyterian lines. Congregations are independent. The supreme court is the synod, consisting of 43 elected and four appointed members. The synod has an executive of nine members. The Evangelical Reformed Church in North-West Germany is a smaller member of the EKD. On the basis of the Concord of Leuenberg the Church is in eucharistic communion with all EKD member churches. It maintains particular relations with partner churches in Togo, Ghana and South Africa and with churches in the GDR, Hungary, Romania and Yugoslavia. It supports the Special Fund of the WCC's Programme to Combat Racism. The themes of 'world peace' and the 'unity of the Church in reconciled diversity' are on its working agenda.

NORTH ELBIAN EVANGELICAL LUTHERAN CHURCH (Nordelbische Evangelisch-Lutherische Kirche)

Nordelbisches Kirchenamt, Dänische Strasse 27/35, 2300 Kiel — Tel: 0431.9911. 2,916,300 members — 665 parishes — 3 dioceses — 3 bishops — 1,244 pastors. Publications: Gesetz- und Verordnungsblatt der Nordelbischen Evan.-Luth. Kirche, NEK-Mitteilungen. WCC (1948), LWF GMC, CEC, EKD. Presiding Bishop: Bischof Karlheinz Stoll.

The church came into existence only in 1977, as the result of the merger of four formerly independent churches — those of Eutin, Hamburg, Lübeck and Schleswig-Holstein. Each of these churches was a founding member of the WCC. The whole region had accepted Christianity since the 9th century. One of the most outstanding personalities of that century was Ansgar, the "apostle of the north". The Reformation was introduced in Eutin in 1535. In Lübeck and Hamburg the Reformation was accepted against the will of the church hierarchy and the city council. The king of Denmark introduced the Reformation in Schleswig-Holstein. Still today about 85 per cent of the area is Lutheran. There is good cooperation with the Reformed Church, the Methodists, Baptists, Moravian Brethren and other small Christian communities.

Members of boards and committees of the North Elbian Evangelical Lutheran Church no longer consider themselves as representatives of the one or the other region, but as representatives of the one Church. The Church is now preoccupied with problems of personnel planning. There has been a great increase in the number of theological students at the University of Kiel. The Church hopes to fill 200 existing pastoral vacancies by 1985. Many of the suggestions made during the "Missionary Year 1980" were taken up and are being carried out. "Mission at our own front door" is recognized as an important task. The Church took an active part in the preparations for the Kirchentag at Hamburg in 1981.

The WCC initiatives on peace and disarmament and the Programme to Combat Racism are crucial concerns in the Church. A committee has been set up for peace work in the region. In spite of financial pressure, the synod decided to continue the annual budget for development — at the rate of 0.1 per cent, with the hope of reaching a total of 3 per cent in 1985. Funds are used for emergency measures of partner churches, for development education and for professional training of young people from overseas. The Church has spent considerable time discussing the political activities of pastors and church groups. The mass demonstration against the construction of a nuclear power plant near Brockdorf led to a special appeal by the Church council which received widespread public attention. This Council sponsored a series of publications on the task and the limits of political activity by pastors.

The Church faces the problem of a large number of people leaving the Church in urban areas. New missionary efforts have to be undertaken to increase church membership and to help the young generation in its search for lasting values. Some congregations are taking up problems of their social environment and do pioneering work, for example with marginal groups.

UNITED GERMAN MENNONITE CONGREGATIONS (Vereinigung der Deutschen Mennonitengemeinden) Sudetenlandstrasse 30a, 3400 Göttingen — Tel: 0551.72152. 7,350 members — 40 parishes — 25 pastors. Publication: Mennonitische Blätter (in German). WCC (1948), WMC. President: Dr Gerhard Hildebrandt — Treasurer: Rev. P.J. Foth, Mennonitenstrasse 20, 2000 Hamburg 50.

At one time a parish priest in Dutch Friesland, Menno Simons (1496-1561) renounced his connections with the Roman Catholic Church in 1536 and joined the Anabaptists, then suffering severe persecution after the attempted kingdom of Saints at Münster. His emphases included adult baptism, a rejection of Christian participation in the magistracy, and non-resistance. Mennonites later rejected any rigid church structure, infant baptism, and the doctrine of real presence in the eucharist. They adopted a congregational church pattern.

The United German Mennonite Congregations were established in 1886. Not all German Mennonites belong to this body. There are various other communities which have their own organization, in particular approximately 10,000 Russian Mennonites who came to the FRG in the 1970s. The community suffered great losses in the East-German congregations. In the FRG there are only 7,350 baptized members of the UGMC.

Until the 19th century Mennonites lived as 'strangers and guests' in the society. In modern society their life has become more demanding and complicated. Their emphasis on tolerance and peace needs new theological foundations, as the community experiences, like other churches, a crisis of identity. Historical research has become more critical of the conduct of Anabaptists during the Reformation. Mennonite congregational and family traditions are undergoing changes in an increasingly secular society. A new orientation challenges Mennonite piety, theology and style of life, as the members are challenged to relate to the exigencies of contemporary Christianity. Love for peace and service of the neighbour have to be tested in the new economic and cultural contexts.

The regional European Mennonite conference from 1970 onwards has been helpful in this search for greater clarity and commitment. The meaning and practice of baptism is being discussed once again, and new emphasis laid on baptism by faith. Similarly the Mennonite rejection of 'taking up the sword' is reinterpreted in the light of the call to discipleship in today's world.

The eleventh Mennonite World Conference will take place in Strasbourg, France, in 1984. The UGMC has heard the call of the Fourth Assembly of the WCC at Uppsala in 1968. It continues to set aside five per cent of its income for development aid. The International Mennonite Organization works in close cooperation with its North American counterpart, and assists in the resettlement of Indians in Paraguay. The Church maintains close contacts with Mennonite communities in the Netherlands, France, Switzerland, Brazil, Paraguay, Canada, and the United States.

GERMAN DEMOCRATIC REPUBLIC

FEDERATION OF THE EVANGELICAL CHURCHES IN THE GERMAN DEMOCRATIC REPUBLIC (Bund der Evangelischen Kirchen in der Deutschen Demokratischen Republik) Oberkonsistorialrat Dr Christoph Demke, Auguststrasse 80, 104 Berlin, DDR.

Evangelical Church in Berlin-Brandenburg
(Evangelische Kirche in Berlin-
Brandenburg)
Neue Grünstrasse 19, 1020 Berlin — Tel:
2000156. 1,500,000 members — 48 districts
— 1,650 congregations — 1 bishop — 4
general superintendents — 800 pastors.
Publications: Die Kirche (Berlin-
Brandenburg edition), Potsdamer Kirche
(weeklies). WCC (1948), AGCK, CEC.
Bishop: Dr Gottfried Forck, Parkstrasse
21, 1120 Berlin — Oberkirchenrat: Gerhard
Linn.

Evangelical Church of Anhalt
(Evangelische Landeskirche Anhalts)
Otto Grotewohlstrasse 22, 4500 Dessau 1.
220,000 members — 1 synod — 5 dioceses
— 200 parishes — 95 pastors. Publication:
Amtsblatt der Evangelischen Landeskirche
Anhalts. WCC (1948), AGCK, EKUDDR.
President: Eberhard Natho — Oberkir-
chenrat: Siegfried Schulze.

Evangelical Church of Greifswald
(Evangelische Landeskirche Greifswald)
Bahnhofstrasse 35/36, 2200 Greifswald —
Tel: 5261. 450,000 members — 362 parishes
— 1 bishop — 148 male and 23 female
pastors. Publications: Die Kirche (weekly),
Amtsblatt der Evangelischen Landeskirche
Greifswald (monthly). WCC (1948),
AGCK, CEC, LWF. Bishop: Dr Horst
Gienke, Rudolf-Petershagen-Allee 3, 2200
Greifswald.

**Evangelical Church of the Church Province
of Saxony** (Evangelische Kirche der
Kirchenprovinz Sachsens)
Am Dom 2, Postfach 122, 3010 Magdeburg
— Tel: 3.18.81. 1,500,000 members — 49
districts — 2,000 parishes — 1 bishop — 8
provosts — 980 pastors. Publications: Die
Kirche (Magdeburger Edition), Amtsblatt
der Evangelischen Kirche der Kirchen-
provinz Sachsen (monthly). WCC (1948),
AGCK, CEC. Bishop: Dr Werner Krusche,
Hegelstrasse 1, 3010 Magdeburg —
Oberkonsistorialrat Christfried Berger.

**Evangelical Church of the Goerlitz Church
Territory** (Evangelische Kirche des
Görlitzer Kirchengebietes)
Berliner Strasse 62, 8900 Görlitz — Tel:
5412. 125,000 members — 75 parishes — 70
pastors. WCC (1948), AGCK, CEC.
Bishop: Dr Hanns-Joachim Wollstadt —
Oberkonsistorialrat: Hans-Eberhard Ficht-
ner.

Evangelical Lutheran Church in Thuringia
(Evangelisch-Lutherische Kirche in
Thüringen)
Dr Moritz-Mitzenheim-Strasse 2a, 5900
Eisenach — Tel: 5226. 1,000,000 members
— 1,432 parishes — 630 pastors. Publica-
tion: Amtsblatt der Evangelisch-
Lutherischen Kirche in Thüringen. WCC
(1948), AGCK, LWF, CEC. Bishop:
Werner Leich — Oberkirchenrat Hartmut
Mitzenheim, Seb.-Bach-Strasse 5a, 5900
Eisenach.

**Evangelical Lutheran Church of
Mecklenburg** (Evangelisch-Lutherische
Landeskirche Mecklenburgs)
Münzstrasse 8, 2751 Schwerin — Tel:
864165. 750,00 members — 320 parishes —
300 pastors (of which 30 female
theologians). Publications: Kirchliches
Amtsblatt der Evangelisch-Lutherischen
Landeskirche, Mecklenburgische Kir-
chenzeitung. WCC (1948), AGCK, LWF.
Bishop: Dr Heinrich Rathke

Evangelical Lutheran Church of Saxony
(Evangelisch-Lutherische Landeskirche
Sachsens)
Lukasstrasse 6, 8032 Dresden — Tel:
4.48.41. 2,350,000 members — 1,163
parishes — 1,110 pastors. Publications:
Der Sonntag, Amtsblatt der Evangelisch-
Lutherischen Landeskirche Sachsens.
WCC (1948), AGCK, LWF. Bishop: Dr
Johannes Hempel.

The present territory of the German
Democratic Republic was progressively
christianized from the south-west (about
750) to the north-east (until about 1150).

Many people followed the converted princes. The Lutheran Reformation of the 16th century was widely accepted. Only small territories at the present west border (Eichsfeld) and in the south-east (Lausitz) remained Roman Catholic. Eisleben, Wittenberg, and the Luther Halle in the territorial church province of Saxony, and Eisenach and the Wartburg in Thuringia are reminders of the 16th century outreach of Lutheranism to many parts of Europe. The confession of faith by princes of small principalities, the reception of French Protestant expatriates and the rule of the Prussian dynasty introduced a Reformed influence, though in a limited way. In 1817 a Lutheran-Reformed Union was concluded through royal order. Both the evangelical churches and the Roman Catholic Church enjoyed until 1918 the status of state churches. Mission from Anglo-Saxon territories in the 19th century resulted in the formation of several free churches, in particular Methodist and Baptist churches.

After the First World War, the history of state churches came to an end. The withdrawal of many among the labouring classes from the church, which had already started in the 19th century, increased after 1918. The period 1933-1945 brought great hardship to all the churches; unfortunately a section of German Protestantism fell to the temptation of the national-socialist ideology. After the Second World War, the churches became involved in the long process of finding their place in a Marxist society.

Among the 17 million inhabitants seven million are Evangelical Christians and over one million Roman Catholics; 50,000 belong to free churches and about 100,000 to the New Apostolic Church.

After the structural separation from the Evangelical Church in Germany in 1969 the eight churches formed the Federation of Evangelical Churches in the GDR. Five of these churches belong also to the Evangelical Church of the Union in the realm of the GDR, namely the churches of Anhalt, Berlin-Brandenburg, Görlitz, Greifswald and Saxony. Three churches belong to the United Evangelical Lutheran Church in the GDR, namely those of Mecklenburg, Saxony and Thuringia. Article 4(4) of the Federation to which the eight churches belong states: "The Federation confesses to belong to the particular community of all evangelical Christianity in Germany. In co-responsibility with this community, the Federation accomplishes the tasks, which all evangelical churches in the German Democratic Republic and the Federal Republic of Germany face, in partnership and freedom through its own organs."

Theological education is provided at the theological sections of six state universities, three church seminaries and two schools for preachers. The churches have, moreover, numerous schools for diaconal and catechetical instruction, church music and other Christian vocations. Diaconal work is carried out by 15,000 full-time workers in a great number of institutions. The churches continue to search for new roles and responsibilities in a socialist society and to face the unsettling prospect of becoming an increasingly minority church, with diminishing human and financial resources. They also address themselves to the task of educating lay people and developing a keen missionary consciousness.

Among the churches' present priorities are:

1. *Congregational renewal:* Enabling lay people to witness to a mature faith in a secular society; Christian education of children trained in communist education in state schools, pastoral work among families and single adults; new orientation of the young generation; evangelism (the regional church rally at Leipzig in 1978 drew 50,000 participants); pastoral care to vacationers; responsible stewardship in view of the churches' limited resources; the publishing of a new church hymnal.

2. *Church unity:* Fostering still closer understanding and partnership among Lutherans and Reformed; efforts to reach a still closer cooperation between the various confessions in the GDR; the involvement of a maximum number of congregations in local and national ecumenical concerns; active participation in ecumenical gatherings on regional and international levels (the

preparation of the WCC Sixth Assembly at Vancouver in 1983 and the LWF Seventh Assembly at Budapest in 1984 in congregations and local ecumenical groups).

3. *Church and society:* The peace and witness of the churches and education for peace; discussion of the ecology problems and new styles of life, the practice of solidarity with the poor; continuing support of the WCC Programme to Combat Racism and the Programme of the Community of Women and Men in Church and Society.

The Evangelical Churches in the GDR maintain the following particular relations with other churches: Evangelical Church of Anhalt — Evangelical Church of the Cantons Thurgau and Frauenfeld in Switzerland; Evangelical Church in Berlin-Brandenburg — Evangelical Lutheran Gossner Church in Chota-Nagpur and Assam (India), Evangelical Lutheran Church in Southern Africa, Evangelical Church A.B. in Poland and the Evangelical Church of the Czech Brethren; Evangelical Church of the Province of Görlitz — Evangelical minority churches in Poland, Czechoslovakia, France and the Evangelical Lutheran Church in Tanzania; Evangelical Church of Greifswald — Evangelical Lutheran Churches in Northern Europe; Evangelical Lutheran Church of Mecklenburg — Church of Sweden; Evangelical Church of the Province of Saxony — four dioceses of the Evangelical Lutheran Church in Tanzania, Netherlands Reformed Church and the Reformed Churches in the Netherlands, United Church of Christ (USA); Evangelical Lutheran Church in Thuringia — Evangelical Church A.B. in Austria and Romania, Evangelical Lutheran Church in Hungary.

FEDERATION OF THE OLD CATHOLIC CHURCH IN THE GDR (Gemeindeverband der Alt-Katholischen Kirche in der DDR)
Georgstrasse 7, 3720 Blankenburg/Harz — Tel: 2297. 3,000 members — 29 congregations — 1 bishop — 3 priests — 1 deacon.

Publication: Auferstehung. WCC (1948), AGCK. President: Mrs Ursula Buschlüter.

The Federation of the Old Catholic Church in the German Democratic Republic is part of the total church in the nation. All its responsibilities and activities have to be seen in this context. It is actively engaged in the Joint Working Group of Christian churches in the country. One of its primary tasks is the pastoral care of church members living in a diaspora situation.

GREECE

CHURCH OF GREECE (Ekklesia tes Ellados)
I Gennadion 14, Athens 140 — Tel: 738.671. 9,025,000 members — 77 dioceses — 7,477 parishes — 85 bishops — 8,335 priests. Publications: Theologia (multilingual), 'Ekklesia' (The Church), 'O Ephemerios' (The Parish Priest), 'Phone Kyriou' (The Voice of the Lord), 'Deltion Plerophorion tes Ekklesias tes Ellados' (Information Sheet of the Church of Greece), all in Greek. WCC (1948), ECCSEC, CEC. His Beatitude Seraphim, Archbishop of Athens and All Greece — Chairman of External Affairs Committee: His Eminence Metropolitan Barnavas of Kitros.

The 'Church of Greece' emerged with the founding of the autocephalous Orthodox Church in Greece in 1833. Before then the history of the church in Greece was inseparable from that of the Ecumenical Patriarchate of Constantinople.

Christianity was first brought to the geographical area corresponding to modern Greece by the apostle Paul. Important church centres, which soon developed into bishoprics, were founded very early, and towards the end of the 2nd century metropolitan sees had arisen in the most important cities. Exarchates, embracing many metropolitan sees, had already formed by the 4th century under the influence of the newly introduced administrative sub-division of the empire. The most important exarchate was East Illyria, which was under the jurisdiction of the bishop of Rome until the time of Justinian I (527-565). East Illyria was finally assigned to the jurisdiction of the Patriarch of Constantinople (732) on the initiative of Emperor Leo III Isauros.

In the 10th century, Macedonia (except for the city of Thessaloniki), Epirus, Thessaly and the rest of the Greek mainland (Sterea Hellas) were occupied by the Bulgarians, who had been Christianized and placed under the archdiocese of Ochrid. After their liberation by Basil II at the beginning of the 11th century, these dioceses were once again attached to the patriarchate of Constantinople.

After the conquest of the Byzantine Empire by the Franks in 1204, Constantinople became a Latin patriarchate, exercising jurisdiction over 68 archdioceses and dioceses. The Orthodox hierarchy was excluded. Although the liberation of Constantinople in 1261 more or less restored the earlier ecclesiastical and political position, several areas still remained under Frankish domination.

The gradual occupation of Greece by the Turks and the conquest of Constantinople in 1453 completely changed the Church's position. The Turks looked upon the church in Greece, as indeed upon the other Orthodox churches in their domain (the Balkans, the Near East), as belonging to the Patriarchate of Constantinople, to which they assigned tasks of a political nature. The Patriarchate was made responsible for the collection of taxes, the observance of the law and for the loyalty of the subjugated Christians.

The Greek revolution of 1821 led to the liberation of southern Greece from the Turkish yoke and, in 1830, to the creation of a kingdom made up of this liberated area. As a result of this the canonical relations with the Ecumenical Patriarchate were broken. The synod of the newly created church in 1833 was later recognized at the synod of Endemusa in Constantinople in 1850. The Church's administration was entrusted to a synod, which consisted of five members. The permanent president was the metropolitan of Athens, and the synod always met in the presence of a royal delegate.

Owing to political changes after the war of 1912-13 the Church of Greece became much more extended. The new territories (divided into 35 metropolitan sees) are administered by the Church of Greece but belong to the jurisdiction of the Ecumenical Patriarchate. Besides the Archbishop of Athens and All Greece, who presides over the synod, twelve metropolitans are today members of the synod.

There are two theological faculties, one at the University of Athens and the other at the University of Thessaloniki. Priests are educated at several theological schools and colleges.

GREEK EVANGELICAL CHURCH
(Helleniki Evangeliki Ekklesia)
24 Markou Botsari Street, Athens 401. 5,000 members — 33 congregations — 17 pastors. Publication: Astir Tis Anatilis (monthly). WCC (1948), CEC, WARC. Moderator: Rev. Nic. Landrou, 20 A Miaouli Street, Korydallos, Piraeus — General Secretary: Mr Antonios Koulouris, 18 Markou Botsari Street, Athens 401.

The Greek Evangelical Church traces its origins to the work of D. Jonas King of the American Board of Commissioners for Foreign Missions. After spending some time in Turkey, King came to Greece, married a Greek woman and settled in Athens in 1828, where he embarked on missionary work. At the instigation of the Greek Orthodox Church, he was arrested, and sentenced to 15 days' imprisonment and expelled from the country. But, on the intervention of the American government, the sentence was set aside, and he continued to live in Greece till his death in 1869.

The Church's first congregation was organized in 1858 by Michael Kalopathakis, a physician who had been so impressed by King that he went to study at Union Theological Seminary, New York, and then returned to Greece as a Protestant missionary. A similar evangelistic movement among Greeks in Turkey had been started in 1815 by the British Mediterranean Mission. Despite the hostility of the Patriarchate and the disapproval of the government, the mission grew. The government later withdrew its opposition and the Protestant Church was officially recognized. After the disastrous Greek campaign in Turkey in 1922, the remnants of these congregations went to Greece as refugees and the Greek Evangelical Church was formed.

It is the sole Protestant Church in the country. It gives ultimate authority to the scriptures and is conservative in theology. Church attendance is very high. Much emphasis is given to the Sunday school and the youth movement. The general assembly of the Church meets every two years while local assemblies, consisting of pastors and elders, meet once every year. Participation of lay persons in Church activities and administration is high. Volunteer workers are engaged in the diaconal work. There are churches, outside Greece, in Cyprus, the FRG and the USA which belong to the synod.

HUNGARY

BAPTIST UNION OF HUNGARY
(Magyarországi Baptista Egyház)
Aradi utca 48, Budapest VI — Tel: 322.332. 20,000 members — 450 parishes — 100 pastors. Publications: Békehirnök (Peace Messenger, weekly, in Hungarian). WCC (1956), ECHC, CEC, EBF, BWA. President: Rev. Janos Laczkovszki — Secretary: Rev. Janos Viczian.

The restoration of the sovereignty of Hungary in 1867 meant religious freedom for the evangelical churches, including the Baptists. Already in 1846, a Baptist missionary from Hamburg had entered the country; a new possibility of mission opened when Joseph Nowotny started

distributing Bibles in 1873. A true pioneer was Heinrich Mayer (1842-1919). In 1874 a German-speaking church, and in 1875 a Hungarian-speaking church were opened. Mayer travelled through the whole country; he was persecuted and imprisoned, but he remained a faithful evangelist. His work had an impact on Romanian-speaking people also.

When the first Baptist preachers, educated at Hamburg, returned to the country, the emphasis shifted from German-speaking congregations to Hungarian-speaking communities. The relation to the state checked the growth of churches.

After the First World War a theological seminary was opened, and the Church gained ground. But during the Second World War the seminary, a home for children and many chapels were destroyed. After the war, the Baptist Union, like other churches, agreed with the government to find its own place in a socialist society. There was a spiritual renewal in 1962.

The Church keenly participates in ecumenical endeavours in Hungary since it became a member of the WCC.

EVANGELICAL LUTHERAN CHURCH IN HUNGARY (Magyarországi Evangélikus Egyház)
Puskin utca 12, 1088 Budapest — Tel: 138.656. 430,000 members — 320 parishes — 2 dioceses — 320 pastors. Publications: Evangélikus Elet (weekly), Lelkipasztor (monthly), Diakonia (biannual) (all in Hungarian). WCC (1948), ECHC, CEC, LWF, CPC. Presiding bishop: Rt Rev. Zoltan Kaldy — Secretary for Foreign Affairs: Rev. Andras Reuss.

The Church is one of the largest Christian communities in the Lutheran 'dispersion' in Eastern Europe. Its long history reflects endurance and vision. Lutheranism began in Hungary in 1518. After about 1550, it was supplanted in many places by the Reformed faith. Both confessions, however, subsequently lost much ground to the Counter-Reformation. Full tolerance was granted to Hungary's Protestants only with the edict of Austria's Joseph II in 1781.

Every parish of the Evangelical Lutheran Church has its own governing council, and the entire Church is governed by a synod, the moderators of which are the general inspector — a lay person — and the presiding bishop. Relations with the socialist government are good, and several churchmen have been elected to high public office (e.g. as members of parliament). Following the nationalization of several hundred church-operated schools in 1948, the ensuing agreement with the government has given the Church freedom within recognized limits. The Church constitution of 1966 and its accompanying code of Church regulations have emphasized the centrality of the gospel in the life of Christians and the Church. In the last twenty years, Hungarian Lutherans have developed a new 'theology of diakonia' — a theology of service which lays great emphasis on the necessity of confessing Christ not only by words but also through deeds of Christian love, by daily witness in a society governed by a Marxist ideology.

The source of the congregation's strength lies in worship, and in the cultivation of its identity in education, an honoured legacy that has enabled Lutherans to produce a great number of church leaders. The Lutheran Theological Academy in Budapest (formerly in Sopron), newly housed in 1975, heads the Church's educational programme. Some 18 diaconic institutions for the elderly and for handicapped children are supported by voluntary contributions. A completely new translation into modern Hungarian of the whole Bible was completed in 1976.

REFORMED CHURCH IN HUNGARY
(Magyarországi Reformatus Egyház)
Abonyi utca 21, Budapest 1146 — Tel: 227.870, 227.878, 227.879 — Cable: Reformed Synod. 2,000,000 members — 4 church districts (synods) — 1,133 congregations — 4 bishops — 1,255 ministers. Publications: Reformatus Egyház (monthly), Reformatusok Lapja (weekly), both in Hungarian, Hungarian Church Press (by-weekly, in English and German). WCC (1948), ECHC, CEC, WARC, CPC. President of the General Synod: Bishop Dr Tibor Bartha — Communication Secretary: Rev. Attila P. Komlos.

By the middle of the 16th century there was a considerable Protestant movement in Hungary. Its main strength was in the eastern part of the country where it enjoyed the protection of the princes of Transylvania. Lutheran in inspiration, the major part of the movement came under Calvinistic influence and the Church became Presbyterian in its polity. But the virulence of the Counter-Reformation, which reached its climax in Archbishop Szelepcenyi's "Bloody Tribunal" of Bratislava, dealt a severe blow to the movement.

It was only the Diet of 1790-1791 which restored civil rights to Protestants. The agreement of 1867 set the pattern of church-state relations till the end of the Second World War.

As to the internal life of the Reformed Church, the 17th and 18th centuries saw the setting up of presbyteries and the acceptance of the elder's dominant position in the life of the Church. The synod of 1881 laid the basis of the constitution which, with additions, is still in force today. One of the Church's peculiarities is its retention of the office of bishop, though it has administrative rather than hierarchical authority.

In 1949, Hungary became a people's republic and adopted a new constitution which separates the church from the state in the interests of liberty of conscience. The population of Hungary numbers ten million, which includes five million Roman Catholics, 400,000 Lutherans and nearly 500,000 Christians belonging to other confessions. The RCH continues to cherish its cultural heritage, which in earlier centuries had made a considerable contribution to the development of the Hungarian language, literature and general culture. Based on Calvinistic features, it still plays an active role in the life of society emphasizing the pluralism of different worldviews and holding up moral norms as in its acceptance of children, the emphasis on the purity of family life and its attitude towards work.

The Church is greatly concerned about the deepening of its theological scholarship, the improvement of diaconal services, extending the dialogue between Marxists and Christians, and participating efficiently in the international ecumenical movement and in Christian peace work. Besides keeping in touch with Hungarian speaking Reformed churches abroad, it maintains close relationships with many churches in Europe, East Africa and the USA.

ICELAND

EVANGELICAL LUTHERAN CHURCH OF ICELAND (Tjóokirkja Islands) Klapparstig 27, 101 Reykjavik — Tel: 15015. 210,580 members — 295 parishes — 113 pastors. Publication: Kirkjuritio. WCC (1960), LWF, CEC. Rt Rev. Bishop Sigurbjörn Einarsson — Secretary for Foreign Relations: Rev. Bernharour Guomundsson.

Iceland's Christian beginnings are traditionally traced to the year 1000, when the Althingi of the republic voted for the acceptance of Christianity. Missionary work by Irish monks had prepared the ground for the event. Highlights during the ensuing ten centuries include the establishment of two dioceses, Skalholt (near Reykjavik) for the south, and Holar for the north; the founding of monasteries which became the seats of culture; and the voting in favour of the kingship union with Norway which in 1380 brought Iceland, together with Norway, under the Danish crown. The introduction of the Reformation had no immediate effect. Some violence and a measure of Danish pressure accompanied the Althingi's adoption of the new church order (1541). Skalholt (1541) and Holar (1552) received Lutheran bishops. Oddur Gottschalkssons' translation of the New Testament (1533-40) was a landmark, as the publication saved the Icelandic language from becoming a Danish dialect. The book of sermons by Jon Vidalin, bishop of Skalholt (1698-1720), was regularly used in family devotions, and even today there are Icelanders who can recite portions of it. During the 19th century, the effects of rationalism were widely felt. Other religious currents like spiritism, theosophy, liberal theology gained a hold in the later years of the 19th century and during the 20th century. Still other forces, like Iceland's crucial role during the Second World War, the continuing presence of Americans, and the ties with the many Icelanders who have emigrated to Canada and the USA, have had their impact on the Church.

Lutheranism is now the official religion of the republic. Relations between church and state are facilitated by a ministry of church affairs. Since 1801, the entire island has been a single diocese. The bishop is elected by the pastors and the theological professors in the university. There are two suffragan bishops. The bishop and clergy meet annually in synod and deal with the Church's concerns. Youth work is promoted widely by the YMCA and the YWCA. The Christian Student Association (1936) received in 1974 its first full-time pastor to assist in its work among some 3,000 students attending the university. Missionary activities include evangelization (inner mission) at home and outreach (overseas mission) abroad. For a while Icelanders participated with Norwegians in work in China. Since the end of the Second World War, they have assumed responsibility for work in a particular area of Ethiopia, among the Konso people. They have also responded generously to development projects on other continents. The movement of people into the capital city has necessitated the construction of new facilities at great cost. Some scattered rural congregations, on the other hand, are too small to support a pastor. Daily religious broadcasts over radio and television, as well as Sunday services, reach a large audience.

IRELAND

CHURCH OF IRELAND

The Church of Ireland House, Church Avenue, Rathmines, Dublin — Tel: 978422. 433,000 members — 520 parishes — 649 pastors. Publications: The Church of Ireland Gazette, Search — a Church of Ireland Journal. WCC (1948), ICC, BCC, CEC, ACC. Archbishop: Most Rev. J.W. Armstrong, The See House, Armagh, N. Ireland — Secretary of the Church Unity Committee: Rev. I.M. Ellis, 6 Ashly Avenue, Armagh, BT60 1HD Northern Ireland.

The Church of Ireland is the direct descendant of the ancient Irish church, and traces its history back to Patrick, who brought Christianity here in the fifth century. Thus the Church of Ireland has a strong Irish identity, but it is also conscious of being part of the worldwide church. As an Anglican church, the church of Ireland is in communion with all other Anglican churches throughout the world, and also with the Old Catholic churches.

Ireland today is a divided island. The north-eastern part, Northern Ireland, is a part of the United Kingdom, and the remainder forms the Republic of Ireland which is a fully independent country, though maintaining close links with the rest of the British Isles. All the churches in Ireland operate on an all-Ireland basis — for historical reasons — and thus they have to speak to the needs of both jurisdictions. Thus they provide a focus for Irish unity, in the broadest sense of that word. The Church of Ireland tries as much as possible to maintain an open, impartial and just position in relation to the political questions in Ireland. It believes it has a contribution to make towards resolving Ireland's problems.

Within the ecumenical context, the Church of Ireland is committed to serious dialogue and active cooperation with all the main churches in Ireland. It faces, at the moment, some difficulties in its ecumenical relationships which in recent years have become rather stagnant. In particular, it will continue to wrestle with the difficult problems which arise in Ireland in situations of marriages between members of the Church of Ireland and the Roman Catholic Church. Protestant-Roman Catholic dialogue has grown over the past decade, a marked feature of which has been the Ballymascanlon talks. Nevertheless, the feeling now is that such dialogue must be able to help Christians in their current problems, both ecumenical and political. The Church of Ireland hopes for significant advances in its relationship with the Roman Catholic Church so that difficulties may be overcome.

METHODIST CHURCH IN IRELAND

3 Upper Malone Road, Belfast BT9 6TD — Tel: 668458. 59,670 members — 292 congregations — 204 ministers. WCC (1948), ICC, BCC, CEC, WMC. President: Rev. Ernest W. Gallagher, 11 Arranmore Road, Dublin 4 — Secretary: Rev. Charles G. Eyre.

The Methodist Church in Ireland owes its origins largely to John and Charles Wesley who visited Ireland on many occasions, beginning with John Wesley's historic visit in 1747. From Dublin the Wesleys journeyed into the Midlands of Ireland and eventually, in 1756, on his sixth tour, John Wesley broke new ground in that he visited the Palatines in County Limerick, penetrated into Connemara and Mayo in the far West, and entered Ulster for the first time.

Today the majority of Irish Methodists live in Northern Ireland, the north-east corner of the country. There are, however, Methodist churches in most of the larger cities and towns in Eire as well.

Although closely linked to British Methodism, the Methodist Church in Ireland is autonomous, with its own president and secretary. There are 292 chapels with 204 ministers of whom 131 are in active work in Ireland itself, the others being retired or engaged in work both within and outside of Ireland. There are in Ireland about 400,000 Presbyterians and 400,000 members of the Church of Ireland, the remainder being largely Roman Catholic.

Irish Methodism has developed a wideranging social work service, largely through the activities of its city missions which are to be found in Dublin, Belfast, Newtownabbey, and Londonderry, with control of several old people's homes, orphanages, and day and night shelters for needy men and women.

Along with other churches, the Methodist Church in Ireland is deeply concerned with the whole question of reconciliation and peace in Ireland. Many of its ministers and people have taken leading roles in movements to establish peace, especially during the last twelve years.

ITALY

EVANGELICAL BAPTIST UNION OF ITALY* (Unione Cristiana Evangelica Battista d'Italia)
Piazza S. Lorenzo in Lucina 35, 00186 Roma — Tel: 6791320 — Cable: Unicebatt. 8,000 members — 80 congregations — 44 pastors. Publications: Il Testimonio and Il Seminatore (in Italian). WCC (1977), IFPC, CEC, CEPPLE, BWA. President: Dr Piero Bensi.

The Baptist work in Italy began about 120 years ago, with the arrival of missionaries from Great Britain (1863) and the USA (1867). They established a few churches in some of the main towns and in some villages. In 1905 a Baptist theological school started work with American and Italian teachers. The school was closed in 1932 under fascist persecution. Until that time the Baptists had published three monthly magazines, two of which had considerable influence upon the religious culture of Italy — "Bylichnis" and "Conscientia".

In 1921 the British retired from Italy, leaving the work in the hands of the Foreign Mission Board of the Southern Baptist Convention of the USA. In 1939

the "Opera Battista" was created, mainly performed by Italian pastors and laymen; in 1956 the Italian Baptist churches organized themselves in the Baptist Union of Italy which is led only by Italians.

The main concerns of the Church are evangelization and social cooperation. The Church has five social centres: Meana (Turin), S. Severa (Rome), Rocca di Papa (Rome), Altamura (Bari), Centocelle (Rome). Two departments, of theology and of evangelization, deal with the burning issues of our time like peace and human rights.

WALDENSIAN CHURCH (Chiesa Evangelica Valdese)
Tavola Valdese, Via Firenze 38, 00184 Roma — Tel: 47.45.537 and 47.41.709. 22,230 members — 129 parishes — 94 pastors. Publication: La Luce (in Italian). WCC (1948), FPCI, WARC, CEC, CEVAA, CEPPLE. Moderator: Rev. Giorgio Bouchard — Rev. Mario Bertinat, 8 de octobre, 3039 Montevideo, Uruguay.

The Waldensian movement had its origins in the 12th century. It owes its birth to the decision of a rich merchant of Lyons, Peter Valdes, to dedicate himself to the preaching of the gospel to the lower classes of society. At the Third Lateran Council (1179) Valdes and his followers sought ecclesiastical recognition. Pope Alexander III expressed approval of Valdes' vow of voluntary poverty, but he and his companions were forbidden to preach except by invitation of the clergy. Valdes and his community refused to obey, and the Council of Verona (1184), under Pope Lucius III, placed the 'poor of Lyons' under the ban of excommunication.

The Waldensians grew rapidly and spread, first in southern France and Spain, then in Germany, Piedmont and Lombardy. In the 16th century the Waldensians made contacts with the Bohemian Hussites. For a brief period they enjoyed in Piemonte a relative measure of freedom and built many churches. After the revocation of the Edict of Nantes (1685), many were compelled, in terrible conditions, to cross the mountains to Switzerland. It was not until 1848 that Charles Albert gave them in Italy real political and religious freedom. Today Waldensians still live as a diaspora, scattered over Italy, Uruguay, Argentina, western Europe and North America.

Waldensians and Methodists have recently merged to become a united church, although both have kept their specific identities. The ecumenical scene in Italy is encouraging today, became of programmes of practical cooperation with the Roman Catholic Church, particularly the plan to publish an ecumenical Bible translation.

Waldensians, mainly located in two regions, the Waldensian valleys and in the south in Sicily and Naples, face increasingly the problems of a secularized society and of political polarization. They have been involved in helping with socio-economic reconstruction and providing moral support to people after the earthquake around Naples. Among its institutions are a theological school, at Torre Pellice (near Turin), a theological faculty in Rome, a religious publishing house, Claudiana (in Turin), the centre of Agape in North Italy (built by international youth teams after the war to provide a meeting place for young people concerned over the renewal of the church), and the centre in the Sicilian village of Riesi bringing hope and help in a scene of poverty and apathy — an example for the nations of western Europe and the world.

NETHERLANDS

EVANGELICAL LUTHERAN CHURCH IN THE KINGDOM OF THE NETHERLANDS (Evangelisch-Lutherse Kerk in het Koninkrijk der Nederlanden) Amsterdamseweg 311, 1182 HA Amstelveen — Tel: 020.434304. 33,200 members — 74 parishes — 48 pastors. Publication: ELK (in Dutch). WCC (1948), CCN, LWF, CEC. President: Rev. W. Bleij, Charl. van Montpensierlann 12, 1181 RR Amstelveen — Secretary: Mr T.R. Seinstra.

In 1966, Dutch Lutherans celebrated their 400th anniversary and reviewed their long history. The first Lutheran congregation fled persecution in Antwerp, where it had begun in 1566 as a unique free church with a confession and a church order. It was reorganized in Amsterdam in 1588. Here the members worshipped in one another's homes until 1600, when the Netherlands, which had become Reformed, began to be tolerant towards both Catholics and Lutherans. By 1605 a congregational polity had developed; a fraternity of six congregations functioned as a synod. The Church grew. Its influence spread to London and to the settlers in New Amsterdam. During the 18th century, the Dutch pastors, educated in Germany, were influenced by the Enlightenment. This caused a break in the Church. The orthodox Lutherans seceded and formed in 1793 the Restored Evangelical Lutheran Church. It was the impact of Dutch Lutheran Missionary Society (1852) that gradually freed the Church from the domination of Rationalism. A return to the sources of the Reformation and a revival of Luther research focused attention once again on justification by faith alone. Extensive literature in various fields of theological study has been developed by Dutch Lutheran scholars since 1945. A new church constitution was adopted in 1955. The Church has a presbyterial structure with a synod meeting twice a year. Of its 36 members, 24 are lay people.

The Evangelical Lutheran Church exists amidst two large Reformed churches. With much effort and sacrifice, it successfully continues to maintain the diaconal institutions established when its membership was larger. There is much awareness of and great interest in the problems of developing countries. The Church's contributions to WCC and LWF projects have been very generous.

Dutch Lutherans support mission work in India and Tanzania. However, the Church has difficulty in meeting its own financial obligations. For over a century the practice of pulpit exchange and intercommunion has gone on between the Lutheran Church and the Dutch Reformed. The relationship with the Roman

Catholics is also positive. Since the Second World War, great interest and concern have been expressed for the Jews, many of whom suffered heavy persecution during the Nazi occupation. The Church maintains a particular relation with the North Elbian Evangelical Lutheran Church, Kiel in the FRG.

GENERAL MENNONITE SOCIETY
(Algemene Doopsgezinde Sociëteit) Singel 454, Amsterdam. 39,000 members. WCC (1948), CCN, MWC. General Secretary: Rev. R. De Zeeuw.

According to Menno Simons (1496-1561), the Reformers overemphasized justification by faith and neglected the sanctification of life (see United German Mennonite Congregations). Mennonites in the Netherlands, as their German brethren, were more radical than the Reformers in rejecting the institutional church, the doctrine of the two sacraments and emphasizing the separation of church and state. They were persecuted because of their withdrawal from society and their strong eschatological expectations.

During the period of the Republic of the Netherlands there was greater tolerance, but divisions surfaced in Mennonite ranks. There was a dearth of educated pastors in the 18th century and a seminary for the training of preachers was founded in Amsterdam in 1735. The General Mennonite Society was inaugurated in 1811. Originally it had little authority, but it has developed into a more central organ in the 20th century. Central Java and New Guinea were chosen as mission fields.

The GMS maintains close relations with sister communities in Germany, France, Switzerland, Brazil, Paraguay, Canada and the United States.

NETHERLANDS REFORMED
CHURCH (Nederlandse Hervormde Kerk) Carnegielaan 9, 2517 KH The Hague — Tel: 070.653915. 2,800,000 members — 1,901 parishes — 1,804 pastors. Publications: Hervormd Nederland (weekly), Woord en Dienst (bi-monthly). WCC (1948), CCN, CEC, WARC, LCC. General Secretary: Rev. Dr R. J. Mooi.

The Netherlands Reformed Church had its origin in the Reformation which stirred the church in Europe during the 16th century. It bore Calvin's imprint, though there were some typically Dutch developments too. The Church and the state of the Netherlands came simultaneously into existence, out of the same struggle and through the same liberation movement from Spanish rule.

The Church was established under the guidance of Prince William of Orange. At its first synods (Emden 1571 and Dordrecht 1578) the teaching of Geneva was accepted together with the confession of Faith (Guido de Brès, 1561), and the Heidelberg Catechism (1563). Consolidation of Reformed Church life took place at the national synod of Dordrecht (1618-19). It was during this period that a group seceded to become the Remonstrant Brotherhood, owing to differences on the doctrine of election. The synod formulated the basic structure of the Church's order, confession and liturgy, and decided on a new translation of the Bible (completed in 1637).

In 1816 King Willem I imposed an order on the Church which was not in accordance with its Reformed nature. The structures of the church were restored in 1945 and 1951, though in contemporary form, emphasizing in particular the missionary and confessing task of the Church as being integral to its whole function.

The structure of the Church is both presbyterial and synodal. The local congregation elects the members of the session. In the session three offices are represented: ministers, elders and deacons. A president is chosen for a session, and he is not necessarily a minister. The country is divided into 54 regions, which are known as *classes*. Every session sends two representatives to the *classis*, and every *classis* sends one delegate to the general synod. The synod has set up a number of advisory bodies which can also undertake independent action. These bodies are concerned with mission, pastoral care, diaconal matters, youth work, finance, relations between the Church and Israel, theology and relations between Church and school, education and formation of church members, in particular for women.

The Church is strongly concerned over social matters. This concern is expressed through a number of organizations which champion the cause of the underprivileged both at home and abroad. There is a training institute called *Kerk en Wereld* in Driebergen.

Much emphasis is laid on confirmation classes (catechesis). The Lord's supper is gaining an ever-increasing importance in church service.

The Netherlands Reformed Church has a strong ecumenical commitment. It describes itself as a manifestation of the One Holy, Catholic or Universal Christian Church. It maintains special relations with the Evangelical Lutheran Church, the Remonstrant Brotherhood and the Mennonite Society. The ties with the Reformed Churches in the Netherlands, the second largest Protestant Church in the nation, are growing ever stronger.

OLD CATHOLIC CHURCH OF THE NETHERLANDS (Oud-Katholieke Kerk van Nederland)
Willemsplantsoen 3, 3511 LA Utrecht — Tel: 030.315018. 10,500 members — 2 dioceses — 29 parishes — 3 bishops — 32 priests — 21 readers. Publications: De Oud-Katholiek (in Dutch), Internationale Kirchliche Zeitschrift (in German). WCC (1948), CCN. Archbishop of Utrecht: Antonius Jan Glazemaker — Secretary: Bishop of Haarlem, Rt Rev. G.A. van Kleef, Papenpad 12, 1506 GR Zaandam.

In an endeavour to find favour with the Catholics, Philip II of Spain secured the creation of five new sees under Utrecht, which was raised to an Archbishopric in 1560. The experiment was a failure, and from 1580 to 1853 the Roman Catholic Church was without territorial bishops, being governed by vicars apostolic or papal legates. From 1583 to 1795 it was subjected by the government to severe penal restrictions. In 1697 accusations of Jansenism were launched from Rome against Roman Catholics in the Netherlands, notably against Petrus Codde (1648-1710), then vicar-general and titular archbishop of Philippi. In 1702 he was officially censured, and a schism began. Codde's followers upheld the continuity of their communion with the national Catholic Church of the past. The support of the French Jansenists, who refused to accept the bull 'Unigenitus' (1713), secured for the Old Catholics as they came to be called the maintenance of the apostolic succession; and the group still survives as a branch of the Old Catholic Church.

The Church was liberated from its isolation when it set up the Utrecht-Union with other non-Roman Catholic churches which emerged in Germany, Austria and Switzerland, refusing to accept the dogmas of Infallibility and universal ordinary jurisdiction of the Pope, as defined by the Vatican Council of 1870. Later the Polish National Church in Poland and in North America also joined the Union. The Old Catholics received episcopal succession from the Church of Utrecht. The first German bishop, J.H. Reinkens (with see at Bonn), was consecrated in 1874, and the first Swiss bishop, E. Herzog (with see at Berne), in 1876.

The Old Catholic communion formally recognized Anglican ordinations in 1925, and since 1932 Old Catholics have been in full communion with the Church of England. A dialogue was started even earlier with the Orthodox churches.

The doctrinal basis of the Church is the Declaration of Utrecht of 1889. Obligatory celibacy was abolished at the beginning of the 20th century. Communion is frequently given in both kinds. Auricular confession is not compulsory. The liturgy is celebrated in the vernacular.

The OCCN has made valuable contributions to the study of ancient hymnology and sponsored the translation of Gregorian chant in Dutch. It still plays a role as a bridge between the Roman Catholic Church and Protestant churches.

Among current concerns are pastoral care of people in a de-Christianized society, the formulation of answers to various social and moral questions, a more intensive training of lay Christians, renewed reflection on the meaning of ecclesiastical offices, and greater commitment to inter-church aid at home and abroad.

REFORMED CHURCHES IN THE NETHERLANDS (Gereformeerde Kerken in Nederland)

Postbus 202, Leusden — Tel: 033.943244 — Telex: 79494 gkn nl. 873,300 members — 830 congregations — 1,099 pastors. Publications: Kerkinformatie (monthly in Dutch), RCN Bulletin (in English). WCC (1971), CCN, CEC, WARC. Dr A. Kruyswijk, Committee for External Ecumenical Relations.

This church came into existence in 1886 separating itself from the Netherlands Reformed Church. Already in 1834 there was a conflict, and a move towards separation. The main issue in both cases was a controversy over the freedom of doctrine involving the liberal and the orthodox sections of the Church. The two denominations born out of these conflicts united in 1892 to form the Reformed Churches in the Netherlands. Especially under the influence of Dr Abraham Kuyper, an energetic Christian emancipation movement arose in the 19th century. It grew rapidly after 1892. Many members of the Reformed Churches have emigrated to America, Canada, Australia and New Zealand, and they have founded independent Reformed Churches with which the Churches in the Netherlands maintain a lively contact. During the last ten years, close cooperation has developed between the Netherlands Reformed Church and the Reformed Churches in the Netherlands; it is hoped that there will come out of this a federal union or even a complete reunion in the future.

Next to the Netherlands Reformed Church, the Reformed Churches in the Netherlands forms the second largest Protestant denomination. Its character is deter-mined by its Calvinistic origin. There are three confessions: the Belgic Confession, the Heidelberg Catechism and the Canons of Dordt. The Calvinistic tradition implies that ruling elders play an important role in the life of the Church. Ordination does not signify a superior position for the minister over the office of the elder or deacon; the latter have in fact gained even greater status during the last few decades. Regional synods are represented in the general synod by two ministers, two elders and one deacon.

The Church is engaged in a continuing struggle to find adequate answers to the challenges of our times. Both Church and theology are characterized by this struggle. The theological faculties at Kampen and at the Free University of Amsterdam are preoccupied with the problem of relating Christian witness to the developments of human society. A missionary centre keeps contact with ministers, physicians, teachers, nurses and other missionary workers in Indonesia, Pakistan, Rwanda, Argentina and Brazil. Congregations and individual church members — the Church has a lay training centre — are encouraged to grapple with the complex problems of daily life. World relief has a dominant place in diaconal activities, covering 80 per cent of this total budget. Concern for the disabled, the isolated, the unemployed, the aged and the drop-outs at home and pro-grammes for them are seen as an essential function of the Church. The fate of migrant workers receives particular attention. Problems of war and peace and nuclear disarmament are high on the Church's agenda in the coming years. The RCN is trying to overcome its former isolation by being engaged in study and action in the fields of ecumenism and evangelization — the preaching of the gospel in a largely secularized nation.

REMONSTRANT BROTHERHOOD (Remonstrantse Broederschap)

Nieuwe Gracht 23, Utrecht — Tel: 030.316970. 12,500 members — 51 congregations — 45 pastors. WCC (1948), CCN, CEC, WARC. Secretary: Rev. G. Bloemendaal.

An indigenous type of Protestantism existed in the Netherlands before Calvinism was introduced from France and the Reformed Church was born in 1568. The latter sought to impose a system of doctrines, against which the more liberal people from the older Protestant circles protested and they found their leader in Armenius. The Synod of Dordrecht (1618-19) expelled the Remonstrants (as they were called, after a remonstrance presented by them in 1610 to the States of Holland, in which they had stated five articles characteristic of a free church), and dismissed 200 ministers, many of whom were banished or imprisoned. These ministers formed themselves into a 'brotherhood', a description later taken over by Remonstrant-Reformed congregations. From 1630, persecution slackened and churches were built. By 1860, the membership of the Brotherhood had fallen to 4,000, but then, as a result of the rise of religious modernism in terms of biblical criticism, modern science and philosophy, response to modern culture, and secularization, the Brotherhood with its evangelical freedom began to appeal to many. Membership increased five-fold. One congregation has been located since 1621 in Friedrichstadt a/d Eider in Schleswig-Holstein, Federal Republic of Germany.

Though not directly engaged in mission work on its own, the Brotherhood shares in the work of the Netherlands Missionary Council. Conversations are in progress with the Netherlands Reformed Church on theological understanding, sharing of ministers and on general cooperation between the two churches. The Church continues to study relations between religion, science and culture, methods to survive the crisis of being the church of Jesus Christ in the world of today and problems of mission and world diaconia.

NORWAY

CHURCH IN NORWAY (Norske Kirke) Postboks 3673, Gamlebyen, St Hallvardspl. 3, Oslo 1 — Tel: 02.193700. 3,600,000 members — 1340 parishes — 10 dioceses — ca. 1250 pastors — 10 bishops. Publications: Kirkeaktuelt (in Norwegian); Church of Norway News (in English). WCC (1948), LWF, CEC, NEI. Bishop of Oslo: Andreas Aarflot — General Secretary, Council on Foreign Relations: Rev. Carl H. Traaen.

Christianity was brought to Norway during the time of the Vikings, around 1000 A.D. St Olav was an outstanding Christian Viking king. King Christian III, ruler of Denmark and Norway during the time of the Reformation, joined the Lutheran Church. The Church of Norway is still a state church, with the king continuing as its official head. The government makes decisions on Church matters like the appointments of bishops and pastors, liturgy, and clerical robes. The parliament is responsible for the church's budget.

The Lutheran missionary organizations have their own structures and depend entirely on voluntary gifts. The Church includes 90-94 per cent of the total population. Among the other churches are the Pentecostal movement which is the largest (40,000), the (Free) Evangelical Lutheran Church (19,600), the Methodist Church (17,000) and the Roman Catholic Church (about 15,000).

There have been tensions between the church and the state for many years. The appointment of bishops and pastors in some instances has created frictions. The Norwegian mass media show a great interest in church matters. There are also a number of church papers which keep many readers well-informed.

The Church of Norway strives to become a more self-ruling body, but there is no clarity yet in the matter of church-state relationships. It is also challenged to face the changing religious situation because of a growing number of migrant workers, in particular Pakistanis who are predominantly Muslim. A profound concern is to reach the young generation with the Christian gospel. The Church puts particular emphasis on confirmation work and the Christian education of young adults under the leadership of the staff of the Church's council. Some mission organizations, together with the Church's council, activate the parishes for more extensive foreign mission work. The Church of Norway maintains close relations with the Scandinavian state churches.

POLAND

EVANGELICAL CHURCH OF THE AUGSBURG CONFESSION IN THE PEOPLE'S REPUBLIC OF POLAND
(Kosciola Ewangelicko-Augsburgskiego w PRL)
ul. Miodowa 21, 00-246 Warsaw — Tel: 315187 — Cable: EWPOL. 80,000 members — 6 dioceses — 122 parishes — 101 pastors. WCC (1948), PEC, LWF, CEC, CPC. Bishop: Rt Rev. Janusz Narzynski.

The Church is the small Polish remnant of a largely ethnic German and mainly Lutheran constituency of evangelical Christians who in 1940 totalled about one million. After the withdrawal or expulsion of the ethnic Germans their number dwindled to about 270,000 in 1946; with further exodus during the early 1970s the number fell to 80,000. The Lutheran Reformation made early gains in the 16th century. The point of entry for Lutheranism was East Prussia — notably the city of Königsberg — where Germans and Poles lived in friendly coexistence. The Lutheran Church in East Prussia continued to use Polish until well in the 19th century. The first translation of the New Testament into Polish was taken up in 16th century Königsberg. However, an aggressive Counter-Reformation erased most of the gains. In 1795, the complete partitioning of Poland by Russia, Austria and Prussia opened a new phase of religious history. In the cities of Warsaw, Lodz and Kracow, large Lutheran congregations were formed. In Prussia's part of Poland, strong congregations developed in an enlarged Silesia. When in 1918 the new Poland emerged as an independent republic, there were seven Evangelical church bodies, mostly Lutheran.

The Church's headquarters are in Warsaw, in a functionally built church centre. It also houses some units of the Christian Theological Academy which is supported by the government. Each congregation is self-governed by a presbytery or parish council; for the Church as a whole, the synod is the decision-making body. The election of Bishop Andrzej Wantula as a vice-president of the LWF (1963-70) was an encouragement to Polish Lutherans

By slow and painful steps a remnant church was reshaped into the present active body. It draws strength from a Polish Lutheran legacy that began with translations of the scriptures four and a half centuries ago, and today includes significant works in theology, hymnody and the church music. There is much involvement in religious literature, and the education of children and young people in a Christian way of life. There is also a concern for the common life, despite the acknowledged differences between the Christian gospel and the official ideology. The Church maintains contacts with other churches throughout Europe and beyond.

OLD CATHOLIC MARIAVITE CHURCH IN POLAND (Staro-Katolickiego Kosciola Mariatowitow wPRL)
ul. Wieczorka 27-29, Plock. 24,100 members — 3 dioceses — 41 parishes — 59 places of worship — 4 bishops — 30 priests — 140 sisters. Publications: Mariawita' (monthly, in Polish). WCC (1969), PEC. Bishop: Stanislaw M. Tymoteusz Kowalski.

This community was founded in 1906 in Warsaw by Jan Kowalski, a diocesan priest, and Sister Maria Felicja Kozlowska of the Third Order of Franciscans. It developed out of the community of sisters founded by the latter in Plock in 1888 and the community of secular priests organized at her instigation by Kowalski in 1893. Both groups adopted the Franciscan rule and aimed at a religious, moral and social renewal of clergy and people. They stressed the veneration of the eucharist and the Blessed Virgin Mary. Because of their mystical bent they were not approved by the Vatican. The new Church recognized the first seven ecumenical councils but rejected papal primacy and infallibility. At a later stage, celibacy of the clergy was made optional, and confession was made voluntary.

Negotiations with the members of the Utrecht Union culminated in the reception of the Mariavites into the Old Catholics at their congress in Vienna in 1909. J. Kowalski was consecrated bishop in the same year. During the Second World War, the Church underwent severe persecution and its membership went down.

Every year the Church makes a pilgrimage on 15 August to Plock. Its highest authority is the synod. The Church operates a home for elderly people in Sobotka near Leczyca, four bakeries, three mineral water factories and seven workshops. Its theological students are educated at a spiritual seminar in Plock and a Christian Theological Academy in Warsaw.

POLISH CATHOLIC CHURCH IN POLAND (Kosciol Polskokatolicki w PRL)
ul. Wilcza 31, Warsaw — Tel: 21.18.42, 28.97.84. 34,250 members — 3 dioceses — 90 parishes — 4 bishops — 126 priests. Publications: 'Rodzina' (Family, weekly), 'Posannictwo' (Mission, quarterly), 'Catholic Calendar' (all in Polish). WCC (1948), PEC. Prime Bishop: Most Rev. Tadeusz R. Majewski.

The PCCP originated in North America as a protest against Irish bishops and priests, under whom American Poles felt abandoned and exposed to Anglo-Saxon Catholicism. Polish members of the Roman Catholic Church demanded from their English-speaking bishops the right to participate in administrative matters and in the election of priests, and more worship services in the Polish language. This led to a schism, and a separate Polish Catholic community was organized. A Polish liturgy and communion with both elements were introduced; clerical celibacy was abolished. Bishops and priests were consecrated by the Old Catholic Church of the Netherlands in Utrecht. After the First World War a missionary campaign was launched in Poland. After the title of the Head of the Church, *Hodur*, members of the PCCP were often named *Hodurowy* (Hodur people).

The three dioceses are: Warsaw, Wrozlaw and Krakow. A considerable number of the members live in the Lublin area. The highest authority is the general synod to which both clergy and lay people belong. Priests are trained at the Christian Theological Academy in Warsaw.

POLISH ORTHODOX CHURCH
ul. Gen. K. Swierczewskiego 52, Warsaw — Tel: 19.34.09. 460,000 members — 233 parishes — 207 places of worship — 430 priests. Publications: 'News of the Polish Orthodox Church' (quarterly, in Polish), 'Cerkovniy Vedomosty' (Church News, quarterly, in Russian). WCC (1961), PEC. His Beatitude Bazyli, Metropolitan of Warsaw and All Poland.

The ancient Slavonic population of the area covering modern Poland became Christian over a thousand years ago. The first Orthodox diocese was established in the tenth century at Uhrusk in the Lublin region. With the marriage of Prince Mieshko to the Roman Catholic Czech princess, Dombrovka, the Polish court gradually fell under the sway of Rome, and Orthodoxy was in consequence severely repressed.

The 1596 Union of Brest, for which the Jesuits were mainly responsible, evoked determined resistance from the majority of the nobility in the east of what was then Poland. The spread of the Uniate Church of the Eastern Rite was thereby held in check.

New monasteries arose and Orthodox brotherhoods were established to defend the indigenous faith. When their churches were commandeered by Uniate priests, the faithful often assembled in unconsecrated buildings to share in the celebration of the Orthodox liturgy. When the country was divided in the second part of the 18th century, the eastern half of Poland became part of Russia and consequently the Orthodox population came under the jurisdiction of the Russian Orthodox Church.

In 1918 an independent Polish state came into being once more and the Metropolitan of the Polish Orthodox Church endeavoured to secure autocephalous status for the church. This was achieved in 1924 through the Ecumenical Patriarchate; it was proclaimed officially in Poland in 1925 and was recognized by the Russian Orthodox Church in 1948.

The period between the two World Wars was accompanied by a number of difficulties for the Orthodox population. With the consent of the Polish state authorities, the Roman Catholic Church seized a part of the properties belonging to the Orthodox Church, and a great number of church buildings were either transferred to Roman Catholic hands or destroyed. Relations with the Roman Catholic Church in Poland remain tense, in spite of the new ecumenical climate.

When the eastern border of the country was altered after the Second World War, a large tract of the country with its Orthodox population became Russian territory and came once again under the Russian Orthodox Church. Consequently the number of Orthodox in the People's Republic of Poland shrank from 5-6 million to less than half a million.

The holy synod, consisting of all the bishops, under the presidency of the metropolitan, is the highest authority. The metropolitan council is the advisory board, made up of representatives of the clergy and the laity, from whom the presidium is elected.

Priests are trained at the theological seminary in Warsaw. The theological academy, also at Warsaw, has an Orthodox section which offers a five-year course. The Monastery of St Onufriy, founded in the 15th century, is located in Jablechna in the Lublin region. The Convent of St Martha Maria in Grabarka in the Bialystok region was founded twenty years ago.

PORTUGAL

EVANGELICAL PRESBYTERIAN CHURCH OF PORTUGAL* (Igreja Evangélica Presbiteriana de Portugal) Avenida Brasil, 92-2° Dt°, 1700 Lisboa — Tel: 764342. 3,000 members — 33 parishes — 18 congregations — 9 pastors and 5 evangelists — 1 synod. Publication: Portugal Evangélico (in cooperation with the Methodist Church of Portugal). WCC (1965), PCCC, UNELAM, WARC, CEC. President: Rev. José da Silveira Salvador — Secretary: Manuel de Sousa Campos.

The Presbyterian Church of Portugal was set up in 1952, but it can trace its history back to 1838 when Robert Kelley, a Scottish physician, opened a small hospital and school, and began to preach the gospel on the Portuguese island of Madeira. Local opposition led to the burning down of the doctor's home and the dispersal of the mission, and many Portuguese Protestants emigrated to Brazil and other countries in the Americas.

Some forty years ago the Protestant Church made a fresh start in Portugal. Missionaries arrived from Brazil and established what was then known as the Presbyterian Church of Lisbon. The work received substantial help from the Presbyterian churches of the USA, and was administered by a Committee on Evangelical Cooperation which represented the Presbyterian Church of Brazil, the Presbyterian Church US, and the Presbyterian Church USA. As for Portugal, the Church's own leadership was with the Junta Presbiteriana, which later became the first national synod of the Presbyterian Church of Portugal.

The first synod met in Lisbon and was attended by representatives from every Presbyterian community in the country. The Church is responsible for St Luke's Presbyterian Hospital, Lisbon. This is a small but modern and well-equipped clinic, where patients are treated without regard to their religious affiliation and may pay for the treatment according to their means.

Activities in other fields depend much on financial support received from abroad. The Church has a programme for old people and continues to seek funds to create a home for them in Lisbon-Marvila. Some small projects are undertaken by local congregations, partly in cooperation with the Portuguese Christian Council of Churches (COPIC) and the Portuguese Ecumenical Centre (CERR). Youth activities are to receive greater attention in the coming years. The Church is handicapped by lack of funds for building or rebuilding of facilities.

The Church continues its relationships with the Reformed Church of France, the Swiss Protestant Church Federation, the Reformed Church of Belgium, the United Presbyterian Church in the USA and the Presbyterian Church in the US.

LUSITANIAN CATHOLIC-APOSTOLIC EVANGELICAL CHURCH* (Igreja Lusitana Católica Apostólica Evangélica)
rua de Elias Garcia 107-1° Dto, 4400 Villa Nova de Gaia. 5,000 members — 17 places of worship. WCC (1962) PCCC, CEC. Rt Rev. Fernando L. Soares.

After the establishment of a constitutional monarchy in 1834, there was a measure of religious freedom in Portugal. Gomes y Togar, a former Spanish priest, who had fled to Great Britain and had been received in the Church of England, came to Portugal and started a small Christian community in 1839, and it used the Anglican

liturgy in Portuguese. The chapel was closed in 1870. In 1868, another Spanish priest, Angel Herreros de Mora, who had been received in the Episcopal Church in the USA, started a congregation in Lisbon along the lines of the Episcopal Church. This congregation acquired official status under the name of Igreja Evangélica Espanhola. Services were conducted according to the American version of the Book of Common Prayer of 1789. At a synod in 1880, presided by Bishop Riley of the American Episcopal Church, a constitution was approved in accordance with the doctrinal and liturgical traditions of the Anglican communion. In the same year a second non-Roman Catholic community in Gaia, near Oporto, was admitted. In 1951, yet another group of independent Evangelical churches joined the Lusitanian Church. Since 1963 the Church has been in full communion with the Church of England on the same basis as the Old Catholic churches. Since 1980 the metropolitan authority over the Church has rested with the Archbishop of Canterbury who is regarded as a visible focus of the unity of the Anglican communion.

The Church runs several schools, open to children of any creed. After the revolution of April 1974 these schools received some financial support from the state. The League of the Good Samaritan is active among the very poor in several neighbourhoods. In spite of its very limited resources, the Church tries to develop a stewardship programme. There is a need for a more effective deployment of ministries and teaching ministries, although the present situation allows only for non-stipendiary or part-time ministry. The experimentation with 'house churches' needs to be extended. There is a project to build a place of worship for the newly formed community of Rio de Mouro, near Sintra. The Lusitanian Church is involved in unity conversations with the Portuguese Methodist and Presbyterian churches and are currently studying plans from overseas in order to learn how fellow Anglicans have been engaged in union negotiations.

ROMANIA

EVANGELICAL CHURCH OF THE AUGSBURG CONFESSION IN THE SOCIALIST REPUBLIC OF ROMANIA
(Biserica Evanghelica CA din RSR)
Gen. Magheru 4, 2400 Sibiu — Tel: 924.13079. 152,000 members — 252 congregations — 160 pastors. Publication: Kirchliche Blätter (in German). WCC (1948), LWF, CEC, CPC. Bishop Albert Klein.

The Church is still in many respects a transplanted German church, an ethnic island with a long history. The first Lutheran writings arrived in Hermannstadt in 1518. Johannes Honterus became the prime leader of a reformation ultimately affecting also the Reformed and the Unitarians. By order of the self-governing Transylvanian council in 1572, the pastors acknowledged the Augsburg Confession. The office of bishop was introduced and has continued without interrruption. The Counter-Reformation made scant inroads. Periodic church renewal was linked to the development of a sound system of education that continued in church hands until the end of the Second World War. The synodal-presbyterial church constitution of 1861 granted a prominent role to the laity and to the congregations, and was revised for the first time in the mid 1970s. The relation between the state and the church, worked out in 1948, seems to work well.

The worship life of the Church continues central to all activities, with church attendance stronger in the villages than in the cities. Children from 6-12 and from 13-14 (confirmation classes) receive a Christian education. Regular Bible studies, an ecumenical week of prayer and regular evening services complete the preaching of the word. A new hymn book is now in use. A new generation of pastors is emerging. The four-year programme of the theological institute in Sibiu (where academic subjects are taught, and no fewer than six languages are offered — Romanian, German, English, Latin, Greek and Hebrew) is supplemented by a fifth year of supervised ministerial involvement, and later self-directed study and conferences. The music school in Sibiu trains organists and cantors for public worship. Like some other churches in Eastern Europe, this Church receives regular gifts of theological books. The spirit of cooperation with the state is evidenced by the participation of the Church in the Front for Socialist Unity, and the contribution it makes during national emergencies.

The mechanization of agriculture and the increasing industrialization of the country have resulted in urban concentrations of population and a dwindling of the rural population. The Church tries to render more service to the shrinking rural congregation. In urban congregations pastoral care and lay training are stressed. Mobility also includes emigration; many people leave to join relatives in Germany. This can create problems, especially when pastors leave.

The Church maintains close relations with Lutheran churches in the GDR as well as in the FRG.

EVANGELICAL SYNODAL PRESBYTERIAL CHURCH OF THE AUGSBURG CONFESSION IN THE SOCIALIST REPUBLIC OF ROMANIA
(Biserica Evanghelica Sinodo-Presbiteriala de Confesiune Augustana din Republica Socialista Romania)
Bulevardul Lenin 1, 3400 Cluj-Napoca — Tel: 951.136.37 — Cable: Biserica Lutherana Cluj. 32,000 members — 40 congregations — 35 pastors. WCC (1948), LWF, CEC. Bishop D. Paul Szedressy.

The Church is spread over a large area extending 400 miles east and west and 280 miles north and south. Its headquarters for administration and ministerial education are in Cluj-Napoca (the former Klausenburg.) The smaller western district of Timisoara (the former Temisvar) is close to the borders with Hungary and Yugoslavia, and near the latter it has five Slovak congregations. The congregation in Bucharest is the only Lutheran one where Romanian is used for Sunday service. Among the Church's members are former Jews who joined the Church under the influence of the long-established Norwegian Israel mission. Given state recognition in 1948, the Church governs its affairs at the congregational and district levels through presbyteries, and at the national level through a general assembly, the highest decision-making body. A bishop (also called superintendent) heads the community, aided by a lay president. The two together chair the general assembly.

The Church's worship life (aided by the introduction of a new hymnal in 1948, with a fourth edition in 1976), its fairly high proportion of communicating members, its careful preparation of young people for confirmation, its accent on the ongoing education of pastors through conferences and self-directed study, and its awareness of its minority status help to keep the ESPC ecumenically alive.

REFORMED CHURCH IN THE SOCIALIST REPUBLIC OF ROMANIA
(Romania Szocialista Kötzársaságban lévö Reformatus Egyház)
Eparhia Reformata Cluj, Str. 23 August nr. 51, 3400 Cluj-Napoca — Tel:1.34.31 — Eparhia Reformata Oradea, Str. Craiovei nr. 1, 3700 Oradea — Tel: 3.17.08. 700.000 members — 687 parishes — 700 active ministers. Publications: Reformatus Szemle, Reformatus Szemle gyülekezeti mellékletë (in Hungarian). WCC (1948), WARC, CEC, CPC. Bishop D. Gyula Nagy — Bishop D. Laszlo Papp.

Members of the Reformed Church of Romania are scattered over the whole of the Republic of Romania, but the majority are in Transylvania. The 15th century Hungarian Hussite translation of part of the Bible is a proof of the early historical connections with Reformed Bohemia. At the time of Luther and Melanchthon, about 150 pastors studied in Wittenberg. The first complete translation of the Bible was made by

Karolyi Gaspar in 1590. The Church's confession of faith came from Wittenberg, Geneva and Heidelberg. The doctrinal writings of Melus Juhasz Peter spurred the synod to organize the Church and, in 1561, the congregations in West-Siebenbürgen set up the first superintendency, followed by a second superintendency in the central region set up in 1564. In 1565, the Heidelberg Catechism was introduced into the schools, and in 1567 the synod adopted the Second Helvetic Confession.

But the struggle for Reformed Church government encountered great difficulties. During the 18th century, puritan pastors, mostly educated in the Netherlands, tried to introduce kirk sessions, the deepening of biblical knowledge, the education of the serfs and the renewal of Christian life. Their movement was suppressed by the feudal powers. The synodical-presbyterian order was introduced only in the second half of the 19th century, following the abolition of serfdom after the 1848 Revolution. Between the two world wars, the Church experienced an inner renewal. A new church constitution was introduced in 1948, with freedom of conscience guaranteed by the state.

The Church has good ecumenical relations with the Orthodox Church and the Roman Catholic Church. It participates in interconfessional theological conferences, and there is much involvement in practical ecumenism at the national and local levels. It maintains special relations with Reformed churches in Great Britain, Scotland, Austria, France, the Netherlands, Switzerland, Hungary, Yugoslavia and Slovakia, and with the Waldensian Church in Italy.

The Reformed Church of Romania hopes to provide better training for its ministers and pastoral care to its young and old members, in particular in rapidly growing urban areas. The rebuilding and the renovation of churches, damaged in the earthquake on 4 March 1977, is almost complete, thanks to generous help from abroad and to financial contributions by the members.

ROMANIAN ORTHODOX CHURCH
(Biserica Ortodoxa Româna)
Palatul Patriarhiei, Aleea Marea Adunare
Nationala nr. 1, Bucharest I, Cod. 70526 —
Tel: 16.34.35. 17,000,000 members — 1
patriarchate and metropolitanate — 4 other
metropolitanates — 4 archdioceses (2 in the
country and 2 abroad) — 6 dioceses — 111
deaneries — 8,161 parishes — 2,478 monks
and nuns — 4 metropolitans — 3 arch-
bishops — 6 bishops — 8 vicar bishops — 2
diocesan vicar bishops — 8,479 priests.
Publications: Biserica Ortodoxa Româna,
Ortodoxia, Studié Theologice, Telegraful
Român (all in Romanian), Romanian Orthodox Church News (quarterly, in English
and French). WCC (1961), CEC, CPC.
Patriarch Justin — Patriarchal Vicar:
Bishop Vasile Tirgovisteanul, Sectorul
Relatii Externe Biseriscesti, Str. Antim 29,
Bucharest VI, Cod. 70666 — Tel: 31.34.13.

According to an old tradition, Christianity in Romania dates back to the
Apostolic Age. It is believed that the gospel
was first preached in this part of the world
by the apostle St Andrew and early Christian missionaries. Fourth-century Christian
vestiges have been found in the area
stretching from Transylvania to the Black
Sea. Bishop Terentius took part in the Second Ecumenical Synod of Constantinople
(381) and Bishop Timothy in the Third
Ecumenical Synod of Ephesus (431). The
Metropolitanate of Wallachia was created
in 1359, the Metropolitanate of Severin in
1370 and the Metropolitanate of Moldavia
in 1401. In 1885 the Romanian Orthodox
Church was granted autocephalous status
through a Tomos issued by the Ecumenical
Patriarch Joachim IV. After Transylvania,
Wallachia and Moldavia united, the
Church organized itself as a patriarchate,
with the Metropolitan of Bucharest as
patriarch. The Church comprises 85 per
cent of the total number of the faithful in
Romania. The country has a population of
over 22,000,000.

Main concerns of the ROC are the Christian way of life, the unity of all churches,
and friendship and collaboration among all
nations. It is engaged in promoting
dialogues with the Roman Catholic, the

Anglican, the Old Catholic and the Protestant churches. Local ecumenical activity is
carried on through interconfessional
theological conferences. Good relationships exist with other Christian confessions
both at the hierarchical and at parish levels.

Because of the escalation of the arms
race in our troubled world, the Orthodox
Church has the question of peace and disarmament high on its agenda. In 1981 it
launched two appeals for peace. The first
was addressed to the Christian churches
and the religious communities in the world
and to people of good will everywhere; the
second to the Romanian Orthodox faithful
abroad. The Church strives to raise the
standard of the missionary and pastoral activities of its priests. It is greatly interested
in Christian literature, and is committed to
bring out new editions of the Bible and the
publication of theological, liturgical and
devotional books, church guides and calen-
dars. The translation of the works of the
holy fathers is now in progress.

SPAIN

SPANISH EVANGELICAL CHURCH
(Iglesia Evangélica Española)
C. Nación 24, Barcelona 13 — Tel:
9.254.0342. 3,150 members — 50 parishes
— 20 pastors. Publication: Carta Circular
(in Spanish). WCC (1948), CEC, WARC,
WMC. Rev. Daniel Vidal Regaliza,
Trevino, 1 dpdo. 3°, 3ª, Madrid 3 —
Secretary: Rev. Enrique Capo Puig.

The severity of the Counter-Reformation prevented the Reformation from taking roots in Spain. There were, however,
communities of Spanish Protestants in exile in many European cities. It was for
their use that the Spanish Bible was printed
in Basel in 1569, and later Spanish translations of Calvin's *Institutes* and of the
Heidelberg Catechism. The SEC is a united
church which is made up of congregations of different origins — Presbyterians, Methodists, Congregationalists and

Lutherans. It was established in 1869 in the wake of the religious tolerance which emerged in Spain following the Revolution of 1868. Its first general assembly was held in Seville in 1872, when it adopted the name Spanish Christian Church. In 1874 the title was changed to Spanish Evangelical Church. By virtue of the Law of Religious Liberty of 1980, the Church obtained for the first time legal status and has now been recognized officially by the Spanish government.

Relations with other Protestant bodies, such as the Spanish Episcopal Church, Baptists and the Plymouth Brethren are on the whole excellent. At present, in the new phase of liberty, new possibilities are opening up for the SEC, making it possible for the Church to take part in decisions concerning problems facing the country.

The Church is committed to the religious instruction of its children. It has also encouraged its young people in the often difficult task of bearing witness to their faith in a Roman Catholic society. Consequently it has given much thought to the work of the laity. Principal aims in the 1980s are the spreading of the gospel in a society which has only been superficially evangelized. New programmes of communication through campaigns and publications are undertaken. Also engaging the attention of the Church are moral problems like divorce, abortion, and the growing incidence of violence and injustice in society.

SPANISH REFORMED EPISCOPAL CHURCH* (Iglesia Española Reformada Episcopal)
Beneficencia 18, Madrid-4. 2,000 members — 15 congregations — 1 bishop — 9 presbyters and 4 deacons. Publication: La Luz (diocesan bulletin, bi-monthly). WCC (1962), ACC, CEC. Bishop Ramon Taibo, Isaac Peral, 52 Madrid 3.

The Church was founded at a synod held in Sevilla in 1880. The first bishop, Juan B. Cabrera, was consecrated in 1894. He died in 1916. Until 1936 the Irish hierarchy carried out the episcopal function. During the Civil War of 1936-1939 the Church suffered greatly. The situation improved after 1945 under the new Spanish law prohibiting prosecution because of religious belief and private worship. Officially, however, no formal ceremonies other than those of the Roman Catholic Church were permitted. Only after the Second Vatican Council and the law on religious liberty in 1967, approved by Franco, did the Church have true freedom of worship. In 1956 the Rev. Santos Molinas was consecrated bishop. He was succeeded in 1966 by the Rev. Ramon Taibo, who was consecrated bishop in the Cathedral of the Redeemer in Madrid in 1967. Celebrating its centenary, the SREC became a full member of the Anglican community, as an extra-provincial diocese, united to Canterbury.

The national synod is made up of ministers and lay people in equal numbers. Each minister in charge of a congregation has a vote. The Church has deacons and elders. Lay people participate in the work of the church as readers, catechists, etc.

The Book of Common Prayer contains the divine services of the Church. The orders of worship reflect Moorish-Arab influences which prevailed in Spain until the adoption of the Roman rite. The Declaration of Doctrine contains the same articles as those of the Church of England, although the articles applicable to the conditions and circumstances of the English church are left out. The SREC has only 38 articles.

Now that it has gone through a stage of reconstruction, the Church is anxious to move ahead and to render a true witness, and serve the nation through various social activities, such as nurseries and homes for the aged. It still depends on spiritual encouragement and financial help from abroad. It maintains close relations with Episcopal churches in Central and South America.

SWEDEN

CHURCH OF SWEDEN (Svenska Kyrkan)

Box 640, S-751 27 Uppsala 1 — Tel: 018.155340 — Cable: Lutherworld, Uppsala — Telex: 760 94 luther s. 7,500,000 members — 13 dioceses — 2,570 parishes — 13 bishops — 3,400 pastors. Publication: Var Kyrka (in Swedish). WCC (1948), SEC, CEC, LWF. Archbishop: Most Rev. Olof Sundby.

Christianity in Sweden traces its beginnings to the missionary endeavours of St Ansgar (801-65), the first archbishop of Hamburg and the 'Apostle of Scandinavia'. Pagan resistance was finally overcome in the 11th century by German and English missionaries. The archdiocese of Uppsala, an influential order founded by St Bridget (at Vadstena) and the University of Uppsala (1477), were signs of the Church's growing strength during the centuries before 1500. In the introduction of the Reformation (1527) under King Gustavus Vasa, the brothers Olavus and Laurentius Petri (both of whom had studied at Wittenberg under Luther) and several others played an important role. Laurentius Petri became the first Lutheran Archbishop of Uppsala (1531), and was consecrated by Petrus Magnus, who had himself been consecrated Bishop of Strägnäs in 1525 while he was in Rome. Through Magnus, apostolic succession was continued in the Church of Sweden. In 1593, the convocation of clergy in Uppsala affirmed the position of the Church of Sweden as Lutheran. The unaltered Augsburg Confession was adopted as the doctrinal norm. King Gustav Adolphus (1594-1632) advanced the Lutheran commitment.

The Edict of Toleration (1781) granted religious liberty to Christians of other confessions seeking to take up residence in Sweden. The 19th century brought upheavals in economic, cultural, political and religious life.

Ever since the Reformation the Church of Sweden has been intimately linked with the state. The great majority of the population still hold membership in the Church. Membership is a civil matter. Organizationally, the Church of Sweden, with its episcopal form of polity and emphasis on apostolic succession, represents a combination of traditional and new structures.

The major functions of the Church as a whole are carried out by boards active in parish development, overseas mission and other fields. Under Sweden's new constitution (1975), the king has been reduced to a figurehead and the time is now ripe for a resolution of the question of church-state relationships.

Many Swedes, now living in one of the most affluent societies in the world, have become conscious both of the needs of the exploited people in the Third World, and of the bad consequences of the consumer attitude at home. Voluntary agencies have been formed within the Church, and these give expression to the new sense of responsibility in positive action. The Swedish National Committee of the Lutheran World Federation raises well over 10 million dollars for development aid overseas largely through a campaign during Lent. The Church of Sweden Mission (1874) remains active in South Africa, Namibia, Zimbabwe, Tanzania, Liberia, Ethiopia, India and Malaysia. The Evangelical National Missionary Society (1856) is active in Ethiopia, Tanzania and India. The Swedish Jerusalem Society (1900) works in Israel. The present archbishop Olof Sundby is a president of the WCC.

ESTONIAN EVANGELICAL LUTHERAN CHURCH (Eesti Evangeeliumi Luteri Usu Kirik)

Box 450 74, 104 30 Stockholm 45 — Tel: 08.206978 and 213277. 55,000 members — 65 parishes — 7 synods — 1 archbishop — 1 bishop — 51 pastors. Publications: Eesti Kirik (in Estonian). WCC (1948), LWF, CEC. Archbishop: Rev. Konrad Veem — General Secretary: Mr Esmo Ridala.

In 1905 Rev. Villem Reiman conceived the idea of an Estonian free people's church to replace the German feudal

Lutheran Church of Estonia. His plan was realized when in 1917 the founding congress of the Estonian Evangelical Lutheran Church met. Its constitution was approved in 1919. The Church in exile arose out of a mass exodus of about 80,000 people from their homeland in the autumn of 1944 — about 30,000 going to Sweden and 50,000 to Germany. Pastors accompanying the refugees included Archbishop Johan Köpp, who went to Sweden. The conditions prevailing there were conducive to a fairly rapid organization of a church in exile. In war-torn Germany, the situation was much more difficult. Eventually the refugees found a place in camps in the British and American zones of occupation. When the opportunity came to emigrate, all but 4,000 left Germany.

In their new countries of settlement — the EELC is widely spread in parishes throughout Europe, North and South America and Australia — the faithful have often contributed significantly to the professions as well as to the life of church and society. Through prayer, worship, witness and pastoral counselling in the Estonian language the Church continues to serve its people. A principal aim is to spread objective information about Estonia, Estonians and its Church as widely as possible.

MISSION COVENANT CHURCH OF SWEDEN (Svenska Missionsförbundet)

Box 6302, 113 81 Stockholm — Tel: 08.15.18.30 — Cable: Förbundet — Telex: 14275 Smfsmu S. 80,000 adult members — 90,000 members of the Swedish Covenant Youth — 11 districts — 1,130 congregations — 590 pastors — 150 youth workers — 30 deaconesses. Publications: Svensk Veckotidning (weekly), Information Bulletin (monthly), Tro och Liv (six times a year), Ansgarius (annually), all in Swedish. WCC (1948), SEC, IFFEC, WARC. General Secretary: Rev. Dr Gösta Hedberg.

The Church, like the Baptist, Methodist and other free churches, was born in the great spiritual revival in the 19th century. The first local church was founded in 1855,

the denomination in 1878. The foundation of the MCCS was a protest against the state church system. Emphasizing the free association of committed believers in local fellowship, the Church adopted a congregational character. It sent its representatives to the first meeting of the International Congregational Council in 1891. It regards the holy scriptures as the sole source of faith, and it has no creeds. Infant and adult baptism are practised. The communion is celebrated by the pastor, but deacons distribute the elements. Pastors have been trained at the Church's own seminary at Lidingö since 1908, or at the theological faculties in Uppsala and Lund. The general assembly is the highest decision-making body. The executive board is elected by the general assembly. The local churches cooperate with the board through the eleven districts and their superintendents, through special conferences for pastors, local leaders and through direct contacts.

The Covenant Church arose among farmers and industrial labourers. Today it is more a middle class church with a rather established position in Swedish society. It is strongly involved in political, social and international questions, with a liberal, social democratic outlook. The MCCS has always been well represented in the Swedish parliament. Members have also held office as Cabinet ministers.

The Mission Covenant Youth is one of the strongest youth movements in Sweden with about 95,000 members. The vigorous youth work has broad contacts in Swedish society and is an effective form of evangelism. In recent years the Church has entered the realm of mass media and many of its members are involved in education and cultural activities. The Church maintains good relations with the Baptist Union and the Church of Sweden. An ecumenical hymnbook has been published by five free churches and a hymnbook for all Christians in Sweden (including Roman Catholics) is in preparation.

Mission work overseas is carried out in Congo-Kinshasa and Congo-Brazzaville, India, Japan and Ecuador. An annual ecumenical development week reminds the

Church of its international responsibility, calling for solidarity with the poor and the oppressed in many parts of the world.

The MCCS has a successful publishing house, and its weekly paper *Svensk Veckotidning* reaches a large readership, beyond the confines of its membership. Every year a special theme for study and action is chosen for the local congregations.

The Church maintains contact with several Reformed Churches and, through the International Federation of Free Evangelical Churches, with many other Christian communities.

SWITZERLAND

FEDERATION OF SWISS PROTES-TANT CHURCHES (Schweizerischer Evangelischer Kirchenbund — Fédération des Eglises protestantes de la Suisse)

SEK/FEPS, Sulgenauweg 26, P.O. Box 36, 3000 Bern 23 — Tel: 031.462511. 3,007,200 members — 1,439 parishes — 2,500 pastors. Publications: Jahresbericht/Rapport annuel, Studien und Berichte des ISE/Institut d'éthique sociale de la FEPS, Publikation des Vorstandes/Publications du Conseil (all in French and German). WCC (1948), ACKS, CEPPLE, KKR, CEC, WARC. President: Rev. J.-P. Jornod — General Secretary: W. Probst.

The Protestant churches of Switzerland — mainly Zwinglian in the German-speaking areas of the country and Calvinist in the French-speaking areas — are products of the 16th century Reformation. They are cantonal churches, distinct and independent from one another. Thus there is no Swiss Reformed Church. Besides John Calvin and Ulrich Zwingli, other Reformers like Heinrich Bullinger, Theodore Beza and Pierre Viret also influenced Christianity in Switzerland. The Helvetic Confession of 1566, drawn up by Bullinger and adopted by most of the cantonal churches, has formed the main link in their spiritual unity. The Evangelical Diet, set up in the mid-16th century, brought together delegates from the Reformed cantons to watch over common concerns and to assist fellow Protestants in other countries for three centuries.

In 1858, a conference of Swiss churches established relations between the cantonal churches and paved the way for the foundation of the Federation of Protestant Churches in Switzerland in 1920. This at first consisted only of national churches, but it soon admitted the Free Evangelical Churches, the Methodist Church and the Evangelische Gemeinschaft. The constitution of the Federation was revised in 1950.

The cantonal churches vary in legal status. Some are still state churches, some are quite independent, and others have a concordat relationship with the state. Diverse in their constitutions, liturgies and manuals of religious instruction, they nevertheless have many points in common. The congregational council constitutes the basic unit. In most cantonal churches the legislative body is the synod and the executive organ the synodical council.

The Federation has a staff of five German-speaking and two French-speaking persons, of whom three are lay persons. There are various departments. Hilfswerk der evangelischen Kirchen der Schweiz (HEKS) works in close cooperation with the WCC Commission on Inter-Church Aid, Refugee and World Service. 'Aktion Brot für die Brüder' is a fund-raising organization. Missionary societies were founded in the 19th century on a private basis. They were later coordinated in the 'Kooperation evangelischer Kirchen und Missionen' (KEM) in the German-speaking part, and in the 'Departement missionnaire romand' (DMR) in the French-speaking part of Switzerland.

Other departments of the Federation are responsible for theological research, problems of migration, diaconia, tourism, church law, finance and administration. Also inner-church questions, like ministry, baptism, eucharist and theological education receive regular attention. On the international scene, the Federation is greatly concerned about human rights, religious liberty, peace and disarmament, social justice and development in the third world.

The Federation maintains many relations with churches in East and West Europe and in South Africa.

OLD CATHOLIC CHURCH OF SWITZERLAND (Christkatholische Kirche der Schweiz)

St Niklausstrasse 61, 4500 Solothurn. 20,000 members — 44 parishes — 41 priests. Publications: Christkatholisches Kirchenblatt (in German), Présence catholique chrétienne (in French). WCC (1948). President: Dr Carlo Jenzer — Bishop Léon Gauthier, Willadingweg 39, 3006 Bern.

As in Germany, the Vatican Council of 1870 was followed by a revolt in Switzerland. Whereas the German revolt was led by theological professors, the Swiss revolt was led by laymen. Two meetings of Roman Catholics — at Solothurn on 29 April and at Berne on 1 May 1871 — passed resolutions rejecting the Vatican decrees, demanding the revision of the constitution for the protection of citizens against clerical demands, and supporting the suspended priests. On 12 May 1872, the proposed revision of the constitution, from which the Old Catholics had hoped much, was rejected. On 28 January 1873, the diocesan conference met at Solothurn, and proceeded to depose the bishop and to invite the cathedral chapter to elect his successor. The first national synod of the Old Catholic Church of Switzerland met at Olten, on 14 June 1875. It declared the constitution drawn up in 1874 to be in force and elected Prof. Edward Herzog as the first bishop. He was consecrated by Bishop Joseph H. Reinkens in the old parish church at Rheinfelden on 18 September 1876.

In several Swiss cantons the OCCS is officially recognized by the state authorities and its priests are paid by the cantons. Slowly a better understanding has developed between the OCCS and the Roman Catholic Church in Switzerland. An Old Catholic Faculty of Theology at the University of Bern also serves theological students of other confessions. Old Catholic priests teach religion at Swiss public schools.

Present concerns of the OCCS are: a more intensive training of lay people, especially women for catechetical teaching, the improvement of the church press service, the coordination of youth work throughout the whole bishopric and the amelioration of pastoral service to the diaspora.

UNION OF SOVIET SOCIALIST REPUBLICS

ARMENIAN APOSTOLIC CHURCH (Hai Arakélakan Yékéghétsi)

Holy See, Etchmiadzin, Armenian SSR — Tel: 5.34.34, 5.23.80. 2,000,000 members — 5 dioceses in the USSR — 500 parishes and monasteries — 500 bishops and priests. Publications: Etchmiadzin (monthly official organ), 'Armenian Church' and 'Mother Church' (Armenian diocese of the USA). WCC (1962), CEC, CPC. His Holiness Vasken I, Patriarch and Catholicos of All Armenians.

According to tradition, the apostles St Thaddeus and St Bartholomew came to Armenia and preached the gospel. From the first century onwards there were Christian communities in Armenia. In 301, during the time of the Armenian King Trdat III (291-330) and of St Gregory the Illuminator (300-325), who was the first Catholicos of the Armenians, Christianity was proclaimed the official state religion. The present Catholicos of All Armenians, Vasken I, is the 130th Catholicos. The historical spiritual centre of this independent national Christian Church is Holy Etchmiadzin, located in the city of Etchmiadzin in modern Soviet Armenia, twenty kilometers from the capital city of Yerevan.

Doctrinally, the Church bases its faith on the Bible, tradition, and on the decisions of the first three ecumenical councils. On the question of christology, it accepts the definition set by the Council of Ephesus, that Christ is "one in the incarnate nature of the word". It does not accept the Council of Chalcedon (451), and also renounces the teachings of Nestorus and the monophysitism taught by Eutyches. The Church's liturgy is substantially that of St Basil, in classical Armenian. The chief vestment is the chasuble, shaped like a cope. For the eucharist unleavened bread is used. Communion is given in both kinds by intinction. The Julian Calendar is followed. The Bible was translated into Armenian at the beginning of the 5th century, immediately after the creation of the Armenian alphabet. This alphabet is still in use today.

In 390 Armenia became divided between the Byzantine and Persian empires, and in 430 the monarchy disappeared; since then the Armenians have been subject to Persians, Arabs, Turks and Russians. They continue to be united by the bond of race, language, literature and religion. The persecutions caused by the power of the Turkish Empire and later by the Russian Empire from 1893 onwards until the socialist epoch were the most severe. In spite of the fact that the AAC lives today in the shadow of the secular state, it still represents the cultural and religious unity of Armenians in their homeland and abroad. Holy Etchmiadzin and other monastic centres have contributed to the advancement of culture, science and the arts for centuries. During the last 25 years many sanctuaries, old monasteries and churches have been renovated. Faithful members in the diaspora have made generous contributions for the renovation of old churches and the advancement of religious activities.

As a result of the historical situation of the Armenian people, three sees were established within the hierarchy of the Armenian Church with local jurisdiction: the Patriarchates of Jerusalem and Constantinople, and the Catholicate of Cilicia in Antelias, Lebanon. The Patriarchate of Jerusalem exercises authority over Armenian monasteries in Israel and the parishes of Jerusalem, Bethlehem, Jaffa, Haifa, Ramlah and Amman. The Catholicate of Cilicia exercises authority over the dioceses and churches in Lebanon, Syria and Cyprus. Since 1956 it is also responsible for the dioceses in Iran and Greece. From 1957 two of the dioceses have been in the USA, in addition to other dioceses which have been there since 1890. At present, approximately three million Armenians live in Soviet Armenia, about one and a half million in the other republics of the Soviet Union, and some two million in diaspora.

During the last twenty years five bishops, 22 celibate priests, 45 married priests and 27 deacons have graduated from the seminary at Etchmiadzin. In recent years the number of baptisms, religious marriages, and church-going believers has gone up.

Among the principal preoccupations of the AAC in the near future are: (1) reorganization of the spiritual life of Armenians and the sustenance of newly formed communities; (b) reorganization of the theological seminary; (c) the preparation for the synod of bishops in 1982 to discuss changes in the ecclesiastical structure of the Church; (d) the preparation for the celebration of the benediction of holy chrism in 1983; (e) the continuation of the ecumenical dialogue with sister churches and other member churches of the WCC; (f) exploration of new ways of active participation in the search and consolidation of world peace.

A new Armenian translation of the New Testament for Armenians in the Soviet Union (third edition: 20,000 copies) and for Armenians in the diaspora (first edition: 50,000 copies) is in preparation. Fifteen biblical scholars have been working for over a year on a new translation of the whole Bible. The construction of a religious museum and library at Etchmiadzin was started in 1979; they will soon be inaugurated. There are plans to publish and distribute widely an official weekly of the AAC in three languages, Armenian, English and French.

ESTONIAN EVANGELICAL LUTHERAN CHURCH (Eesti Evangeelne Luterlik Kirik)

Raamatukogu 8, 200103 Tallinn, Estonian SSR. 225,000 members — 142 congregations — 90 pastors. Publication: Kalender. WCC (1962), LWF, CEC, CPC. Archbishop Edgar Hark.

This Church has its headquarters in Tallinn (Reval) on the southern coast of the Gulf of Finland. The history of Lutheranism in Estonia parallels that in Latvia: christianization and subjection to the Teutonic knights and the Danes — after an unsuccessful revolt, the division of Latvia among Russians, Swedes, Danes and Poles. For nearly a century, until 1710, Estonia was Swedish, but after the Northern War it came under Russian rule (1721-1918). After a brief period of independence following the First World War, the Estonian Soviet Socialist Republic was established; after the Second World War, it became part of the USSR.

Early in the Reformation era, the Estonian towns of Tallinn and Tartu, along with the chief Latvian city of Riga, formed an evangelical alliance. Gradually the Reformation spread among the rural people. The Counter-Reformation and the periodic wars (1558-1629) meant widespread suffering for the young Lutheran Church, especially in southern Estonia which was occupied by Poland. During the Swedish era (until 1710), the Church was reorganized along episcopal lines, a pattern which held until 1832. The Russian Church law of that year recognized Orthodoxy as the religion of the state and placed the Lutheran Church in the category of tolerated churches. With the creation of the Estonian Republic in 1918, the Church was once again reorganized, with first a bishop and later an archbishop at its head. Its legislative body is the synod, its executive unit the consistory.

For many years after 1945, the repair or reconstruction of churches damaged or destroyed during the war was a priority for the Church; it made heavy demands on their giving. As elsewhere in the USSR church property is state-owned, with the congregations paying rent for its use. Among the major problems facing the Church are the need to train a sufficient number of ministers and the question of admitting children to the eucharist. The issue of world peace is high on the Church's agenda. Recently, permission has been given to publish a church journal. Efforts will be made to bring out a quality publication. The Church maintains close relations with the Lutheran churches in Finland and the GDR.

EVANGELICAL LUTHERAN CHURCH OF LATVIA (Latvijas Evangeliski Luteriska Baznica)

Lacplesa 4-4, Riga 226050, Latvia — Tel: 334194 — Cable: Luthchurch, Lacplesa 4, Riga. 350,000 members — 207 parishes — 97 pastors. Publications: Calender-Almanac, Information Message, Archbishop's Feast Messages, Church Hymn Sheets (in Latvian). WCC (1962), CEC, LWF, CPC. Archbishop Dr Janis Matulis.

The Latvian people, inhabiting what was long called Livonia, were converted mainly during the period 1180-1230 and largely by force. In 1524, during the Reformation era, the city of Riga turned Lutheran, with St James Church becoming the first parish. The further spread of the Reformation was slow. The Counter-Reformation, under the Polish king and the Jesuits, offered stern opposition. The first Lettish pastor was not ordained until 1648. The complete Bible in the Latvian language appeared in 1689, and the Lutheran hymnal in 1685.

When Russian rule replaced the Swedish (1721), Peter the Great determined not only that the country would remain Lutheran but also that there should be one Lutheran Church in Russia, comprising five consistories or executive councils: in St Petersburg, Moscow, and the then three Baltic regions of Estonia, Livonia, and (in the coastal south-west) the former German-ruled Courland (a Latvian tribal land).

The people's struggle for freedom culminated in the creation of a Latvian republic in 1918. Of its two million inhabitants, 74 per cent were Letts. The religious distribution was: Lutheran 56 per cent; Roman Catholic 24 per cent; Russian Orthodox 14 per cent; Jews 5 per cent; others one per cent. The Lutheran church was reconstituted, first by government action (1922) and further by a synod (1928). Sweden's Archbishop Söderblom in 1922 consecrated the Church's new bishop, Karlis Irbe, and Peter Harald Poelchau, bishop of the German congregations which were autonomous within the church. In 1940, first the Russians occupied Latvia, then the Germans. More than 200,000 Latvians fled as the war was coming to an end, and ultimately were resettled elsewhere. It was only with great difficulty that the Lutheran Church recovered from the heavy human and material losses it had sustained.

The general synod, consisting of both clergy and lay members, is the highest legislative body of the church. The consistory is composed of seven counsellors and three members of the inspection committee, under the presidency of the archbishop.

Since 1969 the clergy is trained at the Evangelical Lutheran Theological Academy in Riga. There are at present some 50 students. Four women have been ordained so far. Under the leadership of the archbishop an annual conference for pastors is organized.

The ELCL has limited possibilities to issue religious publications. In 1964 the New Testament was reprinted; a revised translation of the New Testament and a new edition of the handbook of worship are in preparation. Two new editions of the Church's hymn book have been published.

The Church participates with the Orthodox Church, the Roman Catholic Church and other churches in ecumenical services, held annually on 9 May, the day of victory and peace. Delegates of the ELCL have participated regularly in theological meetings abroad. The Church maintains close relations with Lutheran churches in Hungary, Czechoslovakia, Finland, Sweden, the German Democratic Republic and the Federal Republic of Germany.

GEORGIAN ORTHODOX-APOSTOLIC CHURCH

4, Sioni Street, Tbilisi 380005, Georgia — Tel: 996930. 5,000,000 members — 15 dioceses — 200 parishes — 5 metropolitans — 4 archbishops — 4 bishops — 180 priests. Publications: Djvari Vazisa, Year-Book Calendar (in Georgian). WCC (1962), CEC, CPC. His Holiness and Beatitude Ilia II, Catholicos and Patriarch of All Georgia — Secretary of External Relations: Boris Gagua.

According to early tradition the Apostle Andrew preached the gospel in Georgia (also known as Iberia, in the South Caucasus). The preaching of the gospel by a Christian slave woman from Cappadocia, St Nina, led to the conversion of the Iberian royal house c. 330, and so to the adoption of the Christian faith as the religion of the country. Whereas the neighbouring Church of Armenia adopted Monophysitism, Georgia remained Chalcedonian, except for a period during the 6th century, when it came under Monophysite control. At first dependent upon the Patriarchate of Antioch, the Georgian Church became autocephalous in the 8th century, and its independence was reaffirmed at a Council of Antioch c. 1057. The Georgians developed a rich Christian literature in their own language, especially from 11th to 13th century. In 1811 the Georgian Church was absorbed by the Church of Russia, but since 1917 it has been autocephalous once more. The head of the Georgian Church has the title Catholicos-Patriarch of all Georgia.

The GOAC is historically a national church embracing the majority of the population. Catholics, Jews and Muslims are minority communities. It remains closely related to society. Many Georgian scholars are taking part in a new translation of the New Testament, in the preparation of several volumes of the history of the Georgian Church and in re-editing the divine liturgy. Microfilms of Georgian manuscripts, preserved in the Gregorian monastery in Greece and in the Vatican library, can now be consulted in Georgia. Artists are involved in the reconstruction and the repainting of Georgian cathedrals and churches. The church in Batumi has been renovated and the cathedrals in Sioni and Svetitskhoveli redecorated. With the help of the government, the cathedral of St Marine has been put to use once again.

The Church hopes to work towards the spiritual strengthening of the Georgian nation and the deepening of bonds with sister churches, expecially in the cause of friendship and peace between the nations. It will also continue the dialogue with the Roman Catholic Church and the Orthodox churches, as well as contribute to the worldwide ecumenical movement.

RUSSIAN ORTHODOX CHURCH

Chisty Perevlok 5, Moscow G-34. 50,000,000 members — 76 dioceses — 20,000 parishes — 30,000 priests. Publications: The Journal of the Moscow Patriarchate (monthly, in Russian and English), Stimme der Orthodoxie (The Voice of Orthodoxy, monthly in German), 'Pravoslavniy Visnyk' (Orthodox Messenger, monthly in Ukrainian), One Church (monthly, in English for parishes in the USA), Messager de l'Exarcat du Patriarcat russe en Europe occidentale (quarterly, in French and Russian). WCC (1961), CEC, CPC. His Holiness Pimen, Patriarch of Moscow and All Russia.

Christian missionaries first preached extensively in Russia in the 9th and 10th centuries. About 988 the Emperor Vladimir was baptized, and he established Christianity as the official religion in his dominions. Anxious to bring Russia into closer relationship with Europe, he brought priests from the Byzantine Empire and established a Greek hierarchy under a metropolitan. From the first the Slav tongue was used in worship and gradually a Russian clergy replaced the Greek. Monastic life began with the coming from Mount Athos of the monk Antony who laid the foundations of the great monastery of Kiev. Monasticism spread rapidly.

In the beginning of the 14th century the metropolitan see was moved from Kiev to Moscow. In 1461, the Russian Church was divided between two metropolitans, centred in Moscow and Kiev. During the 15th and 16 centuries Russian missionary activity continued in the southern and eastern borders of the country. During the reign of Theodore (1584-98) the Patriarchate of Moscow was created in 1589 by Jeremias II, Patriarch of Constantinople. The first Patriarch was Job (1589-1605). Peter the Great (1676-1725), anxious to secure the subjugation of the Church to his authority, abolished the office of patriarch and replaced it with the holy synod, the members of which were nominated by the Emperor and could be dismissed by him at any time.

In 1917-18 a large council of bishops, parish clergy and laity met in Moscow and initiated a thorough reorganization of all aspects of Church life, in particular restoring the Patriarchate. Metropolitan Tikhon of Moscow was elected as Patriarch. Sergius became Patriarch in 1943 after an inter-regnum following Tikhon's death in 1925. Patriarch Alexius was elected in 1945 and Patriarch Pimen in 1971.

At the head of the Russian Orthodox Church preside the Patriarch and the holy synod. The diocesan bishops take part in administering the Church through the synod. There are, besides the Patriarch, three permanent members: the ruling metropolitans of the Kiev, Moscow and Leningrad dioceses. Three members are elected to assist for six months from the geographical groups of south, west, central, north and east. In 1961 the head of the Department of External Church Relations and the bishop charged with the affairs of the Patriarch (called chancellor) were made permanent members. The holy synod elects new bishops.

Priests are educated at three theological schools: the Theological Academy and Seminary Moscow/Zagorsk, the Theological Academy and Seminary Leningrad and the Theological Seminary Odessa.

Abroad, the Russian churches under the jurisdiction of the Moscow Patriarchate are divided into one autonomous Church (Japan), exarchates, deaneries, groups of parishes:

a) The exarchate of Central Europe (an archbishop or a metropolitan resides in East Berlin) which includes the two Republics of Germany and Austria (with a bishop in Vienna who resides in Baden-Baden).

b) The exarchate of Western Europe (an archbishop or metropolitan resides as a ruling bishop in Russia; other diocesan bishops reside in London, Brussels, The Hague and Zürich).

c) The exarchate of Central and South America which includes parishes in Argentina, Chile, Cuba, Mexico (a bishop or an archbishop resides in Buenos Aires).

d) The patriarchal parishes in Canada and the USA.

e) The patriarchal parishes in Finland.

f) The deanery in Hungary.

g) Representations and parishes in different cities: Tokyo, Milan, Jerusalem, Rabat, New York, Alexandria, Damascus, Beirut and others.

The Moscow Patriarchate has had a permanent representative at the WCC in Geneva since March 1962. It also has a permanent representative at the Christian Peace Conference in Prague.

UNION OF EVANGELICAL CHRISTIAN BAPTISTS OF USSR

Malyi Vouzovskii bystr., G.P.O. Box 520, 3 Moscow — Tel: 227.89.47. 1,100,000 members — 5,545 parishes — 5,000 pastors. Publications: Bratskii Vestnik, Calendar (in Russian). WCC (1962), CEC, EBF, BWA, CPC. President: A.E. Klimenko — General Secretary: Rev. Alexei M. Bichkov.

Three factors favoured the introduction of the Baptist witness to Russia in the late 18th century. One was the migration of a large host of Mennonite refugees, who refused to join military service in Prussia. One of their later leaders was Michael Ratushny. A second source was the Molokans, a religious community very much like the Quakers in its teaching. Centred in Tiflis, capital of Georgia, they came under the influence of a German Baptist named Martin Kalweit about 1862. A Baptist community was built up and Basil Pavlov became its preacher. Later, he and Ratushny met, and the two movements of Caucasian Baptists were united into the Russian Baptist Union in 1884. Another influential leader was Nikita Voronin, the 100th anniversary of whose birth was celebrated in 1967. Alexander V. Karev (1894-1971) was a pillar of the Union, and he preached the gospel for sixty years.

The most notable Baptist convert from the Molokans was Ivan Prokhanov. He founded the first Russian Baptist periodical *(Beseda)*, and published a Russian evangelical hymnbook in 1902. He did not wish, however, to work with the Russian Baptist Union and preferred the name 'evangelical' to Baptist. His was the smaller of the two groups in 1914 (with only 8,472 compared with 97,000 in the Russian Baptist Union), but it grew to more than 250,000 in eight years. Prokhanov was elected vice-president of the Baptist World Alliance in 1911.

Both Baptist groups encountered severe persecution from the Russian government. Baptist leaders were exiled to Siberia and the Caucasus like common criminals. By 1905 the persecution was less severe.

During the First World War the mission of Baptist churches was brought to a standstill. Many Russian Baptists refused to fight, although they expressed willingness to do non-combatant work for the army. In this, they reflected the influence of Mennonite teaching.

In many respects the new regime in Russia proved to be a boon to the Baptists. Between 1914 and 1923 the number of Baptists increased from over a hundred thousand to one million. (Some even put the figure at two million.) By 1929, however, the Baptists, like other religious bodies in the country, were subjected to governmental repression. In the revised constitution of the USSR, adopted in 1936, the Communists announced that religious freedom had been guaranteed to all of its citizens. Actually, however, it granted freedom of belief only; propagation of one's faith was still forbidden. During the critical days of the Second World War, a few further concessions were made to win popular support for the military effort.

In 1942, both groups of Baptists (the Russian Union and Prokhanov's Union) made a joint appeal to Baptists throughout the world. They claimed to speak for four million followers. In 1944, they formed the Council of the United Baptists and the Evangelical Christians. In 1945, the Pentecostals joined. The enlarged federation is known as the Council of United Baptists, Evangelical Christians and Pentecostal churches and groups in the USSR. Baptists are spread throughout the USSR, in the central regions, in the far north, and Transcaucasia, the Baltic region, Siberia and the far east.

The spirit of separation and isolation, typical of the early period of the evangelical movement, is being gradually replaced by the spirit of tolerance and friendly attitude towards other Christians. Ecumenical ties with many Christian movements both inside the country and abroad are developing. Mutual visits and conversations and exchange of Christian literature take place with the Russian Orthodox Church. The Union is greatly preoccupied with peace, disarmament, justice and mutual understanding.

UNITED KINGDOM

BAPTIST UNION OF GREAT BRITAIN AND IRELAND
4 Southampton Row, London WC1B 4AB — Tel: 01.4059803. 171,000 members — 2,100 congregations — 1,574 pastors. Publications: Baptist Times, Baptist Union Directory. WCC (1948), BCC, BWA, FCFC, EBF. General Secretary: Rev. Bernard Green.

Organized Baptist life in England had two distinct beginnings. In 1611 Thomas Helwys led back from Amsterdam a little group who, a few years earlier had sought religious freedom in Holland, and had there formed themselves into a separatist church — under the leadership of John Smyth — practising believers' baptism. The successors of Helwys and his friends became known as General Baptists. They were Arminian in theology but their church order was not unlike the Presbyterian. In 1633 a group connected with a Calvinistic separatist church in London broke away on adopting believers' baptism. This was the origin of the so-called Particular Baptists. They remained Calvinistic in theology but their church order was of the more 'independent' type. A 'New Connexion' of the more evangelical General Baptists was formed in 1770 under the influence of the Methodist revival. During the 19th century this section of General Baptists gradually came closer to the Particular Baptists. In 1792 William Carey (1761-1834) was instrumental in the formation of the Baptist Missionary Society which gave a new impetus to missionary endeavour. In 1812-1813 the Baptist Union of Great Britain and Ireland was formed out of particular churches; this gradually drew into its fellowship the General Baptists of the New Connexion and the latter amalgamated with the Baptist Union in 1891.

Membership of churches in the Baptist Union is slightly more than that of the United Reformed Church and about one third that of the Methodist Church. This represents about 0.33% of the total population of the country.

The Baptist Union is engaged in work among Asians and other immigrants. It has a hostel in London for business girls and students. It is engaged in social service of many kinds, is deeply concerned about human rights and religious freedom, and is committed to the responsibility of mission and evangelism at home and abroad. It has separate, though integrated, programmes for youth, women and men. These programmes involve training courses and teaching activities covering a wide spectrum of religious and social concerns.

The primary aim of the Baptist Union is to make known the gospel, through evangelism and mission, in such a way that men and women may know the *wholeness* of Christ's salvation. The most urgent issue facing the Union is to try and make real to a society which is on the whole materialistic and secular in its outlook the reality and the relevance of the Christian gospel to the whole of life. Evangelism is high among the priorities of the local churches. With this goes the endeavour to interpret the gospel in terms of social justice, peace and freedom. The range of concerns is indicated by a list of public issues which came up before a recent Baptist Union assembly: disarmament, unemployment, the nationality law, torture and El Salvador. A thorough assessment has recently been made, in a report entitled 'Signs of Hope', concerning the reasons for the decline in the Church's influence on the life of society in the past few decades. Out of this has come 'A Call to Commitment' to which the local churches have responded well. The 'call' is in six parts: to worship and to pray, to evangelize, to learn, to care, to serve and to release for leadership. It is leading to a new spirit of hope and expectancy and has already brought a new vitality to many of the churches.

CHURCH IN WALES

c/o Religious Education and Communication Centre, Wooland Place, Penarth, South Glamorgan CF6 2EX — Tel: 708234. 1,260,000 members — 664 benefices — 6 dioceses — 727 full-time pastors — 55 non-stipendiary. Publications: Diocesan yearly handbooks. WCC (1948), CCW, BCC, CEC, ACC. Archbishop: The Most Rev. Gwilym Dwea Williams Ty'r Esgob, Bangor, Gwynedd LL57 2SS — Secretary to the Governing Body: B.V. Davies, 39 Cathedral Road, Cardiff CF1 9XF.

The province of Wales was created on 1 April 1920 after the disestablishment and partial disendowment of the Church in Wales by the Welsh Church Acts of 1914 and 1919. These Acts enabled the bishops, clergy and laity to appoint a legislative body with the power to frame constitutions and regulations for the general management of the Church. The Acts also set up a representative body with power to hold property and to exercise financial func-

tions. Since 1920, the Church in Wales has evolved its own identity, bringing together Welsh and English-speaking traditions. Individual members play leading roles in many aspects of Welsh life, whether cultural (National Eisteddfod), political (as members of the House of Commons or county councils), agricultural (chairmanship of the Royal Welsh Show committee) or religious (presidency of the Council of Churches for Wales). There are chaplaincy teams to industry, hospitals, prisons and the university.

The Presbyterian Church of Wales is about the same size, but tends to be more concentrated in the Welsh-speaking areas of north and west Wales, whereas the Church in Wales has an even spread throughout the country. The Free Churches and the Roman Catholic Church are strong in certain places, though their total membership is smaller.

Among the concerns of the Church in Wales in the 1980s are the fostering of more vocations to the ordained ministry while developing the talents of all the people of God to make Christ known; the widespread study of a document on "The Principles of Visible Unity in Wales" and a movement of the covenanted churches towards visible unity; and the completion after forty years of the revision of the Book of Common Prayer without stifling future liturgical growth. The Church in Wales continues programmes covering the consideration of contemporary social and political issues on which the Church should speak; the application of the principles of Christian stewardship; and lay training.

Developments will include the exploration of new forms of ministry, particularly the 'non-stipendiary'; improvement in the methods of policy-making within the synodial framework; and devising more effective support for local initiatives in mission, evangelism and social action.

CHURCH OF ENGLAND

Church House, Dean's Yard, London SW1P 3NZ — Tel: 01.222.9011 — Cable: Chinfo, London SW1 — Telex: 916010 CIO LDN G. 27,200,000 members —

17,460 congregations — 44 dioceses — 13,953 parishes — clergy 18,376 (of whom 5,197 have retired). Publication: Church of England Year Book. WCC (1948), BCC, CEC, ACC. Primate: The Most Rev. and Rt Hon Robert Alexander Kennedy Runcie MC, Lambeth Palace, London SE1 7JU, and Old Palace, Canterbury, Kent CT1 2EE — Secretary General: Mr W.D. Pattinson, Church House, Dean's Yard, London SW1P 3NZ.

The Christian faith was brought to England very early in the Christian era. Augustine became the first Archbishop of Canterbury in 597. In 1534 King Henry VIII claimed the title 'Supreme Head of the English Church', and so brought about a breach with Rome. The attempt to establish one church in England which would include all Christians, those who sought to affirm their continuity with the Catholic tradition and those who were strongly influenced by the Reformation, continued for over a century.

The Bible was translated into English. The English Bible and the Book of Common Prayer gave the Church of England a distinct identity. The Thirty-Nine Articles of Religion expressed the Anglican doctrinal position strongly, but their main thrust was irenic and inclusive. By 1662 the attempt to include all Christians in one church had failed and the Act of Uniformity compelled over 2,000 clergy to leave the Church of England. Since then the established Church of England has existed alongside the Roman Catholic Church and the Free Churches.

The 18th century was marked by the evangelical revival and the creation of voluntary missionary societies. The nineteenth century saw the rise of the Oxford movement with its emphasis on the recovery of the catholic tradition. In the 20th century the church has gradually acquired for itself considerable freedom from state control, and it is now governed by a general synod including bishops, clergy and laity. Liturgical reform has led to the publication of the Alternative Service Book.

Economic pressure and what is sometimes called an 'establishment mentality' have sometimes meant that the Church has put more of its resources of personnel and money in the service of the wealthier and more influential elements of society. However, the Church of England has been able to retain a presence in inner cities, from which some other churches have been forced, by economic pressures, to withdraw. The Church has traditionally been allied with authority and has been a conservative force in society. England, however, escaped the atheistic anti-clericalism which affected some other European countries. All the political parties have Anglicans in their membership, and the Church makes its (often critical) views known on various socio-political issues through debates in its own general synod and in the parliament, and in direct approaches to government.

Among the primary concerns of the Church are (1) maintaining the mission of the Church in rural areas and inner cities (where other religions are growing in influence); (2) encouraging lay education and lay participation in Christian mission; (3) increasing a sense of Christian stewardship, and reliance on the resources of members rather than on endowments from the past; (4) reconsidering the ministry of women in the Church. Among the social issues with which the Church is confronted are: (a) coping with the unprecedented level of unemployment, which has been most severe in the more depressed areas of the country among the unskilled and the ethnic communities of inner cities; (b) attempting to improve relations between different racial groupings; (c) educating people about international trade and aid policies; and (d) responding to social changes in the roles of women and men, and in the field of marriage and divorce.

In the summer of 1981, 17 partners from Anglican and other churches overseas and from churches in Scotland and England were invited to examine the effectiveness for mission of the central agencies of the Church of England, both official and voluntary. Some 60 representatives of those central agencies worked with the external partners to produce an agreed report. This report is being considered by the Church in 1982. In the same year the Church will be asked to decide whether to covenant for unity with the United Reformed, Methodist and Moravian churches in England. It will also receive the final report of the Anglican-Roman Catholic International Commission.

CHURCH OF SCOTLAND

121 George Street, Edinburgh EH2 4YN — Tel: 031.2255722. 2,000,000 members — 1,843 parishes — 2,255 pastors. Publications: Life and Work (monthly), Reports to the General Assembly (annual). WCC (1948), SCC, BCC, WARC. Principal Clerk of the Assembly: Rev. Angus W. Morrison — Secretary of Inter-Church Relations Committee: Rev. Andrew R. Morton.

The Church has its roots in the missionary labours of St Ninian and St Columba, and in the early Celtic Church. It was reformed in the 16th century after the Genevan and Calvinistic pattern. A century and a half of ecclesiastical struggles followed, until in 1690 the Church of Scotland was established in its Presbyterian polity.

Various secessions occurred in the 18th and 19th centuries, but since 1929 the Church of Scotland has been largely reunited. In the declaratory articles which the parliament of the United Kingdom approved as a correct statement of the historic position of the Church of Scotland in matters spiritual, the Church is described as a "national church representative of the Christian faith of the Scottish people". The Church is committed to the modern ecumenical movement and to fostering church union. Its Inter-Church Relations Committee is in conversation with several other denominations, particularly the Roman Catholic Church, and is at present actively engaged in multilateral church conversations in Scotland.

The Church has approximately 957,000 adult communicant members. Its final authority in all matters is the general assembly. It has its own publishing house, the Saint Andrew Press. Its overseas work includes an active force of over 500 missionaries, working in Africa, Asia and the Caribbean areas. Ministers serve in over thirty Scots kirks abroad; various others work in Israel.

Through the Home Mission Committee, the Church is deeply concerned over the declining number of communicant members. There are efforts being vigorously pursued to revive the membership of the Church. The 1981 report of the committee on church and nation to the general assembly documents major concerns for the years ahead: (1) economic and industrial interests (Scotland's industrial base and North Sea oil revenues); (2) international interests (the Brandt report and its implications for the church, disarmament, South Africa, human rights); (3) Scottish interests (proportional representation, Gaelic language, Stornoway NATO base); (4) social interests (penal reform, UN International Year of Disabled People); (5) mass means of communication.

In the field of education, the Church of Scotland continues to devote much attention to the training of ministers and other full-time workers, the instruction of children, youth and adults in the Christian faith and life, and its involvement in schools, colleges and universities. Carberry Tower, near Musselburgh, is maintained as a training and conference centre.

CONGREGATIONAL UNION OF SCOTLAND

1 University Avenue, Glasgow G12 8NK — Tel: 041.3399704. 25,700 members — 107 parishes — 124 pastors. WCC (1948), SCC, BCC. General Secretary: Rev. Robert Waters.

This Church originated in missionary activity stemming from the evangelical revival of the late 18th century. A church orientation which stressed the independence of local churches, the commitment of members and liberality and tolerance in doctrine led by 1812 to the formation of the

Union. Although constituting a voluntary association of fraternal churches, it agreed to form necessary structures for common decision-making. The Union evolved rapidly from a 'church aid and home mission society' to an organized body of churches. However, it never lost its emphases on the local church, mission, and personal commitment to Christ.

Another association of 'independent' churches was also emerging, this one more directly from the Presbyterian branch of Calvinism, with which the Union had much in common. This was the Evangelical Union expelled in 1843 from the United Secession Church, a rigidly doctrinal community. As the two bodies developed, they outgrew their original difference. In 1896 the Congregational Union of Scotland was formed, bringing together the Evangelical Union and the Congregational Union.

The cultural influence of Presbyterianism is evident in many of the churches of the Union and it has helped to give orderly strength to its identity. The quality of membership, emphasis on mission, freedom from state control and the primacy of the local church are all of them still distinguishing marks of the denomination, and these are increasingly seen to be of importance in the ecumenical discussion for the whole Church of Jesus Christ. The Union makes an impressive contribution in many fields. Its primary concerns now are church union, economic justice, rediscovery of contemporary forms of evangelism, and a 'planning for mission' programme. It maintains particular relationships with the Reformed Churches in the Netherlands and the United Reformed Church of England and Wales.

METHODIST CHURCH

1 Central Buildings, Westminster, London, SW1H 9NH — Tel: 01.222.8757. 1,359,900 members — 7,990 churches — 3,506 ministers. Publications: Minutes and Yearbook of the Methodist Conference (annually), Constitutional Practice and Discipline of the Methodist Church, Methodist Hymn Book and Methodist Service Book, various magazines from the Church's national divisions. WCC (1948), BCC, CEC, WMC. Secretary of the Methodist Conference: Rev. Dr Kenneth G. Greet — Convener of the Ecumenical Committee: Rev. John Richardson, 19 Thayer Street, London, W1M 5LJ.

The Methodist Church began through the work of John Wesley (1703-1791) whose itinerant evangelistic work in the British Isles aroused an enthusiastic response among many, both within and outside the Church of England. Wesley's preaching emphasized salvation for all, the effect of faith on character, and the possibility of perfection in love during this life. He organized the new converts locally and nationally, set standards for doctrines in his 'Notes on the New Testament' and '44 Sermons', and enabled his people to sing their theology, mainly through the hymns of his brother Charles (1707-1788). During the 19th century, the Church experienced various divisions, but this was also the period of great missionary expansion throughout the world. The main streams of Methodism came together as 'The Methodist Church' in 1932. Methodism is the largest of the English Free Churches, about three times the size of the next largest, the United Reformed Church. There are Methodist churches in most cities and towns, and in many villages of England and Wales — fewer in Scotland — and so Methodism has a strong local presence. As a national body the Church shares responsibility with other churches to bring Christian insights to the life of the nation at all levels. There are seven national divisions: home mission, overseas, social responsibility, education and youth, ministries, property and finance.

The most urgent tasks according to these divisions are: (a) moving out of a period of decline, both numerical and as regards confidence, to a new sureness and fresh directions in witness; (b) deepening the two-way relationships with other parts of the world church — acting on the Melbourne insights concerning the Church in solidarity with the poor; (c) increasing awareness and giving Christian leadership in the areas of world development and disarmament; (d) offering Christian comments on the nature and purpose of education, including religious education, in a pluralist society, particularly helping the Church to make a positive response to the needs of young people, especially those out of work; (e) recruiting and training ministers able to meet the demands of society with the claims of the gospel, and developing ways of theological education for the whole people of God; (f) encouraging the responsible and flexible use of church property; (g) exercising responsibility in caring for the church's finances in a period of inflation — and studying the ethical issues involved in investment.

Another important priority of the Church is a study of the proposals for covenanting for unity with the Church of England, the Moravian Church and the United Reformed Church. The Methodist Church maintains particular relations with sister churches in Zimbabwe, Sri Lanka, Korea and Chili and United Churches which Methodist Churches linked with Britain have joined (e.g. the Church of South India).

MORAVIAN CHURCH IN GREAT BRITAIN AND IRELAND

5 Muswell Hill, London N10 3TJ — Tel: 01.8833409 — Cable: "Esseffgee" London. 4,050 members — 40 congregations — 29 pastors. Publications: Moravian Messenger (monthly), Daily Watchwords (annual). WCC (1949), BCC, FCFC, IMCU. Chairman: Rev. R.S. Burd — General Secretary: Rev: Fred Linyard.

The Moravian Church came to Britain in the early 18th century and was recognized by act of parliament as an ancient Protestant Episcopal Church, descended from the Unitas Fratrum. The UF came into being in 15th century Bohemia as an offshoot of the Hussite Reformation. The Church in Britain took an active part in the evangelical revival in the 18th century and was a pioneer in modern Protestant missionary work (1732).

Moravians in Britain (as in Europe generally) did not feel called to set up a church in opposition to already existing churches as guardian of some special doctrine, but to work with existing churches. Moravian congregations were established only where there was evident need, and so the Moravian Church in this country has remained small. Up to the mid-20th century, the main emphasis was on overseas missionary work. Even today, though the former mission fields have now become independent provinces of the world Moravian Church, the relationship with them and cooperation in mission remains an important concern. The Moravian Church in Britain maintains particular relations with Moravian churches in Tanzania, India, Labrador and Jamaica. In recent years, the Church has been strengthened by the coming of West Indian Moravians to England.

There is an ordained ministry in which the traditional orders of bishop, presbyter and deacon are preserved. The bishop ordains and gives spiritual leadership but, as bishop, does not hold administrative office. The general oversight of the province is the responsibility of the provincial elders' conference, elected by the synod which, at present, meets every two years. Since 1970 the British province has ordained women into the ministry.

The Moravian Church is ecumenical in outlook. It is one of the five denominations in England engaged in discussions which, it is hoped, will result in a covenant between the five.

PRESBYTERIAN CHURCH OF WALES

Y Berth, Cwmafon, Port Talbot, West Glamorgan SA12 9HS — Tel: 0639.896380. 80,515 members — 1,170 parishes — 210 pastors. Publications: Y Goleuad (in Welsh), The Treasury (in English), Yearbook (bilingual). WCC (1948), BCC, CCW, FFCC, WARC. Moderator elected annually — Clerk of the general assembly: Rev. L.D. Richards.

The Church had its beginnings in the evangelical revival of the 18th century. Its founders, Howell Harris, Daniel Rowland,

William Williams and others (both clerical and lay) were members of the Church of England. Soon after 1735 they established religious societies, similar to the Methodist societies founded in England by John Wesley and George Whitefield. During the years 1735-1752 societies in all parts of Wales were set up under the charge of lay exhorters, and lay and clerical superintendents supervised work. In 1811, under the leadership of Thomas Charles of Bala, an Anglican clergyman, a number of exhorters were ordained. Thus the movement became separated from the Church of England. In 1832, the Calvinistic Methodist Connexion (as it was then called) formulated its confession of faith, rules and discipline, constitution and church government. In general the new Connexion was Presbyterian in polity. The first general assembly of the church was held in 1864. During the 20th century the name of the Church was changed to the Calvinistic Methodist Church of Wales, or the Presbyterian Church of Wales. In 1933, the amended constitution was adopted and received the assent of parliament. The Church has strong ties with the Presbyterian churches in North India and Burma.

Among the primary concerns of the Presbyterian Church of Wales are (a) the decline in membership and the dearth of ministerial candidates; (b) a change in the pattern of social life; there is a major shift from the rural areas where the strength of the witness used to be; (c) the increasingly irreligious nature of society, which affects the traditional methods of witness; (d) a lack of enthusiasm with regard to ecumenical projects.

Programmes related to these issues include: (a) restructuring the ministerial pattern and the lay ministry in order that every parish may receive some pastoral oversight; (b) involvement in interdenominational projects; (c) mission to the young people from spiritual, moral and social perspectives; (d) the strengthening of the administration of the Church by setting up a secretariat with a full-time secretary.

SCOTTISH EPISCOPAL CHURCH

21 Grosvenor Crescent, Edinburgh EH12 5EE — Tel: 031.2256357 — Cable: Episcopal. 71,130 members — 326 congregations — 7 dioceses — 7 bishops — 208 stipendiary priests — 77 non-stipendiary priests. Publication: Outlook (monthly). WCC (1948), SCC, BCC, ACC. Primus: The Most Rev. A.I.M. Haggart, 19 Eglington Crescent, Edinburgh EH12 5EE — Secretary: Ian D. Stuart.

The Episcopal Church was formerly the Established Church of Scotland. It was disestablished and disendowed in 1689 by King William III who set up the Presbyterian Church in its place. Between 1746 and 1792 penal statutes made it illegal for Episcopalians to possess churches or chapels; all public services were forbidden and Episcopalian clergy were not allowed to minister to more than five persons at a time. Nevertheless, throughout the whole period the bishops maintained their continuity. Among the seven bishops today one is elected as Primus by the other bishops. The government of the Church is carried out through a provincial synod and the representative church council which is the administrative body responsible for the 'business side' of the Church's life. It is proposed to replace these two bodies by a general synod within the next two years. Episcopalians comprise some 2.5 per cent of the population.

The membership belongs for the most part to the upper échelons of society, better off than others culturally, educationally and economically. Politically it is very mixed, with people of conservative, liberal and labour leanings and a very small minority of Scottish nationalists. The Church's primary concerns are in the areas of unemployment and the nuclear deterrent. In an inflationary age it is concerned that it should not be locked in the trap of self-survival but rather seek the motivation, energy and resources required to further the Church's mission. There is an active inter-church relations committee. One of the main activities in 1982 is the holding of a partners-in-mission consultation.

UNION OF WELSH INDEPENDENTS
(Undeb yr Annibynwyr Cymraeg)
Ty John Penry, 11 St Helen's Road, Swansea SA1 4AL — Tel: 0792.52542, 52092. 67,500 members — 718 congregations — 330 pastors. Publications: Y Tyst (weekly), Porfeydd (bi-monthly, jointly published with the Presbyterian Church of Wales) (both in Welsh). WCC (1948), BCC, CCW, CEC. President chosen annually — General Secretary: Rev. Derwyn Morris

The Welsh Independent or Congregational Churches stand in the Puritan and Non-conformist tradition. It was the conviction of the Church's founders that the Protestant Reformation which had taken a political turn in England fell short of the reformation called for in the scriptures. The first Congregational Church in Wales was founded at Llanfaches, Gwent, in 1639 under the leadership of William Wroth. A period of persecution followed the civil wars of the forties and fifties, and progress was slow. The Union of Welsh Independents was founded in 1872 for churches worshipping in the Welsh language. The Bible was translated into Welsh in 1588. The preservation of the distinctive language and Welsh culture has always been a major concern of the Church. Today however less than a quarter of the population is able to speak Welsh. The Church also faces considerable indifference, and this in turn affects the Church's life.

The Union has a mission department, and standing committees dealing with moral and social matters, ministry, education and literature, interchurch work and youth. Its primary concern is that its members may be led to a deeper commitment to Christ and one another, and that the congregations may be renewed for their task of worship and witness. In cooperation with other churches, the Union is struggling to proclaim the gospel in all its fullness to the nation. At the 1981 assembly the churches were called to an act of renewed commitment to life in Christ, and to prepare a comprehensive programme of in-service training for their members. Regular coming together of ministers and lay people in retreats for fellowship, Bible study and prayer is a feature of the Church. The appointment of a first full-time youth officer will lead, it is hoped, to the strengthening of the communication with young people.

UNITED FREE CHURCH OF SCOTLAND
11 Newton Place, Glasgow G3 7PR. 11,750 members — 5 presbyteries — 86 congregations — 69 ministers — 3 ordained missionaries — 5 unordained missionaries. Publication: Stedfast (monthly). WCC (1948), SCC, BCC, WARC. General Secretary: David W. Roy.

The denomination is a branch of the Presbyterian Churches in Scotland. There were, in the 18th and 19th centuries, small groups of the Presbyterian order, each independent until some of them formed groupings to become a larger Presbyterian denomination. In 1843, the year of the Disruption, many congregations of the Church of Scotland seceded and became known as the Free Church of Scotland. It existed alongside other Presbyterian denominations, some of which became known later as the United Presbyterian Church of Scotland. In 1900 there took place the union of the Free Church of Scotland with the United Presbyterian Church of Scotland, to become the United Free Church of Scotland. This Church united in 1929 with the Church of Scotland. A small minority continued as the United Free Church of Scotland (continuing) and in 1939 the small denomination decided to go back to the older name — the United Free Church of Scotland. Voluntary support by its members, freedom from state control and religious equality are still distinguishing principles of the Church. Women serve the Church as ministers or elders.

Although small in relation to the Church of Scotland and the Roman Catholic Church, the United Free Church of Scotland maintains an active interest in the cultural, social and political concerns of the whole society. Through its public question committee it is related to a number of organizations which seek to promote the wellbeing of the people. The primary concerns are the desire to promote the Christian gospel, to revive the interest of people in religious matters and to strengthen its association with all who are interested in the promotion of Christian teaching and practice. To this end the Church is currently examining the response of young people to Sunday schools. It is also taking steps to promote evangelistic endeavours, participating through its ministers and members in many efforts that are being planned.

UNITED REFORMED CHURCH IN THE UNITED KINGDOM

86 Tavistock Place, London WC1H 9RT — Tel: 01.837.7661 — Cable: Unichurch, London WC1. 221,150 members — 1,951 congregations — 1,168 pastors (active) — 522 pastors (retired). Publications: Reform (monthly), Year Book. WCC (Congregational and Presbyterian bodies joined in 1948), BCC, CEC, WARC. Moderator: Mrs Rosalind Goodfellow, Kilverstone House, Gordon Road, Claygate, Surrey — General Secretary: Rev. Bernard Thorogood.

Congregational and Presbyterian Churches were established in Britain in the 16th and 17th centuries, and they maintained their separate identities until recent years. The union between the Congregational Church in England and Wales and the Presbyterian Church of England took place in October 1972. In September 1981 the Reformed Association of Churches of Christ was united with the United Reformed Church. The majority of URC congregations have come out of the liberal, middle-class, professional groupings in society, and their major strength is in the suburban areas around the cities. Older, Victorian centres of non-conformity in the city centres have found it a hard struggle to reform their life; the village witness is usually with small congregations who maintain many involvements with the community. Because of this bias in the membership, the URC has been partially sheltered from the great upheavals in British society.

Among the new realitites of its social context are the following: (a) the new racial and cultural mix of the population has not greatly affected the suburban areas; the congregations in inner city areas have been challenged and sometimes renewed in this respect; (b) the economic recession has so far had least effect on the skilled and professional groups; (c) the tide of secularism has affected everyone, and the power of mass media and state education means there is no escape, even for traditionally religious families; (d) the new involvement of ex-colonial Britain in Europe has led the professional groups to retain an internationalist position, though with fears about the loss of independence; (e) the fragility of the family unit has caused much heart-searching as the active community has to shelter a larger aged population and as single-parent families become common.

Among the major concerns of the Church are: (a) Christian education among the church community, with various programmes for children and young people, related to the worship of the church; (b) to revise the programme of ministerial training by taking full account of third world experience, and linking theory and practice more fully at every stage of training; (c) evangelism: groups in the URC are seeking to train and stimulate those with skills in evangelism; (d) the international element in church life; membership in the Council of World Mission has meant that the discussion of mission overseas and mission at home always go together, so that the Church may be as eager to receive from others as to give; (e) Christian unity: the brief history as a united church leads the Church to take very seriously the current search for ways of breaking down the barriers between non-conformist and established episcopal churches; the Church believes that the thrust towards unity and the calling to mission must be held together.

The development of auxiliary ministry is a significant new step for the URC. Traditionally a one-pastor/one-congregation pattern was held to be necessary. Today the Church encourages the development of ministry teams, often serving two or three congregations, in which the auxiliary minister can offer specialized skills. Significant chaplaincy services include ministers from overseas who care for Chinese and African students in London, and those who exercise a mission among white congregations. There is a surprising outburst of hymnody, with a number of gifted authors and composers.

YUGOSLAVIA

REFORMED CHURCH IN YUGOSLAVIA (Reformatska Crke u SFRJ)

Reformed Bishop's Office, Trg M. Tita, 6 Pacir (Backa). 22,410 members — 35 congregations — 23 preaching stations — 31 ministers — 533 elders. WCC (1948), ECCY, WARC.

The Reformed Church in Yugoslavia became an independent church in 1921 when the territory in which it existed became part of Yugoslavia under the peace treaty following the First World War. It covers a narrow strip of territory 700 kilometers in length, stretching from the Romanian border to the Austrian frontier. This geographical situation largely explains the scattered character of the Church. One-third of its members live as a religious minority in the nation. The chief problem, therefore, is organizing on a permanent basis the pastoral care of this diaspora and ensuring the provision of preachers. This calls for a great deal of travelling.

In the smaller and larger congregations, preaching and religious instruction follow the normal pattern. Ninety per cent of the children attend religious instruction. The mother tongue of the Church members is Hungarian. Croatian is the language in one congregation, Czech the langue in two others, while German is the language used in a few remaining German congregations.

The preaching of the gospel and other church work are conducted in these languages.

Congregational diaconia and intensive support for missions abroad may be specially mentioned as features of the life of the Church. Many of the Church members go abroad to work, and a large number do not return, so the Church faces the problem of aging congregations.

There is a shortage of ministers, which means that losses through death and retirement are not being made good from the Church's theological college at Feketic. Orders of service and sermons for each Sunday are provided for use by congregations that have no permanent ministers.

SERBIAN ORTHODOX CHURCH

Holy Synod, Fah 182, Belgrade. 8,000,000 members — 2,974 parishes — 21 bishops — 1,850 priests. Publications: 'Glasnik' (The Messenger), 'Pravoslavni Misionar' (The Orthodox Missionary), 'Pravoslavlje' (Orthodoxy), 'Teoloshki Pogledi' (Theological Views), 'Vesnik' (The Herald). WCC (1965), ECCY, CPC. His Holiness German, Patriarch of Serbia.

Systematic missionary work in Serbia was first undertaken by the Byzantines during the second half of the 9th century, in particular by followers of St Cyril and St Methodius from Moravia. With the baptism of Prince Mutimir (reigned c. 860-91) Christianity became the official religion of the country. For some time the Serbs wavered between Constantinople and Rome, and it was not until the start of the 13th century that their attachment to Eastern Christendom became definite and final. In 1219 St Sava established an autocephalous Serbian Church, of which he was consecrated the first archbishop by the Ecumenical Patriarch in Nicaea (Constantinople being at this time in the hands of the Latins). The Serbian medieval kingdom, and with it the Church, attained its period of greatest brilliance under Stephan Dushan (1331-55). In 1346 the head of the Serbian Church assumed the title 'Patriarch', with his seat at Pec (Turkish: Ipek). The Serbian Patriarchate was recognized by Constantinople in 1375. Along with the Bulgarians and the Romanians, during the Ottoman period the Serbs passed increasingly under the jurisdiction of the Ecumenical Patriarchate, and the Patriarchate of Pec was eventually suppressed in 1766. The Church of Serbia became autocephalous once again in 1879.

The most recent period in the history of the SOC begins after the First World War when all the Serbian regions were included in the new state of Yugoslavia. This rendered it possible to unite all the Serbia regional churches and to re-establish the Serbian Patriarchate. In 1920 the Patriarch of Constantinople recognized the union and the SOC as an autocephalous patriarchate.

But the Second World War brought further suffering. Many towns and villages were destroyed, and many priests were killed. After the war the Church, in spite of all that happened, found its bearings once again. Under the new circumstances of church-state separation it has made every effort to assume its place in the new social and political situation in order to carry out its mission. The SOC has dioceses and parishes in Western Europe, North America and Australia.

The congregation of bishops consists of the Patriarch who is president and all diocesan bishops. It is the supreme hierarchical body of the Church. The synod of bishops consists of the Patriarch as president and four diocesan bishops. It is the highest executive authority. An administrative committee of the Patriarchate is responsible for the financial affairs and a small printing press.

The SOC maintains one theological faculty, four theological colleges (seminaries) and one college for the training of monks. They are all residential institutions, and so the students live and study in the same building. The Church celebrates its feasts according to the old (Julian) calendar.

SLOVAK EVANGELICAL CHRISTIAN CHURCH OF THE AUGSBURG CONFESSION IN YUGOSLAVIA

(Slovenská ev.-kr. a.v. cirkev v Juhoslavii) Karadziceva 2, 21000 Novi Sad. 53,000 members — 65 parishes — 18 pastors. WCC (1963), ECCY. Bishop: Rt Rev. Juro Struharik.

This Church is the largest Lutheran Church in Yugoslavia, speaking the Slovak language. Each congregation is governed by a local council, the entire church by a synod. The bishop is the spiritual head. Its largely rural membership is located in the autonomous province of Vojvodina on the plains south of the Hungarian border. It was earlier a part of the Evangelical (Lutheran) Church in Hungary, but upon the creation of Yugoslavia, it became an autonomous church, with headquarters in Novi Sad. Its pastors are educated at the Lutheran Theological Faculty in Bratislava, along with those of the Slovak Evangelical Church of the Augsburg Confession in the CSSR.

In 1967, this Yugoslav church body was joined by the then 7,000-member Evangelical Church in the People's Republic of Serbia, composed of Hungarian Lutherans. Prior to 1918, that small body had also been part of the Evangelical (Lutheran) Church in Hungary. Between the World Wars, it was part of the German Lutheran Church in Yugoslavia, but after 1945 it became an independent church. As it is located between the Hungarian border and Novi Sad, its merger with the larger Slovak church made sense, although linguistic differences required adjustment. Close links between the Slovak church in Yugoslavia and its much larger counterpart and namesake in Czechoslovakia continue to be maintained.

Middle East

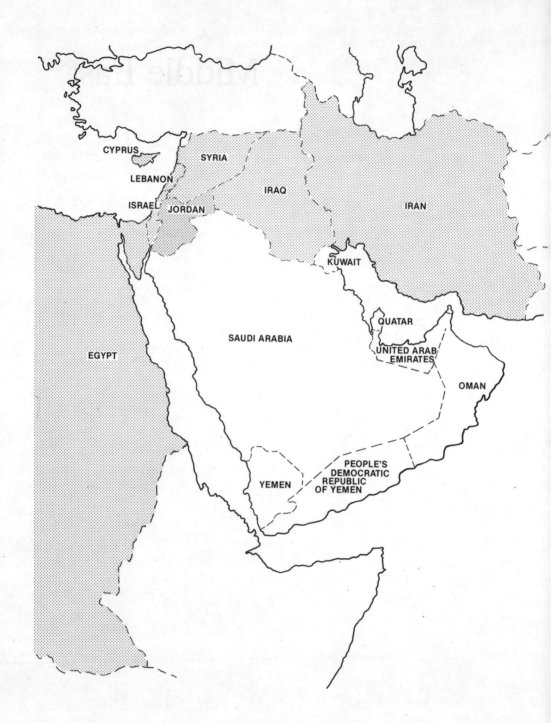

CYPRUS

CHURCH OF CYPRUS

Holy Archbishopric, Nicosia — Tel: 74411 — Cable: Archbishopric — Telex: Archbishopric. 442,000 members — 650 parishes — 6 dioceses — 7 bishops — 1,200 priests. Publication: Apostolos Barnabas (in Greek). WCC (1948), MECC, CEC. His Beatitude Archbishop Chrysostomos, Archbishop of New Justiniana and All Cyprus — Director of the Archbishop's Office: Dr Andreas Mitsides.

"Those who were scattered because of the persecution that arose over Stephen travelled as far as Phoenicia, Cyprus and Antioch" (Acts 11:19). That was in A.D. 37. In A.D. 45 Paul and Barnabas, bringing with them Mark, landed at Salamis and crossed the island to Paphos, where they converted the Roman proconsul Sergius Paulus. The growth of the Church was rapid. Bishops from Salamis, Paphos and Tremithus were present at the Council of Nicaea in 325.

The Orthodox Church suffered much during the Lusignan and Venetian domination (1191-1571), when it was completely under the domination of the Church of Rome. During the Turkish domination (1571-1878) the Church was freed from the domination of its Latin rival. Its archbishops were acknowledged as the official representatives of the Greek Orthodox Church, but the situation in other respects was hardly better. In 1821 Archbishop Kyprianos, the bishops and 486 priests and lay Christians were executed in an act of reprisal against mainland Greek revolutionaries. Great Britain bought Cyprus from the Sultan in 1878 and left the island in 1960 following a five-year guerrilla war for independence under the spiritual leadership of the Ethnarch, Archbishop Makarios III.

Archbishops of the Church of Cyprus are elected by representatives of the towns and villages summoned for that purpose by the holy synod under the presidency of the Metropolitan of Paphos. A new charter for the autocephalous Church of Cyprus was promulgated by the holy synod in January 1980. The Church has many monasteries and in several villages it commemorates a number of local saints. Seventy-eight per cent of the population are Orthodox Christians, 4 per cent Maronite, Armenian and Latin, and 18 per cent Turkish Muslims. There is no aspect of the island's history and society which has not been touched by the Church of Cyprus. For centuries it has acted as a kind of department for social welfare, ministry of justice and ministry of education. After the 1974 invasion by Turkey, 200,000 Greek Cypriots, 49 per cent of the total membership of the Church, were forced to leave their homes in the occupied area and became refugees. Their fate constitutes the primary concern of the Church. The Church has a department for catechesis, youth and women's programmes, a relief service for refugee children, an Archbishop Makarios III Foundation, a council for the administration of the Church property and synodal committees for the revision of church legislation.

EGYPT

COPTIC EVANGELICAL CHURCH — THE SYNOD OF THE NILE (Kaneisat Ai-Akbat Al-Ingiliaa — Sinoudis Al-Nil)

P.O. Box 1304, Cairo — Tel: 904995 and 906633 — Cable: Nilesynod, Cairo. 200,000 members — 314 parishes — 234 pastors. Publication: Al-Huda (in Arabic). WCC (1963), AACC, MECC, EACCSE, WARC. Moderator: Elected every year — General Secretary: Rev. Samuel Habib.

The Evangelical Church in Egypt started in 1854 when the Rev. McCague, a missionary of the Presbyterian Church in the USA, arrived in the country. The Church became independent in 1926. Since its early days it has been serving the local communities. It opened two schools for girls. In 1909 Ramsis College for girls was established, which has at present 2,700 students.

In 1865 the Church established the Assuit American College. Many graduates of this college have played an important role in society. An agricultural department of this college was opened in 1928; it introduced for the first time Jersey cattle in Egypt, and has contributed to the improvement of dairy cattle in the country. In 1914 the Rev. Charles Watson established the University in Cairo; he was its director until 1945. The university has played an important role in raising the standard of education in the nation. The Evangelical Theological Seminary in Cairo trains pastors to serve in various Arab countries. At present there are several Egyptian ministers in the Sudan, one in Bahrain, one in Kuwait, four in Syria and four in Iraq. From the 1930s onwards literacy programmes were organized, following the method of Dr F. Lubach. The ministry of education and the ministry of social affairs participated in the activities of the literacy committee. In 1952 successful literacy experiments were applied to Herz, a village in upper Egypt.

Besides its contribution to education, the Church has also been interested in health care. It established a hospital in Tanta at the turn of the century. This American hospital has now 200 beds; nearly 16,000 people come every year to the dispensary, and some 2,000 cases are treated without charge. Two other hospitals were opened in Assuit and in the Shoubra district of Cairo. The Church has also established four orphanages, one in Foum Al-Khaleig in 1893, transferred in 1915 to Abassia, one in Qualiub in 1927, one in Souhag (Upper Egypt) and one in Helwan in 1942.

The congregations are scattered all over the country: in Cairo there are 26, in Alexandria 5, and in Minia 5. There are fewer congregations in lower Egypt.

Youth centres have become a vital part of the life of the Church. There are five youth centres in Alexandria, one in Port Said and several others in different places of Egypt. A great number of pastoral activities are carried out through old age homes, nurseries and hostels. The Coptic Evangelical Organization for Social Services and the Organization for Developing Church Projects have become important agencies of the Church.

COPTIC ORTHODOX CHURCH

Bishopric of Public, Ecumenical and Social Services, Anba Rueis Building, Ramses Street, Abbasiya, P.O. Box 9035, Nasr City, Cairo. 3,900,000 members — 40 dioceses — 1,200 parishes — 60 bishops — 1,500 priests. Publications: El-Kerazah (weekly, in Arabic), Watany (monthly, in French). WCC (1948), EACCSE, AACC, MECC. His Holiness Pope Shenouda III — For urgent mail: c/o P.O. Box 295, 8034 Zürich, Switzerland. Telex: NACIT 53 388.

The Copts are the native Christians of Egypt and the direct descendants of the ancient Egyptians. Eusebius (died c. 359) records the tradition that the Church in Egypt was founded by St Mark the Evangelist, and Alexandria ranked with Antioch and Rome as one of the chief sees of the early church. The Coptic Church suffered severely in the persecution under Diocletian. In upper Egypt the rapid development of monasticism is attested by the many Coptic "Lives of the Saints" and "Sayings of the Fathers". The Byzantine political dominance and the misunderstanding of the Coptic doctrine caused the Coptic Church to undergo severe sufferings at the hands of the Byzantine rulers.

In 616 the Copts came under Persian domination. In 642 they were conquered by the Arabs, whose rule in varying forms has lasted to the present day. Long periods of comparative peace would suddenly be broken by persecution, e.g. under the Caliph el Hakim (996-1021), who is said to have destroyed 3,000 churches and caused large numbers to apostatize. The Coptic Church is the largest Christian community in the Middle East. The Coptic language is found only in the service books, which provide the Arabic text in parallel columns. The normal liturgy is that of St Basil. Five important fasts are observed: (1) the pre-Lenten fast of Nineveh; (2) the great fast of Lent; (3) the fast of the nativity before Christmas; (4) the fast of the apostles, after the ascension; (5) the fast of the virgin, before the assumption. From the hundreds of monasteries which flourished in the deserts of Egypt, there are now nine left, with 300 monks, and seven convents, with 150 nuns.

Towards the middle of the 19th century the Coptic Church began to undergo phases of new development. Primary, secondary and technical schools for boys and girls were established, some by the patriarchate and the diocesan authorities, others by various Coptic benevolent societies. The theological school for the preparation of pastors and lay leaders was re-established in Cairo in 1875. It is now named the Theological University College, and includes various schools. In 1972 Pope Shenouda III (enthroned in 1971) re-established a branch of the Theological College in Alexandria with about 200 students.

It may be noted that the Coptic language, being the last form or stage of the ancient Egyptian language (originally written in picture-form called hieroglyphics), is indispensable for the study of Pharaonic history and for biblical studies. In the 2nd century A.D. Pantaenus, the principal of the theological school in Alexandria, established the alphabet called Coptic, using the Greek characters and adding seven from the Egyptian which correspond to sounds that do not exist in Greek, in order to record phonetically the vernacular of Egypt. Public interest in theological studies as well as in Coptic history and tradition have led to the foundation of the Institute of Coptic Studies in Cairo by the Church. More than one hundred postgraduate students are currently enrolled in the Institute.

The Coptic laity actively participate in the life of the Church. Parish church councils comprise various sub-committees which cooperate with the clergy to meet the pastoral and social needs of the community. Diocesan communities and parish congregations have established a great number of benevolent societies covering a wide range of spiritual, educational and welfare services.

There is a Coptic church in Kuwait, Jordan, Lebanon, Algeria; there are two in Libya. Five priests serve the Copts in Canada, stationed in Toronto, Ottawa and Montreal; and twelve in the USA. A mission has been working for about 10,000 people in South Africa since 1949. There are five Coptic churches in Australia, three in Sydney and two in Melbourne. Five Coptic priests serve the Copts living in London, Paris, Vienna and Frankfurt. The Coptic Orthodox church maintains close relations with Orthodox churches in Israel and the Sudan.

GREEK ORTHODOX PATRIARCHATE OF ALEXANDRIA AND ALL AFRICA

P.O. Box 2006, Alexandria — Tel: 25196.36839. 350,000 members — 13 archdioceses — 13 metropolitans — 10 suffragan bishops — 147 priests — 176 churches. Publications: Pantainos and Ecclesiasticos Pharos (in Greek). WCC (1948), MECC. His Beatitude Nicolaos VI, Pope and Patriarch of Alexandria and All Africa.

According to tradition the Church of Alexandria was founded in A.D. 64 by St Mark the apostle and evangelist. By the fourth century it had already extended across Egypt and Lybia and had almost a hundred dioceses. The church fathers Athanasius and Cyril fought for the preservation of Orthodox faith at the Councils of Nicaea (325) and Ephesus (431) respectively. The catechetical school was a theological focus for the Christian East at the time.

After the Council of Chalcedon (451) there was a division, and part of the Church joined the Monophysites. Thus two patriarchates arose — the Egyptian, which is known as Coptic, and the Byzantine which, since the capture of Constantinople by the Turks in 1453, has called itself Greek Orthodox.

After the Turkish conquest of Egypt in 1517 the Greek Orthodox patriarchs were forced to seek temporary refuge in Constantinople.

During the Reformation in the West, the Alexandrian patriarchate was administered by the Cretan patriarchs Sylvester, Meletios

I Pegas, Cyril Lucaris, Gerasimus I (1567-1630). The last of them, Metrophanes Kritopoulos, studied in Oxford, Wittenberg and Tübingen, taught Greek in Venice and was elected patriarch in 1630. He bequeathed his books to the patriarchal library, which is one of the most valuable possessions of the church. It contains over 40,000 volumes, over 500 manuscripts and possesses 2,000 rare editions.

Since his election in 1968 the present Patriarch Nicolaos VI hs paid visits to the archdioceses of Johannesburg, Rhodesia, Cape Town and Dar es Salaam, the Sudan, Central Africa, Ethiopia, North Africa, Zaïre and West Africa.

The patriarchate has received fresh impetus from the establishment of new congregations in East and Central Africa, which was principally brought about by the influx of the black indigenous population into the Church. There are already three black African bishops in East Africa.

The Church is governed by the patriarch in conjunction with the synod. It also recognized the right of members to worship in their own language, and so the liturgy is celebrated in Greek in Greek churches and in Arabic in Egyptian Greek Orthodox churches.

Relations with other churches are good. In 1968 Pope Paul VI sent relics of St Mark from Venice to each of the two ancient churches, and observers from the patriarchate were present at the third and fourth sessions of the Second Vatican Council. A council of churches has existed in Alexandria since 1958, and many ecumenical services have taken place in which members of the Orthodox, Catholic and Reformed Churches have participated.

IRAN

EVANGELICAL PRESBYTERIAN CHURCH OF IRAN

P.O. Box 1505, Teheran — Tel: 310831, 311868 — Cable: 'Inculcate'. 3,100 members — 41 congregations — 4

preaching stations — 12 ministers — 2 lay preachers — 70 elders. WCC (1950), WARC. Moderator: Rev. Sh. Isaac.

The Evangelical Presbyterian Church of Iran developed out of the work of American Presbyterians and Congregational missionaries, the first of whom came to Iran in 1834. The work was begun among the Nestorian Assyrian Christians of the Urumia (Rezaieh) district in northwestern Iran. The original hope was that the old churches of the East might be revitalized so that once again, as in the Middle Ages, they would become a powerful and zealous missionary agency. Unfortunately, those members who were touched by the evangelical spirit were forced to leave the old Church and, in 1855, several Protestant congregations came into existence in and around Rezaieh.

The first presbytery was organized in 1862, and other presbyteries were organized later. In the meantime, Presbyterian missionary work in Iran led to the formation of other congregations in various parts of the country, composed of people from different backgrounds — Armenian Christians and converts from Islam, Judaism, and Zoroastrianism.

Today services in Iran's Evangelical congregations are held in the Persian, Turkish, Syriac and Armenian languages. In 1934, all the Evangelical churches in Iran joined together in a union or synod, which became an independent national Iranian Church. In 1963, it adopted a new constitution and took the name of the Evangelical Presbyterian Church of Iran.

IRAQ

APOSTOLIC CATHOLIC ASSYRIAN CHURCH OF THE EAST

7444 North Kildare, Skokie, IL 60076 — Tel: 312.248.0052. 550,000 members — 7 dioceses — 8 bishops — 77 pastors. Publications: Voice of the East (in Assyrian-Aramaic, English, Arabic, Persian and Italian). WCC (1948). His Holiness Mar Dinkha IV, Catholicos Patriarch, P.O. Box 3257, Sadoun, Baghdad, Iraq — Bishop Mar Aprim Khamis, Bishop of the United States and Canada.

The ancestors of the Church were subjects of the Assyrian Empire. When Nineveh was destroyed in 612 B.C., many princes and noblemen of the once vast empire fled northward with their followers to inaccessible mountains where they remained secluded until the dawn of the 20th century.

The Assyrian Church was established in Edessa in the first century of the Christian era. The history of this city is still unclear. Many churches sprang up in the Tigris-Euphrates valley and by the beginning of the third century more than twenty bishoprics had come into being. The Church held Nestorius in high regard, but claimed that it never adopted his teachings and called itself Nestorian only for political reasons to identify itself with those who opposed the Church of Rome. Nestorius defended the doctrine that there were two separate persons in the incarnate Christ, as opposed to the orthodox doctrine that the incarnate Christ was a single person, at once God and man. Opinion is widely divided as to what the doctrine of Nestorius really was and how far it was heretical.

In the sixth century missionaries from the Assyrian Church penetrated as far east as China, and it is possible that Prester John was a Nestorian Khan. Mongol invasions later confined this missionary church to north Mesopotamia. After the Muslim invasion of the Middle East, Assyrian Christians were able to maintain their faith in the mountainous regions of north Kurdistan. In the 16th century a split in the Church took place, and an aspirant for leadership in the Church, Monk Sulaka, joined the Roman Catholic Church.

In 1885 the Archbishop of Canterbury, E.W. Benson, sent out a mission to Qudshanis (then seat of the Assyrian Patriarchate) to assist the Assyrians in educational and other ways. Forced by the Turks to evacuate their country, the Church was temporarily restored to Kurdistan after 1918, but the Christians were again driven out by the Turks; they are now exiles in Iraq, Syria, Lebanon and the USA. A considerable Assyrian community lived in west Iran from early times.

The language of the Apostolic Catholic Assyrian Church of the East, liturgical and colloquial, is a form of Syriac akin to Aramaic, written in east Syrian script. Its liturgies include the rite of Addai and Mari (probably pre-431) which with other liturgical texts, was printed at Urmi by the Archbishop of Canterbury's mission in 1889. It should be remembered that Aramaic was the language of Palestine at the time of Jesus Christ.

JERUSALEM

EPISCOPAL CHURCH IN JERUSALEM AND THE MIDDLE EAST

P.O. Box 19122, Jerusalem — Tel: 282096. 35,000 members — 4 dioceses — 4 bishops — 78 priests. Publication: Bible Lands. WCC (1976), ACC. Rt Rev. H.B. Dehqani Tafti, c/o Anglican Consultative Council, 14 Great Peter Street, London — Secretary: The Ven. Samir Kafity.

The Episcopal Church in Jerusalem and the Middle East was officially inaugurated on January 1976. It succeeded the old Jerusalem archbishopric and was established in accordance with principles settled at the Anglican Consultative Council in Dublin in 1973. It consits of four dioceses: Jerusalem, Egypt, Iran, and Cyprus and the Gulf. Metropolitical authority has been delegated by the Archbishop of Canterbury to the central synod of the Church. The president is elected by the synod from among the diocesan bishops.

Though in no way detracting from the acknowledgment of the position of the Orthodox Patriarch of Jerusalem as the successor to St James as Bishop of Jerusalem and the Church of the Holy Sepulchre as the Cathedral of Jerusalem, St George's under a new constitution has the status of a cathedral church, serving not only the diocese, but also in a unique way the whole Anglican communion, with which it is linked by the episcopal canons who have a share in the government of the cathedral. The Dean of St George's is appointed by a special electoral college on which the episcopal canons are represented. The cathedral ministers both to local and expatriate congregations and to pilgrims, and works with the bishop in fostering good relations with the other churches represented in the parent city of the Christian faith.

While acknowledging the unique place of Jerusalem in the Christian world, the Anglican Consultative Council decided that the general principle by which the Anglican Church in any place is represented by its diocesan bishop should also obtain in Jerusalem and the Middle East, and that the bishop in Jerusalem should therefore, apart from fulfilling his primary function as minister and pastor, be its representative in the holy city. St George's College continues to perform its particular role in providing facilities for study and research; St George's hostel continues to cater for pilgrims and visitors.

The diocese of Iran ministers to Christians of all nationalities in the country. It continues its hospital work and its pioneering work among the blind. The diocese of Egypt, with jurisdiction over North Africa, Ethiopia and Somalia, ministers to small communities of Egyptians mainly in and around Cairo and to expatriate communities in the other countries. The diocese of Cyprus and the Gulf ministers not only to British and American expatriates but also to Pakistanis, Indians, Palestinians and others throughout the area of the Gulf.

The diocese of Jerusalem has considerable responsibilities for schools, welfare centres, and work among the aged and the handicapped. It also ministers to many refugees.

GREEK ORTHODOX PATRIARCHATE OF JERUSALEM

P.O. Box 19/632-633, Jerusalem. 80,000 members — 20 congregations — 16 bishops — 22 priests — 12 monks. WCC (1948), EACCSE. His Beatitude Diodoros Patriarch of the Holy City of Jerusalem and All Palestine.

From its very beginning this Church had to face many difficulties. After the martyrdom of its first bishop, James, and just before Jerusalem was destroyed by Titus in 70 A.D., the Church took refuge in Pella; it returned in 135, when Aelia Capitolina was built on the ruins of Jerusalem. It then entered upon a period of growth, brought about by its bishops, Narcissos and Alexander, who established a school and library. During the early Byzantine Empire the erection of churches on the holy shrines - the holy sepulchre, calvary, the nativity, the ascension, the transfiguration, etc. — led to the founding of the monastic brotherhood 'Spoudaioi' (important monks) whose main task was the guardianship of the holy places and the celebration in them of the divine liturgy. It was in this order of monks that the Brotherhood of the Holy Sepulchre had its origin.

The diocese of Jerusalem was originally under the metropolitan see of Caesarea, but because of historical associations and its importance as a centre of pilgrimage, it soon won the status of an independent church, and by decision of the Fourth Ecumenical Council at Chalcedon in 451 it became known as the Patriarchate of Jerusalem.

The Church of Jerusalem played a distinguished role in the struggle against Arianism (Cyril of Jerusalem), Monophysitism (Patriarch Juvenalis), Nestorianism (Patriarch John III) and Monotheletism (Patriarch Sophronios). The patriarchs were assisted in their struggles by renowned monks who came from all over Palestine — Ephtymios 473, Theoktistos 464, Theodosios 525, Chrysippos 532 and Savvas 533.

Constantine's care for the holy places was continued by his successors Justinian and Heraclius, who expelled the Persians from Palestine, recovered the holy cross from them and erected it in the holy calvary in 629. But Jerusalem was not to remain under the Byzantine emperors for long, and in 637 it was conquered by the Arabs. The Greek Patriarch, Sophronios, handed over the keys of the Holy City to Caliph Omar Ibn El-Khattab and received from him the decree (Omar's Ahtiname) which recognized all the rights and privileges which had been enjoyed by the Patriarch during the Byzantine period — privileges and rights, however, which were to be preserved only at great sacrifice.

The Church of Jerusalem suffered most at the hands of Caliph Hakem in 1009. Through various pacts with the conquerors, however, the Byzantine emperors Constantine VIII, Michael IV and Constantine IX were able to maintain their support and help. During the Iconoclastic Controversy the Church played an important role in the propagation of the Orthodox faith and in the development of church hymnography through the work of St Savvas' Laura, St John Damascene and the brothers Theodore and Theophanes.

The Crusaders brought severe trial. They conquered Jerusalem in 1099, expelled the Greek Orthodox Patriarch Simeon and established a Latin patriarch, who treated the Greek monks very badly. After 88 years, however, in 1177, the Crusaders were expelled from the holy places, which returned to the ownership and control of the Greek Orthodox Patriarchate. In 1517 Jerusalem came under the sovereignty of the sultan of Constantinople and remained under Turkish administration for 400 years, during which time, the Greek Orthodox Patriarchate had to go on defending its claims against the Latins and Armenians for the preservation of its rights in the holy places.

Fortunately, such rights were defined by two firmans which were issued in 1852 and 1853. It was confirmed by international pacts, in 1865 by the Paris convention, and in 1878 by the Berlin conference, and subsequently by the League of Nations and the United Nations.

In 1808 the church of the holy sepulchre was destroyed by fire. It was restored within two years by the Greek nation.

During the British mandate in Palestine the Greek Orthodox Patriarchate was faced with the task of settling its relations with the Arab-speaking congregations. This led in 1958 to the promulgation by the Jordanian government of the law on the Patriarchate. One of the great events in the 20th century history of the Patriarchate has been the restoration of the church of the holy sepulchre. The work began in 1960 and is still in progress. The material costs are being borne by the Greek government.

Priests are educated at the seminary of the Patriarchate. There are 37 elementary and secondary schools in different parishes.

LEBANON

ARMENIAN APOSTOLIC CHURCH
(Hayastaniaytz Arakélagan Yégéghétsi)
Armenian Catholicossate of Cilicia, Antelias, Lebanon — Tel: 410001-3 — Telex: Cilcat 23501 LE. 800,000 members — 12 dioceses — 150 parishes — 14 bishops — 120 priests. Publication: 'Hask' (monthly, in Armenian). WCC (1962), MECC. His Holiness Khoren I, Catholicos of Cilicia — His Holiness Karekin II, Catholicos-Coadjutor of Cilicia.

The diaspora has been a permanent aspect of Armenian history. Since the dawn of their history the Armenians, for one reason or another, have emigrated. Such emigration, often forced and massive, began in the 10th century, with the successive occupation of Armenia by the Byzantines, Seljuk Turks, Persians, Ottomans, and Russians.

After the fall of the Bagradit dynasty in Armenia in the 10th century, many Armenian princes took refuge in Cilicia and formed an independent kingdom which lasted about three hundred years. When this kingdom was finally sacked by the Mamelukes of Egypt, thousands of Armenians went as far west as Poland, Hungary,

Romania and Bulgaria. In 1605 the Persian king Shah Abbas invaded Armenia and took large numbers of Armenians to his capital Ishfahan where they settled and prospered, building their own city of New Julfa. When Sultan Mohammad II occupied Constantinople in 1451, he brought in many Armenians in order to counterbalance the Greek population of that city and give impetus to commerce and crafts. An Armenian patriarchate was subsequently established here along with the Greek one.

Deportation and migration continued in succeeding centuries. But none of the mass deportations of earlier years equalled those that took place in the period 1915-1922. Over one-and-a-half million Armenians were massacred by the Turkish authorities and the rest deported to the Syrian deserts.

The Armenian diaspora remains fluid as the Armenians continue, although at a slower pace, to move from country to country. At present there are about two million of them, mostly in Middle Eastern countries, the United States and Canada, the northern countries of South America, southern and western Europe, and Australia. The Church in diaspora has three centres: the Patriarchate of Constantinople, the Patriarchate of Jerusalem, and the Catholicossate of Cilicia. The Catholicossate of Cilicia, re-established and reorganized in Antelas, Lebanon, in 1930, with its diocesan administrative organization, theological seminary and worldwide ecumenical relations, is *de facto* the spiritual centre of the Armenian diaspora. It also plays a significant role in the cultural, social, and political life of the nation. Its jurisdiction now covers Lebanon, Syria, Cyprus, Kuwait, United Arab Emirates of the Gulf Area, Iran, Greece, and half of the Armenian communities in North America.

Today the Armenian Church in diaspora finds itself in very different contexts and thus faces various problems and challenges. It is truly a scattered church, but this has not affected the integrity and unity of its faith. Deeply rooted in its centuries-old tradition, the Church continues to bear witness to the salvation of human beings in Christ, and to work for the constant renewal of its life, responding to the challenges of the modern world. Translation and dissemination of the Bible, Christian education through courses for youth and adults and popular publications, emphasis on local leadership, both clerical and lay, care of children of broken families, homes for the aged and housing projects for the needy — all these are among the concerns and activities of the Church.

UNION OF THE ARMENIAN EVANGELICAL CHURCHES IN THE NEAR EAST

P.O. Box 110-377, Beirut — Tel:233547 and 349815. 9,500 members — 24 congregations — 13 pastors. Publications: Religious Monthly for Youth, Literary Monthly for Juniors, Devotional Quarterly to Promote Family Worship, Occasional Publications (all in Armenian). WCC (1948), MECC, WARC, MEFEC. Moderator: Rev. Hovhannes Karjian, P.O. Box 112-508, Beirut, Lebanon — Secretary: Rev. Barkev Apartian.

This Church in the Near East is an autonomous body of churches comprising 24 congregations throughout Syria, Lebanon, Turkey, Greece, Egypt and Iran. Beginning in the second decade of the 19th century as an indigenous reform movement within the Armenian Orthodox Church, it developed into an independent community in 1846 in Istanbul, and in subsequent decades registered a membership of 60,000 throughout the Ottoman Empire. After the First World War, when the Armenian population was decimated and the remnant deported from its historic homeland in what is now called Turkey, the Union was reorganized in Syria and Lebanon. The Union is composed of autonomous congregations. Its organizational pattern is a kind of modified congregationalism. The annual convention of the Union is the highest authority. The central committee of 12 members, elected at the convention, acts as an administrative body supervising and coordinating the activities of the member churches and church-related institutions.

From its inception, the Armenian Evangelical Church has stressed the importance of education. It now operates 23 schools and four high schools and owns the only university-level college in the diaspora: Haigazian College, member of the Association of International Colleges and Universities-Europe Inc., with an enrolment of 400 students. It operates, moreover, four conference centres in Syria, Lebanon, Iran and Turkey. Together with the Arabic-speaking Evangelical churches, the Union owns and operates a secondary school in Aleppo and the Near East School of Theology in Beirut (the latter also supported by foreign missionary agencies). With the Armenian Orthodox and Armenian Catholic Catholicossates it operates the old people's homes in Aleppo and Beirut, and a sanatorium in Lebanon.

It has developed ecumenical ties with several churches and fraternal relations with the Armenian Evangelical Union of North America and the Armenian Evangelical Union of France. In spite of grave problems of emigrations and persecution, the Union continues to function with a growing awareness of its mission in its territories.

SYRIA

GREEK ORTHODOX PATRIARCHATE OF ANTIOCH AND ALL THE EAST

(Patriarcat grec-orthodoxe d'Antioche et de tout l'Orient)
c/o The Middle East Council of Churches, P.O.Box 5376, Beirut, Lebanon. 750,000 members — 22 dioceses — 496 parishes — 28 bishops — 408 priests. Publications: The Word (in English), Orthodoxia (in Spanish), 'Al-Kalima', 'An-Nour', 'An Nachra' (in Arabic). WCC (1948), MECC. His Holiness Ignatios IV, Patriarch of Antioch and All the East.

The Orthodox Church of Antioch goes back to the time of the apostles (cf. Acts). In the 4th century the total Christian population of the eastern province of the Roman Empire, of which Antioch was the capital, was under its jurisdiction, and in the 6th century it had more than 150 metropolitans and bishops.

Since then, however, the number has gone down because of the division of the church, the heresies of the 4th and 5th centuries, the granting of independence to the churches of Cyprus and Iberia, the Islamic advance in the 7th century and the formation of the Uniate Church in the 18th century.

Since the beginning of the 20th century, especially after the Second World War, an enormous number of Orthodox people belonging to the church of Antioch have been emigrating or moving from the country to the big towns.

The jurisdiction of the Patriarchate of Antioch and All the East covers all of Syria, the Lebanon, Iraq and Iran, the Arabian peninsula, the whole orient and also certain areas of Turkey. It also extends to the Arab-speaking Orthodox who live in North and South America, Australia and New Zealand.

The holy synod is the highest ecclesiastical authority of Antioch and consists of the Patriarch as president and the metropolitans who are the diocesan leaders as members. Priests are trained at the theological faculty and the theological seminary at Tripoli in Lebanon. Currently there are 300 students.

The Patriarchate is greatly concerned about the suffering in Lebanon, the creation of a Palestinian state, and its responsibilities for its people in the midst of a multi-religious society. An authentic witness to the Christian faith, pastoral care of youth, and reorganization of its establishment in order to express more clearly its apostolicity and its unity, are high on its agenda. Particular emphasis is laid on the coherence of the family which is the centre of the Church and the source of spiritual formation.

NATIONAL EVANGELICAL SYNOD OF SYRIA AND LEBANON

P.O. Box 110-235, Beirut, Lebanon — Tel: 308.545, 309.095 Cable: National Evangelical Synod. 20,000 members — 63 parishes — 23 pastors — 2 licensed preachers. Publication: Annual Report (in Arabic). WCC (1948), MECC WARC. Moderator: Rev. Dr Salim Sahiouny — Executive Secretary: Rev. Ibrahim M. Dagher.

The congregations of the Evangelical Church in Syria and Lebanon are to be found in parts of what has been called the fertile crescent, between the upper waters of the Euphrates and the eastern shores of the Mediterranean. It is the home of the three great monotheistic faiths — Islam, Judaism, and Christianity — and even today it is one of the crossroads of the world.

It was to this area that the American Board of Commissioners for Foreign Missions sent two representatives in 1819. The work then begun met with opposition both from the authorities of the Turkish Sultanate and from the hierarchies of the various Eastern Churches. But in 1848, an Evangelical congregation was recognized by the state and, in 1866, what was to become the American University of Beirut was founded.

In 1920, an independent synod was organized under the more friendly government of the French mandate, though the American Presbyterian Mission continued its independent educational work till 1959, when it was merged with the Church. In its development, the synod has faced three grave problems: the constant loss of leadership by emigration; the top-heavy effect of a powerful mission on a small church; and the innate sectarianism of Levantine Christianity. The Church now shares the problems of rapid cultural change and political instability. Several church buildings have been ruined during the past six years of war. A constant task is the ministry to displaced congregations and families. The national Evangelical synod is deeply concerned about the future of Lebanon and peace with the Muslim neighbours.

SYRIAN ORTHODOX PATRIARCHATE OF ANTIOCH AND ALL THE EAST

Bab Tooma, Damascus, Syria — Tel: 432401. 142,000 members — 28 dioceses — 32 bishops. Publication: 'Journal of the Patriarchate' (in Arabic). WCC (1960), MECC. His Holiness Ignatius Zakka I.

According to tradition, St Peter established the Holy See at Antioch in 37 A.D. and presided over the Church, prior to his journey to Rome. During the first centuries Antioch was the capital of Syria. In the fourth century the Catholicate of the East was established for the administration of the churches in the Persian Empire, Iraq and the Far East. Syrian missionaries went as far as Mongolia, India and China. An outstanding saint was St Jacob Baradaeus (500-578) who revived the spiritual life of the Church in Syria, Armenia, Egypt, Persia and Cyprus. At the beginning of the 13th century the Syrian Orthodox Church had about 20,000 parishes and hundreds of monasteries and convents.

During the 14th century the Church suffered greatly through the Mongol invasions. At the end of the 18th century its strength was further reduced because of the establishment of a separate uniate patriarchate of Antioch (Syrian Catholics), and at the turn of the present century they suffered severe persecution at the hands of the Turks. Since 1964, the Catholicate of the Orthodox Syrian Church of the East in India, vacant for centuries, has been re-established. The seat of the patriarchate, after many moves over the centuries, is now in Damascus.

The SOPA refused to accept the decisions of the Council of Chalcedon about the Person of Christ, on the ground that they had made too many concessions to the Nestorians. Their doctrinal position is thus similar to that of the Armenian, Coptic and Ethiopian churches. Veneration of the saints and prayers for the dead are essential elements of the Church's tradition. The seven traditional sacraments are recognized.

The Old Testament was translated into Syriac during the first century; the New Testament in the second century. The liturgical language of the Church is Syriac, the normal anaphora being that of St James. Other Syriac translations of the Bible were subsequently made by various Syrian scholars. Famous schools of theology were established in Antioch, Nassibeen, Edessa, and Qonnesrin. St Aphrem the Syrian, St Jakob of Sarug, Philexinos of Maboug and Jacob of Edessa graduated from these schools. Many valuable manuscripts of ancient libraries have now been lost or destroyed. Others are still available in libraries and museums around the world. Ignatius Ephrem Barsaum (Patriarch, 1933-57) was the author of a valuable history of Syrian Orthodox literature in Arabic. Since the Church has spread widely during the centuries, vernacular languages like Arabic, Malayalam, Turkish, English, Spanish and Portuguese are today used, alongside Syriac, in religious services.

The SOPA maintains a number of monasteries which are an integral part of its spiritual and cultural heritage. There are two major and three minor seminaries for the training of the clergy. The Church also operates other schools and institutions. It has close relations with the Coptic, Armenian and Ethiopian Orthodox Churches.

TURKEY

ECUMENICAL PATRIARCHATE OF CONSTANTINOPLE
Rum Patrikhanesi, Fener, Istanbul — Tel: 212532, 211921, 239850. 4,700,000 members — 133 bishops — 5935 priests. Publications: Greek Orthodox Theological Review (Brooklyn, MA, USA), Gregorios Palamas (Thessaloniki), Episkepsis (Chambesy/Geneva), Phos (Kavalla, Greece). WCC (1948), CCT, CEC, MECC.

His All Holiness Dimitros I, Ecumenical Patriarch.

The history of Constantinople as a Patriarchate begins in 330, when the Emperor Constantine I decided to move the seat of governmental administration from Italy to the eastern region of his empire and chose this small town of Byzantium along the Bosperus. The Ecumenical Council of Constantinople (381) conferred upon the bishop of the city the second rank after the bishop of Rome. The Ecumenical Council of Chalcedon (451) gave a definite shape to the organization of the Church of Constantinople. From 520 onwards the head of the Church became known as the ecumenical patriarch. After the great schism between Rome and Constantinople in the 11th century, the patriarch became the *primus inter pares* among all the patriarchs of the Orthodox churches.

The Patriarchate of Constantinople is governed today according to the constitution approved (1860-62) by Sultan Abd-ul-Aziz, through a synod under the presidency of the patriarch, and a mixed council of clergy and laity dealing with temporal affairs. The patriarch is elected by an assembly of the synod, made up of 12 metropolitans and lay delegates. The synod is the official organ of authority of the patriarchate, managing spiritual affairs such as the nomination of the metropolitan members of the synod, the election of new bishops, overseeing monasteries and providing teachers. By the Treaty of Lausanne (1923) the Turkish Republic is bound to protect the Greek Christians in Constantinople.

The Patriarchate holds jurisdiction over the faithful in Europe (Great Britain, France, Germany, Austria, Sweden, Belgium, the autonomous church of Finland, and the Russian Exarchy of Western Europe) and the archbishoprics of Australia and New Zealand. The archbishop of New York governs the Greek Orthodox Church of North and South America, which is an autonomous Church, also under the general jurisdiction of the ecumenical patriarch.

The Ecumenical Patriarchate was among the first to participate in the formation and development of the ecumenical movement from 1920 onwards, and it has been involved in the WCC from its beginning. It has had a permanent representative at the headquarters of the WCC in Geneva since 1955. The Patriarchate is currently involved in the preparations for the holy and great synod of the Orthodox churches which is to meet in the near future It is also engaged in official theological dialogues with the Roman Catholic Church, the Anglican Communion, the Ancient Oriental churches, the Old Catholic churches, in bilateral conversations with the LWF, WARC, and WMC, and in theological conversations on a national level in different parts of the world (EKD and others).

North America

CANADA

UNITED STATES OF AMERICA

MEXICO

CANADA

ANGLICAN CHURCH OF CANADA

(Eglise épiscopale du Canada)
600 Jarvis Street, Toronto, Ontario M4Y
2J6 — Tel: 924.9192 — Cable: Marturia,
Toronto — Telex: 065.24128. 2,567,100
members — 1,674 parishes — 30 dioceses
— 2,033 bishops and priests. Publications:
The Canadian Churchman, The Living
Message (both monthly), The Anglican
Church Year Book (annually), The Book of
Common Prayer-Canada (English and
French). WCC (1948), CCC, ACC.
Primate: Most Rev. Edward W. Scott —
General Secretary: Venerable Harry St C.
Hilchey.

The Anglican Church of Canada came
into being as a result of missionary activities on the part of the churches in the
British Isles and particularly the British
Missionary Societies. The Church owes
much to the Society for the Propagation of
the Gospel and to the Church Missionary
Society, both based in London, England,
which sent missionaries and teachers to the
new land in the 18th and 19th centuries.
The first bishop was Charles Inglis who was
consecrated in 1787. Provincial synods date
from the 1860s and the general synod was
organized in 1893. There are now thirty
dioceses organized in four ecclesiastical
provinces. The Anglican Church of Canada
is the third largest Christian communion in
the country, with a census population of
approximately 22 million.

The Church in its leadership is often said
to be middle-class. Included in its membership are large numbers of the original inhabitants of the country — Indian, Eskimo
and Metis (mixed blood). The Church has
long had a special concern for the native
peoples and continues to press the government for settlement of their land claims.
The Church has also a long history of involvement in other social concerns and, for
the past twenty years, through the
primate's World Relief and Development
Fund, has supported a wide variety of
development projects in many parts of the
world.

The primary concerns of the Church, as
identified at the last general synod, are (1)
the nature of our mission and ministry in
an increasingly pluralistic society; (2) a
reawakened interest in evangelism; and (3)
a concern for 'spirituality'. At the present
time the Church has entered upon a major
programme known as "Anglicans in Mission" which will receive a great deal of attention during the next three years. The
programme includes a year of study designed to help the membership gain a clearer
understanding of the Church's mission in
the 1980s. Part of the programme will be a
major financial effort for the support of
mission work both in Canada and overseas.

CANADIAN YEARLY MEETING OF THE SOCIETY OF FRIENDS

60 Lowther Avenue, Toronto M5R 1C7,
Ontario — Tel: 416.922.2632. 1,086
members — 23 parishes. Publication: The
Canadian Friend. WCC (1948), CCC.
Presiding Clerk: Betty Polster, Argenta,
BC VOG 1BO — Secretary: Dorothy
Muma.

The Canadian Yearly Meeting of Friends
is composed of constituent Meetings which
convene for business monthly, quarterly
and half-yearly. Committees of the Yearly
Meeting, representative of all Canadian
Friends, take care, during the year, of activities approved by the Yearly Meeting at
its annual session, and report to it. The
Canadian Friends foreign missionary board
continues to be active in medical and
educational work overseas, in particular in
Kenya, but changing emphases and the impact of the two world wars have resulted in
increased participation through the Canadian Friends Service Committee which was
formed in 1931, in work for war victims
and in peace education as expressions of
the Quaker faith in the worth of all human
beings. The home mission and advancement committee seeks to nurture Meetings,
new and old, and to interpret the religious
emphases of the society, answering en-
quiries, operating a Quaker book service,
and a periodical, the Canadian Friend. The

earlier rural Meetings in Canada have suffered from the general trend of the rural-urban migration, with the result that they are declining, while on the other hand Meetings for worship have registered an upward trend in cities. At the present time there are Meetings in St John's, Newfoundland; Halifax, Nova Scotia; Montreal, Quebec; Ottawa, Kingston, Peterborough, Toronto, Newmarket, Hamilton, Kitchener, Norwich, St Thomas, London, Coldstream, Welland, Muskoka in Ontario; Regina, Saskatoon, Saskatchewan; Calgary, Edmonton, Alberta; Argenta, Vernon, Vancouver, Victoria, White Rock, British Columbia.

There are regular contacts with the Friends General Conference based in Philadelphia and the Friends United Meeting based in Richmond, Ind., both groupings of Friends Yearly Meetings. The association with the CCC and the WCC enables Canadian Friends to keep abreast of ecumenical thinking and actions at national and international levels.

CHRISTIAN CHURCH (DISCIPLES OF CHRIST) IN CANADA

39 Arkell Road, R.R. No. 2, Guelph, Ont. N1H 6H8 — Tel: 519.823.5190. 4,000 members — 30 parishes — 23 pastors. Publication: Canadian Disciple. WCC (1948), CCC, WCCC. Moderator: Dr Russell Legge.

The Christian churches in Canada had their beginnings in the early part of the 19th century through immigration of members of the Scottish Baptist Church from Scotland and the Christian Churches in the USA. These two movements united at the end of the 1840s to form the Christian Church (Disciples of Christ) in Canada. Regional organizations developed in the 1850s in Ontario and in the Maritimes. A western Canada region was formed early in the 20th century and a national structure in 1922. The Church has been involved in the life of the nation ever since its establishment. It has made contributions to the social, cultural and political life of the

nation, far in excess of its numerical strength. It has also been involved in all aspects of the cooperative and unifying forces of Christianity.

Still today the primary concern of the Disciples of Christ is the unity of the church. They continue to seek, along with the United Church of Canada, that visible manifestation of the one church, which spiritually has always been present. Union discussions are therefore one of the Church's most significant programmes. The Christian Church has also a great concern for the liberation of the poor and the oppressed, both in Canada and around the world, and for the defence of human rights in all countries.

EVANGELICAL LUTHERAN CHURCH OF CANADA

247 1st Avenue North, Saskatoon, Saskatchewan S7K 4H5 — Tel: 306.653.0133. 83,315 members — 321 congregations — 299 pastors. Publication: The Shepherd. WCC (1967), LWF. President: Rev. Dr S.T. Jacobson.

Most of the members of this Church are of Norwegian and German origin, though many other backgrounds are also represented. Winnipeg was the major Canadian centre for expansion westward. Not surprisingly, the lure of the Far West drew some to British Columbia, but many others, especially from Scandinavia, entered Canada from the west via Vancouver. The Church, organized in 1967, had begun in 1960 as the Canada district of the newly constituted American Lutheran Church. In the centennial year of Canadian confederation, the ELCC became an autonomous Canadian church body under charter of the parliament of Canada — the first, and to this day the only such Canadian Lutheran Church.

Though small numerically, the Church has contributed significantly to the development of Canadian society, especially through its colleges and schools thousands of whose graduates have gone into the mainstream of Canadian society and continue to bring leadership with a Christian perspective into the various facets of Canadian culture — in the sciences, politics, medicine, business, and educational fields. In addition, the Bible schools have contributed a significant number of missionaries who have taken their skills to various parts of the globe to share the gospel and aid in the development of peoples. In the earlier years and up to the decade after the Second World War, the church not only provided a meaningful cultural link for immigrants but also assisted in the integration of immigrants into the Canadian mosaic.

Three of the prime concerns of the ELCC in the 1980s are Lutheran merger, planting the church in new and expanding locations, and social involvement. The merger process began in the early 1970s with three major bodies participating: ELCC, LCA-CS and LC-C. In the late 1970s the LC-C withdrew but the ELCC and and LCA-CS have set 1985 as the target date for their merger. The 1970s also saw the beginnings of evangelical outreach to the people scattered throughout the Northwest Territories. An airborne ministry, in collaboration with Lutheran Association of Missionaries and Pilots, is reaching many isolated communities in the far north all the way up to Inuvik, NWT. New congregations are still being established in the cities and towns across Canada. A French language ministry has begun in Quebec. The division of social service has provided leadership for the Church in matters of social concern, especially in dealing with questions of justice for the Indian/Metis and other native people of the country. It works through the Indian/Lutheran race relations committees and through collaboration in Project North with other Canadian churches on issues of land claims and development. Through such involvements there is a growing sensitization of the ELCC membership in matters of social justice in Canada and abroad. Globally, there is increasing support for the development and relief work of Canadian Lutheran World Relief and Lutheran World Federation.

Believing that theology must undergird all aspects of its life and mission, the Church is attempting to help all its members towards a greater awareness of the relation of theology to personal, corporate and community life. The many threats in Canadian society to stable and happy family life are being countered by in-depth "caring community courses" for clergy and laity.

EVANGELICAL LUTHERAN CHURCH OF LATVIA IN EXILE (Latvijas Evangeliski Luteriska Baznica Eksila)

5 Valleymede Road, Toronto, Ontario M5S IG8 — Tel: 416.767.2310. 48,000 members — 245 congregations scattered through Europe, North America and Australia — 126 pastors. Publications: "Cela Biedrs", yearly almanach "Gada Gramata" (both in Latvian). WCC (1971), LWF. Archbishop: Most Rev. Arnolds Lüsis.

This fellowship of 245 congregations is spread over 14 countries. Its chief concentrations are in Canada, the USA and Australia. A 21-member church council, with executive powers, assists the archbishop, who is its president, elected for life. The headquarters of the Church in Exile was for about two decades in Esslingen, near Stuttgart, Federal Republic of Germany, where Archbishop Teodors Grinbergs presided over what eventually became an almost global diaspora of his countrymen and women. Expelled from Latvia — in accordance with a secret agreement between Hitler and Stalin (1939) the Baltic States were occupied during the first war years by the Soviet Union — he joined his 120,000 Lutherans in Germany and, with the help of colleagues, organized them into a Latvian Church in Exile. He was an influential member of the first Executive Committee of the LWF.

Since then 43 churches have been built or rebuilt. The Church has made a new translation of the Bible; it has produced a new hymnal and many theological books. It established a mission in Madras, India. One of its major concerns is the training of pastors. The present location of the Church's headquarters in Canada is because of the outsanding role of Canadian Lutherans in promoting the resettlement of Latvians in their country.

PRESBYTERIAN CHURCH IN CANADA

50 Wynford Drive, Don Mills, M3C 1J7, Ontario — Tel: 416.441.1111. 170,000 members — 1,180 parishes — 1,000 pastors. Publication: The Presbyterian Record (monthly). WCC (1948), CCC, WARC. Clerk of Assembly: Rev. Dr Donald C. MacDonald.

The Presbyterian Church in Canada met in general assembly for the first time in Montreal in 1875. Prior to that, there were four independent synods representing various branches of Presbyterianism, largely on the basis of links with mother churches in the British Isles. PCC is a national church, with presbyteries in each of the ten provinces, and, though predominantly English-speaking, it has congregations which use French, Magyar, Italian, Chinese, Ukrainian and even, in the older settlements of Nova Scotia, Gaelic.

In 1925, the majority of Canadian Presbyterians merged with Congregationalists and Methodists, to form the United Church of Canada. But a considerable minority, convinced that certain specific Presbyterian principles had to be maintained, remained in the continuing Presbyterian Church in Canada.

The general assembly of the PCC met in 1975 to celebrate the union of four presbyterian synods in 1875. The Church still remains strong in some parts of the Atlantic provinces, and in the Toronto-Hamilton-St Catharines-Guelph area of Ontario. There are eight synods, corresponding for the most part to the provincial areas of the country.

The Church looks forward to growth in both membership and influence. In 1979 the general assembly resolved to double the membership of the Church in the next ten years. At the same assembly the denomination took steps to become a part of the Vancouver School of Theology. Enrolment at the other two theological colleges of the Church are at record high numbers, and this applies also to Ewart College.

Various boards and committees were restructured through the efforts of the organization and planning task force. An active programme is being carried out overseas, in Taiwan, Japan, Nigeria and other parts of the world.

UNITED CHURCH OF CANADA

(Eglise unie du Canada)
85 St Clair Avenue East, Toronto, Ontario M4T IM8 — Tel: 416.925.5931 — Cable: Weslyana. 903,300 members — 2,388 pastoral charges — 4,265 preaching places — 2,012 pastors. Publication: The United Church Observer. WCC (1948), CCC, WMC, WARC, CCA. Secretary of the General Council: Rev. Dr Donald G. Ray.

The United Church of Canada came into being on 10 June 1925, bringing together the Congregational, Methodist and most Presbyterian (71 per cent) churches in Canada. The new denomination began with over 600,000 members, the largest non-Roman communion in Canada. The membership of the United Church of Canada has grown to one million, with another million or more adherents, out of a total population of 23,700,000. In 1925, the United Church of Canada dedicated itself not only as a united, but as a uniting church. As recently as 1968, the Canada Conference of the Evangelical United Brethren Church joined the Church.

The United Church of Canada has a history of involvement in justice issues both in Canada and overseas, much of this coming from its Methodist tradition of caring for people who suffer economic and social injustice.

In Canada, people moving from rural to urban areas often find themselves living in low-cost, crowded housing. Tensions bring about family breakdown and violence. Churches and mission centres located in the downtown areas minister to these people in a variety of ways, in addition to providing the traditional ministries and pastoral care.

Continuing the traditions of the earlier denominations, it has spoken out strongly and consistently on controversial issues. Current issues under study include abortion, capital punishment, the right of farm labour to organize, racial injustice, guaranteed annual income, land use, refugees and the massive problems of poverty both at home and abroad. In all such matters, educational resources are provided for church groups and official positions are made known to governmental or other agencies.

Support for social justice has been given to groups in Canada. In June 1976, the United Church was part of an ecumenical group called Project North which appeared before Mr Justice Thomas Berger in Ottawa. Project North called for a moratorium on development in the North until native claims were settled, and the native people given the opportunity to set up their own mechanisms for control of land and resources. GATT-Fly, an interchurch project for global economic justice, wrestles with questions of international trade and the struggle for a New International Economic Order. The Task Force on the Churches and Corporate Responsibility (TCCR) coordinates interchurch efforts to challenge corporations and financial institutions (specifically the big five Canadian banks) on issues of corporate social responsibility and policies of trade and finance between Canada and South Africa, Zimbabwe, Chile and Brazil, among others.

MEXICO

METHODIST CHURCH OF MEXICO.
(Iglesia Metodista de México)
Miravalle 209, Apartado 13-538, Col. Portales, Mexico 03570, DF — Tel: 539.36.74. 55,000 members — 370 congregations — 239 pastors. WCC (1948), FEM, WMC. Bishop Ulysses Hernandes B.

The history of Protestant work in Mexico has its roots in the 1810 independence movement led by dissident priests. The introduction of Bibles in Spanish by 1826 and the passage of civil laws and freedoms ratified in 1860 by the Benito Juarez government also played an important role in preparing the ground for Protestantism. All early Protestant missionaries centred their work on small groups, out of which came some of the first pastors.

Methodism was established in 1873 by the two large Methodist bodies in the USA. Bishop John Keener of the Southern Church purchased a place for public worship in the same year. The Methodist Episcopal Church (North) began work a year earlier, following a decision by the council of bishops to send William Butler who had already served 17 years in India. In 1873 the Gante Methodist church building in Mexico City was purchased. The MCM was established in 1930; Dr Juan Pascoe, was elected as its first Mexican bishop. Since 1974 bishops are elected every four years. There are at present two episcopal areas: one in the central area and the other in the northern area.

The principal institutions are the Union Theological Seminary; a deaconess school; a Bible institute; a lay school; a hospital; six social centres; four girls' hostels; 12 grammar schools; secondary, junior college, and teacher's school. In a single year, in 1975, the MCM gained 1,000 members.

UNITED STATES OF AMERICA

AFRICAN METHODIST EPISCOPAL CHURCH
P.O. Box 183, St Louis, MO 63166. 2,500,000 members — 3,050 churches — 3,938 ordained clergy. Publications: AME Christian Recorder, AME Review, Voice of Missions, Women's Missionary Magazine, Secret Chamber. WCC (1948), NCCC-USA, CCC, WMC. General Secretary: Dr Richard Allen Chappelle — Treasurer: Dr Joseph C. McKinney, 2311 M Street, NW Washington, DC 20037.

One of the three largest Methodist groups in the United States, this Church began with the withdrawal in 1787 of a number of members in St George's Methodist Episcopal Church in Philadelphia, in protest against what they considered to be the practice of racial discrimination. Social rather than doctrinal issues were behind the break. They built a chapel with the assistance of Bishop William White of the Protestant Episcopal Church. Francis Asbury dedicated their Bethel Chapel in Philadelphia; he also ordained one of their members, Richard Allen, a former slave, as their minister. A 'Free African Society' was founded not only for the worship of God, but also to care for the sick, the poor and the unemployed, and to promote higher intellectual and moral standards.

The Church was formally organized as the African Methodist Episcopal Church in 1816; in the same year Allen was consecrated as its first bishop, again by Bishop Asbury. It was a church confined, in the years preceding the Civil War, to the northern states; following the war its membership increased rapidly in the South, and today it is found all across the nation.

The AMEC has 13 bishops active in 13 districts, and holds a general conference quadrennially. The general board and the council of bishops meet annually. Foreign missions are supported in South Africa, West Africa, India, the Caribbean, and South America. The Church operates Wilberforce University in Ohio, Allen University, SC, Morris Brown University, Georgia, Paul Quinn College, Texas, Edward Waters College, Florida, Daniel Payne College, Alabama, Shorter College, Arkansas, three seminaries, along with one hospital and one publishing house, 15 housing projects for senior citizens and two nursing homes. It also runs 2,550 Sabbath schools with a total enrolment of 105,250.

AFRICAN METHODIST EPISCOPAL ZION CHURCH

1200 Windermere Drive, Pittsburg, PA 15218. 1,500,000 members — 12 episcopal districts — 6,020 churches — 6,716 ordained clergy. Publications: Star of Zion, Quarterly Review, Missionary Seer, Church School Herald. WCC (1948), NCCCUSA, CCC, WMC. President of the Board of Bishops: Bishop J. Clinton Hoggard, 6401 Sunset Lane, Indianapolis, IN 46260 — Secretary: Bishop Charles Herbert Foggie.

This Church dates from 1796 when it was organized by a group of black members protesting against discrimination in the John Street Church in New York City. Their first church, built in 1800, was called Zion; later it became part of the name of the new denomination. The first annual conference was held in this church in 1821 with six black Methodist churches in New Haven, Philadelphia, and Newark, New Jersey, represented by 19 preachers and presided over by the Rev. William Phoebus of the white Methodist Episcopal Church. James Varick, who led John Street dissension, was elected as their first bishop at this conference. The name African Methodist Episcopal Zion Church was approved in 1848.

The AMEZC spread quickly over the northern states; by the time of the general conference of 1880 there were 15 annual conferences in the south. Livingstone College at Salisbury, North Carolina, the largest educational institution of the Church, was established by that conference. Departments of missions, education, and publications were established in 1892; later came administrative boards to direct work in church extension, evangelism, finance, ministerial relief, etc. Home missions are supported in Louisiana, Mississippi, and in several states beyond the Mississippi, principally in Oklahoma. The Church has sent foreign missionaries to Liberia, Ghana, Nigeria, South America and the West Indies.

There are five secondary schools, two colleges (Livingstone, and Clinton Junior College in Rock Hill, SC) and several foreign mission stations under the Church. It also operates 6,018 Sunday or Sabbath schools with a total enrolment of 193,672 children. The next quadrennial general conference will be held in 1984.

AMERICAN BAPTIST CHURCHES IN THE USA

Valley Forge, PA 19481 — Tel: 215.768.2000 — Cable: AMBAPCHUR-KOPR — Telex: 510-660-2443. 1,600,000 members — 5,874 congregations (USA), 8,270 (overseas) — 9,881 pastors (USA) — 16,855 church workers overseas. Publications: The American Baptist Magazine (monthly), The Baptist Leader (monthly), Foundations (quarterly). WCC (1948), NCCCUSA, NABF, BWA. President: Mr John Mandt, 2180 Washington Blvd, Huntington, WV 25705 — General Secretary: Rev. Dr Robert C. Campbell.

The organized existence of the American Baptist Churches in the USA began in 1814 when a national body of Baptists called the Triennial Convention was formed. Its immediate purpose was to support Adoniram and Ann Judson as missionaries to Burma. Later it became the American Baptist Foreign Mission Society (ABFMS). The second society to be founded was the General Tract Society, formed in 1824. This became the American Baptist Publication Society and still later the American Baptist Board of Education and Publication Society (ABBEP). A third society, the American Baptist Home Mission Society (ABHMS) followed in 1832.

Baptist unity in America was first broken in 1845 over the issue of slavery. The Baptists in the south withdrew to organize the Southern Baptist Convention which has 13,379,000 members today. Following the Civil War, ex-slaves both in the north and the south organized their own churches and conventions on both sides of the Mississippi River. Because they were nationwide, they called themselves National Baptist Conventions, of which there are now three: National Baptist Convention of America (1886); National Baptist Convention, USA, Inc. (1895); and Progressive National Baptist Convention, Inc. (1961). After the north-south schism in 1845, the Baptists of the north maintained the societal structure until 1907, when the Northern Baptist Convention was founded, involving participation by the three societies (ABFMS, ABBEP, ABHMS), on a voluntary basis.

A Ministers' and Missionaries' Benefit Board (M&M) was organized in 1913. The Philadelphia Baptist Association and many state and city associations became affiliated with the Northern Baptist Convention, also by voluntary action.

Two parallel women's boards known as the Women's American Baptist Foreign Mission Society (WABFMS) and the Women's American Baptist Home Mission Society (WABHMS) were founded to do work associated with the American Baptist Foreign Mission Society and the American Baptist Home Mission Society. In 1950 the name of the Northern Baptist Convention was changed to American Baptist Convention — to communicate a theological, philosophical and sociological posture of inclusiveness, racially and geographically. In 1972 the directors of the three national societies (ABFMS, ABBEP, ABHMS) were acknowledged to be the boards of the denomination with the following programme designations: ABFMS/WABFMS (Board of International Ministries), ABBEP (Board of Educational Ministries), ABHMS/WABHMS (Board of National Ministries). The Ministers' and Missionaries' Benefit Board continues as a denominational service agency. This new arrangement was called American Baptist Churches in the USA. It gave American Baptist laity more representational control over the denominational mission as expressed through the Boards.

In 1979 the American Baptist Churches in the USA was further reorganized to provide for covenantal relationships among all denominational groupings of churches — region, state, city, and nation-wide. At present the ABC is the most heterogenous communion in the Baptist denomination. It includes Caucasian churches, black American churches, Hispanic, Asian and Native American Indian congregations, and the Convention of Puerto Rican Churches. The ABC maintains a close fraternal relationship with seven conventions and associations of bilingual Baptist churches of nationality groupings from southern and eastern Europe organized as worshipping communities in the United States. There are also close relations with Baptist churches in Burma, India, Japan, Latin America, Philippines, Thailand and Zaire.

The most urgent issues the ABC faces in the 1980s are in the areas of economic justice in a world of limited resources, international stability and national security, peace and justice: nuclear disarmament, ecology, abortion and homosexuality, and equal rights amendment for women. Significant programmes of the Church include evangelism and church growth; understanding international issues and peace education; Christian education for multiplying the number of available leaders; encouraging the responsible witness of the laity in church and community; and ministry with youth and the revitalization of the denominational programmes with teen-age youth and younger college students.

AMERICAN LUTHERAN CHURCH

422 South Fifth Street, Minneapolis, MN 55415 — Tel: 612.330.3100 — Cable: Madakina Minneapolis — Telex: 29-0766-L and M BLTN. 2,352,430 members — 4,860 congregations — 7,018 clergy. Publication: Lutheran Standard. WCC (1960), LCUSA, LWF. Presiding Bishop: David W. Preus.

The Church was formed in 1960 as the result of the merger of three Lutheran bodies:
— the American Lutheran Church, largely of German backgound, which itself had been the product of a merger in 1930 when the Ohio synod (1818), Buffalo synod (1845), Iowa synod (1854), and the Texas synod (1851) came together;
— the Evangelical Lutheran Church, largely of Norwegian background, which had been formed in 1917 through a merger of three synods: the Hauge synod (1846), the United Church (1890), and the Norwegian synod (1853);
— the United Evangelical Lutheran Church, a much smaller body, of Danish background, which had been formed in 1896 through a merger of the "Blair Church" (1884) and the "North Church" (1894).

These bodies were joined in 1962 by the Lutheran Free Church, also a body of Norwegian background.

The Church is the ninth largest Protestant body in the USA. Although its members live in all parts of the country — only three of the 50 states do not have an American Lutheran Church congregation — its strength is concentrated in the Upper Midwest area: 55 per cent of its members are in the five-state area of Minnesota, Iowa, Wisconsin, and North and South Dakota. The American Lutheran Church is generally known as being a 'middle class' church, with its membership drawn largely from people of Scandinavian and German ethnic backgrounds. Although it has traditionally been strong in rural areas, in recent years a decided attempt has been made to reach more people in urban and inner-city areas. A greater effort is also being made to attract blacks, Hispanics and other minority groups. Although the American Lutheran Church is generally not given to making strong 'official' statements on social issues, it has addressed numerous statements on social issues to its own members, encouraging them to take an active part in political life. Issues that have been addressed include abortion, marriage and divorce, religion in the public schools, stewardship of the land, race relations, South African apartheid, etc.

For a number of years now the American Lutheran Church has been greatly concerned about its declining membership, and it has designated the 1980s as a decade of evangelism in both its broad and narrow senses. The ALC continues to see its main mission as bringing people to Christ, and nourishing and nurturing them with his word so that they may become living members of the body of Christ. The good news of the gospel, the evangel, however, also includes the good news that God wants justice for the people of the world. Therefore, a part of the evangelistic emphasis will also be "teaching them to observe all that I have commanded you". Major future programmes are: (1) nurture: to assist congregations in the nurture of their members so that the Christian faith may be expressed in congregational life and mission; (2) outreach: to make the gospel known throughout the nation and in all areas of the world through the establishment of centres of ministry for the proclamation and demonstration of the word and the celebration of the sacraments; (3) justice and wholeness: to demonstrate the wholeness of the gospel by seeking justice for all persons, by caring for those in need, and by working against the forces which deny health and freedom to people; (4) leadership development: to provide skilled consecrated women and men, both lay and clergy, for ministry in church and society; (5) working together — mutuality of mission: to organize and develop the union of congregations — the ALC — to focus resources on mission.

The ALC maintains particular relations with Lutheran churches in Brazil, Cameroon, Central African Republic, Colombia, Ethiopia, Hong Kong, India, Japan, Madagascar, Mexico, Nigeria, Papua New Guinea, South Africa, Taiwan and Tanzania.

ANTIOCHIAN ORTHODOX CHRISTIAN ARCHDIOCESE OF NEW YORK AND ALL NORTH AMERICA

358 Mountain Road, Englewood, NJ 07631 — Tel: 201.871.1355. 152,000 members — 130 parishes — 2 bishops — 200 priests and deacons. Publication: The World Magazine (in English). WCC (1948), NCCCUSA, SCOBA. Primate: Most Rev. Metropolitan Archbishop Philip (Saliba).

Since the late 1800s, a great many members of the Greek Orthodox Patriarchate of Antioch and All the East have emigrated to different parts of the world. The spiritual needs of those who went to North America were first served through the Syro-Arabian Mission of the Russian Orthodox Church, established in 1892. In 1895 a Syrian Orthodox Benevolent Society was organized by immigrants in New York.

Father Raphael established the first Syrian Greek Orthodox parish in Manhattan, New York. Six years later, in 1902, a larger church building was bought, and consecrated by Bishop Tikhon. 'Bishop of Brooklyn', as he was later called, Bishop Raphael travelled through the country and established new parishes. With the death of Bishop Raphael in 1915, and the chaos in church administration caused by the Bolshevik revolution in Russia, Orthodoxy in North America became disunited. It was not until 1975 that the total jurisdictional and administrative unity was restored among the people of the Antiochian Patriarchate in North America. Metropolitan Philip was recognized as primate and Archbishop Michael as the auxiliary of the one Antiochian Orthodox Christian Archdiocese of North America.

The general assembly of the archdiocese meets biennially. A board of trustees and the Metropolitan's advisory council meet regularly to assist the primate in the administration of the archdiocese.

Departments and commissions of the Church include missionary activity and community development, press and media relations, spiritual vocations, continuing pastoral education, lay ministry, stewardship, inter-Orthodox and interfaith relations, liturgies, sacred music, and administrative duties. Students are educated at St Vladimir's Orthodox Theological Seminary in Crestwood, New York, and at the Holy Cross Orthodox School of Theology in Brookline, Massachusetts. Postgraduate studies are provided at the archdiocesan clergy symposia, held biennially. Each summer six regional parish life conferences are convened which attract many people of all ages.

Three service organizations exist on local, regional and archdiocesan levels: the Society of Orthodox Youth Organizations (SOYO), the Antiochian Orthodox Christian Women of North America (AOCWNA), and the Order of Saint Ignatius of Antioch. In 1978, the archdiocese acquired the Antiochian village — a camp and conference centre located near Ligonier in southwestern Pennsylvania. There are plans for the establishment here of a retreat and learning centre, a retirement village and a monastery.

CHRISTIAN CHURCH (DISCIPLES OF CHRIST) IN THE UNITED STATES

222 South Downey Avenue, P.O. Box 1986, Indianapolis, IN 46206 Tel: 317.353.1491 — Cable: "Go" — Telex: 810.341.3193. 1,217,750 members — 4,362 parishes and congregations — 6,578 pastors. Publications: The Disciple (bimonthly), Mid-Stream: an Ecumenical Journal (quarterly), Yearbook of the Christian Church (annually) WCC (1948), NCCCUSA, CCC, WCCC. General Minister and President: Rev. Dr Kenneth L. Teegarden — Rev. Dr Paul A. Crow, Jr.

The Christian Church (Disciples of Christ) was established on the American frontier in the early 1800s through the coming together of two movements: the "Christians" who were associated with Barton W. Stone in Kentucky, and the "Disciples" who were associated with Thomas and Alexander Campbell in western Pennsylvania. Both groups were established as Christian unity movements, seeking to overcome the historic divisions transplanted from Europe and the British Isles to the North American continent, through an appeal to the restoration of the New Testament faith. In 1832, representatives of the two groups came together in Lexington, Kentucky, to form a single movement with a strong evangelistic witness and committed to weekly celebration of the Lord's Supper, to a rational faith, to a congregational leadership, and to Christian unity expressed in freedom and diversity.

The Christian Church has a total membership of 1.2 million. It is listed as the tenth largest mainline Protestant Church in the United States. Its membership also includes 4,000 Disciples in Canada. As a mainline Protestant church in the North American context, much of the life of the Christian Church is focused upon the broad societal and international issues facing all Christians and churches. Wherever possible and appropriate, the programmes of the Church are carried out through ecumenical channels and organizations.

At its 1981 general assembly, the Church adopted the following priorities as expressions of concerns of "vital importance to the whole church, meriting first attention," to be "proclaimed by its leadership and addressed by its general administrative units, regions and congregations as priorities during the 1982-1985 quadrennium:

A. Pursue peace with justice

The biblical imperative of peace, along with the justice that makes it possible, is at the heart of the Christian gospel. Making peace and therefore being among the blessed is a teaching of Jesus that applies in the congregation, in the region, in the nation, in the world. It is inextricably interwoven with hunger and human rights concerns and is linked to a congregation's life and witness. It means dealing with questions of control of nuclear power, armaments, peace-keeping mechanisms based on the equality and oneness of nations under God, crime, injustice, systemic violence, revolution, freedom, racism, discrimination, and economic inequality. World peace is a new prerequisite for any improvement in the living conditions of the world's people and new redemptive ministries in pursuit of peace are a priority for the church.

B. Reach out globally to alleviate hunger and extend human rights

Life, the most fundamental of human rights, daily is either spoiled or stopped by hunger. The Church is attacking hunger and its causes, but can do more. Other scourges of humanity include repressive governments, exploitative systems, greed, brutality, racism, selfishness and ignorance. Wars, disaster, poverty and persecution smother hope under fear and despair. In the face of such threats worldwide, a continuing priority of the Church is to witness wisely and courageously to its Lord in word and deed.

C. Renew congregational life and witness

Renewed vitality with a rebirth of faith and spirit, rooted in the biblical tradition, though not exclusively a local matter, surely depends on fresh life in congregations. The spark might come from education, effective leadership, ecumenical endeavours, social involvement, personal witness and evangelism, and establishment of new congregations. Enlivening congregations is a continuing priority involving both the Church's innermost being and its outward expressions.''

CHRISTIAN METHODIST EPISCOPAL CHURCH

11470 Northway Drive, St Louis, MO 63136 — Tel.: 314.741.5837. 700,000 members — 1,159 churches — 1,169 ordained clergy. Publications: Christian Index, Eastern Index, Missionary Messenger, Western Index. WCC (1948), NCCCUSA, CCC, WMC. Senior Bishop: Bishop E.P. Murchison — Secretary: Rev. N. Charles Thomas, P.O. Box 74, Memphis, TN 38101.

Known until 1954 as the Coloured Methodist Episcopal Church, this Church was established in the south in an amicable agreement between white and black members of the Methodist Episcopal Church, South. There were at the time at least 225,000 slave members in the Methodist Episcopal Church, South, but with the emancipation proclamation, all but 80,000 of these joined the two independent black bodies. When the general conference of the Methodist Episcopal Church, South, met at New Orleans in 1866, a commission from the black membership expressed the desire to have a separate church of their own. The request was granted, and in 1870 the Coloured Methodist Episcopal Church was organized. They kept this name until the meeting of their general conference at Memphis in May 1954, when it was decided to change it to the Christian Methodist Episcopal Church.

Their doctrine is the doctrine of the parent church; this denomination adds a local church conference to the quarterly, district, annual, and general conferences usual in Methodism. Seven boards supervise the national work, each presided over by a bishop assigned as chairman by the college of bishops. The general secretaries of the various departments are elected every four years by the general conference.

The CMEC sponsors five colleges: Lane College of Jackson, Tennessee; Mississippi Industrial College; Miles College of Birmingham, Alabama; Texas College of Tyler; and Paine College of Augusta, Georgia. Its theological seminary is the Philipps School of Theology of the Interdenominational Theological Center of Atlanta, Georgia. It has 1,057 Sunday schools with a total enrolment of 47,940.

CHURCH OF THE BRETHREN

1451 Dundee Avenue, Elgin, IL 60120 — Tel: 312.742.5100. 194,820 members — 1,061 parishes — 1,911 pastors. Publication: Messenger (monthly). WCC (1948), NCCCUSA. General Secretary: Dr Robert W. Neff.

The Church of the Brethren had its beginnings in 1708, with a church of eight persons in Schwarzenau, Germany. Persecuted, and driven from central Germany into Holland and Northern Germany, one group of the church in Krefeld, Germany, under the leadership of Peter Becker, went to America in 1719 to settle on lands offered free to them by William Penn. They settled in Germantown, near Philadelphia, where they were joined in 1729 by 59 families brought across the Atlantic by Alexander Mack. From Pennsylvania they spread across the country.

Their German speech, their opposition to war, and their emphasis that the inner Christian life is more important than church organization made them suspect from the start. They were opposed to the Revolution on moral grounds; in the Civil War they opposed slavery. The suspicion and misunderstanding subsided gradually; today historians are generous in their praise of the contributions of the Brethren to American democracy. The work of pacifist groups in the Church, the Second World War and their outstanding efforts in relief work in Europe after the War have won for them an honoured place in American Protestantism. In the early years at Germantown the first German Bible in America was made available in 1743 by Christopher Saur I, a friend of the Brethren, and the first religious magazine was launched in 1764 by Christopher Saur II, a Brethren elder.

Overseas churches that were started as the result of missionary activity in Ecuador, Nigeria, and India are now part of autonomous churches in those countries, but the church maintains a cooperative relationship with them.

In doctrine the Church follows the mainstream of Protestant theology, with considerable freedom of thought and great emphasis on practical biblical piety. Its practical teaching is summarized in the following divisions: (1) the doctrine of peace, including refusal to go to war, and a positive peace-making programme that makes members more than war resisters; (2) the doctrine of temperance, under which total abstinence is practised; (3) the doctrine of the simple life, under which unwholesome amusements and luxuries are shunned, and a practical, wholesome, temperate, clean way of personal and family life is stressed; (4) the doctrine of brotherhood, under which all class distinctions are opposed as un-Christian; and (5) the doctrine that religion means loving and willing obedience to Christ rather than obedience to creeds and cults. Christian living is stressed above all else. Baptism is by trine immersion; the love feast is observed, following the pattern of John 13:1-7.

Moderators, lay or clerical, men or women, resident or non-resident, are in charge of local congregations, which enjoy a great deal of autonomy. Pastors are chosen by the local congregation. Above the local groups in the district (there are 24) and the annual conference (a legislative body composed of delegates from the churches and an "upper house" known as the standing committee, made up of delegates from the districts). The annual conference is the overall unifying body.

A general board, composed of 25 members elected by the annual conference, supervises the general church programme, and administers the overseas church programme. It represents the Church in the field of social education, social action, relief and rehabilitation, and carries on a worldwide programme of peace and human welfare. The programme includes a volunteer service in America and abroad for hundreds of young men and women, including conscientious objectors. It supervises church schools, weekday religious education, and summer camps and is loosely related to higher education in six colleges.

EPISCOPAL CHURCH
Episcopal Church Center, 815 Second Avenue, New York, NY 10017 — Tel: 212.867.8400 — Cable: Fenalong, NY. 3,095,080 members — 119 dioceses — 7,417 congregations — 12,978 priests. Publications: Journal of the General Convention, The Episcopalian, The Living Church, The Episcopal Church Annual. WCC (1948), NCCCUSA, ACC. Presiding Bishop: Rt Rev. John M. Allin, D.D. — Ecumenical Officer: Rev. William Norgren.

The origins of the Episcopal Church in the United States of America go back to the British colonial period at the beginning of the 17th century. The Church was an English community, its clergy supported by public tax and by contributions from the Church of England through the Society for the Propagation of the Gospel, and technically under the jurisdiction of the bishop of London. Ministers had to journey to England for receiving ordination, and few could afford it. The limitations of dependence and distance, coupled with the rising tide of the American Revolution, made difficult the situation of the colonial Church of England. Yet membership grew rapidly.

With the outbreak of the Civil War, there was further division in the major Protestant Episcopal Church. A dispute rising out of the Oxford Movement in England resulted in the separation of a group into the Reformed Episcopal Church in 1873, but otherwise Episcopal unity held fast. The Church's mission in the later part of the 19th century was westward in the United States. Overseas mission entered the picture in the 19th century. Overseas work resulted in churches in the Orient, Latin

America, and one diocese in Liberia, some of which have now achieved autonomy.

The Episcopal form of government closely parallels that of the federal government. It is a federal union, now consisting of 119 dioceses, each autonomous in its own sphere, associated originally for the maintenance of common doctrine, discipline, and worship, to which have been added church unity, development and the prosecution of missionary, educational and social programmes on a national scale.

The Church accepts two creeds: the Apostles' and the Nicene. Some Episcopalians are high church people with elaborate ritual and ceremony; other are described as low church people, with more of an evangelistic emphasis. The primary concerns of the Church are missionary — that is, to restore all people to unity with God and one another in Christ. It pursues mission through prayer, worship, proclaiming the gospel, and promoting justice, peace and love. For these purposes it seeks to equip all its members for ministry. The tasks of ecumenism are being stressed in particular, as are issues of hunger, peace, development and ethnic concerns in urban areas. An effective intercommunion has been established among the Anglican, Old Catholic, Polish National Catholic and Philippine Independent Churches, which may prove a first step towards a merger of these bodies.

HUNGARIAN REFORMED CHURCH IN AMERICA

9901 Allen Road, Allen Park, MI 48101. 11,110 members — 40 parishes — 36 pastors. Publication: Mayar Church (monthly) WCC (1948), NCCCUSA, WARC. Rt Rev. Dezso Abraham.

In 1921, the Reformed Church of Hungary transferred its two American classes to the Reformed Church in the United States (later the Evangelical and Reformed Church, and now the United Church of Christ). But certain Hungarian Reformed congregations which refused to accept the Tiffin Agreement concluded between the mother Church in Hungary and the Reformed Church in the US, organized an independent body called the Free Magyar Reformed Church in America on 9 December 1924. There were at that time only six congregations and five ministers.

The Free Magyar Reformed Church emphasized its confessional heritage — for example the Second Helvetic Confession and the Heidelberg Catechism — as the time-honoured basis for the Hungarian Reformed Tradition. One of its objections to the acceptance of the Tiffin Agreement was doctrinal. The Church, of which the other Hungarian congregations had become a part, did not have the second Helvetic Confession as a doctrinal basis. The Free Magyar Reformed Church also emphasized the voluntary church membership principle. The Church developed a mission programme which resulted in the growth of new congregations in many parts of the United States. In 1958, it changed its name to the Hungarian Reformed Church in America.

The church's polity is a combination of Episcopal and Presbyterian elements developed in Hungary in the 18th century. It is made up of three classes — New York, Eastern and Western which form a diocese headed by an elected bishop and a lay curator. There are congregations in ten states: Connecticut, New York, New Jersey, Pennsylvania, Ohio, Michigan, Florida, Kansas, Colorado and California. There are also two congregations in Ontario, Canada.

INTERNATIONAL EVANGELICAL CHURCH

610 Rhode Island Avenue NE, Washington, DC 20002 — Tel: 202.635.8000. 168,100 members — 459 parishes — 646 pastors. Publications: Redemption Faith (in English), Evangel (in English), New Life (in Portuguese). WCC (1972). President: Dr John L. Meares — Bishop Robert McAlister, Caixa Postal 2734, Rio de Janeiro, Brazil 20.000 — Bishop Benson Idahosa, Box 60, Benin City, Nigeria — Rev. Silvano Lilli, Via Appio Claudia 248, Rome, Italy 00174.

The International Evangelical Church was originally known as the International Evangelical Church and Missionary Association. It was chartered to meet the needs of a missionary ministry in Italy which had begun to grow to proportions that called for the structure of a local church. Dr John McTernan founded the International Evangelical Church and Missionary Association. Around the year 1968, quite a number of churches in Italy were a part of that fellowship. Several churches in the United States became a part of the International Evangelical Church and Missionary Association. It reached out and included a group of churches in Brazil under the leadership of Bishop Robert McAlister. About six years ago, there was a revival movement in Nigeria, which was so successful that it had to structure some meaningful on-going care for its many converts. This is headed by Rev. Benson Idahosa of Nigeria.

Nigeria is by far the largest constituency. In Brazil, there are churches in several of the cities, but it is principally centred in the sprawling city of Rio. There are some 17 churches in Rio alone with an average strength of 1,000 people in each. In Italy, church growth is slow. In the USA, there are seven or eight churches ranging in membership from 150 to about 2,500 in size.

In these various nations there are various needs peculiar to the people. For example, in Nigeria thousands of people who are ministered to are illiterate. So the Church has a strong teaching programme. It is establishing schools to educate and train them as well as to minister to their spiritual needs. There is also a strong emphasis on ministering to the physical needs of the people in Nigeria. This is also the case in Brazil. Presently, there is a home being built for elderly people.

The IEC believes that the gospel of the kingdom changes people and motivates them to change their environment. When people really have a meaningful confrontation with the Lord Jesus Christ and come to experience conversion, a strong motivating force arises and brings about radical changes socially, economically and morally.

The Church feels called to assist those in the cities of the USA who are disenfranchized, who drop out of school at a young age and do not belong. Scholarships are provided to enable a number of people to continue their education. Fifteen young people from Nigeria have been received in the USA for higher education. Other church programmes accentuate family life and community involvement.

LUTHERAN CHURCH IN AMERICA
231 Madison Avenue, New York, NY 10016 — Tel: 212.481.8552 — Cable: 'Lutheran' New York. 3,045,380 members — 6,130 parishes — 8,629 pastors. Publication: The Lutheran. WCC (1962), NCCCUSA, LCUSA, LWF. Bishop: Rev. Dr James Crumley — Director for Ecumenical Relations: Dr William G. Rusch.

The Lutheran Church in America was organized in 1962. It grew out of four bodies: the Augustana Lutheran Church (founded in 1860, of Swedish origin); the American Evangelical Lutheran Church (founded in 1872, of Danish origin); the Finnish Evangelical Lutheran Church, or the Suomi Synod (founded in 1890); and the United Lutheran Church in America (founded in 1918 by a merger of church bodies whose antecedents can be traced back to the work of Henry Melchior Muhlenberg and the formation of the Ministerium of North America in 1748). The background of LCA members includes German, Swedish, Danish, Finnish, Norwegian, Icelandic, Slovak, Hungarian, French, Anglo-Saxon, American Indian, African, and Asian ancestries. The congregations are spread across all fifty states of the USA; there are congregations in the Caribbean area as well as in all nine provinces of Canada. Besides pastors and teachers, a large corps of women workers is active in the church. Since 1970 the LCA has ordained women, and today there are over thirty in congregational and other ministries. The LCA organization is synodical, with presbyterial and congregational elements shaping the form of its government and local life.

The Church is the largest Lutheran Church in North America, slightly larger than the American Lutheran Church and the Lutheran Church-Missouri Synod. The Lutheran Church in America is however smaller than the Roman Catholic Church in the US and the United Methodist Church and the total number of Jewish congregations in the US.

The LCA relates to its social setting through the work of church-wide agencies which include the Division for Mission in North America, Division for Parish Services, Division for Professional Leadership and the Division for World Mission and Ecumenism. The LCA sees itself as a global and ecumenical church with an inter-relationship between its life on the North American continent and the life of the church around the world. Through a number of social statements the LCA has addressed itself to such issues as aging, capital punishment, human rights, race relations, religious liberty and world community. The Church's primary concerns in the 1980s include the possibility of a Lutheran merger involving the American Lutheran Church, the Association of Evangelical Lutheran Churches and the Lutheran Church in America; continuing involvement in the ecumenical movement, leading to new formal relationships with other Christians in North America; and continuing concern for a just society. The LCA has historical relations with Lutheran churches in India, Liberia, Guyana, Argentina, Japan, Taiwan, Hong Kong, Singapore and Tanzania. There are ongoing missions with Lutheran churches in Chili, Peru, Uruguay and four Protestant churches in Indonesia.

MORAVIAN CHURCH IN AMERICA (NORTHERN PROVINCE)

69 West Church Street, Bethlehem, PA 18018 — Tel: 215.867.7566. 34,280 members — 105 parishes — 130 pastors. Publications: North American Moravian (monthly), Moravian Daily Texts (annu-

ally). WCC (1948), NCCCUSA. President: Rev. Dr John S. Groenfeldt.

The Moravian Church comes out of the Hussite movement in Bohemia-Moravia in the 15th century. Following the Counter-Reformation the Protestants of that region were given the choice of becoming Roman Catholics or leaving the country. In the 16th century many did leave. Others stayed, outwardly conforming to Roman Catholic practice but secretly reading their Bible and worshipping as Protestants. In the early 18th century a small group of these people learned that they could obtain a certain degree of religious freedom on the estate of a young Pietistic nobleman in German Saxony, named Count Zinzendorf. Zinzendorf had himself taken orders as a Lutheran clergyman, but through his family and his own personal conviction was closely associated with the Pietistic movement. He welcomed the refugees, hoping that they could help him in his desire to bring a new sense of dedication and personal commitment to the established church of Saxony and all of Germany. The Germans referred to the newcomers as "Moravians", from the land of their origin, and the name continued in use in English-speaking lands.

On the continent of Europe the community operates more as a spiritual fellowship and a mission society within the principal churches of the land than as a separate denomination. Elsewhere it is a separate Protestant denomination. The doctrinal position is not substantially different from the Lutheran and Reformed traditions, with which it has close and cordial relationships. The Pietistic heritage is seen in the continued Christ-centred emphasis of the Moravian Church and in its zeal for evangelistic outreach, particularly in the area of bringing the gospel to the most needy sectors of society. Its main doctrinal emphasis may be said to be centred on the love of God manifested in the redemptive life and death of Jesus, the inner testimony of the Spirit, and Christian conduct in everyday affairs.

The Moravian Church continues to place great importance on missionary outreach as an essential part of its calling, as well as on the individual commitment (which Zinzendorf called 'heart-religion') of those who take the name of Christ and call themselves Christians. Worldwide, the Moravian Church is now two-thirds non-white. There are more Moravians in Tanzania than in any other single country. Thus the Church, even though relatively small in numbers, includes people of many races and cultures. The primary concern of the Moravian Church in the decade of the 1980s is to be true to its historic commitment to Jesus Christ as Lord and Saviour, and to share this faith widely with others. The Moravian Church in North America, Northern Province, has designated the 1980s as a decade of development. This refers to the development of the internal life of the Church, the renewed dedication of all its members, and its ministry of outreach both at home and abroad. The emphasis on church growth that has had a prominent place in the life of the Church in recent years is one phase of this decade of development. The Church also maintains a broad ecumenical interest, in the tradition of Zinzendorf who was indeed an ecumenical pioneer.

MORAVIAN CHURCH IN AMERICA (SOUTHERN PROVINCE)

Drawer O, Salem Station, Winston-Salem, NC 27108 — Tel: 919.725.5811. 21,060 members — 53 parishes (including two mission churches) — 78 pastors. Publications: North American Moravian (monthly), Moravian Daily Texts (annual). WCC (1948), NCCCUSA. President: Dr Richard F. Amos.

The Moravian Church in the United States is divided into two provinces, Northern and Southern. Congregations are grouped into provinces and district synods. The highest administrative body in each province is the provincial synod. Composed of ministers and lay people, and meeting every five years, it directs missionary, educational and publishing work,

and elects a provincial elders' conference, or executive board, which functions between synod meetings. Bishops are elected by provincial and general synods. They are spiritual, not administrative, leaders in the Church.

For further information, see Moravian Church in America (Northern Province).

NATIONAL BAPTIST CONVENTION OF AMERICA

954 Kings Rd, Jacksonville, FL 32204. 3,500,000 members — 11,398 parishes — 7,598 pastors. WCC (1955), NCCCUSA, BWA. President: Rev. Dr James C. Sams.

The first black Baptist church in America was organized at Silver Bluff across the Savannah River from Augusta, Georgia, in 1773; other churches followed in Petersburg, Virginia (1776); Richmond, Virginia (1780); Williamsburg, Virginia (1785); Savannah, Georgia (1785); and Lexington, Kentucky (1790).

As early as 1700, white slave-holders in the South were providing religious teaching and places of worship for their slaves; at least most of them did not discourage religious practices. As a rule, however, the black slave sat in the gallery of the white church, identified with the faith of his owner. White ministers, sometimes assisted by black helpers, moved from one plantation to another, holding services more or less regularly; occasionally a black minister was liberated so that he could give full time to religious work among his people. These ministers had great influence; they were consulted by the whites as the respected leaders of their people and were a real power up to the time of the slave rebellion of 1831 led by Nat Turner. For a period following this disturbance it was illegal in some sections of the South for blacks to become Christians or to build meeting houses.

The first black Baptist association, the Providence Baptist Association of Ohio, was formed in 1836; the first attempt at national organization came in 1880 with the creation of the Foreign Mission Baptist

Convention at Montgomery, Alabama. In 1886 the American National Baptist Convention was organized at St Louis, and in 1893 the Baptist National Educational Convention was organized in the District of Columbia. All three conventions were merged into the National Baptist Convention of America at Atlanta in 1895.

Black Baptist doctrine is similar to that of white Baptist churches, though it is a little more Calvinistic. Local churches unite in associations, usually along state lines, for the purpose of fellowship and consultation. There are also state conventions concerned with missionary work, often extending beyond state bounderies. The Church's missionary work continues in Sinoe (Liberia), Jamaica, the West Indies and in the Bahama Islands.

affiliated churches. A board of directors is responsible for the business of the convention between the sessions.

In conjuntcion with the Southern Baptist Convention, the NBC, Inc. operates the American Baptist Theological Seminary in Nashville, Tennessee. It also runs a number of other schools and colleges. It promotes its denomination-wide programme by employing field workers, who serve on a full-time basis for the duration of the cause being promoted.

The old conflict between the National Baptist Convention of America and the National Baptist Convention, USA, Inc. is no longer a serious issue, but no reunion has yet been achieved. Moves have been made, however, towards the union of the National Baptist Convention, USA, Inc. with the American Baptist Convention.

NATIONAL BAPTIST CONVENTION, USA, Inc.

405 E. 31st Street, Chicago, IL 60616. 6,500,000 members — 26,000 parishes — 27,000 pastors. Publication: National Baptist Voice (semi-monthly). WCC (1948), NCCCUSA, BWA. President: Rev. Dr Joseph H. Jackson.

This Church is the parent convention of Negro Baptists. It is to be distinguished from the National Baptist Convention of America, usually referred to as the 'unincorporated' body.

In 1915 a division arose in the National Baptist Convention of America over the adoption of a charter and the ownership of a publishing house. The groups rejecting the charter continued to function as the National Baptist Convention of America, while the group accepting the charter became known as the National Baptist Convention of the USA, Incorporated (incorporated, that is, under the laws of the District of Columbia).

The Convention meets in annual session, usually in September. It may also hold an adjourned session between the regular sessions. Up to 5,000 persons register to attend the session, principally ministers from

NATIONAL COUNCIL OF COMMUNITY CHURCHES

89 East Wilson Bridge Road, Worthington, Ohio 43085 — Tel: 614.888.4501. 153,500 members — 204 congregations — 228 pastors. Publication: The Christian Community. WCC (1974), NCCCUSA, COCU. Executive Director: Dr J. Ralph Shotwell — Moderator of Ecumenical Relations: Dr Robert H. Taylor, 157 Porter NE, Warren, Ohio.

The National Council of Community Churches is comprised of locally autonomous congregations voluntarily covenanting together to share with each other the spirit of Christ as they understand it in their local churches. It came into being in 1950 with the merging of the International Council of Community Churches (organized in 1946) and the Biennial Council of Community Churches (organized in the 1930s). The first was predominantly white and the second predominantly black. While preserving their own autonomy in their local congregations these churches agree to representation in ecumenical councils and to concerted action.

The NCC is directly related to each community in which its local congregations are located and encourages each local church to take an active part in all ecumenical affairs within its community. It seeks to encourage every local church to share its faith with other Christians and people of other faiths. Its stance is that of representing ecumenical Christian religion in the local community. In concert with other mainline religious bodies it seeks to bring the light of Christian faith to bear upon all problems of society, political, social, cultural, etc. Its concept of the "people of God being one in the place where they are" is of great influence in drawing people of different backgrounds together in action to build the good community. Because it was the first significant merger of predominantly white and predominantly black religious bodies (1950) it has always had as one of its major emphases the overcoming of racism. The NCCC does not have its separate "missions" or "outreach" programmes or insitutions but encourages its member congregations to support interdenominational mission programmes or those of other religious bodies.

The NCCC sees racism as one of the major issues it must tackle, along with combating all forms of prejudice, organized and individual. Another of the issues which is considered primary at the present time is that of nuclear armaments and the growing threat of war. Poverty and its effect on people are yet other issues. The application of Christian principles and the Christian faith on these problems is a central concern. Along with these is the emphasis the Council has always laid on ecumenicity, both locally and worldwide.

Increased effectiveness of the Church in local life as well as international life is sought to be promoted through annual conferences in which representatives of the churches come together to offer mutual support and encouragement. Among other major efforts are the upgrading of educational background for its ministers and lay people and the interpreting of ecumenism and the work of the World Council of Churches.

ORTHODOX CHURCH IN AMERICA

Rte 25A, Box 675, Syosset, NY 11791. 1,000,000 members — 440 parishes — 457 priests. Publications: The Orthodox Church (monthly), The Orthodox Herald (monthly), Russian Orthodox Journal (monthly), Yearbook and Church Directory, St Vladimir's Theological Quarterly (all publications in English). WCC (1951), NCCCUSA. His Beatitude Theodosius, Archbishop of New York and Metropolitan of All America and Canada.

The OCA was born in 1794 in Alaska when missionaries came over from the monastery of Valamo in Russian Finland. One of the first missionaries was St Herman, who was also the first to be canonized by the American church. The mission was supported by the Russian Orthodox Church. Churches were already in existence in California by 1812, and in 1858 a bishop's seat was established at Sitka, Alaska. In 1900 the diocese of the Aleutian Islands and Alaska, which had been formed in 1870, became the diocese of the Aleutian Islands and North America.

By the turn of the century there were quite a number of Orthodox Christians on the mainland of the United States, a great many of whom had previously been Uniates. In 1900 many of the texts for public worship were translated into English. Then in 1905-06 the American Archbishop Tikhon, later Patriarch of Moscow, demanded self-government for the church in America and insisted on both the adoption of the new calendar and the use of English in public worship. The Russian Revolution of 1917 had a deeply unsettling effect on the Orthodox Church in America, which was still formally a diocese of the Russian Church. Confusion reigned, authority was undermined, and the seminaries were closed; political emigrants began to arrive, among them a number of the hierarchy and the clergy. In 1921, for the first time different Orthodox ecclesiastical jurisdictions appeared within the same geographical area. In addition to the Russians, there were the other Orthodox, who were divided among themselves according to national and political affiliations and attitudes. In 1931 the Moscow Patriarchate demanded political submission to the USSR as a condition of the restoration of church relations with the metropolitan see. This was a condition which could not be accepted. During the 1940s the Russian church outside Russia came to America. The metropolitan see tolerated its presence but did not unite with it, stressing rather its own consciousness of itself as an American church.

The struggle over the identity and the the unity of American Orthodoxy lasted until 1970. The Russian Orthodox Church granted complete self-government to the metropolitan see whereby it unequivocally became the fourteenth autocephalous Orthodox church in the world. Its jurisdiction extends over the whole of America and Canada, and in 1972 an exarchate was established in Mexico.

The holy synod, to which all diocesan bishops in office belong and which is presided by the Archbishop of New York, meets twice a year, in spring and autumn. When necessary a special session can be convened. In addition there is a lesser synod, of which the Archbishop of New York is the president and to which at least three bishops belong. It can be authorized by the synod to make provisional decisions about specified matters. Priests are educated at St Vladimir's Orthodox Theological Seminary in Crestwood, Tuckahoe, NY, and in St Tikhon's Orthodox Theological Seminary in South Canaan, PA. There are the following monasteries: the Monastery of St Tikhon, South Canaan, PA (1906); the Hermitage of St Eugen the Martyr, Inverness Park, Point Reyes Station, CA (1951); the Monastery of the Ascension, Sifton, Manitoba, Canada; the Orthodox Convent of the Assumption of Our Lady in Calistoga, CA (1942); and the Monastery of the Transfiguration in Ellwood City, PA.

POLISH NATIONAL CATHOLIC CHURCH (Polsko-Narodowy Katolicki Kóściól)

1002 Pittston Avenue, Scranton, PA 18505 — Tel: 717.346.9131 and 717.344.0916. 100,000 members — 5 dioceses — 153 con-gregations — 6 bishops — 126 priests. Publications: Rola Boza (God's Field) and Straz (The Guard, both in Polish and English). WCC (1948), NCCCUSA. Prime Bishop: Most Rev. Francis C. Rowinski.

The Polish National Catholic Church was formed in the USA at the beginning of the 20th century as a result of administrative conflicts between a number of Polish immigrants and the Roman Catholic hierarchy. "Independent" Catholic congregations were established at Chicago, Illinois, and Buffalo, New York, in 1895 by those Poles who demanded a greater role in the management of church properties. Such congregations also emerged in response to the policies of enforced "Americanization" followed by the hierarchy. One dissident leader, Rev. Antoni Kozlowski of Chicago, gained the support of European Old Catholics, who elevated him to the episcopate in 1897. Bishop Kozlowski's "Polish Catholic Church" tried unsuccessfully to establish intercommunion with the Episcopal Church. By the time of his death in 1907, Bishop Kozlowski's church had dwindled considerably in membership.

Much more successful was another dissident leader, Rev. Franciszek Hodur (1866-1953). More daring and radical, Mr Hodur organized an "independent" Catholic congregation at Scranton, Pennsylvania, in 1897, and was excommunicated in 1898. He not only sought administrative reform but also tried to advance the lot of his followers socially and politically. One major innovation was the introduction of a Polish-language liturgy in 1901.

The European Old Catholics consecrated Rev. Franciszek Hodur as bishop in 1907, and the movement spread rapidly. Between 1916 and 1926, the Polish National Catholic Church (PNCC) grew to include 91 parishes with over 61,000 members. By 1936 the PNCC had 118 congregations, and by 1951 156 parishes. With growth came major doctrinal and disciplinary changes, the most significant being the declaration that the "Word of God" is a sacrament (along with the traditional sacraments), the rejection of the doctrine of eternal punishment in favour of a theory of restorationism *(apocatastasis)*, and the abolition of mandatory clerical celibacy. The PNCC however remained essentially Catholic in liturgy and worship. It also spread to Canada and Poland. After the Second World War, the PNCC in Poland became administratively autonomous and changed its name to the Polish Catholic Church.

Following Bishop Hodur's death, the PNCC became more conservative both theologically and liturgically. Church leaders have placed more emphasis on ties with the Old Catholics and on the PNCC's affinities with Catholic Christianity at large. For example, the PNCC had established intercommunion with the Episcopal Church in 1946 but terminated this relationship in 1978 after the latter decided to admit women to the priesthood.

Numerically the PNCC is small in comparison with other American denominations. It continues to see itself as a vehicle for the preservation of Polish culture in American society. Younger members, however, increasingly stress that the PNCC must reach out to people regardless of their ethnic identity. More attention is being devoted to work with the younger generation, and recent years have witnessed several concerted attempts to improve the level of catechetical instruction. Important reforms are currently taking place in the fields of musiç and liturgy. While most of its major concerns are therefore largely internal, the PNCC nonetheless remains committed to the ecumenical movement in the sense that it favours all attempts to bring about greater understanding and cooperation.

PRESBYTERIAN CHURCH IN THE UNITED STATES

341 Ponce de Leon Avenue NE, Atlanta, GA 30365 — Tel: 404.873.1531. 1,700,000 members — 4,159 congregations — 5,631 pastors. Publications: Presbyterian Survey, This Week. WCC (1948), NCCCUSA, WARC. Stated Clerk of the General Assembly: Rev. James E. Andrews.

The Presbyterian Church in the United States came into separate existence in 1861, as a result of tensions connected with the American Civil War and the termination of Negro slavery. The congregations of the denomination today are located in the south-eastern part of the United States, in general south of the Ohio River and extending as far west as Texas, Oklahoma, and eastern Kansas. The major denominational offices are located in the Presbyterian Center in Atlanta, which houses the staff of the General Assembly Mission Board, the Council on Theology and Culture, the Board of Annuities and Relief, the Office of Review and Evaluation, the Board of Publications, and the Office of the Stated Clerk.

The Presbyterian Church in the United States cooperates with overseas partner churches and ecumenical agencies in seventeen countries in Asia, Africa, Latin America, the Middle East, and the South Pacific. Shared personnel and programme funds are extended to these partners for evangelistic, medical, and educational ministries.

Current priorities include leadership development, community projects and mutuality in mission through continued exchanges of personnel and ministry with international students in the United States. The major denominational emphasis outside of the United States has been placed upon partnership in mission with sister churches in Africa. The denomination has achieved an outstanding record in ecumenical involvement, and has been twice cited by the National Council of Churches of Christ for its contributions to ecumenism. Since 1974 the Church has been involved with twelve denominations in the United States and Canada in a project of joint educational development called "Christian Education: Shared Approaches". This venture provides to participating churches four approaches and sets of resources for education in the church: knowing the word, interpreting the word, living the word, and doing the word.

The denomination is currently engaged in union discussions with the United Presbyterian Church in the USA, with a goal of consummating the union in 1983. Through the establishment of union presbyteries, a third of the ministers, members, and local congregations of the denomination are full members of both the Presbyterian Church in the United States and the United Presbyterian Church in the USA. United congregations have also been established in cooperation with the Associate Reformed Presbyterian Church and the Cumberland Presbyterian Church. The Church maintains special relations with the Presbyterian Churches in Korea, Taiwan, Zaire, Brazil, Mexico, the United Church of Christ in Japan, the Reformed Church of Japan, the Moravian Church of Honduras, the United Protestant Church of Belgium, the Episcopal Church of Haiti, the Bangladesh Baptist Union, the Lesotho Evangelical Church and the Korean Church of Christ in Japan.

PROGRESSIVE NATIONAL BAPTIST CONVENTION, Inc.

Savannah Grove Baptist Church, c/o 312 S. Main Street, Sumter, SC 29150. 521,700 members — 655 parishes — 800 pastors. Publication: Baptist Progress (quarterly). WCC (1975), NCCCUSA, BWA. President: Dr Ralph W. Canty — General Secretary: Rev. C.J. Malloy, Jr, 601 50th Street, NE, Washington, DC 20019.

As the result of a dispute in the National Baptist Convention of the USA, Inc., over procedures in the election of convention officers, the Progressive National Baptist Convention, Inc. was organized in 1961. It held its first annual session in Philadelphia in 1962. (No further information has been made available on this body.)

REFORMED CHURCH IN AMERICA

Room 1812, 475 Riverside Drive, New York, NY 10115 — Tel: 212.870.2841 — Cable: Synodical. 350,000 members — 930 parishes — 1,450 pastors. Publications: The Church Herald, Hotline, RC Agenda. WCC (1948), NCCCUSA, WARC. General Secretary: Rev. Arie R. Brouwer.

When the early Dutch settlers arrived in New York, they brought their Calvinistic faith with them. The first Dutch Reformed minister arrived in 1628. This marked the beginning of over 350 years of uninterrupted ministry in the United States. For some years the Reformed Protestant Dutch Church maintained its ethnic identity through Dutch language services and the clergy ordained in the Netherlands. The gradual adjustment to being an American church was accelerated by the American Revolution. In 1819 the name was changed to the Reformed Dutch Church, and in 1867 to the Reformed Church in America. A second immigration of Dutch people in the mid-1800s established a new cluster of churches in the mid-west. The immigrants had withdrawn from the state church in the Netherlands at the price of bitter persecution. They settled in Michigan and in Iowa and, upon learning the Reformed Church here was independent of the state, they united with it. A third wave of immigration took place in the 1950s. This time the Dutch immigrants settled chiefly in Canada and began the double task of integrating themselves into Canadian life and becoming a part of the Reformed Church in America, which had previously existed chiefly in the United States. The Church has grown significantly in California and other parts of the western United States among people of Dutch and also non-Dutch background. The composition of congregations in other parts of the country has continued to change, bringing into the Church people from diverse ethnic and religious traditions.

The Reformed Church in America is Presbyterian in government. It accepts the inspired word of God as its only rule of faith and practice. Important emphases in its theology relate to the covenant and the sovereignty of God. World mission is a priority and active mission fields currently include India, Japan, Arabia, Mexico, Venezuela, and Chinese-speaking populations in various countries. Along with its strong evangelical emphasis, the Church has maintained an interest in examining its role in the social sphere.

The denominational priority the Church has chosen for the 1980s is "Crossing cultural barriers: reaching and receiving in Christ". At home this emphasis is being promoted by the interaction of the varied groups that make up the Reformed Church. They reflect the very diverse backgrounds of the general American population, including Black, Hispanic, Dutch, Asian, and Indian in Canada and the United States. Abroad, the Church is attempting to redefine its still active mission interest with a view to receiving as well as sending missionaries. Other concerns for the 1980s include the search for peace, concern for world hunger, family life, and the roles of women and men in the church and its ministry. An important ecumenical concern is for the black Reformed churches of South Africa.

RELIGIOUS SOCIETY OF FRIENDS: FRIENDS GENERAL CONFERENCE

1520-B Race Street, Philadelphia, PA 19102 — Tel: 215.567.1965. 26,200 members — 400 congregations. Publication: FGC Quarterly. WCC (1948), NCCCUSA. General Secretary: Dwight Spann-Wilson.

The Friends General Conference is the oldest of the five major groupings of Friends in the United States and Canada. It had its beginnings just before 1900 when four Hicksite groups decided to meet annually at the same time and place. These were First Day School Conference, Friends Union for Philanthropic Labor, Friends Religious Conference, and Friends Education Conference.

In 1900, seven yearly meetings which were involved in these groups joined to form Friends General Conference. In the 1950s, when yearly meetings were united, the scope of FGC membership was broadened to include Meetings which had been identified as Orthodox, Conservative, and Evangelical, as well as Hicksite.

Over the years, Friends have found that they come closer to truth when many Friends, rather than a few, are involved in ministry and in decisions. Monthly meetings have joined to form yearly meetings and yearly meetings have joined to form Friends General Conference, Friends United Meeting, and Friends Evangelical Alliance.

Today, Friends General Conference is an association of 12 yearly meetings and some other groups in the Religious Society of Friends. Representatives of these yearly meetings and other groups meet annually as a central committee and serve on programme and administrative committees designed to strengthen and enrich the spiritual dimension of the Society of Friends.

Friends General Conference Friends have historic roots in Christianity. For them, the life and teaching of Jesus are central to their belief and to their day-to-day living. Most are open to the enrichment of theological diversity. FGC Friends believe that everyone has direct access to God through the Inner Light or Inner Christ. Worship is based on expectant waiting upon and communion with God.

RELIGIOUS SOCIETY OF FRIENDS: FRIENDS UNITED MEETING

101 Quaker Hill Drive, Richmond, IN 47374 — Tel: 317.962.7573 — Cable: Fremi. 70,170 members — 569 congregations — 400 pastors. Publication: Quaker Life. WCC (1948), NCCCUSA. General Secretary: Mr Clifford Winslow — Administrative Secretary: Ms Kara Cole.

Quakerism arose out of the religious ferment of the mid-17th century. George Fox, its founder, emphasized the immediacy of Christ's teaching and held that for this consecrated buildings and ordained ministers were irrelevant. By 1655 Quakers had spread throughout Great Britain and Ireland and to the continent of Europe, and in 1682 William Penn founded Pennsylvania on a Quaker basis. From the paramount importance given to the inner light doctrine derives the rejection of the sacraments, the ministry and all set forms of worship. The Society does, however, firmly believe in a spiritual baptism and a spiritual communion. The Friends United Meeting (FUM) was established in 1902 and has grown to include 15 yearly meetings within the United States and around the world.

In the 19th century, Quakers were leaders in the movement to abolish slavery in the United States, and supported it by becoming a part of the underground railroad network. Continuing through the 20th century to live in the deep-rooted belief that *all* people are Children of God, Quakers have been active in relief work throughout Europe, Asia and South America in times of war and anguish, working through such agencies as the American Friends Service Committee. FUM continues to be active overseas in the Middle East, Jamaica, Belize, Japan, Cuba, and East Africa. Schools and meetings for worship have been founded and supported through the efforts of FUM's Wider Ministries Commission. As these areas become more stable in their local leadership and spiritual direction, FUM's role gradually recedes into one of guiding and supporting as it nurtures the extension of a Quaker witness throughout the world.

Within the United States, there is an ever-growing sense of cooperation and community among FUM's diverse member groups. This in turn results in a movement of support within the Society of Friends and in programmes of outreach beyond to neighbouring individuals and communities. Chicago Fellowship of Friends and the Quaker Volunteer Witness have both developed outreach programmes, the former ministering to the inner city and the latter serving in the rural communities.

Friends United Meeting is growing in its awareness of the Lord's power and of its own mission. One of its primary concerns for the years ahead is to make a reaffirmation of its historic commitment to promoting peace.

UNITED CHURCH OF CHRIST

105 Madison Avenue, New York, NY 10016 — Tel: 212.683.5656. 1,736,250 members — 6,462 parishes — 9,870 pastors Publication: A.D. (monthly). WCC (1961), NCCCUSA, COCU, WARC. President: Rev. Dr Avery D. Post — Executive Associate to the President: Rev. Norman W. Jackson.

Pluralistic by nature and design, the United Church of Christ is a uniting and united church. In 1957, the Congregational Christian Churches joined with the Evangelical Reformed Church to become the United Church of Christ. Each uniting denomination represented a merger of an American colonial church tradition with one formed in frontier America.

The Congregational Churches, descended from Puritan and Separatist forebears in England and colonial New England, were born in the 17th century, of the Calvinist theological family and the Free Church Movement. Seeking the simplicity of first century Christianity, on the cusp of the 19th century Second Awakening, the Christian Church arose on the American frontier from three diverse and nearly simultaneous defections from the Methodist, Baptist and Presbyterian Churches. The Congregational Churches and the Christian Church came together in 1931 to become the Congregational Christian Churches.

The German Reformed Church, also with colonial roots, was established by early 18th century Swiss-German refugees from European wars, who had settled in Pennsylvania and nearby colonies. The evangelical synod of North America was born of the Evangelical Church of the Prussian Union, a 19th century Reformed-Lutheran union in the German Palatinate. Emigrants who settled in the American Mississippi Valley during the westward movement of the 19th century, and refugees from social and economic devastation of Napoleonic wars, were gathered into congregations through missionary effort. These two churches of German origin became, in 1934, the Evangelical and Reformed Church.

The 1957 union gathered under one polity reformed and free church traditions and presbyterial and congregational style structures. It united under one covenant, the heirs of Lutheran, Zwinglian, Calvinist, pietist and revivalist theologies to form the United Church of Christ.

There are 39 conferences; associations and conferences elect delegates to the biennial general synod. The general synod, represented *ad interim* by an executive council, sets priorities, recommends policy, votes on budget, makes programme recommendations and allocates monies to the "recognized" and "established" programme instrumentalities, the councils and commissions to be used for purposes emanating from the churches' concerns for mission, evangelism, stewardship, social justice, communication, education and ecumenism.

Three of the four major traditions of the United Church of Christ emerged from European reformation traditions. One was native to US history. Membership is primarily Caucasian, with Black, Asian, Pacific Island, Hispanic and American Indian membership growing more rapidly than Caucasian. It is a middle-class, educated church.

The primary concerns facing the UCC in the 1980s centre on the shaping of the mission in this decade. The Church is concerned about using the strength and values of its diverse membership. The Church began the decade with two priorities, peace and family life, and will attempt to be faithful to Christ by witnessing in special ways by these two issues. In 1983 the general synod is likely to add two more priorities to these two.

UNITED METHODIST CHURCH
Secretary of the Council of Bishops, 223 Fourth Avenue, Pittsburg, PA 15222 — Tel: 412.562.1580 — Cable: Questing. 9,548,450 members — 38,576 congregations — 58 active bishops — 58 retired bishops — 36,283 ordained clergy. Publications: The Interpreter (in English and Spanish) and sixty other periodicals. WCC (1969), NCCCUSA, WMC. Bishop James M. Ault — General Secretary: Rev. Dr Robert W. Huston, General Commission on Christian Unity and Interreligious Concerns, 475 Riverside Drive, Room 1300, New York, NY 10115.

The United Methodist Church, now one of the largest Protestant denominations in the United States of America and with member churches in Europe and Africa and in the Philippines, has its roots in English, Dutch, and German groups working among the early settlers. The Methodist Episcopal Church, following the principles of John Wesley of the Church of England, was officially organized in 1784. During the 19th century Methodism spread across the Atlantic and Pacific through missionary efforts.

The early 20th century brought about various unions. In 1939 the Methodist Episcopal Church (South), the Methodist Protestant Church, and the Methodist Episcopal Church united into the Methodist Church. In 1946 the Church of the United Brethren in Christ and the Evangelical Church became the Evangelical United Brethren Church. In 1968 the Evangelical United Brethren Church united with the United Methodist Church. During the last half century mission churches, especially in Asia and South America, have become autonomous, although the parent denomination maintains close ties with them as it does with its own "mother church", the Methodist Church in Great Britain.

The denomination reflects the diversified society of the nation. Even though the official social creed of the United Methodist Church could be considered a liberal document, individual church members hold views on political and social issues which range from far right to far left. Throughout Methodism's history new congregations in particular communities have been made up of various ethnic groups — black, Asian, European, native American, Hispanic, speaking several languages — sometimes integrated, sometimes not. At the present time the denomination is growing most rapidly in parts of Africa and among newly arrived Asians and Hispanics in the USA. The denomination considers itself to be "an inclusive society without regard to ethnic origin, economic condition, sex or age of its constituents". It is an activist denomination, striving to implement the gospel in the lives of persons and the structures of society and joins in ecumenical efforts to these ends.

The ethnic minority constituency of this Church is larger than that of most other religious bodies which tend to be predominantly white. The priority is the development and strengthening of the work of ethnic minority local churches. Five special programmes for the first half of the decade focus on peace and justice, world hunger, church and campus, Africa, and strengthening local churches through an emphasis on family life and evangelism. These emphases of the quadrennial general conference of 1980 will be reviewed and revised at the 1984 general conference.

The United Methodist Church is involved in the development of ethnic minority local churches; among other priorities are the special emphases on education for awareness and responsibility for world hunger, peace with justice, and television ministry. The denomination's four programme agencies — General Board of Church and Society, General Board of Discipleship, General Board of Global Ministries, and General Board of Higher Education and Ministry — indicate its understanding of the principle concerns. There are also five active general commissions: archives and history, Christian unity and inter-religious concerns, communications, religion and race, and the status and role of women.

The Church has relationships with united churches with Methodist components and with affiliated autonomous churches in Argentina, Belgium, Bolivia, Brazil, Burma, Chile, Costa Rica, Cuba, Dominican Republic, Ecuador, Hong Kong, India, Indonesia, Japan, Korea, Malaysia, Nigeria, Panama, Pakistan, Peru, Singapore and Uruguay.

UNITED PRESBYTERIAN CHURCH IN THE UNITED STATES OF AMERICA

Room 1201, 475 Riverside Drive, New York, NY 10115 — Tel: 212.870.2005 — Cable: Inculcate, New York. 2,434,030 members — 8,832 congregations — 14,502 pastors. Publications: A.D. (monthly), Monday Morning (bi-weekly), Church and Society Magazine (bi-monthly), These Days (bi-monthly). WCC (1948), NCCCUSA, WARC. Stated Clerk: Mr William P. Thompson.

The arrival of French Huguenots in Florida and South Carolina in 1562 marked the first recorded visit of Reformed church people to the New World. After 1600, many Presbyterians fled from Europe to America to escape persecution for their beliefs and to seek religious freedom. As the number of colonists increased, scattered groups formed into congregations. By 1706, the first presbytery was organized in Philadelphia under the leadership of Francis Makemie. In 1789, the first general assembly of the Presbyterian Church was called to order with John Witherspoon appointed to preside at its opening session. Presbyterians took an active part in the formation of American constitutional government. Among the larger US church bodies, the UPC is today eighth in size.

The essential features of the future into which the UPC believes it is being called, and in the light of which it is beginning to plan, are: (1) to be a community that confesses Jesus Christ as Lord and Saviour in its proclamation and in its life and work; (2) to be a community that struggles and suffers; (3) to be a fellowship within which there is diversity; (4) to be open to new perspectives on the Christian faith and life; (5) to take seriously and to work responsibly for moral leadership, understanding itself as a part of the universal church of Jesus Christ.

Significant major programmes and activities of the United Presbyterian Church relate to peace-making concerns including nuclear freeze and Peace Academy;

affirming the good news: reaching persons who have not been reached with the gospel; racial justice and racial ethnic ministries; undocumented aliens and Mexican migration to the USA; advocacy of the poor and disenfranchized; the nature and practice of ministry; the ecumenical commitment; Presbyterian reunion; ministry to and with the aging; joint urban policy for Presbyterian Church in US (PCUS) and the United Presbyterian Church in USA (UPCUSA); mission in higher education; renewed ministries in housing.

The Church participates in mission with churches in over fifty countries.

Oceania

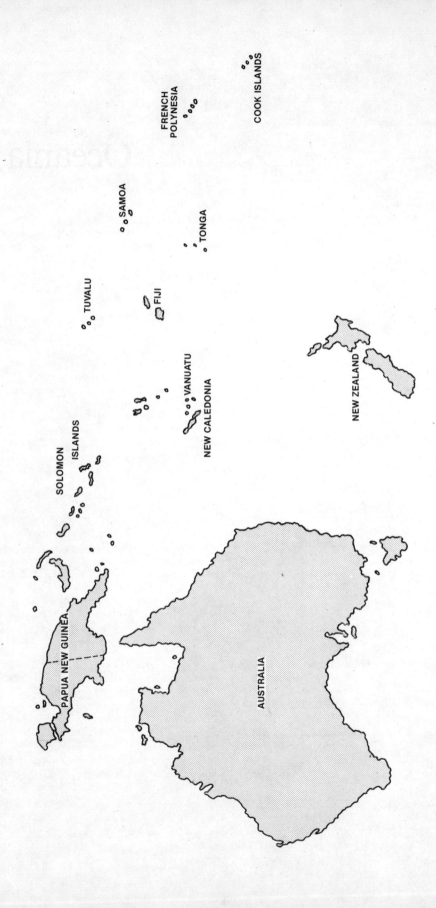

Oceania

COOK ISLANDS

FRENCH
POLYNESIA

SAMOA

TONGA

TUVALU

FIJI

VANUATU

NEW CALEDONIA

NEW ZEALAND

SOLOMON
ISLANDS

PAPUA NEW GUINEA

AUSTRALIA

AUSTRALIA

ANGLICAN CHURCH OF AUSTRALIA

St Andrew's House, Sydney Square, NSW 2000, Sydney — Tel: (02) 2690642 — Telex: COFE 24183. 3,752,220 members — 1,350 parishes — 24 dioceses — 2,400 bishops and priests (in full or licensed connexion). Publication: Church Scene. WCC (1948), ACC, CCA. Primate: Most Rev. Sir Marcus Lawrence Loane, Box Q 190, Queen Victoria Post Office, Sydney NSW 2000 — General Secretary: Mr John Denton (same address as primate).

The Church came to Australia in 1788 with the 'First Fleet', made up, for the most part, of convicts and military personnel. This community was ministered to by the chaplain, the Rev. Richard Johnson. The whole continent of Australia formed an archdeaconry of the diocese of Calcutta in 1824 but in 1836 Broughton was consecrated the first Bishop of Australia and soon after, in 1842, a second diocese, that of Tasmania, was formed. Five years later, three more dioceses were created, and the Bishop of Australia became the Bishop of Sydney. The first general synod was convened in 1972 when the number of dioceses had grown to ten. In the early years of the 20th century, the Church was divided into four ecclesiastical provinces which correspond generally to the States of New South Wales, Victoria, Queensland and Western Australia. The province of South Australia was formed by the general synod in May 1973.

There are now twenty-four dioceses, seven in New South Wales, five in Victoria, five in Queensland, three in Western Australia, three in South Australia; Tasmania is an extra-provincial diocese. The diocese of the Northern Territory was formed in 1968 and the diocese of The Murray in 1969. The diocese of Papua New Guinea had been part of the province of Queensland since its formation, but following proposals authorized by the general synod in May 1973 and the independence of the country, a separate province was formed in February 1977.

On 1 January 1962 the constitution of the Church of England in Australia came into force, having first been approved by the 25 diocesan synods and given legal force and effect by suitable acts passed by the six state parliaments. The general synod is required to meet at least once every four years. The primate is elected from among the diocesan bishops by an electoral college of bishops, clergy and laity.

The Church is intimately related with the culture, social order, political life and all other factors which combine to make up the fabric of the Australian nation. Considerable social welfare programmes and counselling programmes exist across the country.

The most urgent issues the Church faces in the 1980s are: evangelism among contemporary youth; explaining and giving meaning to the gospel in an affluent society; attempting to prepare clergy and laity alike for ministry in Australian society in the eighties; informing the church community and formulating opinion and action concerning social and political questions including the place of the Aboriginal in Australian society; the place of the unemployed and other categories of special need and concern. There is a good deal of concern for adequate relations with the Church in Papua New Guinea, in Melanesia, Polynesia, and in Asia generally, and in Eastern and Southern Africa.

CHURCHES OF CHRIST IN AUSTRALIA

Federal Board of Christian Education, 6th Floor, 177 Collins Street, Melbourne 3000. 40,000 members — 420 congregations — 370 ministers. Publication: The Australian Christian. WCC (1948), ACC, CCA. President: Rev. B. Grear — Secretary: Rev. I.E. Allsop.

Thomas Magarey, from Nelson, New Zealand, founded in 1845 a meeting of Scottish Baptists in Adelaide. His convincing testimony won many to an appreciation of the example of the New Testament Church. The declaration and address of

Thomas Campbell in 1809 also had an impact. In summary he said: "The church is intended to be united. Division in the church is an evil. The way to find out what God wants his church to believe and do is to examine the New Testament."

Land for a building site was purchased, and in the next year a chapel was put up in Franklin Street. By 1865 there were five Christian churches in southern Australia, with a membership of 253.

The first Victorian annual conference was held in 1866. There was a division of opinion over the nature of the conference, but in 1872 the principle of congregational independence prevailed. On appealing for further evangelistic help to Alexander Campbell, two persons were selected. T.J. Gore worked in Adelaide and G.L. Suber in Melbourne. An intercolonial conference at Melbourne in 1889 urged that the colony of Western Australia be evangelized.

A College of the Bible was established at Melbourne in 1907, and another Bible College at Woolwich, a Sydney suburb, in 1942. A year earlier the federal conference had authorized the starting of organized work among Aborigines. A mission station of 20,000 acres was secured in 1945 near Norseman, WA; work was then extended to Carnarvon, WA. Today Churches of Christ are found in New South Wales, Queensland, South Australia, Tasmania, Victoria and Western Australia.

The CCA has a history which parallels the national history as it has been involved in the movements of people first to the rural areas and in recent years to the cities. The churches are alive as local congregations which place an emphasis on lay participation in worship and government. This means that the ethos of theology, liturgy, church programming and evangelism reflects the concerns of the lay membership. The care of congregational life based on the Christian gospel is seen as vital. Sometimes efforts to widen the vision of church members beyond the local congregation are met with limited success.

Among the major issues faced by the CCA are: (a) the enabling of church growth with a theology that is biblical and authentic to Australians; (b) the development of an ethos within the Church that is sensitive to the affluent Australian culture and yet brings to it biblical judgment so as to enable Australians to be obedient to the gospel; (c) to help members towards an understanding of the unity of the Church on the basis of rediscovering a New Testament understanding of the church itself.

The CCA has good relations with sister churches in New Zealand, Western India, Vanuatu, Papua New Guinea, the United Kingdom and the United States.

UNITING CHURCH IN AUSTRALIA

P.O. Box C103, Clarence Street, Sydney NSW 2000 — Tel: (02) 293036 — Cable: Unichurch, Sydney. 2,000,000 members — 3,200 congregations — 7 synods — 2,200 pastors. Publications: Six synod newspapers. WCC (1948/1977), ACC, CCA, WARC, WMC. President of the Assembly: Rev. Prof. R.A. Busch, 6 Longridge Street, Macgregor, Queensland — Secretary of the Assembly: Rev. David M. Gill.

The Uniting Church in Australia, established in June 1977, is the result of a union of the Congregational, Presbyterian and Methodist churches in the country, following five decades of study and negotiation. All three constituent bodies were founding members of the World Council of Churches in 1948. Some Congregationalists and a substantial minority of Presbyterians stayed out of the union, but with about 3,200 congregations and 2,200 pastors the Uniting Church follows the Anglicans and Roman Catholics as Australia's third largest Christian denomination. It is estimated that, out of the country's nearly 15,000,000 people, some 13% claim links with the Uniting Church.

The 1977 union was seen not as an end in itself, but as a step towards wider unity and as a means for renewal in faith, mission and social engagement. In the Basis of Union, the Church "thankfully acknowledges that the uniting churches were members of the World Council of Churches and other ecumenical bodies and she will seek to maintain such membership".

Major issues confronting the Church at present relate to its understanding of baptism and ordination, its image as a predominantly Anglo-Saxon denomination in an increasingly multi-cultural society, the renewal of the congregation in worship and mission, and its deeper involvement in the debate about Australia's goals and priorities.

COOK ISLANDS

COOK ISLANDS CHRISTIAN CHURCH
Takamoa, Rarotonga, Cook Islands — Tel: 2028 K. 12,890 members — 25 congregations — 26 pastors. Publications: Three monthly magazines (in Cook Islands language). WCC (1975), PCC, NCCNZ. President: Rev. Turaki Teauariki — General Secretary: Rev. T. Pitomaki.

The Church had its origin in the work of the London Missionary Society which started in 1820. Rev. John Williams and two pastors from Tahiti began work on the island of Aitutaki. It spread to Atiu, Mauke, Mitiaro, Mangaia and Rarotonga. The first student graduating from the theological college at Takamoa was ordained in 1850. In the following decades Tereora College and the Araura School were established. In 1890, the first Bible translation in the Rarotonga Cook Islands language was completed. During the first decades of the 20th century a ship, "John Williams", occasionally visited the Cook Islands, and thus facilitated the travel to other Pacific islands. Until its independence in 1963 a total of 26 missionaries of the London Missionary Society served the Church. Its constitution was revised in 1968. The CICC has two parishes in New Zealand and exchanges pastors with Tahiti. It is the largest church in the islands, followed by the Roman Catholic Church (2,480).

The Church cherishes its cultural heritage. The liturgy is celebrated in the local language and with indigenous hymns. The social life is similar to life in other Pacific islands. Celebrations and festivals occupy an important place in the church's activities. The CICC has some difficulty in finding its role in the political life of the society.

At present the primary concerns are the training of pastors in order to equip them for a better ministry, and the education of youth leaders. The Church is responsible for its own finances, but it needs more expertise in its whole administration. There are plans to send a few people for training at the Pacific Theological College in Fiji and to the Bible College in New Zealand.

Holy communion is celebrated every month and at Christmas, Lent, Easter and Pentecost. These celebrations are great festivals, with singing, dancing and sharing in meals. October 26 is celebrated as the Gospel Day in the Cooks, the day Christianity arrived on the islands. It is a public holiday during which a religious drama is performed or Bible stories are enacted. The Church sponsors a radio and television programme.

Although the CICC has fewer than 25,000 members, it was accepted as a full member of the WCC, because of its size relative to the total population of the Cook Islands, and also in view of the fact that a considerable number of its members are temporarily living in New Zealand.

FIJI

METHODIST CHURCH IN FIJI (Lotu Wesele e Viti)
Epworth Arcade, Suva — Tel: 24097 — Cable: Methodist, Suva. 170,820 members — 138 circuits — 970 parishes — 168 pastors. Publication: Koniferedi (in Fijian and English). WCC (1976), FCC, PCC, WMC. President: Rev. Inoke Nabulivou — Connexional Secretary: Rev. Paula Niukula.

Christianity came to Fiji in 1830 when three Tahitian teachers of the London Missionary Society arrived in Lakeba. After forty years of work, converted Fijians became keen to be involved in the missionary enterprise, and volunteered to go with Dr George Brown to New Britain in 1875. Ever since, Fijian missionaries have gone to Papua, the Solomons, the High Land of New Guinea and North Australia. When Fiji became a British colony in 1874, a number of Indians were brought under the indenture system to work in cane plantations in Fiji. After their term expired they were allowed to become citizens of Fiji. Today there are more Indians in Fiji than Fijians and this has given rise to many problems.

Methodists are the largest Christian group; after them come the Roman Catholics (49,000), Assembly of God (7,000), Anglicans (5,000), and other churches (7,000); 51 per cent of the population is Christian, 39 per cent Hindu and 8 per cent Muslim.

In 1964 the Methodist Church in Fiji became autonomous. Now it was no longer under the jurisdiction of the Australian Methodist Overseas Mission. In 1977, when the Methodist Church of Australia joined the Uniting Church in Australia, the Methodist churches of Tonga, Samoa and Fiji also became independent churches.

The Church is made up mostly of indigenous Fijians and therefore reflects their culture, communal approach and values. The language is mainly Fijian. Others, including Europeans and Pacific Islanders, communicate in English. The Church's primary concerns are church renewal, evangelism among the growing non-church population, leadership training for clergy and laity and developing church land and property. Church programmes include Christian citizenship and social service, youth fellowships and Sunday schools, women's and men's fellowships, church resources development and congregational education. Besides the Methodist churches in the Pacific, the MCF maintains relations with the Uniting Church in Australia, the United Methodist Church in the USA and the Methodist Church in Great Britain.

MELANESIA

CHURCH OF MELANESIA

P.O. Box 19, Honiara, Solomon Islands — Tel: 893 — Cable: Melanesia Honiara. 90,000 members — 5 dioceses — 5 bishops — 150 priests. Publication: Church of Melanesia Newsletter (in English). WCC (1977), SICA. Most Rev. N.K. Polma — Provincial Secretary: Mr Basil Le Pine Williams.

The Anglican Church first came to Australia in 1788, and to New Zealand in 1814. When in 1858 New Zealand became a separate province, Melanesia became its special responsibility though Australia continued to provide support. In 1861 John Coleridge Patteson was appointed as the first bishop of Melanesia. The diocese of Melanesia became the sixth in the Province of New Zealand. At first the boundaries of the diocese covered New Britain and New Ireland but after the Second World War, New Britain and New Ireland were included in the diocese of New Guinea which had been established in 1898. The Province of Melanesia includes today four dioceses: Central Melanesia (which is also the archdiocese of the archbishop) with four regions: Honiara, Guadealcanal, Makira and Temotu; Ysabel with two regions, Ysabel and Gela-Savo-Russels; and Malaita, which includes Lord Howe Atoll and Sikaiana and the New Hebrides (with New Caledonia). At the second provincial synod held in 1976 the boundaries of the diocese of Central Melanesia and Ysabel were changed, with Gela and Savo leaving the diocese of Ysabel and becoming an additional region of the diocese of Central Melanesia.

The Church receives support from overseas in the form of money and specialist workers. It is an equal partner with other independent Anglican churches throughout the world. Each diocese is governed by its diocesan synod with a diocesan council as the standing committee in the same way as provincial synod and provincial council. The Church of Melanesia continues discussions with the

United Church in the Solomon Islands and (through the South Pacific Anglican Council) with the Episcopal Conference of the South Pacific (Roman Catholic). All decisions about relations between the Church and other churches will be the responsibility of the Church of Melanesia alone, except when other parts of the Anglican Church in the Pacific are also involved. One of the primary concerns of the Church is related to the fact that 57 per cent of the population of the Solomon Islands and the New Hebrides is under 20. Youth work is a clear priority. Its commitment programme is geared to promoting stewardship and pastoral care.

NEW CALEDONIA

EVANGELICAL CHURCH IN NEW CALEDONIA AND THE LOYALTY ISLES (Eglise évangélique en Nouvelle-Calédonie et aux Iles Loyauté)
B.P. 227, 8 rue Leriche, Noumea. 3,700 members — 97 parishes — 65 pastors. WCC (1961), PCC, CEVAA. President: Rev. Jacques Ajapuhnya — General Secretary: Rev. Tella Kasarherou.

As early as 1839, teachers from amongst the Samoan converts of the London Missionary Society were sent to the southern Melanesian islands, then known as Western Polynesia. They were joined in this pioneering work by Rarotongan teachers. Samoan missionaries also laboured from 1839-1845 at Totuma, where the Wesleyan Missionary Society had started work in 1841. Samoan and Rarotongan missionaries pioneered in the mainland of New Caledonia (1841-45), the Isle of Pines and the Loyalty Islands (Mare, 1841; Lifu, 1845; Tika 1852; Uea, 1857). From 1902 onwards the Church registered steady growth, thanks to the work of the Reverend Maurice Leenhardt. It became independent in 1960. It has participated actively in the assemblies of the Pacific Conference of Churches.

The Protestant churches represent about 25 per cent of the population and the Roman Catholic Church 67 per cent. The ECNCLI has 16 per cent, the Free Evangelical Church six per cent, the Tahitian Evangelical Church two per cent and the Anglican and Presbyterian churches one per cent. There are other smaller communities such as the Assembly of God, the Jehovah's Witnesses and others. Three per cent of the population is Muslim.

The Church stresses its cultural identity in a Melanesian context, and particularly through its methods of Christian education. It is engaged in the translation of the whole Bible. The history of New Caledonia is being studied. The Church is greatly concerned about the formation of new leaders, including women and youth, who would communicate the good news to Melanesians. The Church has become conscious of the fact that its worship is still dependent on European forms of liturgy, particularly the liturgy of the Reformed Church of France. It searches for indigenous expressions of adoration, hymnology and prayer, based on local customs and values. Only in this way can the Christian community become the authentic people of God and a true witness to his salvation.

Among the social problems the ECNCLI faces is that of alcoholism.

The ecumenical dialogue, especially with the Roman Catholic Church, is a high priority on the Church's agenda. Close relations are maintained with the Uniting Church in Australia.

NEW ZEALAND

ASSOCIATED CHURCHES OF CHRIST IN NEW ZEALAND
90a Mount Street, Nelson — Tel: 89873. 2,750 members — 42 parishes — 26 pastors. Publication: New Zealand Christian. WCC (1948), NCCNZ. President: Mr L.A. Jacobs, 12 Mascot Place, Christchurch 6 — General Secretary: Mr T.G. Todd.

The first congregation of Disciples in the southern hemisphere was the Church established by Thomas Jackson, of Glasgow, Scotland, who arrived at Nelson, in the north of South Island, in 1843, two years after the founding of the city. All the early members were of English or Scottish origin, but their teachings were those of the Campbells, whose writings were read and circulated.

Conflicts with the Maoris and economic depression drove many of the settlers elsewhere. Thomas Magarey moved to Adelaide and helped open the first church in 1845. Others went to Auckland, now the largest city. In 1884 there were twenty churches, in 1909 forty. At first, the churches cooperated through three conferences — Auckland, Middle District (Wellington and Nelson), and South Island. In 1901, the first dominion conference was held, and others followed at five-year intervals. Since 1921 they have been held annually. The conferences are conducted by delegates appointed by the affiliated churches in numbers proportionate to membership. Prior to conference meetings, matters of special importance are submitted to the congregations, which express their minds in order to guide the voting of their delegates. Inspirational, promotional and devotional sessions play a large role in conference gatherings.

In 1905 overseas mission work was begun in Southern Rhodesia by John Sherriff and F.L. Hadfield. R. Garfield Todd, superintendent on the field, was in 1946 elected to the parliament of Southern Rhodesia and later became prime minister of the state.

Prior to 1927 men were trained to the ministry mainly in the United States and Australia. Since then ministers have been receving their education at Dominion College, set up in Dunedin.

Throughout their existence the Associated Churches have maintained a close connection with those of like faith in Great Britain, the United States, Australia, Zimbabwe and Vanuatu.

BAPTIST UNION OF NEW ZEALAND

P.O. Box 27-390, Wellington — Tel: 844.069 — Cable: Baptist Wellington. 19,370 members — 163 parishes — 240 pastors. Publication: The New Zealand Baptist. WCC (1948) NCCNZ, CCA, BWA. General Secretary: Rev. Dr S.L. Edgar.

The first Baptist church in New Zealand was established in 1851 at Nelson. Others followed. The Baptist Union of New Zealand was formed in 1882. In the early stages many of the ministers — as well as members — came to New Zealand from Great Britain. When the Baptist Church came to New Zealand, the Church of England, and the Presbyterian, Methodist and Roman Catholic Churches were already well established in the country. Growth has therefore been moderately slow. Baptists make up less than 2 per cent of the population. Most of the 20,000 members of the Church are active and very supportive of the work through church attendance, giving and service.

The Baptist Church in New Zealand has developed mainly in middle-class areas, although more recently there has been increased work among the Maori people. Although it has no acknowledged political affinities, in earlier years some of its leaders were outspoken in the labour movement. It is difficult to assess the present political affiliations of members. The Church has sought to meet some of the social needs of the country. Homes for the elderly have been provided, as well as youth camps, halfway houses for psychiatric patients finding their way back into the community, hostels, centres for city mission work, and retirement villages. In earlier years there were problems in relating to certain other sections of the Christian Church, but at present relationships are very good, and the Church participates at all levels in ecumenical affairs.

With regard to internal concerns, the Baptist Union would wish to see a better integration of charismatic and non-charismatic elements in the Church. It would also desire a continuation of ministerial training after ordination, the provision of incentives and skills for service by the laity, with a heightened sense of obligation to commend the gospel to the world, and the development of more acceptable patterns of worship. As far as external matters are concerned, Baptists need to struggle for a Christian answer to the problems of race, law and order, and unemployment. They need to understand more clearly the meaning and implications of responsible freedom.

Major programmes would include an ongoing missionary programme in Asia and South East Asia. The mission work of the Church, which was once confined to India, is now more widespread. Baptists have not sought to enter countries to establish independent missions, but have a policy of aiding existing churches in a number of countries through personnel and the financial support which these need.

Local churches are becoming increasingly involved in social activities. Because of the congregational structure, most of the Church's activities are built into the programmes of local congregations. These include youth work, religious education at all levels, house groups for fellowship, prayer and Bible study, programmes extending into the community, care of the elderly, and other social outreach programmes. The Baptist Union's role is to assist in the development of the above through advice and, when needed and when possible, financial aid.

CHURCH OF THE PROVINCE OF NEW ZEALAND

P.O. Box 320, Christchurch — Tel: 63.098. 1,061,800 members — 383 parishes — 798 priests. Publication: "The Bulletin". WCC (1948), NCCNZ, CCA. The Most Rev. P. A. Reeves, P.O.Box 37023, Parnell, Auckland 1.

The Church of the Province of New Zealand was established as an autonomous church in full communion with the Church of England when its constitution was accepted in 1857. Twenty-nine per cent of the population are Anglican, and it is the largest denomination in New Zealand.

The controlling body of the Province is the general synod which meets in alternate years. While the general synod is not in session there is a standing committee which under the canons must meet at least every year when the general synod does not meet. Each diocese has its own synod, which must meet once at least every year. By an act passed by the parliament of New Zealand in 1955, the general synod has power to define the extent, nature and terms of the association of missionary dioceses with the Church of the Province of New Zealand. In 1955 the general synod enacted a new canon and this is now operative. The diocese of Polynesia is an integral part of the Church of the Province of New Zealand.

Since 1964, negotiations have gone on with the Associated Churches of Christ, the Methodist Church, the Presbyterian Church and the Congregational Union with regard to church union. In 1978 the general synod agreed to enter into a covenant agreement with the five negotiating churches, involving a statement of shared faith and a commitment to work towards more visible unity. However, proposals for the unification of ministries were defeated in 1980. In 1976 the general synod made canonical provision for the ordination of women to the priesthood. In six dioceses, women have now been ordained.

A great deal of work is carried out among the Maori people. There are four secondary schools under the Church of the Province which cater mainly for Maori pupils. At the 1978 session of the general synod of the Church of the Province of New Zealand, the bishopric of Aotearoa was established. The bishop is now licensed by the primate to share with the bishop of each diocese the episcopal oversight of the Maori people.

There are many institutions run by the Church of the Province of New Zealand — children's homes, old people's homes, rescue homes for girls, city missions, hostels for students, etc. Chaplains are provided often on an ecumenical basis, in universities, hospitals, prisons and, more recently, in industry under the Inter-Church Trade and Industrial Mission. Many schools, both boys' and girls', secondary and primary, provide education with a religious background. Bible lessons are now given in most of the state schools, but for many years this was not allowed. The theological training of candidates for ordination is now carried out at St John's College, Auckland, in cooperation with the Methodist Church of New Zealand. The overseas mission work of the Church is coordinated under the New Zealand Anglican Board of Missions. The most comprehensive gathering of clergy and laity in the history of the New Zealand Anglican Church was held in August 1981 in order to re-evaluate the Church's role in evangelism and social issues.

METHODIST CHURCH OF NEW ZEALAND

P.O. Box 931, Christchurch — Tel: 66.049. 24,030 members — 194 parishes — 365 pastors. Publication: "Focus". WCC (1948), NCCNZ, CCA, WMC. General Secretary: Rev. A. Woodley.

Wesleyan missionaries from Australia began work in New Zealand in 1822, ministering to the large Maori population and the few whalers and traders in coastal areas. In the early years Methodism in New Zealand was part of the Foreign Mission enterprise of the British Methodist conference. The first New Zealand annual conference of the Australasian (Australia and New Zealand) Wesleyan Methodist conference was held in 1874. Also active in New Zealand were the United Methodist Free Churches and the Bible Christian Church. These groups came together with the Wesleyans to form the first United Methodist Conference in 1897. Separation from the general conference of Australia followed in 1913 and in the same year the Primitive Methodist Church in New Zealand and the existing United Methodist Church joined to form one Methodist Church. Itself a product of union, the Methodist Church has in recent times voted strongly in favour of union with four other

denominations, the Anglican Church, the Presbyterian Church, the Congregational Church and the Church of Christ. According to the census Methodists (173,526) are about 5.5 per cent of the total population which numbers just over 3 million. Church members number about 24,000. This makes New Zealand Methodism the fourth largest denomination in the country. (Anglican 29 per cent, Presbyterian 18 per cent, and Roman Catholic 15 per cent).

Methodist churches in New Zealand are strongest in the suburban areas of the four main cities, and in the larger provincial towns. There are city missions in major centres and since 1973 a Maori division has come into being with a distinct life of its own but integrated into the total life of the Church, which has meant a great deal of mutual enrichment. Ecumenical cooperation, a feature of New Zealand church life, has created some difficulties for the smaller denominations such as Methodism. Over 75 per cent of Methodist circuits are involved in cooperative ventures or are part of union parishes. This represents some 20 per cent of the membership and means that the union parishes are almost like another denomination. There are however very positive gains in these ventures and they encourage creative approaches to the needs of the eighties.

New Zealand Methodism sees itself as one of the churches of South-East Asia and the Asian links are strong. Overseas missions are united under a joint board of mission with the Presbyterian Church and strategies are evolving which stress more mutual caring between the older "giving" and "sending" churches and the new indigenous churches as in New Guinea, Papua, and the Solomon Islands. The same joint board is actively involved in issues of justice and peace.

PRESBYTERIAN CHURCH OF NEW ZEALAND

P.O. Box 10-000, The Terrace, Wellington — Tel: 602.014. 577,000 members — 437 congregations — 392 preaching stations — 648 ministers — 7,259 elders — 48,825

Sunday school teachers. WCC (1948), NCCNZ, CCA. General Secretary: Rev. W.A. Best — Convener of Ecumenical Affairs Committee: Rev. Eric Chapman, 6 Nelson Street, Wanganui.

The PCNZ dates from 1840, when the 'Bengal Merchant' brought the Rev. John Macfarlane and 122 Scottish immigrants into Port Nicholson, on which the city of Wellington now stands. In 1848, the Otago Presbyterian Church settlement was founded under the leadership of Rev. Thomas Burns. For the next half century, the two organizations developed independently. The Otago settlement embraced the southern part of the colony and was administered by its own synod. The rest of the country was cared for by the Northern Church's general assembly. In 1901, an act of union merged them in what is now the PCNZ.

The Church's 25 presbyteries cover the whole country and include a growing number of Pacific Island parishes and a Maori synod which cares for the Maori people. About two to three per cent (73,014) of New Zealanders are on parish rolls as members, but if one includes those under pastoral care, this figure is closer to ten per cent, making this Church the largest after the Anglican Church. Despite a decline in membership, it maintains a well-trained parish ministry, overseas mission in partnership with the various indigenous churches, and a very active programme of social service. The latter is the largest welfare organization outside the state, providing care for children and the aged, and an increasing range of community services. Through its committees on public questions, race relations and international relations the Church plays an active role in the nation's affairs.

The place of women in the Church has received increasing recognition, and women take their place in all the church courts as elders and ministers; 1979 saw the election of the first woman as moderator of the general assembly. Another recent development is the union negotiations into which the Church has entered with the Anglican Church, Associated Churches of Christ, the Congregational Union and Methodist Churches. At the parish level the Church is involved in 143 (out of 439) union and cooperating parishes.

PAPUA NEW GUINEA

UNITED CHURCH IN PAPUA NEW GUINEA AND THE SOLOMON ISLANDS

Assembly office, P.O. Box 3401, Port Moresby — Tel: 211744 — Cable: Unichurch, Port Moresby. 211,350 members — 1,260 congregations — 7 bishops — 1,020 ministers and pastors. Publication: United Church News (in English, Pidgin and Motu). WCC (1971), MCC, SICA, PCC, CWM (UK), CCP. Moderator: Rev. Albert Burua — Assembly Secretary: Rev. Dick Avi.

The London Missionary Society began its work in Papua New Guinea in 1872. The committed leadership of several missionaries — in particular W.G. Laws and James Chalmers — enabled the Church to expand through the Papuan mainland. Led by George Brown, some Fijians and Samoans, the Australian Methodist Church responded to the Church's request for further pioneering work. In 1902 church work began in the Western Solomons under the leadership of Rev. Goldie. The Methodist Church covered three independent areas, which were then called 'districts'. These three districts joined together in 1950 in the mission work in the southern highlands. In 1962 a United Synod was established. A theological college was opened in 1964. In 1966 three Methodist districts formed themselves into an independent Methodist Church and Conference in Melanesia. The United Church was established in 1968 and six bishops were appointed as pastoral heads of each region. The Church maintains relationships with the Uniting Church in Australia, the Joint Board of Mission in New Zealand (Methodist and Presbyterian), the Methodist Church in Fiji and in the UK, the United Methodist Church in the USA, the United Church of Canada, the Reformed Church in the Netherlands and a few other churches.

The United Church represents a sixth of the population while the Roman Catholic and Lutheran Churches represent a third each. The Anglican Church comes next. There are also a few other smaller Christian communities.

The Church emphasizes a ministry to the whole person and the education of people in their social, cultural and political situations. There is a growing awareness of the need for greater contextualization in theological training. An urban ministry to street roamers, school drop-outs and juveniles has been developed.

POLYNESIA (French)

EVANGELICAL CHURCH OF FRENCH POLYNESIA (Eglise évangélique de Polynésie française — Ekalesia Evanelia no Polynesia Farani)
403, Bld. Pomare, B.P. 113, Papeete, Tahiti — Tel: 20029. 80,000 members — 79 parishes — 41 pastors. Publication: Ve'a Lien (in Tahitian and French). WCC (1963), PCC, CEVAA. President: Rev. Marurai Utia — General Secretary: John Doom

The gospel was preached in Tahiti from the year 1797. Missionaries faced various difficulties, among them the hard task of mastering the Polynesian language. The 'Tahitian week of Christianity' in 1819 was a great event. After 1843 the Church was without outside help for twenty years, as the missionaries of the London Missionary Society had gone back. The Paris Missionary Society took over the work in 1863.

The ECFP received its juridical structure in 1884, which was modified in 1927. The Church became autonomous in 1963; its constitution was twice revised, in 1971 and 1976. It is a founding member of the Evangelical Community for Apostolic Action (CEVAA).

Out of the total population of 135,000 people, 80,000 belong to the ECFP, 45,000 to the Roman Catholic Church and 10,000 to other communities (Adventists, Mormons, etc.). The official language is Reo Maohi (Tahitian). One parish, in Papeete, is French speaking, and another parish, in the same city, Chinese speaking. The ECFP preserves the traditional songs ('Himene Torava'). Its pastors are all indigenous, with the exception of the pastors of the French and Chinese speaking parishes. The Church has a synodical-presbyterial structure and is financially independent.

Much emphasis is laid on the formation of the people of God at the local parish level and on innovative work among the young people. The Church struggles with problems of cultural identity, social development, alcoholism and the nuclear threat. It operates a centre for young girls and a centre for re-education of youth, and has a wide programme of Christian education at all levels.

SAMOA

CONGREGATIONAL CHRISTIAN CHURCH IN SAMOA
P.O. Box 468, Apia, Western Samoa — Cable: Conchris. 18,700 members — 244 parishes — 300 pastors. Publications: Church Chronicle, Worship Book, Bible readings (in Samoan). WCC (1961), PCC, CWM, WARC. General Secretary: Rev. Galvefa Aseta.

The Congregational Christian Church in Samoa traces its beginning to the arrival of Rev. John Williams of the London Missionary Society in Samoa in August 1830. He and his friends were the first missionaries to come to the islands. A nation weary of warfare was willing and ready at the time to accept the Christian gospel of peace. The missionaries were officially accepted by King Malietoa, a reigning monarch in the 1830s. Now the people also accepted Christianity as their new religion.

Within the next two years, the whole of Samoa was converted to Christianity. The missionaries gave Samoa its first written language and then a translation of the Bible; they introduced the first newspaper called the "Church Chronicle" and translated a number of books into the local language.

By the end of the 19th century, a pattern of ministry had emerged. It was modelled on the Samoan village setting and aimed at preserving, as much as possible, the value systems of the Samoan way of life.

The newly converted nation was conscious of the fact that the missionaries had come all the way from England to bring them the message of salvation, and this in turn awoke in them the zeal to go out to evangelize other lands. It resulted in a remarkable outpouring of offers for overseas mission. From 1839, the Church has been sending missionaries to the neighbouring islands, Niue, Rotuma, Fiji, Kiribati, Tuvalu, Vanuatu, New Caledonia, Solomon and Papua New Guinea. Mission work was established in some of these islands and continued till the 1960s when the churches in these islands achieved an independent status.

The Church at home, during this period of mission work elsewhere, was engaged in "the social redemption of humanity". This vision was based on the Church's understanding of God's sovereignty. It saw the divine purpose of redemption not in individual terms only but in corporate, social and political terms as well. Its newly acquired faith had its focus on the transformation of total life and society. That legacy remains a motivating force in the nation's idealism as well as in the Church's commitment to active social efforts. Consistent with its commitment to education the Church has been able to maintain two colleges, two high schools, one primary school and one theological college (the first institute of learning established in Samoa). In 1977, the Church assembly gave formal endorsement to the establishment of the University of Samoa.

The CCCS presently has in its membership more than 60 per cent of the population in American Samoa, and over 75,600

in Western Samoa. Like Congregational churches elsewhere, the Church has entered into ecumenical relationship with other churches both in and outside Samoa.

METHODIST CHURCH IN SAMOA*
(Ekalesia Metotisi i Samoa)
P.O.Box 199, Apia, Western Samoa — Tel: 22283 and 21985. 30,150 members — 7 synods — 128 parishes — 168 ordained ministers and probationers. WCC (1975), PCC, WMC. President: Rev. Faatauvaa Tapuai — General Secretary: Rev. Sione U. Tamaalii.

When Rev. Peter Turner arrived at Manono in 1835, some 2,000 Samoans were already calling themselves 'Lotu Tonga' (Tonga Religion). They worshipped in rough chapels, observing a few basic Christian practices in a way which they had been taught by Salevaaia, a Samoan chief, who had embraced Christianity in Tonga and on his return become a missionary to his own people. In 1839, it was ordered that Methodism be abandoned, and Turner left the country. Some Methodists returned to paganism, and some went over to the Roman Catholic faith.

But Methodism survived, and for 18 years it was served by Tongan and Samoan teachers. In 1856 the conference in Australia decided to resume the work in Samoa, and the Rev. Martin Dyson was sent in 1857. Towards the end of the 19th century Samoa was badly ravaged by civil wars and political conflicts. During these years Rev. George Brown was in charge of the Methodist mission. The beginning of the 20th century was marked by various developments. The Church began to realize that its task is to be a 'sending church', not only a 'receiving church'. It sought financial independence, developed indigenous leadership and established schools to meet the challenge of illiteracy and ignorance. The political independence of Samoa in 1962 was followed by the independence of the Methodist conference in 1964.

Since then notable changes have taken place. The number of ordained ministers increased; laity gained participation in the work of the Church. Present programmes of the Church extend to areas of land development and home economics. There is a great evangelistic zeal and a growing enthusiasm for missionary outreach. The life of the Church is based on the culture and tradition of the people. The total population of Samoa according to the latest census is over 160,000. Education of the people at all levels is a high priority. The Church maintains close relations with Methodist churches in New Zealand, Tonga, Fiji, the USA, the Caribbean and the Uniting Church of Australia.

TONGA

FREE WESLEYAN CHURCH OF
TONGA (Ko e Siasi Uesiliana Tau'ataini 'o Tonga)
P.O. Box 57, Nuku 'alofa — Tel: 21.622 and 21.632 — Cable: Methodist. 35,260 members — 177 congregations — 124 pastors. Publication: Ko e Tohi Fanongo-nongo (in Tongan). WCC (1975), TNCC, PCC, WMC. President: Rev. Dr V.H. Mo 'ungaola — Connexional Secretary: Rev. John M. Connan.

The first missionaries came to Tonga in 1787. In 1885 the Wesleyan Church split. In 1924 a partial reunion was achieved. The word 'Free' in the name of the Church indicates that the Tonga conference is completely independent, and the word 'Wesleyan' expresses the gratitude of the Tongan people to the ministers of the Wesleyan Church who evangelized the islands. Tonga was a conference within the Methodist Church of Australasia until 1977 when the Methodist Church entered the Uniting Church in Australia and the three Pacific conferences of Tonga, Samoa and Fiji became autonomous. The Church represents 47.4 per cent of the total population.

The relation between the king and the Free Wesleyan Church has been strong since the foundation of modern Tonga under Tuafa 'ahau Tuou I in 1845. The reigning monarch confirms constitutionally the elected president in office. The Church is often seen as the state religion, though this is not so. Yet the influence of the monarch and the hereditary nobility remains strong in the Church, and prevents it from exercising a full critical ministry in matters related to culture, society and politics.

Education and evangelism have been strong features of the work of the Church. The government is responsible for almost two-thirds of primary education and the churches for one-third of which the Wesleyan Church is carrying almost the entire load. It operates 29 primary schools, 21 intermediate schools and 8 secondary schools. From 1828 it has been involved in carrying the good news beyond Tonga, and still has missionaries at work among the Aborigines in North Australia and with the United Church in Papua New Guinea and the Solomon Islands. There are also ministers in Fiji, New Zealand, Australia, Hawai and the West Coast of the USA.

The Church faces a population growth of some 3 per cent, with half of the population under the age of 17. Legally all land must be distributed in inheritable 3.34 hectare plots, but in 1976 more than 65 per cent of those eligible held no land. Migration from the country is currently estimated at 30,000. The growth of a money economy and tourism have affected traditional loyalties and structures of the family and society. The Church is rather slow to come to grips with the emerging signs of alienation and injustice in society.

The Church maintains close relations with the Uniting Church in Australia and the Methodist Churches in Fiji, Samoa, New Zealand, the United Kingdom and the USA.

TUVALU

CHURCH OF TUVALU* (Ekalesia Tuvalu)
Funafuti, Tuvalu — Cable: Tuvchurch, Funafuti. 8,508 membres — 12 congregations — 16 pastors. Publications: Tuvalu New Testament, "Lama" Quarterly

Church Magazine. WCC (1980), PCC, CWM. President: Rev. Panapa Makini — Acting General Secretary: Puafitu Faaalo.

The Church of Tuvalu was founded in 1861. Its existence was consolidated in 1864 by the London Missionary Society. It became autonomous in 1968. The Church is of the congregational tradition. About 98 per cent of the population are members of the Tuvalu Church. The other 2 per cent belong to various groups — the Bahia, Seventh-Day Adventists, New Apostolic Church and the Jehovah's Witnesses.

The Church plays an important role in the cultural, socio-political and religious development of society. It has fostered education in the life of the country. Future aims are to develop women's work in the Church, to set up a seamen's centre and to establish a lay theological training centre. The creation of this centre will be of great importance for the revival and spiritual growth of the Church. Presently Bible study courses are carried on to strengthen the evangelistic zeal in Tuvalu.

The Church has fraternal relations with the Methodist Church in Fiji, the Congregational Christian Church in Samoa and the Uniting Church in Australia.

VANUATU

PRESBYTERIAN CHURCH OF VANUATU (Presbitirin Jyos long Vanuatu)
P.O. Box 150, Vila, Vanuatu — Tel: 2722. 45,000 members — 49 parishes — 59 pastors. Publications: "On the Move" (occasional), Annual Assembly Proceedings. WCC (1961), PCC, WARC. Moderator: Rev. Peter Hanley — Assembly Clerk: Rev. Philip Shing.

The Presbyterian Church of Vanuatu (New Hebrides) was inaugurated in 1948 at a session of the New Hebrides Presbyterian mission synod which marked the mission's centenary. The Presbyterian churches of Nova Scotia, Australia, New Zealand and Canada, and the Free and Reformed Presbyterian churches of Scotland had all contributed to this work.

Vanuatu consists of 12 large islands and many smaller ones in a 400-mile long chain which runs south-east from the Solomon Islands in the West Pacific. Difficult communications, a sparse population, and a variety of cultures and languages are among the problems faced. The general assembly of 1949 was an important first step in building up a sense of unity among the Christians of Vanuatu. The PCV is the largest church, followed by the Roman Catholic Church (16,000), the Anglican Church (15,000) and several other very small religious communities.

Vanuatu gained independence as a nation in 1980. Five Presbyterian pastors and two elders are represented in the government.

Primary concerns in the 1980s are the development of a strong leadership, mission and education. An average of five pastors graduate every year from the theological college. It is hoped that this number will increase to at least ten. A Bible college offers various courses for lay people. It is planned to amalgamate the theological college and the Bible college on one campus. The PCV also maintains a high school in Onesua and the Navota farm school where young men are trained in agricultural programmes and farm techniques. Facing modern problems like the breakdown of marriage, alcoholism, the conflict between tribal and individual possession of land, the conflict between the young generation which has received a modern education and their parents, the Church is called to play an active role in the socio-economic and human development of the nation.

It maintains strong relations with the Presbyterian Churches in Australia and in New Zealand, the Methodist Church in New Zealand and the Uniting Church in Australia.

South America

ARGENTINA

CHURCH OF GOD* (Iglesia de Dios)

Miralla 453, 1408 Buenos Aires — Tel: 642.9298. 40,000 members — 100 parishes — 100 pastors. Publications: Fuego Pentecostal, Dimension de Fe (in Spanish). WCC (1980), CLAI, UNELAM. President: Dr Gabriel O. Vaccaro.

This Church grew out of the two evangelical Pentecostal missionary movements from the USA and Sweden, and was founded in 1952. It has been recognized as an autonomous church body since 1955. It strongly believes in the sustaining power of the Holy Spirit. In line with Baptist tradition the Church lists 10,000 full members, but the total community is close to 40,000. Since 1977 an evangelistic movement "vision de futuro" has been closely associated with the Church of God. When communities growing out of this movement have sufficiently matured, they are incorporated in the Iglesia de Dios.

The Church is now established in the provinces of Chubut, Buenos Aires, Santa Fé, Cordoba, Entre Rios, Corrientes, Misiones, Chaco, Formosa and in the Republic of Paraguay. There are other church organizations working with the Church of God in San Luis, Mendoza, Tucumas, Santa Fé and Cordoba.

A Bible institute was founded in 1971, besides a centre for the preparation of Christian leaders, called "Emmanuel". Courses here are given on three levels and lead to the degree of bachelor of theology. The Church of God participates actively in the work of the Bible Society of Argentina, and has made several contributions to the Movement of Evangelical Unity in Latin America (UNELAM). It broadcasts four radio programmes under the title "Dimensions of Faith".

CHURCH OF THE DISCIPLES OF CHRIST* (Iglesia de los Discipulos de Cristo)

Federico Lacroze 2985, 1426 Buenos Aires. 600 members — 8 congregations — 11 ministers. WCC (1975), CLAI. President: Rev. Luis Parrilla, Juan A. Garcia 2044, 1416 Buenos Aires.

The Church was established by a missionary, Willie Burner, and his family in a suburb (Belgrano) of Buenos Aires in 1906. The first baptism took place in the following year. In 1910 two other missionaries arrived to strengthen the mission.

Disciples in Argentina have become known for their educational work in kindergartens and the Villa Mitre school. Together with the Methodists, they established in 1918 Ward College, and in the same year, together with the Methodist Church and the Waldensians, a theological seminary. By 1923, the missionary work had expanded to include the suburbs of Belgrano, Colegiales, Paternal, Villa Devoto, Saavedra, Villa Crespo and Villa Lynch. National ministers assumed the direction of the congregations which had been previously administered by North American missionaries. In 1926, the Church participated in the first congress of FAIJE, the Argentine Federation of Evangelical Youth.

The 1930s were marked by a slower growth, but cooperation in ecumenical affairs increased. During the next decade the Disciples opened a new area of work in the province of Chaco. In 1959, the Missionary Society of the USA decided to hand over the entire administration of the CDC to the community itself. During the 1960s and the 1970s there were new opportunities for the development of the Church, and service and socio-educational programmes were extended. Although the CDC remains very small, its work is many-faceted, and specially strong in the areas of ecumenical mission and education.

Among the Church's programmes the following should be mentioned: (1) Covifac — Orientation Centre for Community and Family Life, founded twenty years ago, aims at helping people find their identity in family, work and community. It offers assistance in the fields of medicine, obstetrics-gyneocology, pediatrics, psychology and education. (2) The Tablada Community Centre: this Centre is located in an industrial area offering many social and recreational activities for children and adolescents. (3) Aidet-Isadet is the place where pastors and other leaders are trained, together with Methodists, Waldensians, United Lutherans of the River Plate, Anglicans and Scottish Presbyterians.

Together with five sister churches the CDC operates the Aurora Publishing House. Many evangelical books in Spanish, expressing Protestant culture and thought, have been published. Also together with other denominations, the Church is engaged in JUM (United Board of Missions). This board is very active in the province of Chaco rendering service to small indigenous communities, and more than 1,000 families are taking part. The Church continues to participate in the Consultative Council of Churches whose major objective is to reflect together on the policies and goals of various programmes in which the denominations are involved.

EVANGELICAL CHURCH OF THE RIVER PLATE (Iglesia Evangélica del Rio de la Plata)

Esmeralda 162, 1035 Buenos Aires — Tel: 45.7520. 60,000 members — 32 congregations — 37 ordained pastors — 12 nonordained pastors. WCC (1956), LWF, AFEC. President: Rev. Rodolfo R. Reinich.

The Church was established in 1843. It is a 'union church' including people of Swiss as well as German origin, whose confessional composition is about 90 per cent Lutheran and 10 per cent Reformed. During the 19th and 20th centuries, Esmeralda 162 was the address for German church outreach into many parts of Latin America. Its membership was largely rural, but there were also congregations in larger cities like Montevideo, Uruguay (1846) and Asuncion, Paraguay (1893). Organized in 1899 as the German Evangelical La Plata Synod, it slowly disengaged itself from German ties. In 1956, it became independent from the foreign office of the Evangelical Church in Germany. In 1965, it dropped

the "German" and took its present name. There are now a great number of congregations spread throughout Argentina and the neighbouring countries of Uruguay and Paraguay.

In the 1960s, the Church became ecumenically active, joining the WCC, and — overcoming much of what keen observers called a cultural Protestantism — took a leading part also in the promotion of unity among Lutherans by cooperating in such projects as theological education and resettlement of displaced persons. Pastors of the Church are in part still supplied from Germany, but a new generation of ministers is being trained at the Instituto Superior Evangélico de Estudios Teologicos. The ECRP participates in the Argentine Federation of Evangelical Churches, the Christian Communications Centre, and the Lutheran Council of the River Plate.

EVANGELICAL METHODIST CHURCH OF ARGENTINA (Iglesia Evangélica Metodista Argentina)

Rivadavia 4044, Buenos Aires. 8,940 members — 101 congregations — 60 pastors. Publication: El Estandarte Evangélico (in Spanish). WCC (1971), WMC, AFEC. Bishop Federico Pagura.

In 1825 the Missionary Society of the Methodist Episcopal Church in New York proposed the establishment of a mission in South America. Rio de Janeiro, Buenos Aires and Montevideo were visited. The 1836 general conference recommended that work be established in the first two of these cities. The work in Buenos Aires flourished, and soon a church building was put up. Until 1867 it was forbidden by local regulations to preach the gospel in Spanish. Once the prohibition was withdrawn, the work of the Methodist Church, followed in course of time by other denominations, spread throughout the country. The missionary thrust went beyond the borders, and centres were opened in Peru, Bolivia, Paraguay, Uruguay and Southern Brazil. All these were later organized into the

South American annual conference. In 1884 the first secondary school was established in cooperation with the Waldensian Church. It became the nucleus of the first seminary which developed into the Facultad Evangélica de Teologia; by merger with the Lutheran Seminary it became the Instituto Superior Evangélico de Estudios Teologicos. Social work in various forms was undertaken, and an active literature programme as well, based on the Methodist Printing House, Methopress.

The work in Uruguay was organized separately from the River Plate annual conference. The work in Argentina continued with two conferences: one took the name of Argentina annual conference; the other, created a few years later, became the provisional annual conference of Patagonia. Both became a part of the Iglesia Evangélica Metodista Argentina in October 1969.

The small Church is recognized for its ecumenical spirit and social awareness. It has several educational centres and shares with seven other churches one of the best theological institutions of the continent. High on its agenda are evangelization and church growth, and the struggle for social justice and human rights. For these the development of a qualified leadership of laypersons has become a prerequisite. Social and missionary work is undertaken among the indigenous population — in the north with the Tobas and in the south with the Mapuches. Also nursery services in Christian communities in various regions of the country are built up. The Church maintains strong relationships with Methodist churches in Europe and North America.

UNITED EVANGELICAL LUTHERAN CHURCH* (Iglesia Evangélica Luterana Unida)
Simbron 4661, 1417 Buenos Aires — Tel: 53.8615 . 5,760 members — 22 parishes — 27 pastors. Publication: Luz y Verdad. WCC (1969), LWF, AFEC. President: Rev. Raul E. Denuncio.

This Church, organized in 1948, is the youngest and the smallest of the three Lutheran church bodies in Argentina. Its main strength lies in the Buenos Aires area, with congregations also some 200 miles to the south, in the northern tip — the Misiones region — and elsewhere. Begun in 1908 by one of the antecedent bodies of the present Lutheran Church in America, the "Unida", as the UELC is commonly called, has for seven decades seen its task as evangelizing the secularized Spanish-speaking Argentinians. But with the resettlement of European refugees after the Second World War, the Unida became very much involved in ministries which today include the use of Latvian, Estonian, Hungarian, Slovak and German as well as Spanish. This diversification has proved helpful to people with special needs, but it has also tended to keep the Church small and struggling, as well as scattered. Moreover, the reduction of help from the Lutheran Church in America, as a result of changing trends in mission and the Church's desire to stand on its own feet, has put severe strains on Unida's leadership.

Meanwhile, it continues to take a strong part in theological education, maintains programmes for the training of lay leadership in the congregations, and provides special services to the aging and persons in need. In this decade evangelization remains the primary objective of the Church. As it is now self-supporting, it receives aid only for special projects.

BOLIVIA

EVANGELICAL METHODIST CHURCH IN BOLIVIA* (Iglesia Evangélica Metodista en Bolivia)
Landaeta 423, Casilla 356, La Paz — Tel: 342702 and 352732 — Cable: Metodista. 5,000 members — 75 parishes — 25 pastors. Publication: Avance (in Spanish). WCC (1971), UNELAM, WMC. Rt Rev. Rolando Villena Villegas.

In 1891 Karl Beutelpacher, a lay preacher, founded the first Methodist Sunday school in Oruro, Bolivia. Because of the 1899 revolution and later through the Liberal Party in 1906 reforms were effected in the Bolivian constitution which permitted freedom of worship, creating conditions for establishing Protestant work in Bolivia. Francis Harrington, an American missionary, opened the doors for Methodism in 1906 and founded the first Protestant school in La Paz in 1907. In 1969, the EMCB became autonomous and elected its first national bishop, Mortimer Arias. In 1975 a popular Aymara movement, representing the majority of church membership, initiated a historical process of change. At an extraordinary session of the fourth general assembly in 1976, three national executive secretaries were elected, responsible for national and international ecumenical relations, for life and mission (including education and promotion of the interests of women), and social services (including rural ministry and health services).

The EMCB seeks to deepen the faith of its members and create a commitment to love and justice. It is in the process of evaluating its social ethic goals and preparing an overall missionary strategy for the next ten years. It is also committed to the re-evaluation of native cultures. It stimulates basic education and social-economic development, evangelization and general social welfare — always in the context of the Bolivian situation and with the purpose of remaining faithful to Jesus Christ and the mission of the Church.

The EMCB maintains two hospitals and administers two others. Its main emphasis today is on promoting public health. Through a formal agreement with the Bolivian government, the Church sustains and directs seven educational centres, with an emphasis on primary, secondary, vocational and adult education. It carries out broad programmes of rural and community development. It supports various ecumenical programmes such as a centre of educational research and a centre of social studies and documentation. Through seminary extension classes, it seeks to update the education of its local and national

leaders. It owns one of the most important Protestant book stores in Latin America and a centre to promote native handicrafts. There are 50 national workers and 13 missionaries. The Church maintains a close relation with the United Methodist Church in the USA.

BRAZIL

EPISCOPAL CHURCH OF BRAZIL
(Igreja Episcopal Do Brasil)
Caixa Postal 2684, 90.000 Porto Alegre, RG — Tel: 49.36.58. 42,770 members — 117 congregations — 6 bishops — 105 priests. Publications: Estandarte Cristão, Sementes (both in Portuguese). WCC (1966), NCCB, ACC, SAAC, CLAC. Primate: Rt Rev. Arthur Kratz — General Secretary: Rev. Plinio L. Simões.

This Anglican province covers the whole territory of Brazil, and was inaugurated in 1965. There are British chaplaincies in central and northern Brazil. With its enormous geographical area, Brazil is a country of great contrasts. The nation is facing serious economic and social problems, and the Church has an important contribution to make to the spiritual life of the Brazilian people as a church which is both catholic and reformed. The synod of the Church meets every two years, and it functions through the executive council of the synod which meets twice a year.

Theological education is supervised by a national board of which all bishops are *ex officio* members, with clerical and lay representation from each diocese. Two large schools, Southern Cross and St Margaret's, both coeducational, are run by the Diocese of Southern Brazil. *Estandarte Cristão*, published since 1893, contains articles and news about the life of the Church at local, national and international levels. The Church is actively involved in the ongoing work of the National Council of Churches in Brazil (CONIC). Primary concerns for the 1980s are education, youth work and financial autonomy.

EVANGELICAL CHURCH OF LUTHERAN CONFESSION IN BRAZIL
(Igreja Evangélica de Confissão Luterana no Brasil)
Rua Senhor dos Passos, 202-2° andar, Caixa Postal 2876, 90.000 Porto Alegre, RS — Tel: (0512) 21.3433 — Cable: Eclesia — Telex: 0512064 Fuis BR. 800,000 members — 32 districts — 1,300 parishes — 366 pastors. Publications: Boletim Informativo da IECLB, Informação IECLB (both in Portuguese), Jornal Evangélico, Annuário Evangélico (both in Portuguese and German). WCC (1950), UNELAM, ECB, LWF. President: Rev. Augusto Ernesto Kunert — General Secretary: Rev. Rodolfo J. Schneider.

The first German immigrants arrived in southern Brazil in 1824, bringing with them their evangelical faith. The settlement in São Leopoldo became the German Protestant stronghold and the base for progressive expansion. Later, similar projects with immigrants were launched in the neighbouring states of Santa Catarina and Paraná. Commercial and other interests drew Germans to Rio de Janeiro, to the states of São Paulo, Minas Gerais, Espirito Santo, and elsewhere. These were restricted to the ethnic and cultural German community. Until the independence of Brazil, the Portuguese government barred non-Portuguese immigrants from entering the country.

The first permanent general body was the synod of Rio Grande do Sul (1886). It was followed by the Lutheran synod (1905), the synod of Santa Catarina and Paraná (1911), and the Middle Brazilian synod (1912). The hardships of the pioneering days and the setbacks resulting from chaotic local conditions were gradually overcome. Organizational consolidation and confessional identity advanced hand in hand. The present Church, the result of the fusion of several synods, was inaugurated at its general council meeting at São Paulo in 1968. It represents less than one per cent of the total population of 121 million who continue in the Roman Catholic faith. Yet the Church is the largest among the Evangelical churches, in membership only surpassed by the Pentecostal churches. It has increasingly become a part of the Brazilian as well as the ecumenical scene.

The last-minute decision not to hold the LWF Assembly in Brazil in 1970, owing to widely reported violations of human rights in the country, was a serious setback for the ·Church. But it stood the test. It has spoken out for human rights, and become increasingly concerned about social issues, in particular through its programmes of lay education and its attempts at missionary outreach in frontier areas. Its work among young people, university students, and the uprooted population which in recent years have migrated to the cities, is challenging the Church to complete its transition from German to Portuguese.

The board of directors has established five priorities, around which the life of the Church turns: (1) unity in theological plurality; (2) internal and external evangelization; (3) proportional contribution by its members; (4) support of the indigenous (Indian) cause; and (5) agrarian reform.

EVANGELICAL PENTECOSTAL CHURCH "BRAZIL FOR CHRIST"
(Igreja Evangélica Pentecostal "O Brasil para Cristo")
Caixa Postal 4054, 01000 São Paulo, SP — Tel: 262.3442. 1,100,000 members — 200 parishes — 300 pastors. WCC (1969), ECB, UNELAM. Rev. Manoel de Melo — Secretary: Enilson Rocha Souza, Caixa Postal 041, 4000 Salvador.

From the earliest days of Pentecostal revival, Brazil has been a centre of activity for both American and Scandinavian missionaries. The first Pentecostal Church in Brazil was organized in Para in 1910, with eighteen members, when Gunnar Vingren and Daniel Berg, Swedes living in the United States, arrived to conduct a programme of missionary evangelism. Since that time the Pentecostal movement has grown steadily; it now has more than 4,000 churches with an estimated membership of

16,4 per cent of the total population. The principal concentration of Pentecostals is in Rio de Janeiro, Recife, Para and Manaos.

The EPC was founded in 1955 by Manoel de Melo, a migrant from Brazil's impoverished north-east. The headquarters temple, dedicated on 1 July 1979, is described as the "world's largest evangelical church". The Church's cornerstone was laid in 1962, at the height of opposition from traditional Protestant denominations. It was built solely from contributions from Brazilian sources, especially the Church's own membership. The EPC is the largest member church in Latin America of the World Council of Churches.

From Pernambuco, where M. de Melo was active as pastor of the Assembléias de Deus, his course took him to Sao Paulo. A few years later he broke away from the Assembléias there and put his extraordinary gifts as an evangelist and his inexhaustible capacity for work at the service of the Cruzada Nacional de Evangelização. There were gigantic gatherings at his evangelization meetings in tents, in open places and in parks, which often resulted in astonishing cures of the sick.

Attending an interdenominational symposium on "The Holy Spirit and the Pentecostal Movement" in 1965 Rev. de Melo said: "Rome has brought to the world idolatry, Russia the terrors of communism, the USA the demon of capitalism; we Brazilians, nation of the poor, shall bring to the world the gospel."

As an observer of the assembly at Uppsala, 1968, he remarked that he felt like "Ezèkiel in the valley of dry bones". In his view, as far as worship was concerned the World Council was pedalling a bicycle in the age of jet aeroplanes. Nice services are not enough, de Melo argued. "While we convert a million, the devil de-converts ten millions through hunger, misery, militarism and dictatorship." He mentioned the Roman Catholic bishop Helder Camara as the model of a true evangelist.

Ever since the EPC has been eager to have the help of the WCC to fulfil its function as a prophet and a reviver of social and political conscience. It has made valuable contributions in bringing socio-economic help and educational opportunities to large numbers of people in Brazil.

LATIN AMERICAN REFORMED CHURCH (Igreja Reformada Latino Americana)

Caixa Postal 1251, 01000 Sao Paulo. 19,000 members — 11 parishes — 11 pastors. WCC (1972), ECB, UNELAM, WARC. General Secretary: Rev. Janos Apostol.

The LARC began in 1932 as the missionary enterprise of the Reformed Church in Hungary. Congregations were gradually organized in Sao Paulo, Parana, Rio de Janeiro, and in the vast hinterland of Brazil. Communities were also organized in Argentine and Uruguay. The Church started among immigrants from Central Europe and used the Magyar language. It continues its special care of immigrants; at the same time, it has enlarged its sphere to become a national church with services in Portuguese. During the Second World War, it became an autonomous, self-supporting body which, in 1945, received its official name Igreja Crista Reformada do Brasil.

The Church accepts the second Helvetic confession, the Heidelberg catechism and — as a special and historic confession — the profession of faith of the first "Igreja Reformada" organized in Brazil in the year 1557 by ministers sent by John Calvin. It follows the Presbyterian system. The Church's ministers are usually educated in Brazilian theological faculties, though candidates for the ministry are also sent to take postgraduate courses abroad.

METHODIST CHURCH IN BRAZIL (Igreja Metodista Do Brasil)

Rua Visconde de Porto Seguro 442, 04642 Santo Amaro, Sao Paulo; Caixa Postal 55202-01000 Sao Paulo — Tel: 011.247.7669, 521.6747 and 548.5623. 68,000 members — 6 dioceses — 1,200 congregations — 6 bishops — 550 pastors. Publications: Expositor Cristao, Voz Missionaria, Bem-Te-Vi, Flâmula Juvenil, No Cenaculo (in Portuguese). WCC (1948), NCCB, CIEMAL, WMC. Bishop Sady Machado da Silva — President of the General Council: Dr Elizeu Constantino.

The Church was started in Brazil by missionaries of the board of missions of the Southern Methodist Episcopal Church and the Methodist Episcopal Church in the USA. After an unsuccessful attempt in 1835 another missionary enterprise began in 1867. Several congregations were established and the Church grew steadily. The Church became autonomous in 1930, when the MCB became an independent body, though in close relation with American Methodism. Now there are six bi-annual conferences each one electing its own bishop. During the time between regular meetings, decisions are taken by a council elected for a two-year term.

The Catholic Church claims 90 per cent of the Brazilian population. All Protestant churches together total less than one fifth of Pentecostal membership in the country.

From its very beginning the Methodist Church in Brazil had laid great emphasis on education. As a result there are several schools, some more than a hundred years old. The Methodist University of Piracicaba, in the state of Sao Paulo, was inaugurated in 1976.

Pastors are prepared in a school of theology and in three Bible seminaries. Many Methodist schools play an important role in the Brazilian educational system. Today there are almost as many pupils in the various Methodist schools as there are members in the Church. In the last few years Methodists have realized that their schools should not simply echo the official government ideology, but should operate in different ways, seeking the transformation of society. New methods of education are still a controversial issue.

In the field of social work, the MCB has also been a pioneer in establishing centres of aid, shelters for children and people in the slums. More programmes need to be developed, such as specific projects for community action, the structuring of new youth movements and work with indigenous communities. The preparation of new ministers with missionary zeal and an ecumenical vision is another priority for the 1980s. The Church maintains good relations with the United Methodist Church in the USA, the United Church of Canada and the Evangelical Methodist Church in Germany.

CHILE

EVANGELICAL LUTHERAN CHURCH IN CHILE (Iglesia Evangélica Luterana en Chile)
Avenida Ricardo Lyon 1483, Casilla 15167, Santiago — Tel: 2255816. 2,000 members — 5 congregations — 5 communities in formation — 7 pastors. Publication: Boletin Informativo de la IELCH (in Castilian). WCC (1963), CECH, CLAI, LWF. President: Rev. Stefan Schaller.

In 1849, some German and Swiss families began their pioneering on arable land between the towns of Valdivia and Osorno, some 500 miles south of Santiago. Within a decade, about 700 families had settled there. As non-Roman Catholics they were only permitted to worship in private, a restraint which over the decades induced in them a certain religious and cultural ghetto mentality. Hard work, economic success, and readiness to perpetuate their inherited faith marked the life of this first congregation (1853) and of those that later came to other parts of the country, including the capital city. Pastors came from Germany, and a general oversight was exercised from Berlin (Evangelical Church of the Old Prussian Union) via Buenos Aires. A synod of congregations, formed in 1904, later became the German Evangelical Church in Chile (1937). German immigrants after the First World War, and again German as well as Hungarian, Baltic, and other refugees after the Second World War, were added to the church's membership. A new constitution (1959) dropped the "German" from the title and adopted the confessional designation "Evangelical Lutheran Church in Chile". A president (or provost, on occasion also called bishop) heads the church; the synod is the legislative body, and the church council the executive unit.

Troubles in the church came to a head with the downfall of the Allende regime in September 1973. Tensions between pastors and laity were not new. The pastors, most of them supplied on a short-term basis by the foreign office of the Evangelical Church in Germany, and some of the laity tended to have a broader understanding of human rights issues than the rank-and-file members of the congregations. The latter, mostly self-made people, tended to be conservative in politics and against a social application of the gospel, especially if this aided people on the political left. The mediating efforts of Helmut Frenz, the duly elected head of the ELCC, sprang from his Christian faith and his own experience as a Second World War German refugee. His heading of an ecumenical effort to aid Chilean political refugees and their families, along lines authorized by the Pinochet government, triggered reaction in his church. He was later expelled by the Chilean government in 1975. The break in the ELCC was now complete. Most of the pastors remained with the remnant church and elected a new president. Of the church's 12 parishes, eight seceded, taking with them church properties and all but 2,000 of the 25,000 members.

The Church has close ties with the Evangelical Church in Germany and the Lutheran Church in America.

METHODIST CHURCH OF CHILE*
(Iglesia Metodista de Chile)
Sargento Aldea 1041, Casilla 67, Santiago de Chile — Tel: 56.6074. 6,000 members — 131 churches — 1 bishop — 52 pastors. Publication: El Cristiano (in Castilian). WCC (1971), CIEMAL, CLAI, WMC. Bishop Isaias Gutiérrez V.

In 1877 William Taylor began his controversial plan for self-supporting missions on the west coast of South America, separately from the work of the board of missions of the Methodist Episcopal Church. The work came under the Methodist Episcopal Church in 1893, when the South America conference was organized with Chile as one of six districts. In 1901 the Chile district became an annual conference.

The conference was supervised from the United States for many years, but in 1920 Chile proposed a division of the work in Latin America into two episcopal areas and the creation of a central conference. The general conference of 1924 approved the latter request and the Latin America central conference met that same year. In 1932 the central conference was permitted to elect bishops.

The Methodist Church of Chile became autonomous in 1969. The new Church maintains ties with the United Methodist Church and with that Church's Board of Global Ministries.

Pentecostal or holiness groups, with a Methodist background, have been very active in Chile and have by far the largest constituency of any Protestant body. They claim a membership of about six per cent of the population of Chile, with one church in Santiago of 2,000 members.

Extensive evangelization and human promotion, in particular among the poor peasants and workers, remains a primary aim of the MCC.

PENTECOSTAL CHURCH OF CHILE
(Iglesia Pentecostal de Chile)
Calle Peña 1103, Casilla de Correo 2, Curico — Tel: 1035. 90,000 members — 350 congregations — 145 pastors. Publication: La Voz Pentecostal (in Spanish). WCC (1961), CLAI, CECH. Bishop Enrique Chavez Campos.

The Church was founded in 1945. From the beginning its headquarters were in Curico, about 200 km to the south of Santiago. Its founder, Bishop Chavez, came out of the Methodist Pentecostal Church. The growth of the Church has been the result of an intensive evangelistic campaign among the population of Chile, in particular among its working classes, marginal groups and the poorest sectors of society. Labourers who flocked from the countryside to the cities responded to the Church's transforming message. The Church proclaims and lives by the power of the Holy Spirit, whose presence is felt among the faithful in different ways. The Church is also open to cooperation and communication with other churches and religious organizations.

The Pentecostal Church is governed by the general assembly which elects an executive committee. Pastors are nominated and sent by the bishop.

The Church faces many challenges. The education of children, youth and adults is a priority. The young generation in Chile is poorly educated. Adults need a clear vision of the society in order to search in creative ways for solutions to the problems faced by the nation. The Christian community needs to be strengthened by a sense of solidarity.

The Church has participated actively in the creation and ongoing work of Evangelical Christian Aid whose principal objective is to promote social action programmes among the most needy of the community. To this effect several projects are undertaken — the creation of homes for students, lunch rooms for children of poor families, practical schools for women giving instruction in health, nutrition, sewing, weaving, literacy, etc., the teaching of new agricultural techniques, programmes to support members of congregations who belong to labour unions defending the rights of people.

The Church is also committed to Christian unity. It is convinced that only a united church can tackle the social and economic problems of the nation.

PENTECOSTAL MISSION CHURCH

(Mision Iglesia Pentecostal)
Av. Pedro Montt 1473, Casilla 5391, Correo 3, Santiago — Tel: 568657. 12,000 members — 17 parishes — 32 preaching localities (in Chile) — 8 parishes — 12 preaching localities (in Argentina). Publication: Sembrando (in Spanish). WCC (1961), CLAI. President: Rev. Narciso Sepulveda Barra — Secretary: Rev. Arturo Palma Cher, Casilla 618, Los Angeles.

The Church was founded in 1952 by a group of 120 people who had left the Evangelical Pentecostal Church, one of the largest Pentecostal denominations in the country which had sprung from the Methodist Episcopal Church in 1909. From the beginning the Church emphasized its readiness to relate to other churches in order to fulfill the tasks of evangelization and Christian service. It participated from the outset in the Evangelical Christian Aid. It is also one of the founders of the Evangelical Theological Community of Chile. Missionary work was extended to neighbouring Argentina, concentrating mainly on Chilean immigrants. There was also a mission in Uruguay, but this work has been passed on to the Waldensian Church. The membership is 1.27 per cent of the Protestant population of Chile. As other Pentecostal churches in Chile, the Pentecostal Mission Church has taken roots mostly among the poor sectors of society, both urban or rural. The interpretation of the Christian faith and the celebration of Sunday worship reflect this fact. There is an increasing commitment to service among the poor and marginalized in society.

A central preoccupation at present is the search for new forms of Christian education and theological reflection, adapted to the reality of the congregations. New forms of pastoral work and a new style of evangelization are being explored.

PERU

METHODIST CHURCH OF PERU*

(Iglesia Metodista Peruana)
Apartado 1386, Lima 100 — Tel: 245970 — Cable: Metodista. 3,800 members — 47 congregations — 20 pastors. WCC (1972),

UNELAM. President: Bishop Marco A. Ochoa.

William Taylor set up one of his self-supporting missions in Peru in 1877-1878. In 1886 Francisco G. Penzotti visited the country and in 1890 he was thrown into prison for selling Bibles. This case became internationally known because the principle of religious liberty was involved, and Penzotti was released after eight months.

The self-support principle resulted in the development of several schools. The Lima high school for girls is one of the well-known schools in South America, with some 700 girls. The Victoria school for boys and girls, also in Lima, has 750 students. At Callao there is a coeducational school with an enrolment of 1,000. There are three other Methodist schools in the country. There are 6,000 Sunday school pupils.

The Peru Annual Conference of the Methodist Church became autonomous in 1970, and organized itself as a church — Iglesia Metodista Peruana.

SURINAM

MORAVIAN CHURCH IN SURINAM

P.O. Box 219/1811, Paramaribo — Tel: 73073. 57,400 members — 57 congregations — 38 pastors. Publication: Kerkbode (in Dutch). WCC (1975), CCC. Chairman of the Surinam Provincial Board: Rev. Th. A. Darnoud — General Secretary: B.J. Parabirsing.

The mission in Surinam started from Herrnhut in 1732 and was continued after 1928 from Zeist in the Netherlands. Mission among the American-Indians started in 1748 and later among the (African) slaves and the bush negros (fugitive slaves). The first bush negro to accept baptism was Arabi (1771). After 1835 several congregations were built in Saramacca, Nickerie, Albina, Groningen, Grote Stad, Wanica, Noorderstad en Zuiderstad. Mission

among the East Indians (Hindustanis) began in 1873 and among the Javenese in 1909. As several members of the Moravian Church in Surinam emigrated to the Netherlands Antilles and Holland, especially after the Second World War, the Church in Surinam is also working in these countries. In 1963 the Church became independent, with its own synod meeting every three years. The provincial board, the governing body of the Christian community, is assisted by two other boards, one for church affairs and the other for mission affairs.

The Moravian Church has several departments — for boarding schools, socio-diaconal service, medical assistance to the bush negros and the Indians, agricultural promotion. Clergy and evangelists are trained in study centres. Some 800 teachers teach 2,500 pupils in several kinds of schools. Pastoral work is undertaken by ten ordained clergymen and evangelists. Missionary work is carried on by 41 clergymen and evangelists.

URUGUAY

EVANGELICAL METHODIST CHURCH IN URUGUAY* (Iglesia Evangélica Metodista en el Uruguay)

San José 1457, Montevideo — Tel: 4.42.36.40.08.37. 1,000 members — 8 pastors — 4 laymen. Publication: Boletin Metodista (in Spanish). WCC (1971), CLAI, CIEMAL, WMC. President: Miss Margarita Grassi.

Methodism was introduced to Uruguay and Argentina in 1838. In 1842 the work had to be closed; it did not start again until 1870. The arrival of Thomas B. Wood in 1876 marked the official establishment of Methodist work. Throughout its early years, Methodist work in Uruguay was a part of the mission based in Buenos Aires. When the South America conference was organized in 1893, Uruguay became a district.

Educational work was established early, and today the outstanding institution is Crandon Institute, founded in Montevideo in 1879, with a branch now in Salto. Among notable institutions in the country is Good Will Industries, the first of its kind to be set up outside the United States.

In 1952 the general conference separated Argentina and Uruguay, and the latter became the Uruguay provisional annual conference. In 1960 it became a regular annual conference. Then in 1968 the conference asked for and received authorization to become an autonomous church. The EMCU districts have been eliminated and an executive committee of 12 — 6 ministers and 6 lay people — exercise supervision over the entire church.

Among the primary concerns are active participation in the national ecumenical movement and the strengthening of relations, in particular with Pentecostals and Roman Catholics; a more intensive programme of theological education of ministers and lay persons; more creative Sunday school work and better communication with youth; and better articulated programmes of evangelism.

The EMCU has fraternal relations with the Evangelical Methodist Church in Argentina, the United Methodist Church in the USA, the Reformed Churches in the Netherlands and the Uniting Church in Australia.

Constitution and Rules of the World Council of Churches concerning membership

as approved by the Fifth Assembly, Nairobi, Kenya,
23 November-10 December 1975, and amended by the Central Committee,
Geneva, Switzerland, 28 July-6 August 1977

CONSTITUTION

Basis

The World Council of Churches is a fellowship of churches which confess the Lord Jesus Christ as God and Saviour according to the scriptures and therefore seek to fulfill together their common calling to the glory of the one God, Father, Son and Holy Spirit.

Membership

Those churches shall be eligible for membership in the World Council of Churches which express their agreement with the Basis upon which the Council is founded and satisfy such criteria as the Assembly or the Central Committee may prescribe. Election to membership shall be by a two-thirds vote of the member churches represented at the Assembly, each member church having one vote. Any application for membership between meetings of the Assembly may be considered by the Central Committee; if the application is supported by a two-thirds vote of the members of the Committee present and voting, this action shall be communicated to the churches that are members of the World Council of Churches, and unless objection is received from more than one-third of the member churches within six months the applicant shall be declared elected.

RULES

Membership of the Council

Members of the Council are those churches which, having constituted the Council or having been admitted to membership, continue in membership. The term "church" as used in this article includes an association, convention, or federation of autonomous churches. A group of churches within a country or region may determine to participate in the World Council of Churches as one church. The General Secretary shall maintain the official list of member churches noting any special arrangement accepted by the Assembly or Central Committee.

The following rules shall pertain to membership

1. Application

A church which wishes to become a member of the World Council of Churches shall apply in writing to the General Secretary.

2. Processing

The General Secretary shall submit all such applications to the Central Committee (see Art. II of the Constitution) together with such information as he or she considers necessary to enable the Assembly or the Central Committee to make a decision on the application.

3. Criteria

In addition to expressing agreement with the Basis upon which the Council is founded (Art. I of the Constitution), an applicant must satisfy the following criteria to be eligible for membership:
a) A church must be able to take the decision to apply for membership without obtaining the permission of any other body or person.
b) A church must produce evidence of sustained independent life and organization.
c) A church must recognize the essential interdependence of the churches, particularly those of the same confession, and must practise constructive ecumenical relations with other churches within its country or region.

4. Associate membership

A church otherwise eligible, which would be denied membership solely under Rule I.3(d), may be elected to associate membership in the same manner as member churches are elected. A church applying for associate membership must ordinarily have at least 10,000 members. An associate member church may participate in all activities of the Council; its representatives to the Assembly shall have the right to speak but not to vote. Associate member churches shall be listed separately on the official list maintained by the General Secretary.

5. Consultation

Before admitting a church to membership or associate membership, the appropriate world confessional body or bodies and national council or regional conference of churches shall be consulted.

6. Resignation

A church which desires to resign its membership in the Council can do so at any time. A church which has resigned but desires to rejoin the Council, must again apply for membership.

Index by countries

Names of member churches

English names of member churches

Abbreviations

AACC	All African Conference of Churches
AAICC	All African Independent Church Council
ABF	Asian Baptist Fellowship
ACC	Anglican Consultative Council
ACC	Australian Council of Churches
ACKBD	Arbeitsgemeinschaft christlicher Kirchen in der Bundesrepublik Deutschland und Berlin (West) (Joint Working Group of Christian Churches in the Federal Republic of Germany)
ACKS	Arbeitsgemeinschaft christlicher Kirchen in der Schweiz (Joint Working Group of Christian Churches in Switzerland)
AEPB	Alliance des Eglises Protestantes du Burundi (Alliance of Protestant Churches of Burundi)
AFEC	Argentine Federation of Evangelical Churches
AGCK	Arbeitsgemeinschaft christlicher Kirchen (Joint Working Group of Christian Churches in the German Democratic Republic)
AK	Arnoldshainer Konferenz (Arnoldshain Conference)
ALICE	All African Lutheran Churches' Information and Coordination Center
AMC	Austrian Missionary Council
BeCC	Bengal Christian Council
BiCC	Bihar Christian Council
BoCC	Botswana Christian Council
BCC	British Council of Churches
BuCC	Burma Council of Churches
BWA	Baptist World Alliance
CAN	Christian Association of Nigeria
CCA	Christian Conference of Asia
CCC	Canadian Council of Churches

CCC	Caribbean Conference of Churches
CCC	Curaçao Council of Churches
CCCE	Council for the Co-operation of Churches in Ethiopia
CCEA	Council of Churches of East Asia
CCG	Christian Council of Ghana
CCI	Council of Churches in Indonesia
CCL	Christian Council of Lesotho
CCM	Christian Council of Madagascar
CCM	Council of Churches of Malaysia
CCM	Conselho Cristao de Moçambique (Christian Council of Mozambique)
CCN	Christian Council of Nigeria
CCN	Council of Churches in the Netherlands
CCT	Christian Council of Tanzania
CCT	Christian Council of Trinidad
CCW	Council of Churches for Wales
CCZ	Christian Council of Zambia
CEC	Conference of European Churches
CEC	Consejo Ecumenico de Cuba (Ecumenical Council of Cuba)
CECH	Concilio Evangelica de Chile (Evangelical Council of Chile)
CEPPLE	Conférence des Eglises Protestantes des Pays latins d'Europe (Conference of Protestant Churches of South-European Countries)
CEVAA	Communauté évangélique d'action apostolique (Evangelical Community for Apostolic Action)
CIEMAL	Consejo de Iglesias Evangélicas Metodistas de América Latina (Council of Evangelical Methodist Churches in Latin America)
CLAI	Consejo Latinoamericana de Iglesias (Conference of Latin American Churches)
COCU	Consultation on Church Unity
CPC	Christian Peace Conference
CPR	Conseil Protestant du Rwanda (Protestant Council of Rwanda)
CUC (SA)	Church Unity Commission (South Africa)
CWM	Council for World Mission
DEFAP	Département Evangélique Français d'Action Apostolique. Service protestant de mission et de relations internationales (French Evangelical Department for Apostolic Action)
DMC	Danish Missionary Council
DMPB	Département missionnaire protestant de Belgique (Protestant Missionary Department of Belgium)
EACCSE	Ecumenical Advisory Council for Church. Service in Egypt
EAD	Evangelical Alliance of Denmark
EBF	European Baptist Federation

ECB	Evangelical Confederation of Brazil
ECCA	Ecumenical Council of Churches in Austria
ECCCS	Ecumenical Council of Churches in the Czech Socialist Republic
ECCSEC	Ecumenical Commission for Church and Society of the European Community
ECCY	Ecumenical Council of Churches in Yugoslavia
ECD	Ecumenical Council of Denmark
ECF	Ecumenical Council of Finland
ECHC	Ecumenical Council of Hungarian Churches
EKD	Evangelische Kirche in Deutschland
EKU	Evangelische Kirche der Union (Evangelical Church of the Union)
EKUDDR	Evangelische Kirche der Union - Bereich DDR (Evangelical Church of the Union - GDR)
FCC	Fiji Council of Churches
FCFC	Free Church Federal Council (British)
FEM	Federación Evangélica de México (Evangelical Federation of Mexico)
FEMEC	Fédération des Eglises et Mission Evangéliques du Cameroun (Federation of Churches and Evangelical Missions of Cameroon)
FFCC	Federal Free Church Council
FIEU	Federación de Iglesias Evangélicas del Uruguay (Federation of Evangelical Churches of Uruguay)
FPCB	Federation of the Protestant Churches in Belgium
FPCI	Federation of Protestant Churches in Italy
FPF	Fédération Protestante de France (Protestant Federation of France)
GCC	Guyana Council of Churches
GMC	German Missionary Council
HKCC	Hong Kong Christian Council
ICC	Iran Council of Churches
ICC	Irish Council of Churches
IFFEC	International Federation of Free Evangelical Churches
IFPC	Italian Federation of Protestant Churches
IMCU	International Moravian Church in "the Unity"
JCC	Jamaica Council of Churches
KKR	Konferenz der Kirchen am Rhein (Conference of Churches along the Rhine)
LCC	Leuenberger Church Community
LCUSA	Lutheran Council in the USA
LWF	Lutheran World Federation
MCC	Melanesian Council of Churches

MECC	Middle East Council of Churches
MEFEC	Middle East Fellowship of Evangelical Churches
MWC	Mennonite World Conference
NABF	North American Baptist Fellowship
NCCB	National Council of Churches Bangladesh
NCCB	National Council of Churches in Brazil
NCCI	National Christian Council of India
NCCJ	National Christian Council of Japan
NCCK	National Christian Council of Kenya
NCCK	National Council of Churches in Korea
NCCL	National Christian Council of Liberia
NCCNZ	National Council of Churches in New Zealand
NCCP	National Council of Churches in Pakistan
NCCP	National Council of Churches in the Philippines
NCCS	National Council of Churches of Singapore
NCCSL	National Christian Council of Sri Lanka
NCCCUSA	National Council of the Churches of Christ in the United States of America
NEI	Nordic Ecumenical Institute
NHCC	New Hebrides Christian Council
OOCC	Oriental Orthodox Communion of Churches
PCC	Pacific Conference of Churches
PCCC	Portuguese Council of Christian Churches
PCR	Protestant Council of Rwanda
PEC	Polish Ecumenical Council
PICOPUI	Philippine Inter Church Organization for the Promotion of Unity, Inc.
RBBRD	Reformierter Bund in der BRD (Reformed Alliance in the FRG)
SAAC	South American Anglican Council
SACC	South African Council of Churches
SCC	Scottish Churches Council
SCC	Sudan Council of Churches
SCOBA	Standing Conference of Canonical Orthodox Bishops of the Americas
SEC	Swedish Ecumenical Council
SICA	Solomon Islands Christian Association
SLUCC	Sierra Leone United Christian Council
SPCF	Swiss Protestant Church Federation
TNCC	Tonga National Council of Churches
UJCC	Uganda Joint Christian Council
UNELAM	Unidad Evangélica Latino Americana (Movement of Evangelical Unity in Latin America)
VELKD	Vereinigte Evangelisch-Lutherische Kirche Deutschlands (United Evangelical Lutheran Church in Germany)

WARC	World Alliance of Reformed Churches
WCC	World Council of Churches
WCCC	World Convention of Churches of Christ
WMC	World Methodist Council

	Anglican	Baptist	Disciple	Independent	Lutheran	Methodist	Old Catholic
Africa	17,333,000	735,000	—	6,250,000	2,302,000	2,256,000	—
Asia	5,059,000	1,008,000	98,000	—	3,518,000	1,178,000	—
Caribbean	1,780,000	—	—	—	—	314,000	—
Europe	28,980,000	1,700,000	12,000	—	40,182,000	1,486,000	147,000
Middle East	35,000	—	—	—	—	—	—
North America	8,100,000	22,544,000	1,241,000	—	5,570,000	31,955,000	282,000
Pacific	90,000	—	—	—	—	235,000	—
South America	43,000	—	—	—	802,000	231,000	—
	61,420,000	25,987,000	1,351,000	6,250,000	52,374,000	37,655,000	429,000

continent and sub-continent *

Eastern Orthodox	Oriental Orthodox	Pentecostal	Reformed	United	Others	Total
—	14,000,000	—	5,104,000	1,872,000	54,000	49,906,000
25,000	1,600,000	—	8,196,000	6,426,000	5,000,000	32,108,000
—	—	—	48,000	37,000	109,000	2,288,000
97,610,000	2,000,000	—	14,085,000	17,294,000	569,000	204,065,000
6,395,000	5,492,000	—	225,000	—	—	12,147,000
1,152,000	—	200,000	7,230,000	3,911,000	403,000	82,588,000
—	—	—	166,000	380,000	—	871,000
—	—	1,215,000	19,000	65,000	57,000	2,432,000
105,182,000	23,092,000	1,415,000	35,073,000	29,985,000	6,192,000	386,405,000

*These figures represent total membership in WCC member churches.

Issues that matter — Books that count

John Poulton
THE FEAST OF LIFE

A theological reflection on the theme "Jesus Christ — the Life of the World"

This book draws upon and continues the reflection on the assembly theme within a eucharistic framework.

A "Risk" book, paperback Sfr. 7.90, US$3.95, £2.25

IMAGES OF LIFE
An invitation to Bible study

Study resources on seven biblical images of life: The way of life. Birth. The house of living stones. The bread of life. The treasure of life. The crown of life. The water of life. The resources come in a wallet, along with some notes for group enablers and a set of 14 pictures. Also available is a set of seven posters.

Sfr. 6.50, US$3.50, £1.90

Leon Howell
ACTING IN FAITH
The World Council of Churches since 1975

The story of what the WCC has been doing in recent years and of the faith that undergirds the work. It is written, says the author, "for those who are not insiders by one who is definitely not an insider".

Paperback, Sfr. 9.90, US$4.95, £2.75

Philip Potter
LIFE IN ALL ITS FULLNESS

The general secretary of the WCC reflects on the central issues of today's ecumenical agenda. Anchored in the biblical faith, tested in the storms of a turbulent world, his vision of the imperatives of Christian unity makes for stimulating reading and issues a forthright challenge to all who seek life in all its fullness.

"Dr Potter's book will help the attentive reader to understand what really makes the WCC tick."
Church Times

Paperback, Sfr. 15.90, US$7.50, £3.95

Rod Booth
THE WINDS OF GOD

The Canadian Church faces the 1980s

A fascinating look into church life in Canada, written by the communications director of the United Church of Canada in British Columbia.

A "Risk" book, paperback Sfr. 7.90, US$3.95, £2.25

AN ORTHODOX
INTERPRETATION
OF THE ASSEMBLY THEME

Studies on life based on patristics, iconography, hymnology and spirituality.

Paperback approx. Sfr. 7.90, US$3.95, £2.25

These publications can be ordered from WCC Publications, P.O. Box 66, 1211 Geneva 20, Switzerland, or from its distributors in various parts of the world.

World Council of Churches
PUBLICATIONS

Issues that matter — Books that count

BAPTISM, EUCHARIST AND MINISTRY

The statement published here marks a major advance in the ecumenical journey. The result of a fifty-year process of study and consultation, this text on baptism, eucharist and ministry represents the theological convergence that has been achieved, through decades of dialogue.

Paperback, Sfr. 6.90, US$3.50, £1.95

GROWING TOGETHER IN BAPTISM, EUCHARIST AND MINISTRY

A study guide written by William H. Lazareth for lay study groups.

Paperback, approx. Sfr. 6.90, US$3.50, £1.95

ECUMENICAL PERSPECTIVES ON BAPTISM, EUCHARIST AND MINISTRY

A volume of theological essays edited by Fr Max Thurian which provides doctrinal and liturgical scholars with fuller treatment of the technical issues involved.

Paperback, approx. Sfr. 15.—, US$7.50, £3.95

BAPTISM AND EUCHARIST: ECUMENICAL CONVERGENCE IN CELEBRATION

Edited by Fr Max Thurian, offers priests and pastors some appropriate resources and adaptable models for Christian worship.

To be published April 1983. Paperback, approx. Sfr. 10.—, US$4.95, £2.75

Hans-Ruedi Weber
EXPERIMENTS WITH BIBLE STUDY

A unique standard work, which pastors, students, lay-people in Bible study groups and religious educators cannot afford to miss.

Paperback, Sfr. 27.50, US$13.95, £6.95

Ulrich Duchrow
CONFLICT OVER THE ECUMENICAL MOVEMENT

Confessing Christ today in the universal church

How does the unity of the church come to concrete expression in the world today? This fundamental issue in the doctrine of the church, which has been at the heart of ecumenical discussion for many years, is the burden of this penetrating study.

Paperback, Sfr. 24.50, US$11.50, £5.95

MAJOR STUDIES AND THEMES IN THE ECUMENICAL MOVEMENT

Edited by Ans J. van der Bent

This book describes all the important ecumenical studies which have been undertaken by various sub-units of the WCC since 1948, and lists themes chosen by WCC assemblies, central committees, regional conferences of churches, etc.

Paperback, Sfr. 11.50, US$5.95, £2.75

YOUR KINGDOM COME

Mission perspectives

The official report of the world conference on mission and evangelism, held in Melbourne 1980.

Paperback, Sfr. 18.90, US$10.90, £4.75

THE BIBLE

Its authority and interpretation in the ecumenical movement

Edited by Ellen Flesseman-Van Leer

This book contains all the major reports on this issue. They reflect the thinking of many theologians in various cultures, situations and times and reveal the ongoing dynamic of biblical understanding in each new age.

Paperback, Sfr. 8.50, US$4.95, £2.25

SPIRIT OF GOD, SPIRIT OF CHRIST

Ecumenical reflections on the filioque controversy

Edited by Lukas Vischer
Paperback, Sfr. 22.50, US$10.95, £6.50

These publications can be ordered from WCC Publications, P.O. Box 66, 1211 Geneva 20, Switzerland, or from its distributors in various parts of the world.

World Council of Churches
PUBLICATIONS